Transactions
of the American Philosophical Society
Held at Philadelphia for Promoting Useful Knowledge
Vol. 85, Pt. 1

A Sixteenth-Century Spanish Bookstore:

The Inventory of Juan de Junta

WILLIAM PETTAS

American Philosophical Society
Independence Square ■ Philadelphia
1995

Copyright © 1995 by the American Philosophical Society

Cover illustration: Page from Erasmus's New Testament (Froben, Basle, 1521). In *Printing Types, Their History, Forms, and Use,* Daniel B. Updike (Cambridge: Harvard, 1922).

Library of Congress Cataloging in Publication Data

Pettas, William
A Sixteenth-Century Spanish Bookstore
Includes index

1. Inventory, literature 2. Booklist 3. Spanish bookselling
4. Sixteenth century Spain

ISBN:0-87169-851-X   94-78553
US ISSN 0065-9746

Introduction

An article published in 1952 on early foreign printers in Burgos mentioned the existence in that city's archives of a 1556 document concerning the shop of the printer-bookseller, Juan de Junta, an Italian by birth, son of the famous Florentine publisher Filippo di Giunta. The document is a legal contract written in 1556 by the notary Pedro de Espinosa for the lease of the Junta bookstore and print-shop in Burgos and also contains "a very interesting inventory of everything which was in the shop in that year."[1] Giovanni di Giunta, the third son of the famous Florentine humanist publisher, Filippo di Giunta, and nephew of the prolific and extremely successful Venetian publisher of liturgical and legal works, Lucantonio di Giunta, by 1556 had been a citizen of Burgos, an important ecclesiastic and commercial center in Northern Spain, for over 30 years. There are very few contemporary documents which give us as much primary evidence for the kinds of materials a 16th-century Spanish bookstore contained as this document does, for it provides the titles of all of the books in the stock, the number of copies of each title, the prices of the individual books, in most cases the format of the book, and, in many cases, the city of publication or the name of the publisher. In addition, the document provides financial details of the costs of paper and labor for printing, and rich insights into the agreements which governed the book trade.

EARLY SPANISH PRINTING AND BOOKSELLING

Printing in Spain was primarily for the local market and did not even satisfy local demand, since many books were imported from Lyons, Basel, Paris, Antwerp and Venice. The books produced by Spanish publishers in the 16th and 17th centuries were not widely exported to Europe. The market for their output, unlike that of their counterparts in Italy, France and Germany, was Spain and the New World. The great distances to overseas markets, the scarcity and high cost of skilled labor and paper and other printing materials, and competition from cheaper imports resulted in generally smaller press runs and a market which was chiefly domestic. The Castilian cities of Burgos, Salamanca and Medina del Campo developed active book trades, although Medina's trade was confined to the import and exchange of books and it did not become a major printing center. Among the printers and booksellers who came to Spain in the late 15th or early 16th

---

[1] Luisa Cuesta Gutiérrez, "Los tipógrafos extranjeros en la imprenta burgalesa, dès[de] Alemán Fadrique de Basilea al italiano Juan Bautista Varesio," *Gutenberg Jahrbuch* (1952) pp. 67-74. The document, unpublished until now, is written in a script which varies from fairly good to almost illegible.

century to engage in the growing book trade were a significant number of Italians--with names such as Liondedei, Bonhomini, Lavezaris de Genoa, Gazani, Gentilis, Gazini, Liarcari, Porralis, Portonariis, Millis, Varesio and Giunta. They were good businessmen for the most part and some were knowledgeable in the new craft of printing. Most important, they brought with them an entrepreneurial spirit, knowledge of accounting methods, skill in record-keeping, familiarity with international transportation, contacts with their countrymen scattered throughout Europe, and, not least, access to capital. These craftsmen and merchants were following in the footsteps of their earlier countrymen who had gone to Germany, France and Switzerland to engage in the manufacture of paper. Like their co-nationals, the Italian bankers and merchants who had agents throughout Europe, the Italian booksellers in Spain maintained trade ties with Italian merchants in Spain, France, Italy and elsewhere.[2]

The first known printer in Burgos was Fadrique de Basilea, who can probably be identified with Friedrich Biel, a printer from Basel.[3] His first dated work in Burgos was produced in 1485, and he continued to publish there until 1517. A few years after the arrival of Fadrique, a book was finished by the city's second printer, Juan de Burgos, in 1489. Little is known about this printer, whose production was not extensive. In 1500 and 1501, Juan de Burgos left the city for employment in Valladolid, returning in 1502, the year of his last dated work. Juan de Burgos was succeeded in 1503 by Andrés de Burgos, possibly his son, who published a total of seven works between 1503 and 1505. Norton suggests that Andrés was probably unable to compete with the well-established firm of Fadrique de Basilea, and so later moved on to Salamanca and Granada. The next known printer-publisher in Burgos was Alonso de Melgar, who first worked with Fadrique, and then, in time-honored fashion, married his daughter Ysabel and succeeded him when he died in 1517 or 1518. Melgar, himself, died a few years later, in 1525, and his widow soon married Juan de Junta.

---

[2] For Italian banking and especially the international activities of the Strozzi, see Melissa M. Bullard, *Filippo Strozzi and the Medici: favor and finance in sixteenth-century Florence and Rome*. Cambridge and New York: Cambridge University Press, 1980. The classic work in this area is that of Raymond de Roover. See his essay "The organization of trade," in the *Cambridge economic history of Europe*, vol. 3, *Economic organization and policies in the Middle Ages* (Cambridge, 1965), 42-118, esp. 43-46 and 70-93, and his *The Medici bank: its organization, management, operations and decline* (New York: N.Y. Univ. Press, 1948).

[3] Much of the data on the printers in this section was taken from the works of Cuesta Gutiérrez, and from F. J. Norton's *A descriptive catalogue of printing in Spain and Portugal, 1501-1520* (Cambridge, 1978), and the British Library's *Catalogue of books printed in the XVth century now in the British Museum. Parts I-X.* (London, 1908-1971). *Part X: Spain. Portugal.*

INTRODUCTION

Juan de Junta set out for Spain about 1520, leaving behind his older brothers Bernardo and Benedetto, who had undertaken to carry on their father's printing, publishing and stationery business in Florence after his death in 1517. Juan's move undoubtedly had to do with the bookselling and stationery business that his father Filippo and uncle Lucantonio had prospered in since the 1480's.[4] At about the same time that Juan set out for Spain, his cousin Giacomo was sent to Lyons (perhaps accompanied by Juan) by their uncle Lucantonio under a limited partnership agreement known as an *accomandità*.[5] Giacomo's commission was to engage in bookselling (and other profitable trade) in the booming book market in Lyons, a center for legal and medical education in the 16th century, and to act as a representative for the distribution of the products of Lucantonio's press in Venice.[6] Giacomo spent the rest of his life in Lyons,[7] acting as an agent in the distribution of the liturgical and theological books from his uncle Lucantonio's press in Venice and becoming a major publisher of legal, medical and theological works in his own right. We know that Giovanni di Giunta was in Spain about 1521,[8] representing family interests at the Medina del Campo fairs, and that he published his first signed book in Burgos in 1526,[9] using the hispanicized form of his name he was henceforth to be known by, Juan de Junta.

---

[4] Both Henri-Jean Martin in *The coming of the book: the impact of printing, 1450-1800* (London, Verso Editions, 1984), pp. 122-123, and Luisa Cuesta Gutiérrez have erred in describing the Giunta family as wealthy wool merchants. The tax records of Florence during the 15th century show them to be of modest circumstances. (Archivio di Stato di Firenze, Catasto 752, ff 36-37, 952, f. 68, 866, f. 138.) Furthermore, Lucantonio did not begin his business in Florence, as Martin stated, but in Venice, where he had gone in 1477 when he was about 20 years old to seek employment in the stationery business. It was his good luck to get into the business of bookselling and then publishing as this industry was just coming into its own. His success led him to encourage his unemployed older brother Filippo to open a stationery store in Florence. The great wealth of the family and its associated partnerships was due to Lucantonio and not to his forbears.

[5] For the text of their agreement, see William Pettas, *The Giunti of Florence; merchant publishers of the sixteenth century* (San Francisco, Bernard M. Rosenthal, 1980), p. 298.

[6] It was argued by the French bibliographer Antoine-Augustine Renouard (*Annales de l'Imprimerie des Aldes*. 3rd ed. Paris, 1834) that the Lyons firm of Giacomo Giunta was engaged in the counterfeiting or pirating of Aldine editions, but Paolo Camerini refuted that charge, successfully I believe, in *Difesa di Lucantonio Giunta* (Padua, 1937).

[7] For a catalogue of the publications of Giacomo in Lyons, and some information on his activities there, see Henri Baudrier, *Bibliographie lyonnaise; Recherches sur les imprimeurs, libraires, relieurs et fondeurs de lettres de Lyon au XVIe siècle*. Lyons: Librairie ancienne d'Auguste Brun, 1895-1921. 12 vols. in 11. Vol. VI. p. 77 ff. The history of the Giunta firm in Lyons offers a fertile field for future investigation.

[8] Pettas, *The Giunti of Florence*, p. 109.

[9] *Las sergas de Esplandián*. The Beinecke Library at Yale University and the Biblioteca Central, Barcelona possess rare surviving copies.

What drew Juan de Junta and other foreign merchants and agents to Burgos, a city which, unlike most 16th-century centers of European commerce, was neither a major port nor a center of non-agricultural production? We cannot answer this question with certainty, but it is tempting to suppose that his uncle Lucantonio, who by 1520 had become one of the wealthiest publishers in the world, with agents and correspondents throughout Europe, was aware that Burgos presented a good business opportunity after the death of its only major publisher, Fadrique de Basilea. The 16th century was a period of growing population, political influence and prosperity for Burgos. When Juan arrived in Spain, the first generation of German printers had mostly passed from the scene in Castile. Burgos did, however, have a serious drawback for commerce, being situated about a hundred miles from Bilbao and Santander, the nearest major outlets for Burgos' trade on the north coast of Spain, accessible from Burgos only by horse or mule. But it had long been a center for the collection, preparation and sale of wool because of its proximity to the starting point of the Iberian sheep grazing regions and the royal favor it enjoyed under the Catholic Monarchs increased its importance as a center for the wool trade. Merchants there specialized in the purchase of wool from Castilian sheepherders and prepared it for export. After the wool was prepared for market in towns such as Burgos, it was sold to merchants and exporters at the biannual trade fairs in Medina del Campo and then carried overland by mule or horse for shipment from Bilbao, Santander or other Biscayan ports.

Burgos was also an important ecclesiastic center, and many pilgrims made their way to its beautiful Gothic cathedral. In the 15th and 16th centuries it was one of the exempt bishoprics of old Castile, but the increasing importance of the city and the eminence of its church prelates led to the recognition of the see as an archdiocese in 1572.[10] Besides the market created by the cathedral, there were important convents such as the Cistercian convent in Las Huelgas, the Carthusian monastery in Miraflores, the convent of San Pedro de Cardeña and the monastery of Silos. It was one of the oldest cities in Castile, the seat of warrior rulers who defended the borders against Moslem domination and gradually established the kingdom of Castile. Until the Court was permanently established in Madrid in 1561, Burgos was an important administrative center and home of many officials of the Crown. But the city's prosperity was most closely linked to the wool trade and above all, to the trade fair in Medina del Campo, some 150 kilometres away. Medina del Campo's trade fair, like that of Lyons, was a crucial factor in the economy of Castile in the 16th century, attracting large

---

[10] Mansilla, Demetrio. Creación de la Metrópoli de Burgos." *Historia de la Iglesia en España. III. La Iglesia en la España de los siglos XV y XVI*, ed. by José Luis Gonzalez Novalín. Madrid: Biblioteca de Autores Cristianos, 1980. pp. 14-15. The bishoprics of Burgos León and Oviedo were "exempt" in the sense that they did not belong to an archdiocese.

numbers of international traders.[11]

Burgos, then, although it had a well-established press, was not a major book publishing center in the four decades before Juan de Junta arrived and began his involvement in the book business there. But printing and publishing in Castile were at a major disadvantage by comparison with other parts of Europe such as Lyons and Venice. France and Italy had a much larger paper production than Spain, and since this heavy material had to be brought to Burgos by land, it was a costly article for publishers. Moreover, Lyons, which as we shall see from the books in the inventory, played a major role in supplying the Burgos book market, was the more prosperous city, and its much larger book trade had attracted more skilled labor and more capital investment in publishing.[12]

THE BOOKSTORE OF JUAN DE JUNTA IN BURGOS

Attempts to reconstruct the business history of a 16th-century firm such as that of Juan de Junta are usually hampered by the lack of account books, correspondence, legal contracts, and notarial and private documents. Our knowledge of early printing and publishing is also incomplete because of the subsequent loss and deliberate destruction of many of the books that were produced.[13] Smaller press runs and the later pressures of censorship may have resulted in the loss of a larger percentage of the titles printed in the Spanish peninsula, but due to the durability of rag paper and an attitude of reverence for books, much has survived, though often in remote places and in single or fragmentary copies. The antiquarian interests of booksellers and collectors in the 18th and 19th centuries and the more recent growth of interest in bibliography and textual criticism in the 20th century have done

---

[11] The basic works on the fairs are both old, but still useful. For Lyons, see H. Brésard, *Les Foires de Lyon au XV et au XVI Siècle* (Lyons, 1914), and for Medina del Campo see Cristóbal Espejo and J. Paz, *Las antiguas ferias de Medina del Campo* (Valladolid, 1912). See also Alberto Marcos Martín, *Auge y decline de un núcleo mercantil y financiero de Castilla la Vieja: evolución demográfica de Medina del Campo durante los siglos XVI y XVII* (Valladolid, 1978).

[12] It appears that the major source of imported books in the Junta bookstore was Lyons. Publishers in Basel, Antwerp and Paris also produced many of the works. The books may have been purchased directly from publishers in those cities, but it is likely that many of them came through the book dealers who came with their wares to the fairs at Medina del Campo.

[13] The likelihood of a work surviving the ravages of fire, flood, ordinary usage, and the destruction resulting from civil or religious prohibitions and censures is lower when most of this output is concentrated in only one country. By contrast, the publications of the Giunti in Florence were probably destined to survive in greater numbers, since copies of these editions were routinely sent not only throughout the Italian peninsula, but to family and agents in important export centers such as Venice and Lyons for redistribution to an even wider market.

much to save early printed materials from obscurity or destruction.[14] We also have some useful documentary evidence such as letters,[15] contracts for printing,[16] laws,[17] civil and ecclesiastic court records, guild records, wills and testaments, and the current document, which grew out of a conflict between two booksellers.

In addition to the information the document provides about the activities of the principals to the contract, it contains a careful listing of the bookstock of the Burgos store, with, as we have said, prices for each book and the number of copies, a catalogue of the furnishings of the print-shop, and the terms of the leasing of the bookstore and press to another printer-publisher. The inventory of the Junta bookstock in the Burgos store is perhaps the best example of a record of the holdings of a large Castilian bookstore in the turbulent period immediately prior to the publication of the Spanish *Index* by the Inquisitor-General Fernando de Valdés in 1559.

At the time of the preparation of this inventory *cum* contract we are told that Juan de Junta was in Lyons, engaged in urgent business and unable to return to Spain both for reasons of personal health and because of political instability. The document does not indicate the reason for Juan's going to Lyons, but it could be that he was there to purchase books, to buy the better quality paper to be had in France, to pursue debtors, to handle business matters with the heirs of Giacomo di Giunta in Lyons,[18] or to acquire other supplies for printing such as type founts or matrices. Acting on his behalf in Spain during his absence was Matías Gast, a printer of Flemish

---

[14] Luigi Balsamo discusses the interesting phenomenon in *Bibliography, the history of a tradition* (San Francisco: Rosenthal, 1991), pp. 124-42, 158-60. A praiseworty undertaking in Spain has been the compilation by the Departament of Bibliography at the Universidad Complutense de Madrid of *Repertorio de impresos españoles perdidos o imaginarios* and *Respuestas ... Nuevos impresos a buscar* (Madrid, 1982, 1983), a work which has focused attention on missing editions and led to the rediscovery of a number of them.

[15] One of the best examples of a publisher's correspondence in the sixteenth century, at least for its sheer size, is the *Correspondance de Christophe Plantin* (Antwerp, 1863-1918) 9 vols. in 8.

[16] Pérez Pastor, *La imprenta en Medina del Campo*, op. cit., and Klaus Wagner, "El negocio de las 'Siete Partidas,'" *La Bibliofilia*, LXXVIII (1976) 67-82, are among the sources of 16th-century Spanish book printing and publishing contracts.

[17] Horatio Brown, *The Venetian Printing Press 1469-1800: an historical study based upon documents for the most part hitherto unpublished.* London, 1891. This collection of documents and laws on Venetian printing and bookselling is invaluable.

[18] Giacomo Giunta died in December, 1546, leaving as heirs his second wife, Catherine, a daughter, Jeanne, and a daughter Jacqueline, born three months after his death, but no male heir.

origin who was established in Burgos before 1554.[19]

Gast appears to have entered the employ of Juan or to have entered a contractual relationship with him, and soon thereafter he married Juan's daughter; during Juan's absence from Spain he was representing the family's business and legal interests in Burgos and Salamanca. We learn from the document (f. 3) that Juan's printshop and bookstore in Salamanca had been left for some time in the hands of Alexandro de Cánova, a printer long associated with Juan,[20] while the printshop and bookstore in Burgos had been left with Martín de Eguía.[21] By the time of this document, Eguía was dead and had been replaced with a bookseller named Rodrigo de la Torre at the initiative of Cánova.

During Juan's absence, suspicion and disagreement had arisen between the Junta family and Alexandro de Cánova. Both Gast and his mother-in-law Ysabel were residents of Salamanca at the time, and one might wonder why the Junta store in that city was left in Cánova's hands. It is possible that Juan decided that it would be less complicated and probably prevent future problems if Gast, who had a bookstore and printshop of his own in Salamanca by this time, were not responsible for the operation of his business.[22] Moreover, it appears that Alexandro de Cánova had been responsible for the supervision of the business in Salamanca since the beginning of the partnership between him and Juan de Junta some 25 years

---

[19] In 1554, Juan de Junta published *De inuentione dialectica, Libri tres* by Rudolf Agricola, and on the verso of leaf +[1] of this work is a preface by F. Arcisius Gregorius thanking the recently arrived Mathias Gast, "recentem quidem typographum, sed quem novi bonarum literarum iampridem studiosissimum, ut quam primum illos suis typis excuderet." On the verso of leaf +[ii] is a preface written by Gast, dated November 1554.

[20] In *La imprenta en Medina del Campo*, pp. 420-22, Pérez Pastor has provided the text of two documents relating to a dispute over payment for the purchase by Juan de Junta and Alexandro de Cánova of a press from Pierre Tovans in Salamanca in 1532. The purchase of the press probably marked the establishment of the Junta bookstore and press in Salamanca, and the beginning of a partnership between the two printers.

[21] Eguía or Yguía is first mentioned as a "criado" (servant) of Juan de Junta in the *Tractatus perutilis*, a theological work of Martinus de Frías, a professor in the University of Salamanca, which was published by Juan de Junta in 1528 or 1529. It seems likely that he was related to Miguel de Eguía, a well-known printer in Castile in the early sixteenth century and an important figure in the printing of works by Erasmus in Spain. See Marcel Bataillon. *Erasmo y España: estudios sobre la historia espiritual del siglo xvi*. 2nd ed. Mexico-Buenos Aires: Fondo de Cultura Economica, 1966.

[22] It is also possible that Juan had been absent from Spain for a number of years. From documents relating to a dispute between a neighbor and Isabel de Basilea in 1551, we learn that "Juan de Junta ... ha muchos dias que no esta en esta ciudad." See A. Rumeau, "Isabel de Basilea, 'Mujer Impresora'?" *Bulletin Hispanique* [Bordeaux] LXXIII (1971) 231-247. 244.

earlier.[23]   In any case, in order to allow Gast to resolve the dispute with the Cánovas, on September 12, 1555, Juan sent from Lyons a document giving him power of attorney. It is interesting that the power of attorney was written in Latin, the legal language of Lyons and the international language of Europe, and that this seems to have presented a problem for the parties in Spain; the first step therefore was an appeal for the court to appoint a translator to render an accurate Spanish version.[24]

Gast alleged in the opening statements on behalf of Juan de Junta and Ysabel de Basilea,[25] that Alexandro de Cánova and his son Juan had on numerous occasions improperly entered (and by inference removed assets from) the Junta store in Burgos. He further charged that Cánova had even caused other parties to enter that store, something he had no authority to do. Gast therefore demanded first of all that a careful accounting of the contents of the press and the bookstore be made. This was duly prepared, and constitutes the bulk of the document.

What do we learn from the inventory of the bookstore and printshop? First, it appears that the inventory was undertaken with a twofold purpose, first to clear up the disagreement with Alexandro de Cánova and second to have a firm starting place with Juan Gómez de Valdivielso, "librero resydente en esta ciudad," with whom an agreement had been reached for the lease of the Burgos store. Bookstores in 16th-century Spain were something of a cross between a warehouse (where large numbers of copies of individual works were held for wholesale distribution), a workshop (where books were printed and bound), and a retail store (where printed books, paper, parchment, eyeglasses and other articles were sold). After the listing of the books is an inventory of the furnishings and equipment of the press and the living quarters. If we assume that the arrangement of materials in the store was like that of the inventory, the Latin works were shelved separately from those in Spanish, and the bound books were separated from both, but not segregated by language. The works were shelved alphabetically, either by title or author. Presumably the materials were arranged on the shelves by

---

[23] Pérez Pastor has published two documents relating to a legal action between the printer Pierre Tovans and Juan de Junta caused by the latter's failure to pay for a press Tovans sold to him and Alexandro de Cánova in 1532. *La imprenta en Medina del Campo* (Madrid, Est.-tip. sucesores de Rivadeneyra, 1895), pp. 420-422.

[24] This may point to the fact that Latin was less known at this time among the merchants in Castile than was the case with the customers of the book market in Lyons.

[25] After Fadrique's death, his enterprising and strong-willed daughter, Isabel, carried on the business and soon married one of her father's associates, Alonso (or Alfonso) Melgar. The latter died in 1525 and Isabel once again carried the business forward, styling it as that of an "honesta[e] vidua[e]" in the first book published after her husband's death. A. Rumeau, op. cit., makes a compelling refutation of Cuesta Gutierrez's thesis that Isabel played a major role in directing the book business in Salamanca.

the shopkeeper in the manner he could most easily retrieve them for his customers.

The book collection was of considerable size, consisting of 15,827 volumes. Of these, 15,214 were unbound, 6,261 were in Latin and 8,953 were in Spanish. The 613 bound volumes constituted a relatively small part (4%) of the total stock, probably typical for bookstores of the period since it was customary for retail buyers to have books bound to their taste and pocket-book when purchased, and wholesale buyers normally found unbound books safer and easier to transport and cheaper to buy. We can get an idea of the cost of binding by comparing the cost of the unbound and bound versions of a few of the titles. The unbound octavo *Formulare instrumentorum*, for example, was priced at 34 *mrs.*, while the bound copy was 68 *mrs*. The unbound quarto *Loores del monte Calvario* cost 117 *mrs.*, while the bound copy was priced at 187 *mrs*. The folio-sized *Castillo inexpugnable* was 51 *mrs.* unbound, 85 *mrs.* bound.[26] The total value of the stock of bound volumes was 55,772 *maravedís*, or about 6% of the value of the entire bookstock. The total number of titles in the stock was 1,579. Of the titles, 1,037 were in Latin and 527 in Spanish. Greek and Italian works number six each and there are two Hebrew titles and one Arabic.[27] The total value of the combined bookstock was 1,045,725 *maravedís*[28] and that of the equipment and furnishings of the press and living quarters, 511,000, for a total of 1,556, 725 *mrs.*, or 4,151 *ducados*. The value of the bookstock was therefore twice the total value of the printshop and the contents of the house where the workmen lived.[29]

A complete classification of the kinds of books in the large stock would be difficult because of the number of titles and because it is not possible to identify all of the titles listed. It might, however, be useful to mention a few of the characteristic or important works in the list, with no attempt at completeness. Works on theology, devotional works for the pious, and works required for the conduct of church services constitute the largest part of the Junta bookstock. The primary market for these books was the church hierarchy, the parish clergy and monastics.

1. Among the many works in theology are those by Cano, Bouelles, Arnaldus de Villanova, Salicetus, Pico, Denis le Chartreux, Pierre le

---

[26] I cannot explain the fact that some titles with the same format and presumably of the same edition are listed at the same price in both the unbound and the bound sections.

[27] The Hebrew and Arabic titles are dictionaries.

[28] The *maravedí* was a unit of Spanish money, both a unit of account, and an actual coin, usually of copper, but sometimes of silver. Thirty-four maravedís made one *real* and 375 equaled one gold florin.

[29] Henri-Jean Martin, op. cit., pp. 111 ff.

Vénérable, works on St. Thomas Aquinas by Vio and commentaries by St. John Chrysostom. Decisions of church councils, diocesan constitutions, rules for religious orders, and polemics attacking the teachings of heretics by Castro, Arelatanus, Eck, and Smith are prominent.

2. For the use primarily of clergy in the performance of the public and private worship of the clergy, we find breviaries, missals, diurnals, books of canonical hours, hymnals, psalters, books of sermons, concordances, confessionals, catechisms, the *Baculus clericalis*, *Aviso de curas*.

3. There are Bibles (folio editions from Cologne, Antwerp and Louvain), Gospels, Epistles and individual books of the Bible (in Latin and in Spanish); Bible commentaries by Tittelmans, St. Ambrose and St. John Chrysostom; commentaries on the Epistles of St. Paul by Theophylactus and Petrus Lombardus; commentaries on the Psalms by Pedro de Castrovol; and commentaries on Petrus Lombardus.

4. Devotional works include those by Martinez de Toledo, Alonso de Madrid, Vives, Maldonado, Osuna (*Abecedario espiritual*) Savonarola (*De simplicitate vitae* and *Exposicio del pater noster*), *Contemptus mundi*, *Luzero de la vida*, *Mysterios de la missa*, *Luz de religiosos*, St. Jerome, *Vita Christi*, *Scala Celi*, and *Meditaciones y soliloquios* of St. Augustine.

5. One of the surprising findings is the large number of works by Erasmus, which it now appears were readily available in pre-*Index* Burgos in spite of the well-known hostility of the Church to him, especially by the 1550s.[30] A comparison of the inventory with the Spanish *Index* reveals a number of other authors' forbidden titles, which I have indicated in footnotes. The works of Erasmus include the *Enchiridio militis christiani*, *Tratado de Oración*, *Hyperaspistes*, *De pueris statim ac liberaliter instituendis*, *De recta Latini Graecique sermonis pronuntiatione*, *De octo partium orationis constructione*, *Dialogus Ciceronianus*, *Moriae encomium*, *Adagiorum epitome*, *Apologia*, *Apophthegmata*, *De matrimonio christiano*, *De misericordia Dei*, and *De paraphrases in epistolam Pauli*. The stock also includes works attacking Erasmus by Alberto Pio, and works of anti-Erasmians such as Melchor Cano.

6. Works of philosophy and logic include editions of the texts of Aristotle (and commentaries by St. Thomas Aquinas, Ciruelo, Occam, and

---

[30] I hesitate to say that we find in the inventory evidence for Junta sympathies with the Illuminists or *alumbrados*, but the ready availability of works emphasizing internal piety and individual faith represented by authors such as Sts. Anselm and Augustine, the *Imitatio Christi*, works of Erasmus such as *Enchiridio militis Christiani*, etc., does indicate that there was a strong market for these interests in Burgos.

Themistius), the works of Boethius, Tittelmans, and Agricola.

7. Utilitarian and professional works include instructions for notaries (*Ars notariatus*), arithmetic books (Ghaligai, Texeda, Gutierrez), calendars, almanacs, a cookbook, collections of laws, commentaries on civil and canon law by Duaren, Castillo, Brant, and numerous printings of individual decrees or *pragmáticas*, books of medicine by early writers such as Galen, Dioscorides, Hippocrates and Avicenna, and modern writers such as Luiz, Cartagena, Ganivet, Gazio, and Cuellar. There are works on surgery by Guy de Chauliac and Guido Guidi as well as works on medical botany and pharmacy.

8. Books of instruction include Budé on the Greek language, grammars of Latin by Donatus, Cordier, Priscian, Nebrija and Sulpitius, Greek grammars by Gaza and Hummelberger, a Hebrew grammar by Santi Pagnino, Greek dictionaries by Calepinus and Hesychius and a polyglot dictionary (*Vocab. 7 linguarum*). Music instruction was represented by works such as *Arte de canto llano* of Martínez de Bizcargui and books on playing the vihuela by Mudarra and Narváez. The interest in Greek and Hebrew reflects the impetus given by Cisneros to the study of the scriptures in the original languages in his new university at Alcalá de Henares.

9. Classics and literature include Virgil, Cicero, Martial, Macrobius, Bembo, Machiavelli, Ovid, Quintilian, Plautus, Livy, Catullus, Suetonius, Marcus Aurelius, Seneca, Poliziano, Pindar, Sophocles, Aulus Gellius, Theocritus, Xenophon, Petrarch, Sallust, Bruni, Quintus Curtius, Plutarch, Valerius Maximus. Popular classical authors published in Castile in the first four decades of the 16th century were Seneca, Sallust, Aesop, Livy, Apuleius, and Plautus.

10. Light entertainments are represented by Boccaccio's *Fiammetta*, collections of *Coplas*, Aesop's fables, romances, the *Crónica del Cid*, Marco Polo, *Orlando Furioso*, and *Cárcel de amor*, Don Clarian de Landanis, Amadís de Gaula, *Arderique*.

11. Histories and biographies include Justinus, Nebrija, Vasaeus, Eusebius, *Relación de las Indias*, *Repertorio de Cortés*, Chronicles of various sorts, *Crónica del rey don Pedro*, *Crónica del rey don Rodrigo*.

Table 1 on page 24 shows the titles with the largest numbers of copies, and their values. From Table 2 on page 25, we see that a very large amount of the Junta capital in the Burgos operation was invested in a single title,

Missale burgense.[31]   There were 510 paper copies of this expensive title, valued at 680 *maravedís* each, and 10 copies on parchment at 3,750 *maravedís*, for a total of 384,300 *maravedís*. This represents over a third of the total value of the bookstock. From the number of copies, it appears that Juan was either the publisher or a major financer of the work. The substantial price of individual copies is an indication that these were aimed at an affluent market, the Church, backbone for many 16th-century publishers.

The Latin books in the inventory are listed first, followed by those in Spanish and then a list of the bound books. The preponderance of the unbound titles (756 titles) was in Latin, with only 447 in Spanish. There were 376 bound titles. Liturgical and devotional works such as breviaries, missals, confessionals, psalters, Bibles, books of hours, lives of the saints, and sermons dominate the Latin stock. Other Latin titles include legal and philosophical works, classics and grammars. Among the Spanish works we find, as one would expect, matter for parish clergy and the devout lay person as well as for merchants and other middle-class persons. There were works of personal edification, devotional works, practical texts for notaries, doctors and lawyers, collections of laws and editions of individual laws (*pragmáticas*) for trades-persons, grammars, romances, poetry, drama, histories, works of Erasmus and Savonarola, and books of hours.

A brief word might be said also about the books which cannot be identified, or may not have survived. In the first place, not all of the titles which have not been identified have disappeared. Some will be well known to subject specialists familiar with the literature of the 16th century, and others to bibliographers and librarians. In general, however, it seems that large-format works, especially those in the areas of medicine, theology, philosophy and law have had a higher survival rate than the smaller works such as vernacular works of piety, breviaries and missals for personal use, entertainments and ephemera. This is not surprising since it is a human tendency to take greater care of more expensive articles on the one hand, and also because these editions were usually printed on better quality paper, bound better, and housed in better conditions.

OTHER INVENTORIES OF SPANISH PUBLISHERS

To help the reader evaluate the Junta inventory in relation to other

---

[31] I have not been able to identify this work with certainty, but a good possibility is the *Missale secundum cōsuetudinem Burgen[sis] ecclesie*, which Juan de Junta published in Burgos in 1546. It is a large folio volume, over 35 cms. in height, with a great deal of rubrication. It contains 340 leaves, with much music notation, woodcuts, and is printed on unusually good paper for a Burgos publication. The British Library has a copy of this work. If this is the work, then another question is raised about why such a large number of copies remained unsold after ten years.

booksellers of the period, it might be useful to consider other Spanish inventories. The inventory of the books in possession of the Valencian bookseller Juan Rix de Cura at the time of his death in 1490 is impressive, especially for this early date. The list includes grammars, classic authors, Bibles, missals, sermons, lives of saints, history, medicine and popular romances.[32] On June 7, 1529, an inventory of the property left by Jacobo Cromberger, the recently deceased German printer in Seville, was completed by Lázaro Norambergo, a German merchant in Seville and Jacobo's son-in-law.[33] Cromberger had been a successful merchant in Seville and his estate was extraordinary, having a value of 12,000 *ducados*, while his bookstock in Seville consisted of over 160,000 items.[34] The inventory reveals that at the time of his death, a large sum of money was owed him, primarily by booksellers in other parts of Spain and Portugal. The inventory also reveals that much of the bookstock in Cromberger's possession was not from his own production, but, as was the case with the Junta bookstore in Burgos, came from other publishers. In the long list of his debtors,[35] 53 were identified as booksellers and probably some of the others were also.

We are also fortunate to have, for purposes of comparison, an inventory of another Spanish bookseller from the same year as the Junta inventory. The document, published by Blanco Sánchez,[36] provides us with the transcription of the 1556 inventory of the assets of the Toledo printer-publisher Juan de Ayala. Ayala's period of activity, 1530 to 1556, very closely parallels that of Juan de Junta, who published in Burgos and Salamanca from 1527 to 1557. At the time of Ayala's death in 1556, his

---

[32] José Enrique Serrano y Morales, *Reseña histórica en forma de diccionario de las imprentas que han existido en Valencia* (Valencia, 1898-1899), pp. 489-496.

[33] José Gestoso y Pérez, *Noticias inéditas de impresores sevillanos* (Seville, 1924) as quoted in Thelma Eaton, "The Wandering Printers of Spain and Portugal, 1473-1536," diss., U. of Chicago, 1948. See also the excellent work on the Cromberger firms by Clive Griffin, *The Crombergers of Seville; the history of a printing and merchant dynasty* (Oxford: Clarendon Press, 1988), pp. 20-70.

[34] Griffin, op. cit., p. 70.

[35] Ibid., pp. 43-54. Eaton correctly remarked that printers were often drawn to cities where booksellers were already established, in hope of securing employment or financial backing. The point is often overlooked that the new technology of printing and the business of publishing depended heavily on the older business of stationery, binding, etc. Clive Griffin, *op. cit.*, p. 4-5, points out that there was an active trade in foreign manuscripts in Castile before printing and that it continued long after printing was well established. It is easy to lose sight of the fact that printing did not create bookselling and the book trade was not completely identified with printing.

[36] Antonio Blanco Sánchez, "Inventario de Juan de Ayala, gran impresor toledano (1556)" *Boletín de la Real Academia Española*, 67 (1987) 207-250.

inventory of books amounted to the impressive total of 72,048. In his work on printing in Toledo, Pérez Pastor identified 60 books from the press of Ayala.[37] Blanco Sánchez notes that the inventory of Ayala's store included 248 titles, in addition to many printed reams, song books (*cancioneros*), and chap-books of ballads (*pliegos de coplas*), and concludes that the number of titles printed by Ayala might be much greater. We cannot, of course, identify with certainty which of the titles are the work of Ayala and which are the work of other printers.[38]

Marcel Bataillon reports on an inventory of the Salamanca publisher Domingo de Portonariis (Sr.) which was done when he left Spain for France in 1547, leaving his stores in Salamanca and Medina del Campo in the care of his son Andrés.[39] The Archivo de Protócolos de Salamanca has the inventories of both stores and the 1552 inventories which Andrés commissioned in order to give a financial report on his activities. These inventories would be of great use to us, but unfortunately, they have not to my knowledge been published.

PRESSES, PRINT MATERIALS AND FURNISHINGS

In an excellent article on Spanish book production of this period, D. W. Cruickshank has pointed out that even major printers in Spain usually did not own punches, but either owned or borrowed matrices (molds for casting type) for the production of replacement type.[40] The same appears to have been true of the press of Juan de Junta. A check of the Junta inventory reveals no mention of punches. Eighteen typefounts were listed,[41] but only two sets of matrices, a number with which it would be impossible to supply the type needs of even a modest press. What is surprising is the quantity of type. Cruickshank has calculated the total weight of the various founts to be over two metric tons, an amount which would be found only in a press of considerable size.

---

[37] Cristóbal Pérez Pastor, *La imprenta en Toledo*. Madrid, 1887.

[38] The value of the Ayala inventory includes his property in Vizcaya, Medina del Campo and Toledo, and the value of his accounts receivable. The Junta inventory by contrast includes only the assets of the bookstore in Burgos.

[39] Bataillon, op. cit., p. 503, note 7. I have not seen this inventory and do not know of any other research done on it. Although we do not know the contents of the inventories, Bataillon notes the existence of significant numbers of Erasmus' works in the 1547 inventories and fewer in the 1552 inventories. The inventories contain none of the prohibited works.

[40] Cruickshank, D. W., "Some Aspects of Spanish Book-production in the Golden Age," The Library, XXXI (1976) pp. 1-19. See p. 6.

[41] Lectura vieja, lectura nueva, lectura antigua, cartilla nueva, cartilla vieja, glosa de la cartilla, breviario antigua, breviario nuevo, breviario viejo, canon, nomina, romance nuevo, romance viejo, romance pequeño, missal, antigua del tamaño del romance, conteros, and cursiva.

INTRODUCTION

Two printing presses were in the shop as well as another press for dampening paper ("de mojar papel") (f. 59) and a large number of ornaments and plates, (*cornettes, regletes, renglones, guarniciones* and *viñettas*), coats of arms (*armas reales, armas de Juan de Junta*), ornamental woodcut initials (*principios*) and woodcuts of the Crucifixion. There were also appurtenances for preparing ink and a large stone for preparing vermillion (for red ink). Cruickshank describes the material owned by Barcelona printer-founder Hubert Gotard from about this time. Gotard owned 10 sets of matrices and 16 founts of type, but no punches. [42]

The inventory also mentions a room called the "carpenteria" where the tools were kept and tells us that the retail store contained the equipment used in bookbinding. Many other items of furnishings and equipment for the press are listed as well as materials for the binding of books.

The publisher of the 16th century often had a large number of people who lived on the premises, both the workmen of the press and those of the retail operation. Among the many items of furnishings, the inventory refers to five candelabras, a wardrobe of pine, a chest "where the workmen sleep," two wooden beds, four muskets, a mattress, three screens, four sieves and various items for cooking. One item, a round table with chess game, suggests that life in the print shop was not without recreational pastimes.

THE NEW LEASE AGREEMENT

Following the inventory in the document is a section setting forth a series of conditions or clauses which form the lease agreement that the new tenant, Juan Gómez de Valdivielso, promised to observe. Some of the most significant or interesting clauses are worth noting. The first required that Gómez sell the books in the Junta shop in Burgos at the prices listed in the inventory. If any were sold for more than the list price, Gómez could keep the difference, but if any sold for less, he would have to pay the difference. The second clause fixed the term of his tenancy-agency at one year, beginning from the current date. He was to keep all the income he might make from binding books in the shop, with the understanding that he must maintain all the binding tools in good condition. In the fourth clause he was enjoined from buying books on credit from other publishers or incurring any new debts without written permission from Gast or Junta, except for the purchase of paper and other materials needed in printing. The fifth clause required that he sell to Juan de Junta as many copies as the latter desired of

---

[42] Cruickshank, op. cit., p. 7. Dr. Cruickshank pointed out to me that the weight of the type in the inventory was calculated in *arrobas*, each of which weighed twenty-five *libras* (nearly equivalent to the English pound), meaning that the Junta type materials weighed over 4,300 lbs.

every work Gómez printed. For this Gómez was to receive the following prices: 375 *maravedís* for the printing of each ream in black, and 525 per ream for any printing in two colors. Gómez was to bear the cost of the freight to the place the books were being sent, and was directed to retain 50 copies of each work he printed in the store for retail sales. It appears that this represents the major part of his income, since he was obligated to pay from it all of the costs of the store and the press, including the salaries of the workmen and the costs of paper and supplies as well as the costs of the house. The Junta firm was to reimburse him only for the printed reams at the rate agreed upon in the previous clause.

The seventh clause, inserted no doubt to protect the Junta firm in Salamanca from competition with its lessee in Burgos, forbade Gómez from shipping books, either at wholesale or retail, to the cities of Valladolid, Salamanca, Medina del Campo or Segovia. Boundaries were also set for the distribution of the products of the Junta press in Salamanca in order to protect Gómez's market. The eighth clause mandated that if the cost of paper (*marquilla* or *bastardo*) exceeded 7 *reales*, Gómez would either be paid more for each printed ream or not be required to print that particular work on that paper. Since the value of the *real* was 34 *maravedís*, the cost component for the ream of paper was 238 *maravedís*, or about 63% of the price a printer received for printing in black. This dropped to 45% for the more labor-intensive two-color product. These high paper costs confirm the statements of Robert Kingdon, Raymond de Roover and others, that paper costs far exceeded labor costs in 16th-century printing.[43]

Among the most significant instructions in the remaining clauses, we learn in the ninth clause that Gómez was prevented from printing *libros de obispados* (probably liturgical works in large format), either on paper or parchment, for any bookseller except Juan de Junta without written permission. He was directed to place at the beginning or end of each printed book a title [page] indicating that the book was printed *en casa de Juan de Junta*, together with the year, month and day of completion, even though the book was printed on commission for a private person.[44] Gómez was to pay 9,000 *maravedís* and nine pair of hens each year to the mayordomo of the Cathedral of Burgos, the first payment to be due on the feast of St. John Chrysostom and the second on Christmas. He was, however, to receive for his own the rental income from three dwellings below the Junta premises as

---

[43] Robert M. Kingdon, "The Plantin Breviaries: A case study in the sixteenth-century business operations of a publishing house," *Bibliothèque d'Humanisme et Renaissance. Travaux et documents*, (1960) 133-150; and Raymond de Roover, "The business organisation of the Plantin press in the setting of sixteenth century Antwerp," *Gedenboek*, p. 235 and ff.

[44] This should sound a warning to historians of the book to exercise caution when making assumptions about the identity of the printer on the basis of printed statements alone.

well as from the "room in the front." He was accorded free use of the presses and bookbinding tools. If the contract was renewed, Gómez would be responsible after four years for replacing the type founts he had used with new ones. Gómez was prohibited from entering partnerships with other publishers and from buying type, matrices or printing equipment. Everything he printed or received in income would belong to Juan de Junta. He was not to have authority to extend credit to anyone, and were he to do so, he would be obliged to cover in cash within six months of the expiration of his contract any bad debts he incurred.

The sixteenth clause obligated Gómez to keep accurate detailed accounts by year, month and day of everything he printed, recording the name of each book, the number of its *pliegos*,[45] and the number of copies printed. The same records were to be kept for all books sold from the shop, those named in the inventory and those "miscellanies ... entrusted to the honesty of Gómez." Half the profits from the sale of printed books would belong to him and half to Junta. That is, if a book sold for 14 *reales* per ream, the 11 *reales* already agreed upon as his income were to go to Gómez but the other three were to be equally divided by Gómez and Junta. In the eighteenth clause, Gast and Junta promise to pay for the binding of up to 25 of the good, salable books such as "missales del obispado," gospels, epistles, and books of hours. The twentieth clause repeats the prohibition against Gómez's buying books from third parties, stating that it would be the responsibility of Juan de Junta to supply him with the bookstock needed for the store. The final clause stipulated that at the conclusion of the contract, Juan de Junta would buy all of the remaining stock printed by Gómez at the agreed prices of 375 *maravedís* per ream for printing in black alone, and 525 for those in black in red. If Gómez preferred to take them for his own, however, he would pay 11 *reales* per ream.[46]

Censorship and the Spanish Inquisition

In addition to the economic problems of production and distribution, booksellers and printers in mid-16th-century Spain faced extraordinary obstacles of a political nature from the civil and religious authorities. These came in the form of new requirements for approbations and licenses which were necessary prior to publication, as well as new strictures occasioned by the Holy Office of the Inquisition for books already printed.

At the time the inventory of the Junta bookstore in Burgos was prepared,

---

[45] The gatherings of printed leaves which were folded and sewn together.

[46] It was customary to reckon a ducat at 375 *maravedís*, though more precisely it was 374 *maravedís*, i.e. 11 *reales* at 34 *maravedís* per *real*. A number of the prices listed in the inventory are calculated in multiples of 17 *maravedís*, i.e. half a *real*.

the most repressive laws governing printing had not been enacted. Spain had one of the earliest laws governing the press and a relatively greater sensitivity to this issue than did other countries. In 1492, during the reign of Ferdinand and Isabella, the Crown had placed prohibitions on vernacular translations of the Bible, and in 1502 the first law specifically governing the press was promulgated, requiring printers and publishers to obtain a license before printing any work.[47] In Burgos, this was to be issued by the bishop of Burgos. Any new book was to be read and approved by "un honesto letrado" before the license was issued; after the printing, it was to be compared to the original before being marketed. In the first half of the 16th century the Office of the Holy Inquisition issued a number of licenses, but without a clear legal authority from the State to do this. In 1550, however, the Crown forbade the Holy Office from issuing any more licenses, and in 1554 the Consejo Real issued a mandate declaring that in the future all licenses for printing were to be granted by the President of the Consejo.[48] The sanctions of the lists of prohibitions issued by the faculty of Theology at the University of Paris in 1544 and by the University of Louvain (Netherlands) in 1546 added to the tension. In 1551, the first official Spanish catalogue of prohibited books was published by the local offices of the Inquisition in Valencia, Sevilla, Toledo, and Valladolid.[49] Two years after the Junta inventory was prepared, a harsh law governing printing and bookselling was published by the Crown, on September 7, 1558. It acknowledged that both the civil measures for prior approval of new books and the efforts of the Holy Office to control the sale and ownership of heretical books had proven inadequate and called for the publication of a list of works already forbidden by the Inquisition and its prominent display in all bookstores of the realm. Strict controls were ordered on the importation of Spanish works, including those from other parts of Spain. Publishers were henceforth required to obtain a license from the Consejo Real and to print it in the front matter of each book, along with the author's name, the place and date of printing, and the price of the book. The law also provided for authority for the inspection of bookstores and private libraries by the church authorities and local judiciaries. In 1559, two variant editions of the Spanish

---

[47] De Bujanda, J. M. *Index des livres interdits*, (Sherbrooke, Québec.: Centre d'Études de la Renaissance, 1984). v. 5, *Index de l'Inquisition espagnole, 1551, 1554, 1559*, pp. 42-43. The student of Spanish literature and the sociopolitical history of Spain is deeply indebted to Prof. De Bujanda and others at the Centre d'Études de la Renaissance (Sherbrooke, Québec) for the work they have carried out on the Spanish *Index* of 1551, the *Censura Bibliorum* of 1554 and the *Index* of 1559, reproducing and transcribing the original texts and providing a thorough bibliographical and historical analysis of them.

[48] De Bujanda, op. cit., p. 44.

[49] According to Henry Kamen, the 1551 *Index* was "simply a re-issue" of the University of Louvain's strictures. *The Spanish Inquisition* (New York: New American Library, 1965), p.88. Clive Griffin notes that a suppositious *Index* of 1547 is a fiction. Griffin, op. cit., p. 121. See also De Bujanda, V, pp. 58-63, "L'index fantôme de 1547."

Index[50] were published, and the Roman *Index* of Pope Paul IV also made its appearance in Spain. This marked a new phase in the history of publishing, but it is one beyond the bounds of the current article.

The Junta firm could not have been unaware of the growing pressures for church reform in Spain, the struggles between the Erasmians and the traditionalists, the cases tried by the Office of the Inquisition in Spain, and the several lists of prohibited books. Of the works in the inventory which have been identified, 82 titles, or 673 books, with a total value of 38,896 *mrs.*, fall under the prohibitions of 1559. The value of these items, just under 4% of the total value of the bookstock, is not an exceedingly large amount. But the question must still be raised why there are so many works in the inventory which would provoke the ire of the anti-Erasmians and the church hierarchy. The ready availability of these books could be explained by the firm's espousal of Erasmian ideals, but the ready availability of works of scholastic theologians and anti-reform authors makes the more likely explanation the bookseller's normal profit incentive, satisfying the Burgos market's demand for these, and any works. Old Castile was one of the centers of Illuminist activity in Spain and in the 1520s and 1530s the adherents of this movement became increasingly sympathetic to Erasmian ideas. The sense of danger to the firm for handling these materials was evidently not sufficiently strongly felt at this time to cause the firm to dispose of them.[51]

Conclusion

The spread of printing and the international traffic in printed books was aided in the 16th century by factors such as a common language of scholarship (Latin), the patronage of wealthy humanists and ecclesiastics, the growth of middle class literacy, the rise of cities, and the increase in number and influence of universities. The geographic path followed by the new technology ran generally from Germany to Italy, and thence to France and Spain. The earliest printers and publishers in Spain, often German, Flemish or French, operated in an environment with little consistent government

---

[50] Or, more exactly, *CATHALOGVS librorũ, qui prohibētur mandato Illustrissimi & Reuerend. D.D. Ferdinandi de Valdes Hispalen. Archiepi, Inquisitoris Generalis Hispaniæ.*

[51] It should be noted that the Spanish *Index* did not prohibit all of Erasmus' work as did the Roman *Index* of Pope Paul IV in the same year, but limited the restriction to the most controversial works. Erasmus had enjoyed a reputation at some of the highest levels in Spain, even enjoying the support of the Inquisitor-General Manrique in the 1530's. The climate changed somewhat after Valdés came to this post in 1546. Bataillon, op. cit., pp. 173-174. See also Stephen Haliczer, *Inquisition and society in the kingdom of Valencia, 1478-1834* (Berkeley: University of California Press, 1990), pp. 280-281.

control, and a lack of restraints from a guild structure, but increasingly they became dependent on booksellers and merchants, often Italian, for both the capital and the expertise needed for production and wide distribution. Printing was established early in university towns such as Paris and Salamanca to replace the *pecia* system of book production by scribes, and in centers of civil or ecclesiastic government (e.g. Lyons, Madrid), in centers of commerce (e.g. Venice, Amsterdam, London, Frankfort, Medina del Campo) and in religious communities (monasteries, convents).

Castile proved to be a hospitable venue for the young Florentine immigrant Juan de Junta. His arrival in Castile was well timed. Universities and enrollments were growing in number, literacy was on the rise and the consumption of luxury goods was favored by the concentration of wealth in the hands of the nobility and the church. The Catholic Monarchs were acting in ways that benefited Burgos, and the political turmoil of the rising of the *Comuneros* that had troubled the cities of Castile in 1520-1521 were past. Both Salamanca and Burgos were well positioned in relation to the Medina del Campo fairs and had good, though distinct book markets, the former supplying the needs of the students and masters in the several colleges of Salamanca, while the Burgos store purveyed to the ecclesiastic, administrative and mercantile communities of the city and the region. The capital assets Juan brought with him were probably modest, but he possessed valuable experience with the wool trade and the book trade and had family and business connections to the very successful Giunta firms in Venice and Lyons. To these were added the assets of the young Ysabel, widow of the publisher Alonso Melgar and heir of the Burgos proto-typographer Fadrique de Basilea. In the course of some 35 years in Spain and France, Juan maintained close business relations with Giunta family firms in Venice, Lyons and Florence, producing books in Salamanca and Burgos, exporting wool and hides to Italy, and importing and selling books from Italy, France and Germany. Some of his output is very well printed, although beautifully produced works were not his hallmark. The capital invested in some of the works, such as the *Missale Burgense* is quite impressive and gives an idea of the acumen and resources he possessed. The value of the Burgos bookstore exceeded 4,000 gold *ducados*, and represented only a part of Juan's total wealth, which would have included the Salamanca bookstore and perhaps other real estate and capital assets.

The document examined is interesting for the detail it provides about the bookstock and equipment of a major 16th-century Spanish bookselling firm. Its value is heightened by the fact that it closely precedes the harsh restrictions of the 1558 edict of Philip II,[52] the 1559 Spanish *Index* of Valdés and the actions of the Holy Office which probably caused the disappearance of many works from bookstores and private collections. It gives a detailed look at the bookstock of a major 16th-century Spanish firm before the full effects of the 1559 *Index* were felt and the destruction of large quantities of printed books by the Holy Office occurred. There is no evidence for a clandestine book trade in Spain such as that of Geneva, Amsterdam or London, and after the 1560's the extraordinary effectiveness of the Inquisition meant that Spain was to be even more isolated than other Catholic countries from exposure to diversity of beliefs, new philosophical ideas and information about new scientific investigations. The document shows us what a bookstore in Burgos might contain at mid-century. It was primarily the product of market demand, what sold best, including a great range of materials on all subjects. But increasingly it came under pressure from the Crown and the Holy Office to adjust to other norms.

---

[52] On September 7, 1558, princess doña Juana de Austria promulgated a law in the absence of her brother King Philip II establishing measures for the control of the press in order to stop the spread of heresies. Regulations governing the importation and sale of forbidden materials were set forth, as well as the procedure for royal licensure for printing a book. De Bujanda, V, pp. 38-41. The text of the law is given on p. 122.

Table 1. **Titles with large numbers of copies**

Sheet	Number of copies	Title	Value in *maravedís*
f. 17	330	*Carmina Mancinelli*	1,980
f. 19	208	*Conjuros*	10,608
f. 23	49	*Gramática clenardi*	2,499
f. 24	39	*Glosa del Cyfuentes*	2,652
f. 25	236	Levinus Lemnius	8,024
f. 26	626	Maldonatus, *De senectute*	15,650
	885	ibid. *Vitae sanctorum*	30,090
	58	ibid. *De civilitate morum*	986
	105	ibid. *Parenesis*	1,260
	226	ibid. *Hispaniola*	4,520
	135	ibid. *Pastor bonus*	1,620
f. 27	510	*Missale burgense*	346,800
f. 28	52	*Officium de nomine Jesu*	104
f. 29	62	*Psalterium burgense*	2,176
f. 31	64	*Repeticio Urzurro*	3,264
f. 36	47	*Abecedario espiritual, libro tercero*	3,995
	36	*Abecedario espiritual, libro segundo*	3,060
	109	*Arte de canto llano*	1,526
	89	*Aranzeles*	4,539
f. 37	535	*Computus*	3,198
	179	*Cruz de Christo*	3,043
	50	*Confessionario del Tostado*	1,250
f. 38	83	*Cortes de Valladolid*	4,233
f. 39	33	*Deseoso*	2,805
	318	*Desafio del rey de Francia*	1,908
	35	*Deliberacion en casa delos pobres*	1,190
f. 40	139	*Epistolas y evangelios*	9,452
	239	*Excelencias de la fe*	12,189
	164	*Espejo de illustres personas*	1,640
f. 41	194	*Forma libellandi*	3,291
	124	*Horas*	9,920
	100	*Horas*	1,700
f. 42	41	*Introduction de Vives*	1,025
	40	*Leche de la fe*	9,520
	32	*Leyes del estylo*	5,576
	103	*Leyes de Toro*	1,751
	158	*Leyes de abogados*	2,686
f. 44	651	*Ordenanças del Calzado*	7,812
	151	*Perla preciosa*	1,208

f. 45	100	*Pragmatica de lana*	1,200
	127	*Pragmaticas de ladrones*	1,016
	176	*Pragmaticas de lanas y panos*	4,400
	84	*Questiones del Tostado*	7,140
f. 46	38	*Reprobacion de astrologia*	646
	500	*Sucesso de Inglaterra*	500
	160	*Thesoro de devocion*	1,600
	148	*Tratado de cuentas de Castillo*	2,516
f. 47	201	*Vergel de virginidad*	10,251
f. 49	103	*Calendarium franciscanorum passado*	0

Table 2.
Titles with the largest total value

maravedís

Missale burgense	346,800
Missale burgense (parchment)	37,500
Maldonado, *Vitae sanctorum*	30,090
Maldonado, *De senectute*	15,650
Excelencias de la fe	12,189
Conjuros	10,608
Vergel de virginidad	10,251
Horas	9,920
Epistolas y evangelios	9,452
Levinus Lemnius	8,024
Missale burgense (bound, parchment)	7,976
Ordenanças del Calzado	7,812
Questiones del Tostado	7,140
Leyes del estylo	5,576
Aranzeles	4,539
Pragmaticas de lanas y panos	4,400
Cortes de Valladolid	4,233
Cruz de Christo	3,043

Table 3.

Most expensive titles	Unit price in *maravedís*
Aristoteles *De animalibus cum Theophrasto*	510
Biblia folio Antuerpie	544
Biblia (folio, Lovanii)	2,040
Bernardi *opera*	1,122

Cyrilli *opera* folio	1,122
Con[sili]a generalia in 3 bus	2,448
Cronica Sabellici (folio)	510
Ciceronis *opera* (8º)	1,020
Cronica Antonini (folio)	680
Concordantie biblie (folio)	510
Commentaria Budei in linguam grecam (folio)	510
Cursus Canonicus (8º)	510
Canones Consiliorum (folio)	510
Dioscorides (folio)	510
De Bassolis *sup[er] sentencias* (folio)	1,020
Eusebii *opera* (folio)	680
Epistole Hieronymi (folio)	510
Guliel. Rubio *super sentencias* (folio)	1,020
Index operum Tostati (folio)	1,020
Missale carmelitanum	510
Missale burgense	680
Missale burgense (parchment)	3,750
Missale burgense (4º)	750
Orantius	510
Paraphrasis Erasmi	750
Promptuarius juris	850
Plinius (Froben)	750
Quodlibeta Henrici a Gandauo	510
Repeticio Benedicti	510
Supplementum cronicorum	510
Suetonius	612
Theosophia arborei	680
Cronica de Florian do Campo	510
Morales de San Gregorio	544
Tostado *sobre Eusebio*	1,020
Bassolis *super sentencias* (folio)	1,020
Bernardi *opera*	918
Isagoge Sanctis Pagnini	510
Missale burgense (bound, parchment)	3,988

INTRODUCTION

Notes on the transcription of the contract and inventory

A few words of explanation of the procedures I have followed in dealing with this document are in order here. First, since the text is in more than one style of script, my transcription undoubtedly contains a number of errors. In some places I have placed a question mark when I was unsure of the reading. In other places I have entered information within brackets if I was fairly confident of my reading and believed that this would assist the reader in understanding the entry. The format followed by the makers of the inventory is as follows: The number of copies in the stock is the first column, followed by the title or description of the work, then the format and the price of one copy in *maravedís*. The last column records the total value of the stock of that title. At the end of each sheet is a running total and at the end of each alphabetical section a total for that letter. The inventory is arranged, probably as the store was, with books in Latin (and Greek) first, followed by those in Spanish and then by the list of bound books, both Latin and Spanish.

In the transcription of the inventory which follows this article, I have tried to identify titles in the Junta bookstore which would have fallen under the specific prohibitions of the 1551 and 1559 *Index* by comparing it with the texts of the indexes reproduced in De Bujanda. I have also tried to keep in mind the general censures such as those against "All sacred scriptures, in whichever vernacular language," "All Bibles and all New Testaments in whichever vernacular tongue," and "All works of Joannes Oecolampadius." Many titles in the Spanish *Index* are not sufficiently described, however, to firmly identify them, especially if no copy has survived, and the same is true of the list of titles in the Junta inventory. The provision of publisher names or place of publication for many of the items in the Junta inventory proved a great assistance, and it was possible to identify many authors and works and to get a good idea of subject matter, language and selling prices.

I have attempted to identify as many of the works as possible, a task which was easier when elements such as author, printer, place of publication and format were indicated in the inventory.[53] These identifications are to be considered only as suggested possiblilties rather than definitive. The task becomes even less certain when the inventory provides only a generic title and there are many known surviving editions. In identifying or commenting on the titles in the inventory, I have made extensive use of the bibliographical works which I have listed below. Finally, I have depended on the work of De Bujanda for identifying titles on the Spanish *Index*, the publication some scholars prefer to call the Valdés *Index*.

---

[53] My limited acquaintance with other inventories suggests that this list is unusual in the amount of bibliographic information it provides.

Bibliographies and Catalogues

Bataillon, Marcel. *Erasmo y España: estudios sobre la historia espiritual del siglo xvi*, 2nd ed. Mexico-Buenos Aires: Fondo de Cultura Economica, 1966.

Baudrier, Henri. *Bibliographie lyonnaise; Recherches sur les imprimeurs, libraires, relieurs et fondeurs de lettres de Lyon au XVIe siècle.* Lyons: Librairie ancienne d'Auguste Brun, 1895-1921. 12 vols. in 11.

Bonilla y San Martín, Adolfo. "Erasmo en España." *Revue Hispanique*, XVII (1907), 378-548.

British Museum. Department of Printed Books. *General catalogue of printed books. Photolithographic edition to 1955.* London: Trustees, 1959-1966. 263 vols.

Camerini, Paolo. *Annali dei Giunti.* Florence: Sansoni, 1962- . 2 vols.

De Bujanda, J. M. *Index des livres interdits.* Vol. 1, *Index de l'Université de Paris* and Vol. 5, *Index de l'Inquisition espagnole, 1551, 1554, 1559.* Sherbrooke, Québec.: Centre d'Études de la Renaissance, 1984, 1985.

Durling, Richard J. *A Catalogue of Sixteenth Century Printed Books in the National Library of Medicine.* Bethesda, Md.: 1967.

Eisenberg, Daniel. *Castilian romances of chivalry in the sixteenth century; a bibliography.* London: Grant & Cutler, 1979.

Gil Ayuso, Faustino. *Noticia bibliográfica de textos y disposiciones legales de los reinos de Castilla, impresos en los siglos XVI y XVII.* Madrid, 1935.

Griffin, Clive. *The Crombergers of Seville; the History of a Printing and Merchant Dynasty.* Oxford: Clarendon Press, 1988.

Guerrero, José-Ramón. "Catecismos de Autores Españoles de la primera mitad del s. XVI (1500-1559)." in *Repertorio de historia de las ciencias eclesiásticas en España.* 2 (Salamanca: Instituto de Historia de la Teologia Española, 1971), pp. 225-260.

Martín Abad, Julián. *La imprenta en Alcalá de Henares (1502-1600).* Madrid: Editorial Arco Libros, 1991. 3 vols.

National Union Catalog, pre-1956 Imprints; a Cumulative Author List Representing Library of Congress Printed Cards and Titles Reported by Other

American Libraries. London: Mansell, 1968-1981. 685 vols.

Palau y Dulcet, Antonio. *Manual del librero hispano-americano; bibliografía general española e hispano-americana desde la invención de la imprenta hasta nuestros tiempos con el valor comercial de los impresos descritos.* Segunda edición corregida y aumentada por el autor. Barcelona and Oxford: A. Palau, 1948-1977. 28 vols.

Paris. Bibliothèque Nationale. *Catalogue général des livres imprimés: Auteurs.* Paris: Impr. Nationale, 1900-1981. 231 vols.

Penney, Clara Louise. *Printed Books (1468-1700) in the Hispanic Society of America.* New York: Hispanic Society of America, 1965.

Pérez Pastor, Cristóbal. *La imprenta en Medina del Campo.* Madrid: Est.-tip. sucesores de Rivadeneyra, 1895.

___. *La imprenta en Toledo; descripción bibliográfica de la obras impresas en la imperial ciudad desde 1483 hasta nuestros días.* Toledo: Inst. Prov. de Investigaciones y Estudios Toledanos, 1984. (facsim. reprint)

Pettas, William. *The Giunti of Florence; Merchant Publishers of the Sixteenth Century.* San Francisco: Bernard M. Rosenthal, 1980.

Rhodes, Dennis E. *Catalogue of Books Printed in Spain and of Spanish Books Printed elsewhere in Europe before 1601 now in the British Library.* 2nd ed. London: British Library, 1989.

Ruiz Fidalgo, Lorenzo. *Libros e impresores en Salamanca 1501-1550.* Pontevedra, 1990.

Smith, David Eugene. *Rara arithmetica.* 4th ed. New York: Chelsea Publishing, 1970.

Spain. Biblioteca Nacional. *Catálogo colectivo de obras impresas en los siglos XVI al XVIII existentes en las bibliotecas españolas.* (Edicion provisional). Madrid: Ministerio de Educación y Ciencia, Dirección General de Archivos y Bibliotecas, 1972-

Wagner, Klaus. *Catálogo abreviado de los libros impresos de los siglos XV, XVI y XVII de la biblioteca de las facultades de filología y geografía e historia de la Universidad de Sevilla.* Seville: Bib. univ., Universidad de Sevilla, 1987.

Weale, William Henry James. *Bibliographia liturgica; catalogus missalium ritus latini, ab anno M.CCCC.LXXIV impressorum.* Londini: Apud Bernardum Quaritch, 1928.

Abbreviations

@	arroba
in fol.	folio size
ligat.	sewn?
mrs.	*maravedí*(s)
pp	small format books (parvuli?)
pre	?
qqtqrijs	with commentaries (cum commentariis)
qto.	commentary
qqto.	with commentary (cum commentario)
sine qto.	without commentary
4.to	quarto
8.vo	octavo

Archivo Histórico Provincial, Burgos. Protócolo de Pedro de Espinosa, Número 5542, Año 1557, ff. 100-134v.

Juan de Junta
la enprenta   +

Sepan todos esta carta y publica escritura vieren, como yo   Matias Gast mercader de libros, vezino dela cibdad de Salamanca resydente esta cibdad de Burgos en nombre de Juan de Junta mi señor e suegro, vezino de la dicha cibdad de Salamanca, por virtud del poder que d'el tengo traduzido de latin en rromance signado de Tomas publicano, que thenor del qual es este que se sigue:

En la muy noble ciudad de Salamanca a veynte y un dias del mes de Abrill año del señor de mill e quinientos y cinquenta e seys años, ante muy magnifico señor licenciado Gonzalo de Tapia teniente de corregidor en la dicha ciudad por el muy magnifico cavallero Pero Gomez de Porras corregidor yn la dicha ciudad por Su magestad y ante mi Alonso de Paz escrivano de Su magestad y uno de los del numero de la dicha ciudad de Salamanca por Su Magestad y de los testigos de yuso escriptos parecio presente Diego Perez en nombre de las dichas Francisca Perez, muger de Alexandro de Canova y Ysabel de Basilea muger de Juan de Junta sus partes en el pleyto y causa que tratan con Juan Maria de Terranova sobre la excaicion que le pidio presentó una peticion del tenor siguiente---

Muy magnifico señor Diego Perez en nombre de Francisca Perez e Ysabel de Basilea mis partes en el pleyto de excaicion que trata con Juan Maria [de Terranova] librero digo que el poder original que presente en Latin tengo necesidad de traduzir de latin en el rromance pido a vuestras mercedes, nombre una persona perita en la lengoa latina para que lo traduza de latin en rromance e traduzido me mande dar del dicho poder un traslado dos o tres o mas signados en publica forma y para todo ello mande enstar la parte adversa y para ello, etc.

Otrosi pido avra merced que quedando un traslado del dicho poder ansi en latin como en rromance vuestra merced me mande dar el original por que a mi parte a menester el dicho poder para (f. 2) las demas cosas en el contenidas y para todo publico avra merced se cite la parte adversa, etc.
E ansi presentada la dicha peticion de suso encorporada luego el dicho Diego Perez en los dichos nombres dijo e pidio lo en ella contenida e justicia testigos Pero Gomez y Diego Rio escrivanos vezinos de Salamanca. El dicho señor teniente dijo que avia e obo [i.e. hubo] por presentada la

dicha peticion e mando que el dicho poder se traduza de latin en rromance e para ello nombró al bachiller Antonio Sobrino al qual mandó notificar lo acepte y aga bien e fielmente que Su merced le mandera pagar Su trabajo y quedando un traslado del dicho poder en Latin y en rromance yn este proceso mandósele de el original e que se le de el dicho poder sacado en rromance signado en publica forma e manera que haga fe e para todo se cite la parte contraria e se le notefique testigos dichos, etc.

E despues de lo suso dicho en la dicha ciudad de Salamanca este dia yo el dicho escrivano notifique lo suso dicho a Mateo de Benavides procurador de Juan Maria en Su persona. Y le cite en Su persona para todo lo contenido en el pedimiento del dicho Diego Perez e mandamiento del dicho juez, testigos dichos,

E despues delo suso dicho en la dicha ciudad de Salamanca a veynte e tres dias del mes y año dicho, yo el dicho escrivano notifique todo lo suso dicho al bachiller Antonio Sobrino en su persona testigos dichos, etc.

E luego el dicho bachiller Antonio Sobrino dijo que ello aceptava e acepto e dijo que estava presto y aparejado de acer y cumplir lo que por el dicho señor teniente le es mandado, testigos dichos etc.

E despues delo suso dicho en la dicha ciudad de Salamanca a veynte y tres dias del dicho mes de abril del dicho año de mill e quinientos e cinquenta e seys años en audiencia publica ante el dicho señor teniente y ante mi el dicho Alonso de Paz escrivano publico e testigos parecio presente el dicho bachiller Antonio (f. 3) Sobrino en cumplimiento delo mandado por el dicho señor teniente e dijo que el avia traduzido el dicho poder de latin en rromance segun e como por su merced le hera mandado que lo presentava e presentó en la forma y manera siguiente,

En el nombre de Dios amen. Por este presente publico ynstrumento sea a todos evidentemente notorio y manifiesto como sea que el honrado y prudente varon Juan de Junta hijo que fue de Felipe de Junta ciudadano y mercader Florentino rresidente que ser solia en la ciudad de Salamanca del reyno de castilla nacion de España y agora lo es aqui en Leon de Francia teniendo casa y tienda de ynpresion de vender e conprar libros yn la dicha ciudad de Salamanca y otra en la ciudad de Burgos tan bien de la dicha nacion de España la administracion de la qual tienda de Salamanca hubo dado al senor Alejandro de Canova borgoñes mercader de libros rresidente en la misma ciudad y la dela casa y tienda de Burgos a Martin de Yguia ansi mismo librero abitante en el dicho lugar la qual administracion los dichos Alejandro de Canova e Martin de Yguia rrespitivamente por largo tiempo an fecho segun que el dicho Alejandro de Canova aun agora haze el qual por muerte del dicho Martin de Yguia ubo cometido la administracion de la casa y tienda del dicho Juan de Junta que esta en el dicho lugar de Burgos a Rrodrigo de la Torre. A los quales Alejandro de Canova y Rrodrigo de la Torre y otras personas el dicho señor Juan de Junta deseara tomar cuenta Pero por las guerras que ay entre los principes y yndispusicion de su persona no se puede seguramente venir a España y ala dicha ciudad de Salamanca E ynpedido e ocupado en otras sus ciertas urgentes negocios queriendo no menos prober en sus cosas confiando de la bondad e lealtad de la señora Ysabel de Basilea su muy amada muger estante agora en la dicha ciudad de Salamanca y tan bien del honrrado varon Matias Gaste mercader de libros rresidente ansy mismo en la dicha ciudad de Salamanca en presencia de mi el notario (f. 4) y publico y rreal abajo signado y de los testigos ynfra escriptos estantes personalmente constituydo el sobre dicho señor Junta de Junta el qual asaviendas de su gracia y voluntariamente con todos aquellos mejores modos que mejor pido y debo e puede y debe ser fecho no rrevocando los poderes por el dados a la dicha señora Ysabel de Basilea su muger antes los conformando y rrevocando todos los otros procuradores por el fechos en el tienpo pasado agora de nuevo hizo, crio, constutuyo y hordeno e por el tenor del presente ynstrumento [h]aze, cria, constituya y solenemente hordena sus procuradores generales y mensajeros especiales con tanto que la generalidad no derogue a la especialidad ni por el contrario conviene a saver ala sobre dicha señora Ysabel de Basilea su muy amada muger y al dicho Matias Gaste ausentes como si fuesen presentes presentados deste poder e qualquier dellos yn solidum especial y espresamente para que en nonbre del dicho señor constituyente y por el puedan pedir y rrequerir al dicho Alexandro de Canova e sus herederos e a otras quales quier personas a quien convenga buena cuenta y las otras cosas de la administracion por el hecha en la tienda de la libreria del dicho Juan de Junta en el dicho lugar e ciudad de Salamanca, e ansi mesmo de todos los libros e mercanzias por el avidas e rrecibidas del dicho señor constituyente y de lo que han rrentado semejantemente de la venta e compra de los libros y de las otras cosas dependientes de la dicha tienda de Salamanca y tan bien de todas e quales quier sumas por el rrecibidas e pagadas e quales quier espensas por el fechas por rrazon de la dicha tienda de Salamanca e Otrosi de la administration de la casa e tienda de ympresion y libreria pertenecientes al dicho senor constituyente en el lugar de Burgos de la nacion de España la qual administracion el dicho Alexandro de Canova tomo en si por su autoridad privada despues de la muerte del dicho Martin de Yguia defunto y en el mismo lugar cometio al dicho (f. 5) Rrodrigo de la Torre y ansi mismo de todos y quales quier bienes muebles e alhajas de la casa e ynpresion los quales entonces estavan en las mismas casa y tienda en la quel el dicho Alexandro de Canova y Juan de Canova su hijo muchas vezes entraron y otras diversas personas por mandado del dicho Alexandro de Canova aun que yn ellos ningun derecho tenia ni en los bienes y mercanzias de los libros e alhajas de la casa tienda e ynpresion ni en los enprestidos y deudas dellas. Antes totalmente pertenezce segun pertenece al dicho señor constituyente como lo certifica e afirma ser verdad o para que puedan hazer que el dicho Rrodrigo de la Torre de la dicha cuenta, a costa del dicho Alexandro de Canova que lo cometio, e ver y rrever, contar, arrestar y averiguar las dichas cuentas. E pedir y aver, rrecibir y rrecaudar de los dichos padre y hijo Alexandro e Juan de Canova. E Rrodrigo de la Torre e de cada uno dellos e de sus herederos e otras personas que convenga quales quier sumas, mercanzias, deudas, enprestidos, bienes, muebles e rrayzes e alajas de la casa e ynpresion y otras quales quier cosas de que los dichos Alexandro y Juan de Canova e Rrodrigo dela Torre o qual quier dellos quedare deudor o fueren deudores del dicho señor constituyente ansi por la averiguacion de las dichas cuentas que se hiziere como en otra qual quier manera y por qual quier causa o ocasion que sea y de lo que ovieren recibido, avido e cobrado e delo que hubieren, rrecibieren, y cobraren dar por libres y quitos a los susodichos y qual quier dellos rresplitiva mente (sic) y a otras personas.

A quien tocare e acer e pasar quitanca e quitancas e cartas de pago ante notarios y testigos e por sus proprias manos y si necesario fuere, de y sobre lo suso dicho e alguna cosa dello puedan hazer con cierto conposicion y concordia y conprometer en arbitos arbitadores y amigables tratadores de paz e concordia sinple- (f. 6) mente. Y por via de pena y azer e pasar quales quier ynstrumentos de concierto concordia e conpromiso en nonbre del dicho señor constituyente y rratificar las sentencias arbitatorias que sobre ello fueren pronunciadas, y apelar d'ellas para el arbitrio de Buenbaron o en otra manera. Y obligar al dicho señor constituyente e a quales quier sus bienes de guardar lo contenido en los dichos ynstrumentos y sentencias arbitrarias y casometer a todas las justicias y rregidores con las rrenunciaciones y clausulas que en tales casos se suelen poner y Otrosi para que puedan pedir e rrecibir de quales quier otras personas deudores del dicho señor constituyente todas e quales quier sumas de dinero y de oro e plata y cantidades de mercancias que le son debidas y pertenecientes o se le devieren y pertenecieren ansi por obligaciones, cedulas publicas, bulletas, parcellas, partidas, cuentas, libros de cuentas, como en otra qual quier manera y por qual quier causa y ocasion que sea y pedir y rrecibir, usar y gozar las casas, posesiones, tierras, vinas e las otras cosas tocantes e pertenecientes al dicho señor constituyente ansi en las dichas ciudades de Salamanca y Burgos como fuera d'ellas y las posesiones y frutos d'ellas y delo que fuere rrecibido y cobrado dar por libres e quitos como arriba es dicho y dar una o mas cartas de pago e pedir e rrequerir que sean parado en los dichos bienes y demas d'esto pedir e rrequerir en nonbre del dicho señor constituyente y por a quales quier notarios y personas publicas y provadas todas e quales quier escrituras, ynstrumentos, documentos y otras cosas para la conservacion delos derechos y aciones del dicho señor constituyente de sus bienes, muebles e rrayzes, mercanzias, deudas, en prestados sumas, quantias y de las otras cosas a el tocantes e pertenecientes y que le pertenecieren y acer que les sean desenbaracados y de- (f. 7) librados e semejantemente para que puedan rrecaudar del dicho Alexandro de Canova y de sus herederos y de otras personas que convengan todos y quales quier libros de cuentas, escripturas publicas e privadas, cedulas, obligaciones, cuentas, y otras quales quier escripturas fechas y pasadas entre los dichos Juan de Junta y Alexandro de Canova y que quedaron en manos e poder del dicho Alexandro de Canova e las que quedaron yn manos e poder del dicho Alexandro de Canova verlas y rreverlas, tenerlas y poderlas, y si necesario fuere dar e sacar copia d'ellas que sirvan alos derechos y aciones que el dicho Juan de Junta pretende contra el dicho Alexandro de Canova y contra otras quales quier personas o azer, depositar, e rrequerir que se depositen los dichos libros de cuentas y escripturas en manos de alguna persona ydonea. Y sobre lo suso dicho o alguna cosa d'ello constrenir y conpeler e azer que sean constrenidos y compelidos por todas las vias y maneras juridicas y deuidas, los dichos Alexandro y Juan de Canova, padre y hijo, y el dicho Rrodrigo de la Torre y otras quales quier personas. Y si necesario fuere en nonbre del dicho señor constituyente parecer y presentarse ante quales quier señores justicias e juezes oficiales y sus lugares tenientes e que tengan sus veces y defenderle a el y a sus derechos e dar e hacer quales quier pedimientos por palabra o por escripto y rresponder a los en contrario dados y hechos e pedir que se rresponda a los suyos y el pleyto o pleytos, contestar y ver, contestar y jurar de calunia y malizia y verdad dezir en anima del dicho señor constituyente y helegir domicilio y domicilios y dar e presentar caucion e cauciones [several words crossed out] e presentar testigos autos y escripturas e otros quales quier generos de prueba en modo de provanca e dezir e poner tachas a los en contrario presentados e concluyr en la causa o causas e oyr derecho ynterlocutorias y sentencias difinitivas y pedir que sean dadas (f. 8) e promulgadas y provocar e apelar d'ella y d'ellas y de otro qualquier agravio hecho e que se hiziere y seguir sus apelaciones y si necesario fuere rrenunciarlas e pedir tasacion de quales quier costas e siendo tasadas averlas, rrecibirlas e rrecaudarlas e de lo que rrecibieren dar cartas de pago en la manera suso dicha e hazer e procurar quales quier otros autos a los pleytos e causas necesarios y oportunos y sostituyr ansimismo uno o mas procuradores en su lugar y de cada uno d'ellos e aquel e aquellos rrevocar e otros de nuevo sostituyr quedando todavia este poder en su fuerca y generalmente para que puedan azer y exercir y procurar todas las otras cosas y cada una d'ellas cerca de lo suso dicho e de alguna cosa d'ello necesarias y oportunas que el mismo señor constituyente aria y podria hazer si personalmente se [h]allase presente a lo suso dicho aun que fuesen tales cosas que de si rrequiriesen mas especial poder de lo que aqui va espresado e promete el dicho señor constituyente por su juramento que le hizo tocando las escripturas e so obligacion e ypoteca de todos y quales quier sus bienes de aver e que perpetuamente [h]abra por rrato en rrato e firme todo aquello y qual quier cosa que por los dichos sus procuradores e sostitudos fuere autuado dicho y fecho a procurado cerca delo suso dicho y de alguna cosa d'ello e deuo venir contra ello o rrelevar alos dichos procuradores y sostituidos e a los quales rrelevo y rrelieva por la presente de toda carga de satisfacion y otra qual quier que sea y presentando caucion de rrado por ellos prometio de estar en juyzio e pagar lo juzgado con los sometimientos, rrenunciaciones y clausulas e portunas de lo qual que dicho es el dicho señor constituyente quiso y quiere que por mi el dicho notario publico apostolico y rreal abaxo signado le sea fecho a el e a los dichos procuradores e sus sostitudos e a cada uno d'ellos un ynstrumento o ynstrumentos publicos el qual le prometi que aria y hize (f. 9) so la presente forma fecho y dado yn Leon de Francia en la casa de la morada de mi el notario apostolico y rreal abaxo signado a doze dias del mes de setienbre año del Señor de mill e quinientos y cinquenta e cinco, estando presentes por testigos para esto llamados y rrogados, maestre Claudio Marihan notario rreal, ciudadano de Leon de Francia e Antonio Muboy clerigo abitante tanbien yn Leon,

E yo maestre Juan Piguino clerigo ciudadano de Leon de Francia notario publico por las autoridades apostolica y real y notario jurado del audiencia del señor oficial de Leon por que fuy presente a todo lo suso dicho e a cada cosa e parte dello al tiempo del otorgamiento d'ello juntamente con los dichos testigos e lo vi e oy todo ansi pasar y lo tome en nota por ende este publico ynstrumento por mano de otro fielmente escripto rrogue e signe y espedi en fe delo qual dicho es siendo rrequerido e rrogado Juan Piguino

Nos el que tiene cargo del Sello comun rreal para los contratos constituydo en la vallyva de mascon y sinescalia de Leon de Francia hazemos saver e publicamente afirmiamos como maestre Juan Piguino arriba nonbrado el quale rrecibio si no y espidio el ynstrumento de poder arriba escripto es verdadero legal y fidedino notario por las autoridades apostolica y rreal e a sus escripturas e ynstrumentos publicos sienpre se a dado y da critesa e yndubitable fe en juyzio e fuerza d'el en fe e testimonio delo qual que dicho es pusimos el dicho Sello comun rreal fecha y dada en el año, dia suso dichos de sarge

Yo el bachiller Antonio Sobrino notario vezino de Salamanca doy fe que saque e traduzi este poder de su original sacada de latin en rromance e que concierta con su original (f. 10) sin mudar, añadir, ni quitar cosa alguna de la sustancia segun que yo mejor lo puede traduzir y entender en fe delo qual lo firme de mi nonbre fecho en Salamanca a veynte y tres dias del mes de Abrill de mill e quinientos e cinquenta e seys años el bachiller Antonio Sobrino notario.

Ansi presentado el dicho poder traduzido de latin en rromance de suso encorporado en la manera que dicho es el dicho bachiller Antonio Sobrino juro por Dios nuestro señor todo poderoso e por una señal de cruz tal como esta + en que puso su mano derecha y por las palabras de los santos quoatro (sic) evangelios do quier que mas largamente estan escriptos yn forma de vida e de derecho que el dicho poder esta bien fiel y verdaderamente traduzido de latin en rromance segun Dios e su conciencia y en lo que el en ello alcança, Y que si ansi es verdad que Dios nuestro señor le ayude. Y si es al contrario que el se lo demande e ala fuerça y confusion. Del dicho juramento dijo, si juro y amen, testigos dichos

Lo qual todo que dicho es paso delante de Mateo de Benavides procurador contrario, testigos dichos.

El dicho señor teniente lo obo [i.e. hubo] por presentado e rrecibio el dicho juramento y mando que se de signado a las partes del dicho Diego Perez yn publica forma e manera que haga fe una y dos e tres y mas vezes tantas quantas fuere menester. Y a la validacion de todo ello el dicho señor teniente dijo que ynterponia e ynterpuso su autoridad e decreto judicial tanto quoanto podia e de derecho devia y no mas ni aliende. Y lo firmo de su nonbre testigos dichos el licenciado Tapia va entre renglones (o Diz/do y enmendado) vezes el no arri/ vala todo/ Y yo el dicho Alonso de Paz escrivano publico fuy presente, fize Aqui mi sino que es a tal en testimonio de verdad Alonso de Paz

(f. 11)

Sostitucion

Yn la muy noble ciudad de Salamanca a [blank] dias del mes de [blank] año del señor de mill e quinientos y cinquenta e seys años. Ante mi Alonso de Paz escrivano de su magestad en la su corte y en todos los sus Reynos y señorios y uno de los escrivanos publicos del numero de la ciudad de Salamanca por su Magestad Y de los testigos de yuso escriptos parecio presente Matias Gast librero vezino de la ciudad de Salamanca en nonbre y por virtud del poder que [h]a y tiene de Juan de Junta su parte sinado de mi el presente escrivano y por virtud del dicho poder y en el dicho nonbre del dicho Juan de Junta y por virtud d' este poder y en la via e forma que mejor [h]aya lugar de derecho y al dicho su parte mas conventa util e provechoso le sea dijo que sostituya e sostituyo a Cesar de Blanquis, canonigo en la Santa yglesia de Burgos y a Francisco Alzedo, scritor de libros y a Pedro de Estremiana, herrador, vezinos de la ciudad de Burgos, especial y espresamente para que por el en nonbre de su parte puedan, poder guardar, y guarden poner e pongan a Recaudo e guarda la casa y hazienda del dicho

Juan de Junta su parte ansi libros como prensas, pergaminos ajuares de casa y otras cosas y otros quales quier bienes del dicho Juan de Junta su parte muebles, rayzes semovientes. Y que le pertenezcan y puedan pertenecer e sean suyos del dicho su parte y de Ysabel de Basilea su muger los quales puedan poner e pongan a rrecaudo, guarda y encomienda por ante justicia e sin ella y de palabra o amigablemente segun y como el podria [h]aze llo por virtud del dicho poder que a y tiene del dicho su parte y en ello e sobre razon d'ello puedan parecer ante quales quier justicia e juezes de quales quier partes, ciudad, villas, y lugares d'estos Reynos y ante ellos y qual quier d'ellos podades hazer y aga del todos los autos, deligencias, pedimientos, requerimientos (f. 12) que sean necesarios y al caso convengan y dar las ynformaciones necesarias como el podria por el dicho poder la qual dicha casa y hazienda y todo lo demas de suso espresado el dicho mi parte y su muger [h]an y tienen en la ciudad de Burgos que para ello vos doy poder amplido y el que yo he y tengo, Y vos trasmito mis vozes y vezes, derechos y aciones y Otrosi sostituyo para todos lo pleytos, causas, negocios, ceviles [sic] y criminales, movidos e por mover que los dichos sus partes tengan y otros contra ellos contenidos en el dicho poder y no para mas a Roate Frias y Pero Gomez de Cerezo y Miguel de Pino procuradores en la Real Audiencia de Burgos a todos siente juntamente y a cada uno y qual quier d'ellos ynsolidum a cada uno segun y como para lo que va sostituydo y no para otra ninguna cosa segun dicho es y obligo la persona e bienes del dicho su parte a el obligados por el dicho poder de aver y que el dicho su parte y el en su nombre [h]avran por bueno y firme ysta Sostitucion y lo que por virtud d'ellos suso dichos hizieren y autuaren cada uno por lo que de suso es y que no yra ni veria contra ella agora ni en tienpo alguno ni por alguna manera e si contra ello fuere yo, o el, o otra persona que no nos vala sino que sienpre se cumpla esta Sostitucion y lo que se hiziere por virtud de ella y los relevo en forma de derecho segun el es relevado so la clausula que dize Judicium sisti judicatun solui, con sus clausulas en testimonio de lo qual otorgo ansi ante mi esta sostitucion yl dicho Matias Gast, dia mes y año susodicho siendo ello presente por testigos llamados y rogados para lo que dicho es Juan de Polanco y Francisco de la Pena vezinos de la ciudad de Salamanca Y yo el dicho escrivano doy fe que conozco al dicho otorgante el qual lo firmo. Aqui de su nombre (f. 13) y otrosi el dicho Matias Gast otorgante dijo que queria que los dichos Cesar de Blanquis canonigo y Francisco Alzedo y Pedro de Ystramiana [h]ayan y tengan este dicho poder y sostitucion. Para lo que dicho es de suso declarado y cada uno d'ellos yn solidum y que todos los yn esta sostitucion contenidos usen d'ella juntos y cada uno yn solidun ynneventun que muera o sea muerto Alonso de Medina su fator a quien el dejo en la dicha casa de Burgos y no en otra manera. Por que siendo vivo el dicho Alonso de Medina lo suso dicho no es necesario y ansi lo otorgio todo ante mi el dicho escrivano dia, mes, y año suso dichos. Y lo firmo de su nonbre testigos los dichos va hemendado Cerezo o Vala,

Matias Gast, Y yo el dicho Alonso de Paz yscrivano publico fuy presente fize aqui mi signo en testimonio de verdad, Alonso de Paz (f. 14) Quien de por virtud del dicho poder que suso va yncorporado y usando d'el yo el dicho Matias Gast en nombre del dicho Juan de Junta mi señor y suegro digo que por quanto yo estoy convenido y concertado con dicho Juan Gomez de Valdivielso librero resydente en esta ciudad questa y se presente de estar en factoria encomienda y manificiacion la casa y enprentas tienda y libreria que el dicho Juan de Junta y Ysabel de Basilea su muger tienen en esta ciudad de Burgos, el ynventario de todo lo qual es este que se sigue que se sigue (sic)

(f. 15)

Inventario de los libros, ymprentas muebles de casa e otras cosas que Matias Gast en nonbre de Juan de Junta mercader de libros vezino de la ciudad de Salamanca da en manificiacion y fatoria a Juan Gomez de Valdivielso librero natural de Hoz de Valdivielso hijo de Pero Gomez defunto resydente en esta ciudad. Son los siguientes:

2 Apuleus de asino aureo[54] in 8º Floren. falto,	68	136
14 Anto[nio] corduben[sis] de detractatione[55] in 4to,	51	731
14 Anto[nio] cordub[ensis] de indulgentijs[56] in 4to,	136	1,904
1 Authoritates Philosophorum[57] in 8º,	10	010
1 Arnal[dus] de Villanova[58] in fol. falto	306	306
4 Authores qqto.[59] in 4to	85	340

---

[54] Apuleius, Lucius. *De asino aureo*. This was published by the Giunti in Florence in February, 1512 (i.e. 1513).

[55] Córdoba, Antonio de. *Libellus de detractione (sic) et famae restitutione* (Compluti, Ex officina Ioannis Brocarii, 1553). 4.to. Bibliothèque Nationale, Paris. Biblioteca Nacional, Lisbon. Univ. of Illinois, Urbana. Martín Abad, p. 614, no. 444. *Catálogo colectivo*, A, 1673. Palau, 61831.

[56] Ibid. *Opus de indulgentijs* (Compluti, Ex officina Ioannis Brocarii, 1554). 4.to. Martín Abad, p. 633, no. 470. *Catálogo colectivo*, A, 1674. Palau, 61832, cites another edition (Salmanticae, In Officina Andreae à Portonariis, 1554).

[57] *Auctoritates philosophorum* (Lugduni, Johannes de la Place, 1527). Archivo de la Corona de Aragón, Barcelona. *Catálogo colectivo*, A, 2762.

[58] Arnaldus de Villanova, d. 1313? Folio editions of his *Opera* were published in Lyons (Fradin, 1504, 1509, 1514; Huyon, 1520); Venice (Locatellus, 1505); and Lyons (de Gabiano, 1532).

[59] *Auctores cum suis commentis* (Lugduni, Anthonius du Ry, 1531). 4.to. Biblioteca del Palacio, Madrid. The Biblioteca Nacional also has quarto editions published in Lyons in 1501 (Lugduni, s.i.) and 1505 (Lugduni, per Stephanum baland).

1 Anto. luda med. olyssi opera[60] in fol. 306		306
2 Alphonsina de Vergas[61] in fol. 68		136
4 Annothomia mundini[62] in 4to 51		204
2 Annota[tiones] oroschii[63] in Ætum in fol. 85		170
3 Acta consilij tridentini[64] in 4to 95		285
12 Actiona Christiana in 4to 85		1,020
1 Anto[nius] cartagenen[sis] de peste[65] in fol. 119		119
1 Aristo[teles] mystica ph[ilosoph]ia. in 4to 68		068
1 Angelus de maleficijs[66] in 4to 306		306
2 Articella qqto.[67] in 4to 204		408
3 Apophthegm[atum] Erasmi[68] in 8° gr[yphius] 85		255
1 Adagiorum epitome[69] in 8° gr[yphius] 85		085

---

[60] Luiz, Antonio, d. 1565. *Antonii Lodovici medici Olyssipponensis de re medica opera qvae hic seqvntvr* (Olyssippone, impressa apud Lodovicum Rotorigium, 1540). Folio. Santander Rodríguez, pp. 283-285. Durling, no. 2867.

[61] Enríquez, Alfonso. *Alphonsina acutissimi ac clarissimi illustris viri Domini D. Alphonsi Enriquez in sacra theologia baccalaurei ... Per doctissimum virum magistrum. Franciscum de Vargas: eiusdem Alphonsinae priorem: correcta* (In complutensi achademia. Per Arnaldum Guillelmum de Brocario [1523]). Folio. Trinity College, Dublin. Biblioteca Nacional, Madrid. Biblioteca Colombina, Sevilla. Martín Abad, p. 290, no. 107. Palau, 79781.

[62] Mondino dei Luzzi, d. 1326. *Anothomia [sic] Mundini* (Salamanca, Pedro de Castro, 1540). 4.to. There are several possible quarto editions. Ruíz Fidalgo, no. 64.

[63] Orozco, Cristóbal, 16th cent. *Annotationes in interpretes Pauli Aeginetae* (Venetiis, in officina Luceantonio Junta, 1536). Folio. National Library of Medicine. John Crerar Library. Camerini, I, p. 271. Durling, no. 3413.

[64] *Decreta et acta sacrosancti oecumenici et Generalis Concilii Tridentini* (Metinae, apud Stephanum Palatiolum, 1553; [at end:] Vallisoleti, apud Franciscum Cordubensem, 1554.). 4.to. Palau, 69495. *Catálogo colectivo*, D, 232.

[65] Cartagena, Antonius de. *Liber de peste, de signis febriū et de diebus criticis. Additus est etiā huic operi libellus eiusdē de fascinatione* (Compluti, in aedibus Michaelis de Eguia, 1530). Folio. British Library. Biblioteca Nacional, Madrid. Palau, 46271. Martín Abad, p. 400, no. 234. *Catálogo colectivo*, C, 832.

[66] Gambilionibus, Angelus de. *De maleficiis* (Lugduni, Stephano Gueynard, 1521; Lugduni, apud A. du Ry, 1530). 4.to. Bibliothèque Nationale, Paris. Baudrier, XI, p. 252. The Giunti firm of Lyons published octavo editions in 1532, 1542 and 1555. The author was commonly known as Angelus *Aretinus*.

[67] See footnote 72.

[68] Prior to 1556, Sebastián Gryphius of Lyons published editions of Erasmus' *Apophthegmatum* in 1538, 1539, 1541, 1544, 1547, 1548, 1550, 1554 and 1555.

[69] Erasmus, Desiderius. *Adagiorvm ... epitome* (Lvgdvni, apvd Seb. Gryphivm, 1544, 1550, 1553). Baudrier, VIII, pp. 183, 235, 264.

INVENTARIO DE LOS LIBROS

2 Aulus gellius[70] in fol. pre 170		340
1 Architectura dureri[71] in fol. pre 85		085
2 Articella[72] in 8° Lion 68		136
1 Appollogia Erasmi[73] in fol. ale[maña] 187		187
1 Altercatio Synagoge[74] in fol. 136		136
1 Aristo[teles] de animalibus cum Theophrasto[75] ale[maña] 510		510
5 Antidotarius anime[76] in 8° Lion 51		255
1 Aristo[teles] meteora[77] in fol. 68		068

/8,506/

(f. 16)

2 Anselmus sup[er] mattheum[78] in 8° 68   136

---

[70] Gellius, Aulus. *[Noctes Atticae]*. Folio editions were published in Paris by Badius in 1519, 1524, 1530; by Roigny in 1536; and in Cologne by Cervicornus in 1526. Editions in octavo were published in Lyons by Gryphius in 1532, 1534, 1537, 1539, 1542, 1546, 1550 and 1555.

[71] Dürer, Albrecht. *A. Dureri pictoris et architecti ... de vrbibvs, arcibvs, castellisqve ...* (Parisiis, ex officina C. Wecheli, 1535). Folio. British Library. Bibliothèque Nationale, Paris.

[72] Articella. *Articella nuperrime impressa* (Lugduni, ... impensis Jacobi q. Fran. de Giuncta, 1534). 8.vo. Baudrier, VI, p. 154. Palau, 230680. The Giunta firm of Lyons also produced octavo editions of this work in 1515, 1519, and 1525.

[73] Johannes Froben published several editions of Erasmus' *Apologia ...* in Basel in the 1520s. This may be *Apologiae Erasmi Roterodami omnes* (Basileae, Apud Ioannem Frobenium, 1522). Folio. Biblioteca Nacional, Madrid.

[74] Folio editions of *Altercatio Synagogae et Ecclesiae* were published in Cologne by Melchior Novesianus in 1533 and 1540. British Library.

[75] Aristoteles. *And. Cratandri lectori S. En tibi candide lector, Aristotelis et Theophrasti historias, quibus cuncta fere quae Deus Opt. Max. homini cõtemplanda & usurpanda exhibuit ... complectuntur: creaturas inquam omnes, & sensu praeditas, quae animalia dicuntur* (Basileae, Apud A. Cratandrum, 1534). Folio. British Library.

[76] Salicetus, Nicolaus, d. ca. 1493. *Anthidotarius animae. Meditationvm, confessionvm, ac deuotarum orationum insignis libellus* (Lugduni, apud Iacobum Giunta, 1542; and another, apud Theobaldum Paganum, 1554)). Both 8.vo. This work was also published by the Giunta firm in Venice in 1508. Baudrier, IV, p. 257 and VI, p. 196. Camerini, I, p. 138.

[77] Aristoteles. *Libri Meteororum ... cum commentariis d. Thomae de Aquino* (Venetijs, in aedibus Lucaeantonij Iunte, 1532). Folio. Camerini, I, p. 253. Another edition of St. Thomas Aquinas' commentary on this work was published by the same firm in 1547. Other folio editions were published in Venice and Paris.

[78] Anselm, Saint, Abp. of Canterbury, 1033-1109. *Divi Anselmi in Matthaeum evangelistam commentarius* (Antuerpiae, excudebat J. Gravius, 1551). 8.vo. Bibliothèque Nationale, Paris.

5 Avicenna de viribus cordis[79] in fol. 68	340
1 Alciati emblemata[80] in 8° 25	025
2 Amicus medicorum[81] pp. 30	060
1 Arithmetica[82] en Toscano 34	034
1 Argumenta Vet. et Nove Testamenti 34	034
1 Ars notariatus[83] in 8° 85	085
1 Arelatanus de Hereticis[84] in 8° 34	034
1 Acta consilij Tridentini[85] in 8° pre 17	017
1 Ambrosius in epistolas Pauli[86] in 8° 119	119
1 Almanach perpetuum[87] in 4to 204	204
3 Annothomia in 8° 25	075
2 Arithmetica brevis in 8° 25	050
1 Aristo[teles] de animalibus grece[88] in 4to 306	306

---

[79] Avicenna, 980?-1037. *De viribus cordis cum cōmentarijs Jacobi Lupi Bilbilitani.* The Hispanic Society of America owns a copy of this title published in Toulouse by Jacobus Colomies in 1527.

[80] Alciati, Andrea. *Emblematvm Libellus.* Octavo editions were published in Lyons by G. Rovilius in 1548, 1550, 1551, and 1566; and by Iacobus Modernus for Jacobus Giunta in 1545. Baudrier, VI, p. 209; IX, pp. 144, 173, 187, 307. Rovilius also published a Spanish translation in 1540 and 1549 (Maggs, 26).

[81] Ganivet, Jean, fl. 1431-1434. *Amicvs medicorvm Magistri Ioannis Ganiveti, cum opusculo, quod inscribitur, Caeli enarrant* (Lugduni, Apud Gulielmum Rouillium, 1550). 16.mo. Bibliothèque Nationale, Paris. British Library. Baudrier, IX, p. 169.

[82] Ghaligai, Francesco. *Practica d'Arithmetica* (Firenze appresso Bernardo Givnti, 1548; Appresso i Giunti, 1552). 4.to. Newberry Library. University of Michigan. *Rara Arithmetica*, pp. 132, 514. This may also be the 1521 printing, the first edition, titled *Summa d' Arithmetica*.

[83] *Ars notariatus.* Incunable editions of this work were published in Rome and Milan; 16th-century editions in Cologne, Speyer, Lyons. This may be the Lyons edition of 1546 or 1550 (Apud Ioannem Frellonium). Baudrier, V, p. 203, 217.

[84] Nicolaus Arelatanus, Joannes (or Nicolas d'Arles). *De haereticis aurevs tractatus.* ([Lugduni], apud Vincentium Portonarium, 1536). 8.vo. Bibliothèque Nationale, Paris. Baudrier, V, p. 459.

[85] Trent, Council of. *Acta concilii Tridentini vnà cum annotationibus piis* ([Basel?] 1546). 8.vo. British Library.

[86] Ambrosius, Saint, bp. of Milan. *Commentarij in omnes divi Pauli epistolas, ex restitutione Desiderii Erasmi, ... diligenter recogniti* (Coloniae, excudebat J. Gymnicus, 1532). 8.vo. Bibliothèque Nationale, Paris. University of Minnesota.

[87] Zacuto, Abraham ben Samuel. *Almanach perpetuū siue tacuinus, ephemerides τ diariū* (in laribus venetis, L. A. Iunta, 1525). 4.to. British Library.

[88] Aristoteles. Περί ζώων ιστορίας βιβλία θ' (Florentiæ, per haeredes P. Iuntæ, 1527). 4. tp. British Library. Legrand, 3, p. 313.

INVENTARIO DE LOS LIBROS

1 Ausonius grece[89] in 8° 68	068
1 Ausonius gallus[90] in 8° 25	025
2 Astudillo in libros physicor[um][91] in fol. 102	204
2 Aristo[teles] dialectica[92] in 8° 85	170
1 Ars notariatus[93] in 8° 85	<u>085</u>
	2,071
/ x,dlxxvij /	<u>8,506</u>
	L. 10,577

1 Breviarium medinense falto in 8°	----
5 Breviarium Carthusianum[94] in 8° 153	765
1 Breviarium Romanum[95] in 8° Lion falto	----
12 Baculus clericalis[96] in 8° Alcala 51	612
13 Breviarium Cisterciense[97] pp uno muy roto 102	1,326
4 Breviarium conceptionis[98] in 8° 68	272
5 Breviarium predicator[um] de novis[99] pp 187	935

---

[89] Ausonius, Decimus Magnus, ca. 310-394. *Dicta Sapientum Graeciae cum Erasmi Roterodami enarratione* (Lugduni, 1544). Bibliothèque Nationale, Paris.

[90] Ibid. *Avsonii Galli poetæ disertissimi Omnia opera* (Florentiæ, sumptu P. Iunte, 1517). 8.vo. British Library.

[91] Astudillo, Diego de. *Quaestiones ... super octo libros Phisicorum et super duos libros de Generatione et corruptione Aristotelis* (Vallis Oleti, in officina Nicolai Tyerri, 1532). Folio. Bibliothèque Nationale, Paris. Palau, 19179.

[92] Aristoteles. *Dialectica.* The British Library has octavo editions by Gryphius (Lugduni, Apud S. Gryphium, 1551) and by Vincentius (Lugduni, Apud A. Vincentium, 1553).

[93] See footnote 83.

[94] *Breviariū ord. Carthusiensis* (Lyons] per Simonem beuelaqua, [1506]). 8.vo. Baudrier, II, p. 12.

[95] Theobaldus Paganus published editions of the Roman breviary in Lyons in 1542, 1544, 1545, 1547, 1548, and 1555. Baudrier, IV, pp. 226, 231, 233, 236, 239, 261. The Giunta firm of Venice published editions in 1547, 1548, 1549, 1550, 1551, 1553, 1554, 1555. Camerini, I, p. 527 et passim.

[96] Cucala, Bartolomé. *Obra muy prouechosa ... llámase Baculus Clericalis* (Alcalá de Henares, en casa de Joan de Brocar, 1550, 1554). 4.to. Hispanic Society of America. Palau, 65830. Martín Abad, p. 559, no. 384. See also footnote 116.

[97] Small-format breviaries were common. Bohatta lists a Cistercian breviary in 12.mo (Parisiis, Thielman Kerver, 1534); a 16.mo by the same publisher in 1508; and a 32.mo (Parisiis, Expensis Anguilberti et Gofredi de Marnef, 1516). Bohatta, 1360, 1346 and 1354.

[98] *Breviarium secundum Ordinem Inmaculatae Concepcionis* (Compluti, In domo Ioannis Brocarii, 1551). 8.vo. Biblioteca Nacional, Madrid. Palau, 35662. Martín Abad, p. 572, no. 393.

[99] *Breviarium Praedicatorum* ([Venice, heirs of Lucantonio Giunta] 1554). 16.mo. This is the reformed breviary for the Dominicans. Camerini, I, p. 404.

SIXTEENTH CENTURY SPANISH BOOKSTORE

9 Breviarium Santi Petri pp 202	918
9 Breviarium Romanum[100] pp falto	----
1 Bucolica Virgilii qqto.[101] falto	----
4 Breviarium de las plagas[102] in 8° 238	952
1 Breviarium Romanum de las armas in 8° 170	170
1 Breviarium Roma[num][103] 8° Valencie falto	
1 Biblia[104] in fol. Colonie 408	408
1 Biblia[105] in fol. Antuerpie 544	544
2 Biblia[106] in fol. Lovanii 1020	2,040
1 Bernardi opera[107] in fol. ale[maña] de novis 1122	1,122
16 Breviarium predicato[rum] de primis pp 136	2,176
1 Breviarium del Calice[108] in 8° una 238	238
3 Breviarium Carmelitanum 102	<u>306</u>
	12,784

(f. 17)

2 Breviarium carmelita[num][109] in 8° 170	340

---

[100] *Breviarivm Romanvm* (Uenetijs, In officina heredum Luce Antonij Iunte, 1550). 16.mo. Camerini, I, p. 377.

[101] Virgilius Maro, Publius. Possibly the *P. Virg. Maronis Bvcolica. Cum commentariis Richardi Gorræi Parisiensis* (Lvgdvni, apud Guliel. Rouillium, 1554). 8.vo. Baudrier, IX, p. 218.

[102] Griffin cites two entries in the 1540 inventory of the Crombergers' stock for "breviarios romanos delas llagas." Could this be the same? Griffin, Appendix One, no. 439.

[103] *Breviarium secundum consuetudinem ecclesie Valentine* (Valentie, Arte et peritia Francisci Romani, 1533). 8.vo. Biblioteca de la Catedral, Toledo. *Catálogo colectivo*, B, 2445. Palau, 35712.

[104] Folio editions of the Bible were printed in Cologne in 1527 and 1529. British Library.

[105] The *Censura generalis contra errores quibus recentes haeretici sacram scripturam asperserunt* (Valladolid, 1554), specifically names folio Bibles printed in Latin in Antwerp by Merten de Keyser (Caesar, 1534), Joannes Steelsius (1541), and Antonius Goinus (1540). De Bujanda, V, p. 276-77. The British Library has the folio edition printed in Antwerp (M. Caesar, sumptu G. Dumaei, 1534) and one printed in Louvain (Ex officina B. Grauii, 1547).

[106] *Biblia ad vetustissima exemplaria nunc recens castigata* (Louanii, Ex officina B. Grauii, 1547). Folio. 3 vols. British Library.

[107] Bernard, Saint, Abbot of Clairvaux. *Opera quae colligi potuere omnia* (Basileae, per I. Heruagium, 1552). Folio. British Library. St. Vincent College, Latrobe, Pa.

[108] The Giunti firm of Venice published an octavo edition of the Roman Breviary in 1555 which has an illustration of the holy chalice on the title page. Camerini, I, p. 406.

[109] *Breuiarium Carmelitarum cum annotationibus in margine* (Venetijs, apud heredes Luceantonij Junte, 1543). 8.vo. Camerini, I, p. 348.

Inventario de los libros

2	Bartholo[maeus] anglicus de proprieta[tibus] rerum[110] in fol. 272		544
1	Blondus de Roma triumphante[111] in fol. 102		102
3	Belial de Consolacione[112] in fol. 85		255
1	Breviarium Salmaticense[113] in 8° 272		272
3	Breviarium Romanum pp una 170		510
2	Breviarium Hieronimi in 8° 272		544
2	Breviarium de la paloma in 8° Lion 170		340
3	Breviarium Romanum in 8° 153		459
1	Beroal[do] in questiones tusculanas Tullii[114] in 4to 68		068
1	Baldus sup[er] feudis[115] in 4to 68		068
11	Baculus clericalis[116] in 4to 51		561
1	Biblia[117] in 8° ale[maña] 272		272
			4,335
			12,784
	xvij,cxix		L. 17,119

---

[110] Bartholomaeus Anglicus, 13th cent. *De proprietatibus rerum*. Editions in Nüremburg, Cologne, Lyons, Basel, Strassburg, Seville, etc.

[111] Biondo, Flavio, 1388-1463. *De Roma triumphante libri decem* (Basileae, per Hier. Frobenium, Ioan. Heruagium & N. Episcopium, 1531). 2 vols. Folio. Newberry Library. New York Public Library.

[112] Palladinus, Jacobus, de Theramo, bp. of Spoleto, 1349-1417. *Liber Belial de consolatione peccatorum noviter impressus* (Vicẽtie, Henrici de Sancto Ursio, 1506). Folio. British Library.

[113] Juan de Junta published an octavo edition of *Breuiarium secundum consuetudinem alme ecclesie Salmanticensis* in Salamanca, 1541. It contains over 600 leaves printed in two columns, with much printing in red, and this would explain the relatively high price for an octavo work. Biblioteca Nacional, Madrid. Bohatta, *Breviere*, 2658. *Catálogo colectivo*, B, 2438.

[114] Beroaldo, Filippo, 1453-1505. His commentary on Cicero's *Tusculanae quaestiones* was published in Bologna (Benedictus Hectoris, 1496), Venice (Simone Bevilacqua, 1502), Paris (Jean Petit, 1509), Venice (Philippo Pincio Mantuano, 1510), Venice (Agostino de Zannis de Portesio, 1516), Venice (per Benedictum Augustinumque Bindonos, 1525), Paris (Apud M. Vascosanum, 1533), Paris (I. Roigny, 1549). The Petit and Roigny editions are in quarto.

[115] Baldo degli Ubaldi, 1327?-1400. *Baldus Super feudis. Opus aureum* (Lugduni, Jacobi Myt, 1522). 4.to. Bibliothèque Nationale, Paris.

[116] Cucala, Bartolomé. *Obra muy prouechosa, no solo para los Reuerẽdos Sacerdotes, rectores, Curas y vicarios: mas tãbien para los mismos penitẽtes: y en fin para todo fiel Christiano. Llamada Baculus Clericalis* (Çaragoça, por Diego Hernandez, 1548). 4.to. Palau, 65827.

[117] This may be *Biblia sacrosancta* (Basileae, Apud N. Bryling[erum] 1551). 8.vo. British Library. Brylingerus also published the 5-part *Biblia graeca et latina* in an octavo edition in 1550.

3 Castro de iusta herecticor[um] punitione[118] in fol. 300		900
2 Comedia de Samaritano evangelico[119] in 4to qqto 25		050
4 Cronica nebrissensis[120] in fol. 408		1,224
1 Castro in beati quor[um][121] in 8° 51		051
7 Covarubias Sup[er] 4to[122] in fol. 170		1,190
1 Con[sili]a Bellonii[123] in 8° 85		085
10 Cronica Vasei[124] in fol. 238		2,380
330 Carmina mancinelli[125] in 4to 6		1,980
1 Confessio theologica 51		051
1 Catalogus Sanctorum[126] in 4to falto		----
1 Comenta[ria] in Aristo[teles] logi[cam][127] Lovanienses	476	476
2 Concordantie biblie[128] in 4to gr[yphius]	375	750
1 Consilium cardinalium in 4to ale[maña]	10	010

---

[118] Castro, Alphonso. *De iusta hæreticorum punitione* (Salmanticae, in officina Ioannis Giuntae, 1547). Folio. Palau, 49077. British Library. First edition.

[119] Papeus, Petrus. *Samarites Comœdia de Samaritano Euãgelico* (Toleti, Ioannis ab Ayala, 1542). 4.to. British Library. Maggs, 713. Palau, 211793. Rhodes, p. 148. The commentary is by Alejo Vanegas de Busto.

[120] Nebrija, Elio Antonio de. *Aelii Antonii Nebrissensis rerum a Fernando et Elisabe hispaniarũ foelicissimis Regibus gestarũ decades duas. Necnõ belli Nauariẽsis libros duos. Annexa insuper Archiepi Roderici Chronica, aliisq; historijs antehac non excussis* (Apud inclytam Granatam, s.i., 1545). Folio. 3 parts in 1 vol. Biblioteca Nacional, Madrid. Bibliothèque Nationale, Paris. Palau, 189342.

[121] Castro, Alphonso de, 1495-1558. *Fratris Alfonsi a Castro, Ordinis Minorũ, super psalmũ Beati quor. remisse sunt iniquitates* (Salmanticæ, in officina Pedro de Castro, 1540). 8.vo. Palau, 49074. British Library. Harvard University Library. Library of Congress.

[122] Covarrubias y Leyva, Diego de, Abp., 1512-1577. *In librum Quartum Decretalium Epitome, ex secunda autoris recognitione* (Salmanticae, Excudebat Ioannes Iunta, 1545; 1550; Joannis de Canova, 1554). All folio. Palau, 64178, 64179. Biblioteca Univ., Sevilla. Trinity College, Dublin. Univ. of Chicago, Regenstein Library.

[123] Belloni, Niccolò. *Consiliorum liber primus* (Lvgdvni, Apud Hæredes Iacobi Giuntæ, 1550). 8.vo. Baudrier, VI, p. 265.

[124] Vasaeus, Joannes, d. 1550. *Chronici rervm Memorabilivm Hispaniae. Tomus prior* (Salmanticae, Excudebat Ioannes Iunta, 1552). Folio. British Library. Hispanic Society of America. Yale University. Palau, 352991.

[125] Perhaps one of the editions of *Carmen de floribus* by Antonio Mancinelli (1452-1506?). The Bibliothèque Nationale, Paris, has quarto editions published in Paris in 1499 and 1506.

[126] Natalibus, Petrus de. *Catalogus Sanctorum* (Ueneũt lugd. apd Iacobũ Giũcti, 1543, 1545). 4.to. Baudrier, VI, pp. 201, 210.

[127] This may be Porphyry's *Isagoge*, a commentary on the Categoriae and other parts of the Organon of Aristotle which was published in Greek in Louvain (Lovanij, Apud T. Martinum, 1523). 4.to. British Library.

[128] *Concordantiæ maiores Sacræ Bibliæ* (Lugduni, Apud S. Gryphium, 1535, 1540, 1545 and 1551). 2 parts. 4.to. Baudrier, VIII, pp. 82, 133, 193, 249.

7 Catullus Tibul[lus] Proper[tius][129] in 8°	51	357
12 Contemptus mundi[130] pp	25	300
3 Compendium musices[131] in 8° una	51	153
5 Cyprianus in psalm. 130[132] in 8°	10	050
1 Calepinus g[raecu]s[133] gr[yphius] viejo falto		----
1 Compendium previlegior[um] fratrum minor[um][134]	51	051
1 Confessionale Savonarole[135] in 8°	51	051
57 Conjugationes in 4to	4	228
1 Ciceronianus Dialogus Eras[mi][136] in 8°	25	025
1 Catolico[137] gr. pre	272	272
1 Conª Guidonis[138] in 8°	85	085

---

[129] Catullus, Gaius Valerius [and others]. *Catullus Tibullus Propertius*. Numerous octavo editions of this collection of Latin elegiac poetry were published in Paris, Lyons and Florence. This may be the 1531, 1535, or 1542 edition published by S. Gryphius in Lyons. Baudrier, VIII, p. 58, 82 and 159.

[130] Probably the work of Pope Innocent III, *De contemptv mvndi siue miseria conditionis humane* (Lvgdvni, apud Theobaldum Paganum, 1555). 16.mo. Baudrier, IV, p. 262.

[131] *Compendiū musices confectū ad faciliore instructione cantum choralē* (Uenetijs, Lucantoniū de Giunta, 1513). 8.vo. Camerini, I, p. 155.

[132] Huelga, Cipriano de la. *Commentarius in Psalmum CXXX* (Compluti, Ex officina Ioannis Brocarij, 1555). 8.vo. Palau, 116615. Martín Abad, p. 647, no. 486.

[133] Calepino, Ambrogio. This may be *Dictionarium ... Adiectai sunt latinis dictionibus, Hebraecae, Graecae, Gallicae, Italicae, Hispanicae et Germanicae* (Lugduni, Apud. Seb. Gryphium, 1531). Palau, 40359 note. Baudrier also lists 1546 and 1553 editions. Another possibility: *Ambrosii Calepini Bergomatis Lexicon* (Lvgdvni, Sebastianvs Gryphivs Germanvs excvdebat, 1533). Folio. Baudrier, VIII, p. 67, 198, 264.

[134] Franciscans. *Compendium previlegiorum fratrum minorum*. Probably the 1530 edition of Juan Varela (Hispali: in domo Joānis Varela Salmāticeñ) or that of de Porras (Salmantice in edibus Ildephonsi Porres, 1532). Both 4.tos. British Library. John Carter Brown Lib. Rhodes, p. 81. Ruíz Fidalgo, no. 28.

[135] Savonarola, Girolamo. *Confessionale pro instructione confessorum*. Octavo editions were published in Venice in 1507, 1517, 1520, 1524, 1537 and 1543. The Bibliothèque Nationale, Paris, has octavo editions published in Paris in 1510 and 1517.

[136] Erasmus, Desiderius. *Dialogvs qui titul. Ciceronianvs siue, de optimo genere dicendi* (Complutensi Vniuersitate, Apud Michaelem Eguia, 1529). 8.vo. Martín Abad, p. 383, no. 217. Palau, 80356.

[137] Balbi, Giovanni, d. 1298. *Catholicon*. There are a large number of folio editions, both incunable and sixteenth-century, from Strassburg, Venice, Lyons, Leyden, Nüremberg, and Augsburg. The British Library and the Bibliothèque Nationale, Paris, both have several editions. The first edition was printed in Mainz in 1460, perhaps by Johann Gutenberg.

[138] La Pape, Guy de, 1402-1487. *Cōsilia Guid. pape. Guidonis pape. I.* (Lugd. apud Iacobū Giūcti, 1550). 8.vo. Baudrier, VI, p. 207. The Harvard School Law Library has copies of the 1542 and 1544 editions and the Bibliothèque Nationale, Paris, has an octavo edition published in 1533 (Lugduni, in officina Joannis Crespin).

1 Cyrilli opera[139] in fol. ale[maña] 1122   1,122
1 Chyrurgia Vido Vidii[140] gr 680   680
                                                 12,521

(f. 18)

17 Castro Sup[er] miserere[141] in 8° 34   578
1 Canones consilior[um][142] in fol. Colonie falto   ----
13 Confessionale Antonini[143] pp. Lion 51   663
1 Con[sili]a generalia de novis in 3^{bus}[144] Colo[nie]. 2448   2,448
5 Cronica granatensis in fol. 51   255
3 Calendarium Romanum Stofflerini[145] in fol. 136   408
2 Cateronis officia pp. 34   068
2 Confessionale Jacobi Phillipi in 8° 25   050
1 Cicero de oratori[146] in 8° Florencie 85   085
1 Cathena sup[er] Psalmos[147] in fol. pre 306   306

---

[139] Cyrillus, Saint, Patriarch of Alexandria, d. 444. *Opervm Divi Cyrilli ... tomi qvatvor qvorvm postremvs nvnc recens accedit, ex græcis manuscriptis exemplaribus fideliter latinitate donatus* (Basileae, apud Ioannem Hervagium, 1546). Folio. 4. vols. Columbia University Library. British Library.

[140] Guidi, Guido, or Vidius, Vido, 1500 (ca.)-1569. Probably the folio edition of *Ars chirurgica* (Venetiis, Heredes L. A. Iuntae, 1546) or his *Hippocrate. Chirurgia e graeco in latinum conversa, Vido Vidii ... interprete* (Luceciae [sic] Parisiorum, Petrus Galterius, 1544). Both folio. National Library of Medicine. Bibliothèque Nationale, Paris. Durling, no. 2204.

[141] Castro, Alphonso de. *In psalmū miserere mei deus secundum magnam misericordiam tuā* (Salmanticae, In officina Ioannis Giuntae, 1547). 8.vo. Biblioteca Universitaria, Sevilla. British Library. Ruíz Fidalgo, no. 143. Rhodes, p. 49. Another octavo edition was published in Salamanca in 1537: *Homiliae uigintiquinq[ue] sup. Psalmum, Miserere mei deus* (Rodrigo y Gonzalo Castañeda). Ruiz Fidalgo, no. 47. Palau, 49072.

[142] *Concilia omnia tam generalia quam particularia* (Coloniae, P. Quentell, 1538 and 1540). Folio. British Library.

[143] Antoninus, Saint, Abp. of Florence, 1389-1459. *Summa Confessionalis Do. Antonini Archiepiscopi Florentini* (Lugduni, apud Theobaldum Paganū, 1546). 16.mo. Baudrier, IV, p. 235.

[144] This is the three-part edition (Coloniae, P. Quentell, 1551) of the above work (footnote 142) on the councils of the church. Folio. British Library.

[145] Stoffler, Joannes. *Calendarium Romanum* (Oppenheym, I. Kobel, 1518). Folio. British Library.

[146] Cicero, Marcus Tullius. *De oratore ad Q. Fratrem* (Florentiæ, sumptibus Philippi Giuntæ, 1514). British Library.

[147] Bible. Psalms. *Cathena aurea super Psalmos* ([Paris] C. Wechel, 1530). Folio. British Library.

1 Caieta[nus] in primam 2e Sancti Thome[148] in 8°   68   068
1 Cronica Sabellici[149] in fol.   510   510
2 Caietanus sup[er] Evangelia[150] in 8° pre   187   374
3 Caieta[nus] in epistolas Pauli[151] in 8° pre   187   561
1 Chrysostho[mus] Sup[er] epistolas Pauli[152] in 8° pre   306   306
1 Chrysostho[mus] Sup[er] evange[lia] et Acta
                                  aposto[lorum][153] 8° 238   238
1 Chrysostho[mus] sup[er] mattheum opus
                                perfectum[154] 8° 153
                                                                             153
6 Comentaria Cesaris[155] in 8° Gryph[ius] 85   510
3 Corona florida[156] in 8°   51   153

---

[148] Vio, Tomaso de, called Gaetano, *cardinal*. There are several editions of St. Thomas Aquinas' *Prima secundae partis Summae theologicae* with the commentary of Vio, but I have not identified one in octavo printed before 1556.

[149] Sabellico, Marco Antonio, 1436?-1506. *Historia rerum Venetarum* (Venetiis, Andreae de Toresanis de Asula, 1487). Folio. Bibliothèque Nationale, Paris. The inventory copy of this work on the history of Venice may have been a later edition, but I do not know of one.

[150] Vio, Tomaso de, called Gaetano, *cardinal*. *Evangelia cum commentariis reverendissimi domini Thomae de Vio*. I have not located an octavo edition.

[151] Ibid. Perhaps the *Epistolae Pauli et aliorum Apostolorum* (Parisiis, Apud Hieronymum & Dionysiam de Marnef Fratres, 1546). 8.vo. New York Public Library.

[152] Chrysostomus, Joannes, Saint, patriarch of Constantinople, d. 407. *D. Ioannis Chrysostomi ... Enarrationes, partim antehac, partim nunc primum traductæ & editæ, in D. Pauli Epistolas* (Antuerpiæ, in ædibus Ioan. Steelsii, 1544). 2 vols. Another possibility: *Commentariorum D. Joannis Chrysostomi in omnes D. Pauli Epistolas* (Parisiis, apud A. Girault, 1545). 8.vo.

[153] Ibid. *Commentarium in Acta apostolorum. Desiderio Erasmo Roterodamo interprete.* (Antverpiae, in aedibus I. Steelsii, 1542 and 1550). 8.vo. Bibliothèque Nationale, Paris. Princeton Theological Seminary has a copy of *D. Ioan. Chrysostomi ... commentarij ... in Euangeliū secundum Marcum & Lucam* (Parisiis, Apud Ioannem Roigny, 1543) which is bound with his *Commentarium in Acta Apostolorum* (Parisiis, Apud Ioannem Roigny, 1542).

[154] Ibid. *D. Ioan. Chrysostomi archiepisc. Constantinop. Avrevm commentariorum in Euang. Matthaei opus hactenus inscriptvm opvs imperfectvm* (Antverpiae, I. Steelsius, 1542, 1548). 8.vo.

[155] *C. Ivlii Caesaris commentariorvm* (Lvgdvni, Apvd Seb. Gryphivm, 1538, 1540, 1543, 1547, and 1551). 8.vo. Baudrier, VIII, pp. 110, 132, 174, 211, 248. Gryphius also produced several 16.mo editions.

[156] Gazio, Antonio, 1449-1528. *Corona florida* (Lugduni, apud J. Giunta, 1548). 8.vo. Bibliothèque Nationale, Paris. The National Library of Medicine also has a 1534 edition by S. de Gabiano and a 1541 edition by J. de Giunta. Baudrier, VI, p. 194. Durling, no. 2034.

1 Caietanus in libros regum[157] in 8° 170		170
1 Concordia evangelica Janseni in 8° 68		068
2 Ciceronis questiones tusculane[158] in 8° 34		068
1 Corasius de Sacerdotio[159] in 8° 68		068
1 Cardanus de Immortalitate[160] ale[maña] in 8° 34		034
2 Cravetta de antiquitate[161] in 8° 119		238
1 Cepola de edilitio [sic][162] in 8° 85		085
1 Ciceronis opera[163] in 8° rob[erti] 1020		1,020
3 Compendium ethices in 8° ale[maña] 85		255
2 Castrovol sup[er] phisica[164] in fol. 136		272
7 Castrovol sup[er] psalm. quicumque[165] in 4to 34		238
1 Cronica Antonini[166] in fol. 680		680
1 Concordantie biblie[167] in fol. 510		510

---

[157] Vio, Tomaso de. *In omnes authenticos veteris testamenti historiales libros commentarii. In Iehosuam Iudices, Ruth, Reges, Paralipomena, Hezrum, Nehemiam et Ester* (Parisiis, Apud Carolum Guillard, 1546). 8.vo. Biblioteca Nacional, Madrid. Bibliothèque Nationale, Paris. Other editions were published in Paris by Bogardus and by Johannes Roigny and Poncet le Preux.

[158] Cicero, Marcus Tullius. *Quaestiones tusculanarum* (Florentiæ, sumptibus Philippi Giuntæ, 1514). 8.vo. British Library.

[159] Coras, Jean de, 1513-1572. *In universam sacerdotiorum materiam ...* (Parisiis, per A. Angelicum, 1551). 8.vo. Bibliothèque Nationale, Paris. Harvard University Library has a quarto edition produced by de Portonariis in 1548.

[160] Cardano, Girolamo, 1501-1576. This is the *Liber de immortalite animorum*, but I do not know of a probable edition from Germany. Seb. Gryphius published an octavo edition in Lyons, 1545. Bibliothèque Nationale, Paris.

[161] Cravetta, Aimone. *Tractatus de antiquitate temporis. Omnia summa fide recognita* (Lvgdvni, haeredes I. Giuntae, 1550). 8.vo. Baudrier, VI, p. 264. Library of Congress. Harvard Law School Library.

[162] Cipolla, Bartolomeo, d. ca. 1477. *Commentaria ... De ædilitio edicto* (Lugduni, apud Haeredes Iacobi Giuntae, 1550). 8.vo. Baudrier, VI, p. 266. A work on canon law.

[163] Robert Estienne published a 9-volume octavo edition of the works of Cicero in Paris, 1543-1550. Bibliothèque Nationale, Paris.

[164] Pedro, de Castrovol. *Incipit tractatus super libros phisicorum [Aristotelis]* ([no printer or place] 1489). Folio. Palau, 49095.

[165] Pedro, de Castrovol. *Tractatus sup[er] psalmum: "Quicumque vult" nominatum* (Pāpilone [no printer or date]). 4.to. Bibliothèque Nationale, Paris. Hispanic Society of America. Penney, p. 106. Palau, 49099.

[166] Antoninus, Saint, Abp. of Florence. There are several folio editions known. This may be the 1543 edition, *Chronica Antonini. Prima (-Tertia) pars Historiarum Domini Antonini* (Lugduni, apud Aegidum et Iacobum Huguetan, 1543) or the 1527 edition, (Lugduni, I. Myt). 3 vols. British Library.

[167] Bible. Concordances. *Biblia. Concordantiae in eadem* (Lugduni: per Iohannem Crespin, 1540). Folio. Baudrier, IV, p. 31.

INVENTARIO DE LOS LIBROS

2 Columella de re rustica[168] in 4to 204		408
2 Cano de penitentia[169] in 4to 85		170
2 Cano de sacramentis[170] in 4to 34		068
1 Chyrurgia Guidonis[171] in fol. 102		102
1 Clypeus thomistarum[172] in fol. 136		136
2 Compendium fratrum minor[um][173] in 4to 51		102
3 Compendium orationum[174] pp. 51		153
1 Commentaria Budei in ling[uam] grecam[175] in fol. 510		510
22 Colloquia tyrann. hessi[176] in 8º 30		660
2 Centum modi argumentandi[177] in 8º 119		238
5 Comentaria Cesaris[178] pp. 68		340

---

[168] Columella, Lucius Junius Moderatus. *De re rustica libri xii*. Editions in octavo were published in Lyons by S. Gryphius in 1537, 1541 and 1548; and in Paris by Estienne, 1543. Bibliothèque Nationale, Paris.

[169] Cano, Melchor. *Relectio de Poenitentia habita in Academia Salmanticensi anno M.D.XLVIII ... super .14. distinctione quarti sententiarum* (Salmanticae, Andreas de Portonariis, 1550 and 1555). 4.to. Biblioteca Nacional, Madrid. University of Pennsylvania. *Catálogo colectivo*, C, 342, 343. Palau, 42330 note.

[170] Ibid. *Relectio de sacramentis in genere habita in Ac. Sal. anno. 1547* (Salmanticae, Andreas de Portonariis, 1550). 4.to. Biblioteca Nacional, Madrid. *Catálogo colectivo*, C, 346. Palau, 42330. University of Pennsylvania.

[171] Guy de Chauliac, ca. 1300-1368. *Ars chirurgica Guidonis Cauliaci ... lucubrationes chirurgicae, ab infinitis prope mendis emendatae* (Venetiis, Apud Iuntas, 1546). Folio. British Library. National Library of Medicine. Durling, no. 2235.

[172] Petrus Nigri, ca. 1434-ca. 1483. *Clypeus thomistarum* (Venice, 1487). Folio. Harvard University has a 1481 edition of this work and the Bibliothèque Nationale, Paris, an undated edition.

[173] See footnote 134.

[174] Salicetus, Nicolaus, d. ca. 1483. *Meditationum, confessionum, ac deuotarum orationum insignis libellus, omnibus Christifidelibus summe necessitatis* (Lugduni, Iacobum Giunta, 1542). 13 cms.

[175] Guillaume Budé's *Commentarii linguae graecae* was published in folio editions by Josse Badius (Paris, 1529), Bebelli (Basel, 1530), Soter (Cologne, 1530), Giunta (Venice, 1530) and Estienne (Paris, 1548). Camerini, I, p. 238.

[176] Schottenius, Hermann. *Colloquia sive confabvlationes Tyronum Literatorvm* (Lugduni, Apud Theobaldum Paganum, 1547 and 1554; Lugduni, Apud J. et F. Frellonios, fratres, 1539 and 1545). 8.vos. Baudrier, IV, pp. 237, 258. Other octavo editions were published in Antwerp by Steelsius in 1540 and in Paris by Ruelle in 1543.

[177] Everardi, Nikolaus. *Centum modi argumentandi* (Venetijs, apud haeredes Lucaeantonij Iuntae, 1544; Lvgdvni apvd Gvilielmvm Rovillivm, 1545). 8.vo. Camerini, I, p. 352. Baudrier, IX, p. 124.

[178] Caesar, Caius Julius. *C. Ivlii Caesaris rerum ab se gestarum commentarii* (Lvgdvni, apvd Seb. Gryphium, 1546). 16.mo. British Library. Baudrier, VIII, p. 201.

SIXTEENTH CENTURY SPANISH BOOKSTORE

3 Cuellar in predicationes Hyppocratis[179] fol. 238   <u>714</u>
    15,041

(f. 19)

1 Cosmographia Appiani[180] in 4to	119	119
8 Cathacumenus Romanus in 8° una	34	272
9 Compendium accentuum[181] in 8°	25	225
3 Cicero de oratore[182] in 8° Gryph[ius]	40	120
1 Caieta[nus] sup[er] psalmos[183] in fol. pre	306	306
2 Comenta[ria] Schodrensis in Plinium in fol.	119	238
1 Chyrurgia Guidonis[184] in 4to	68	068
1 Claudianus poeta[185] in 4to	51	051
1 Consuetudines premonstratenses in fol.	102	102
1 Cornelius celsius[186] pp.	51	051

---

[179] Cuellar, Enrique. *Enrici a Cuellar medice facultatis professoris primi: opus insigne: ad libros tres predictionum Hippocr. Cōmento etiā Gal. aposito et exposito. Anotationes eiusdem sup primo libro que interlegēdum occurrere* (Conimbrie, Ex offi. Iohānis aluari & Ioānis barrerii Calcographor., 1543). Folio. Biblioteca Nacional, Madrid. Santander Rodríguez, pp. 163-164. *Catálogo colectivo*, C, 3759.

[180] Apianus, Petrus. *Libro de Cosmographia, el qual trata la descripcion del Mundo, y sus partes, por muy claro y lindo artificio, augmentado por Gemma Frisio, doctor en Medecina, y Mathematico excellentissimo* (Antwerp, Gregorius Bontius, 1548). 4.to. Maggs Bros. *Catalogue no. 495*, 47. Rhodes, p. 14. The Hispanic Society of America owns an earlier Antwerp edition printed by Aegidius Copenn in 1540. Penney, p. 31. There were also quarto editions in Antwerp in 1529, 1539, 1545, 1550 and 1553 and a Paris edition in 1551.

[181] Robles, Franciscus. *Ratio accentuum omnium fere dictionum difficilium tam linguæ latinæ, quā hebraicæ nonnullarūque græcarū* (Toleti, apud fretres Ferrarienses, 1552). 8.vo. British Library. Rhodes, p. 166. Pérez Pastor, *Toledo*, p. 103, no. 261.

[182] Cicero, Marcus Tullius. *Marci Tvllii Ciceronis De Oratore Libri III* (Lvgdvni, Apvd Seb. Gryphivm, 1540, 1543). 8.vo. Baudrier, VIII, p. 138, 180.

[183] Folio editions of Tomaso de Vio's commentary on the Psalms, *Psalmi Davidici ad hebraicam veritatem castigati*, were published in Venice (Venetiis, in aedibus Luceantonii Iuntae, 1530) and Paris (I. Badii, I. Parui & I. Roigni, 1532). Camerini, 335.

[184] Guy de Chauliac. *Chyrvrgia ...* (n.p., n.d., but with printer's mark of the Lyons printer Vincent de Portonariis the elder). 4.to. National Library of Medicine. Durling, no. 2233.

[185] Claudianus, Claudius. Gryphius published *Cl. Claudiani poetae celeberrimi opera* in Lyons, 1535 and in 1548 in octavo, but I have not found a likely quarto edition.

[186] Celsus, Aulus Cornelius. *De re medica libri octo* (Lugduni, Apud Joan. Tornaesium & Gulielmum Gazeium, 1549). 16.mo. There was reprinted in 1554. Durling, no. 914, 916.

INVENTARIO DE LOS LIBROS

1 Conclusiones bouilli[187] in fol. 102	102
2 Castillo in leg. Tauri[188] in fol. 306	612
2 Cornazanus de re militari[189] in 8° 34	068
1 Canzoni de Petrarcha[190] in 8° 34	034
1 Comentaria Cesaris[191] in 8° Florencie 68	068
1 Consonantie Christi et Prophetarum in 8° 25	025
2 Cicero de natura deorum[192] in 8° Florencie 68	136
1 Carpius contra Eras[mum][193] in 8° 34	034
1 Constitutiones dominice pp. 34	034
5 Cathonis disticha[194] in 8° 25	125
208 Conjuros en papel 51	10,608
3 Conjuros en pergamino 119	357
1 Copie Verborum[195] in 8° falto	----

---

[187] Bouelles, Charles de. *Theologicarum conclusionum ... libri decem* (Paris, Venundantur a Badio, 1515). Folio. British Library.

[188] Juan de Junta published a folio edition of Diego del Castillo de Villasante's *Las leyes de Toro glosadas ... Didaci Castelli... super leges Tauri* in Burgos (Burgis: in officina eximij viris Joanis juncte, 1527). British Library. Boston Public Library. Palau, 48462. Rhodes, p. 47.

[189] Cornazano, Antonio. *De re militari* (Firenze, per li heredi di Philippo di Giunta, 1520). 8.vo. British Library.

[190] Petrarca, Francesco. Perhaps the 1515 octavo edition of *Canzoniere et triomphi* by Filippo Giunti in Florence. Fitzwilliam Museum, Cambridge.

[191] Caesar, Caius Julius. *Commentaria*. Editions of this were published by Filippo Giunti in Florence in 1508 and 1514; and by his heirs in 1520.

[192] Cicero, Marcus Tullius. *De natura deorum*. Probably the 1516 edition by Filippo di Giunta in Florence. 8.vo. BNazionale, Firenze.

[193] Alberto Pio, prince of Carpi. *Alberti Pii Carporvm ... tres et uiginti libri in locos lucubrationum uariarum D. Erasmi Rhoterodami, quos censet ab eo recognoscendos et retractandos* (Venetiis, in aedibus Lucae Antonii Iuntae, 1531). Catholic University of America. The Library notes that leaves 36-51, containing a reply by Erasmus, have been cut out. De Bujanda, V, p. 249. Camerini, I, p. 244.

[194] Cato, Dionysius, pseud. *Disticha de moribus, nomine Catonis inscripta* (Lugduni, apud Ioannem et Franciscum Frellonius fratres, 1543). 8.vo. Palau, 50338. An earlier octavo edition with Erasmus' commentary was produced in Lyons by Seb. Gryphius in 1536, 1537, 1540, 1541 and 1550 and another by T. Paganus (Payen) in 1538. Baudrier, IV, p. 219; VIII, pp. 89, 132, 143, 238.

[195] Erasmus, Desiderius. *De duplici copia verborum ac rerum*. Octavo editions were produced in Lyons (Seb. Gryphius, 1535, 1543 and 1555; Stephanus Dolet, 1540; de Portonariis, 1536; S. Vincentius, 1535) in Paris (Simon Colines, 1530, 1536 and 1539; C. Wechel, 1535, 1539; R Stephanus, 1546), in Cologne (M. Gymnicus, 1530, 1535, 1545 and 1551) in Basel (N. Bryling, 1555) and in Alcalá de Henares (M. de Eguía, 1529). This may also be the work of Oldendorp, Johann, 1480-1567, *De copia verborum et rervm in ivre civili* (Lugduni, Apud Seb. Gryphium, 1543, 1546). 8.vo. Baudrier, VIII, pp. 176, 202.

3 Colloquia Vives[196] in 8°	25	075
1 Cursus Canonicus in 8° pre	510	510
1 Canones Consilior[um] in fol. de novis ale[maña]	510	510
		14,850
		15,041
/ xlii,cmxij /		12,521
		L. 42,412

2 Deliberatio Sotonis in causa pauperum[197] in 4to	51	102
6 Diurnale Romanum[198] pp Alcala	60	360
2 De ratione studii[199] in 8° ale[maña]	85	170
10 Dialectica agricola[200] in 8°	68	680
1 Duarensis de verborum obligationibus[201] in fol.	170	170
1 Diurnale de S. Pedro pp.	45	045
9 Diurnale Romanum de novis[202] pp.	60	540
153 Doctrina mense Sulpitii[203] in 4to	6	918
1 Duareni opuscula[204] in fol.	306	306

---

[196] Vives, Juan Luis, 1492-1540. *Colloquia sive linguae latinae exercitatio*. The University of Illinois possesses a copy printed in Basel by Ioannes Oporinus which they date c. 1560. If that is the work in question, it must be dated before 1556.

[197] Soto, Domingo de. *In cavsa pavpervm deliberatio* (Salmanticæ, In officina Ioãnis Giuntæ, 1545). 4.to. Biblioteca Nacional, Madrid. Houghton Library, Harvard. Palau, 320086. *Catálogo colectivo*, S, 1734.

[198] No copy of an Alcalá de Henares edition appears to have survived. Martín Abad, no. 502.

[199] Erasmus, Desiderius, d. 1536. *De ratione studii deque vita iuuentutis instituenda opuscula diuersorũ autorum* (Basileae, B. Lasius, 1541). 8.vo. Other octavo editions of his were published in Germany in Leipzig (Lipsiae, in aedibus V. Schuman, 1521), Mainz (Moguntiae, in aedibus Ioannis Schoeffer, 1521) and Strassburg (Argentorati, apud Iohannem Hervagivm, 1524; [and:] apud Iohannem Knoblouchum, 1521 and 1526). British Library.

[200] Agricola, Rudolf, 1443-1485. *De inuentione dialectica Libri tres* (Bvrgis, Excvdebat Ioannes à Iunta, 1554). 8.vo. Biblioteca Nacional, Madrid. *Catálogo colectivo*, A, 258.

[201] Duaren, François, 1509-1559. *Comentarivs in lib. XLV Pandectarvm, Tit. de verborvm obligationibvs* (Lvgdvni, Apvd Gvliel. Rovillivm, 1554). Folio. Baudrier, IX, p. 214.

[202] The Giunti firm of Venice published a 16.mo edition of the Diurnum Romanum in 1542. British Library.

[203] Sulpitius, Joannes, Verulanus, 15th cent. This small work is a much-reprinted book on table manners for boys. The large number of copies indicates a publication date close to the 1550s.

[204] Probably the folio edition of Duaren's works published by Rovilius in Lyons, 1554, *Opera omnia ... cum quibusdam aliis opusculis*. It is bound with his *De verborum obligationibus*.

INVENTARIO DE LOS LIBROS

2 Dioscorides[205] in fol. una el uno falto	510	1,020
1 Declaratio arboris consanguinitatis[206] 4to	17	017
2 De usu Pharmacopolis[207] pp.	34	068
	4,396	4,396

(f. 20)

3 Dialogi Castallionis[208] pp.	34	102
17 De Residentia episcoporum[209] pp.	25	425
2 De Bassolis sup[er] sñas[210] in fol. pre	1,020	2,040
3 Dialectica de Naveros[211] in 4to	34	102
2 Diatriba de Justificatione[212] in 8°	85	170

---

[205] The Giunti firm in Florence published folio editions of Dioscorides' *De medica materia libri sex. Interprete Marcello Virgilio*, in 1518 and Feb. 1523 (i.e. 1524). (Florentiæ, per hæredes Philippi Iuntæ). National Library of Medicine. Durling, no. 1141, 1142.

[206] Andreae, Joannes, d. 1348. *Declaratio arboris consanguinitatis*. This work on marriage law was published several times in the incunable period and early 16th-century, primarily in Germany.

[207] Fusch, Remaclus, ca. 1510-1587. *Plantarum omnium quarum hodie apud pharmacopolas usus est* (Parisiis, Ex officina Dyonisii Janotii, 1544). 12 cms. Durling, 1731. Martinus Nutius (i.e. Nucio) published a similar title of Fusch in Antwerp the same year.

[208] Châteillon, Sébastien, 1515-1563. *Dialogorum sacrorvm ad linguam simul & mores puerorum formandos libri IIII* (Medinae, Apud A. Gemard, 1551). 16.mo. Newberry Library. This collection of Bible stories was much reprinted in the 17th and 18th centuries, especially in England, Scotland and Germany. The work was condemned by the Spanish *Index* of 1559. De Bujanda notes that the Index de l'Université de Paris condemned the 1549 Lyons edition of Theobaldus Paganus and that the author was condemned in the Venice *Index* of 1554 and the Roman *Index* of 1559. De Bujanda, I, p. 169; V, p. 344.

[209] Carranza de Miranda, Bartolomé. *Controversia de necessaria residentia personali Episcoporum et aliorum inferiorum Pastorum* (Metinae, Apud Adrianum Ghemartium, 1550). 16.mo. Biblioteca Nacional, Madrid. Pérez Pastor, *Medina del Campo*, p. 68, no. 71. *Catálogo colectivo*, C, 762.

[210] Bassolis, Joannes de, d. ca. 1347. Perhaps his *In tertiũ (-quartũ) sentẽtiarũ* [of Petrus Lombardus] (Parhisius, N. de Pratis, sumptibus F. Regnault 7 I. Frellon, 1516, 1517). Folio. 2 vols. British Library.

[211] Naveros, Jacobus. *Preparatio Dialectica* (Compluti, excud. Joãnes Brocarius, 1542). 4.to. Palau, 188814 note. Martín Abad, p. 499, no. 329. San Lorenzo de El Escorial.

[212] Smith, Richard, 1500-1563. *Diatriba de hominis justificatione aedita Oxoniae in Anglia ... adversus Petrum Martyrẽ vermelinũ* (Lovanii, Apud Antonium Mariam Bergaigne, 1550, i.e. 1551). 8.vo. British Library. Harvard University.

2 Dominicale de Ossuna[213] in 8° 238		476
13 Dialectica de Naveros[214] in 8° 34		442
4 Declamantio sive regule Augustini in 8° 17		068
3 Didacus alvarus in parab. Arnaldi[215] in fol. 85		255
1 Decacordium christianor[um][216] in 8° 68		068
12 Diurnale predicator[um][217] pp. los 3 faltos 51		612
3 Diurnale Cisterciense pp. 51		153
3 Dominicus pico de conversione peccatoris[218] 204		612
4 Decreta Augustana in 4to 25		100
3 Diurnale Hieronymi pp. 51		153
1 Diurnale predicatorum in 8° una 102		102
1 De plantis ecclesie in fol. 306		306
13 Differentie ex Laurentio Valle[219] in 4to 17		221
1 Diurnal de Astorga pp. 51		051
2 Decius de reg[ulis] juris[220] de primis in 8° 52		102
1 De divinis traditionibus in 8° 85		085
1 Dionis[ius] de fide orthodoxa[221] in 8° pre 187		187

---

[213] Osuna, Francisco de. *Pars Meridionalis Euangeliorum Dñicalium totius anni* (Cæsarauguste, in aedibus Ioãne Millian, Viduæ Didaci Hernandes quondam, 1549). 8.vo. British Library. Palau, 206844. Rhodes, p. 145.

[214] Naveros, Jacobus. *Preparatio Dialectica* (Compluti, Per Ioannem Mey Flandrum, 1552). 8.vo. Biblioteca Universitaria, Sevilla. Martín Abad, p. 598, no. 424.

[215] Arnaldus de Villanova, d. 1313. *Commentum novum in Parabolis divi Arnaldi de Villa Nova ... editum per egregium doctorem Alvari Chanca* (Hispali, impressum per Iacobum Cromberger, 1514). Folio. National Library of Medicine. Library of Congress. The commentary is by Diego Álvarez Chanca. Griffin, Appendix One, no. 106. Durling, no. 315.

[216] Vigerius, Marcus. *Decachordū Christianū; controuersiaq[ue] De instrumētis dominice Passionis* (Parisij, In aedibus Iodoci Badij Ascensij, 1517). 2 parts. 8.vo. British Library.

[217] *Diurnum vna cum psalmis nocturnis feriarum secundū consuetudinē ordinis fratrū predicatorū sancti Dominici*. The Giunta firm of Venice published the Dominican diurnal in 1509, 1541, 1547. Camerini, I, p. 139, 328, 370.

[218] Pico, Domingo del. *De ordinaria conversione Peccatoris recedentis a Deo Patre* ... (Caesaraugustae, in aed. Barth. de Nagera, M.D.XLIX). Folio.

[219] Nebrija, Elio Antonio de, ed. *Differētie excerpte ex Laurētio valla* (Lugduni, I. de Platea, 1512). 4.to. Palau, 349458. British Library.

[220] Decio, Felipe. *De Regulis juris* (Lugduni, 1525, 1528, 1534) or Valencia, 1531. Baudrier, IV, p. 26. Palau, 69357.

[221] Denis le Chartreux. *Svmmae fidei orthodoxae* (Parisiis, apud Hieronymum & Dionysiam de Marnef, 1548). 8.vo. 2 vols. Library of Congress.

INVENTARIO DE LOS LIBROS

1 Dictionarium juris[222] in 8° 25		050
2 Decisiones Cassadori[223] in 8° in 2^{bus} 119		238
3 Distinctiones Vincentii in 8° 119		357
1 Dullart Sup[er] phisicam[224] in fol. 85		085
2 Dionys[ius] Areopagita[225] in 8° 119		238
3 De modo celebrandi generalis Concilii[226] in 4to 51		153
14 De constructione octo partium[227] in 8° qqto. 34		476
3 De constructione octo partium sine qto.[228] 17		051
1 Dioscorides[229] pp. 68		068
3 De corrupti lat. sermo. emendatione[230] 8° 85		255

---

[222] This may be *Dictionariolum Iuris Ciuilis, Ex IIII lib. Theophilinarum Institutionum ... Pontio à Quadraginat, Lorigena Avtore* (Lugduni, Apud Mathiam Bonhomme, 1552). 8.vo. Baudrier, X, p. 224.

[223] Cassador, Guilielmus, bp., 1477-1527. *Decisiones ac intelligentiae ad regvlas cancellarie* and *Decisiones seu cōclvsiones avreae*. This 2-volume work on canon law was published in Lyons by Portonariis in 1546 and by Petrus Compater and Bladius Guido in 1547. There are other surviving editions from Paris and Venice.

[224] Dullaert, Joannes, c.1470-1513. *Joannis de Janduno ... super octo libros Aristotelis de Phisico* (Venetiis apud Iuntas, 1551). Folio. Bibliothèque Nationale, Paris.

[225] Dionysius, *Areopagita. D. Dionysii Areopagitæ scripta, cū D. Ignatii martyris Epistolis: & aliis quæ D. Dionysii scriptis annectuntur* (Compluti apud Ioannem Brocariū, 1541). 8.vo. This may also be the octavo edition done by the Giunta firm in Florence in 1516. British Library. Newberry Library. Biblioteca Nacional, Madrid. *Catálogo colectivo*, D, 1041. Rhodes, p. 67.

[226] Durantis, Gulielmus, bp. of Mende, c. 1237-1296. *De modo generalis concilij celebrandi ... Tractatus, in generali Viennae Concilio ... nunc primū aeneis typis missus* (Lugduni, Excudebat J. Crispinus, 1531). 4.to. Newberry Library.

[227] Erasmus, Desiderius. *De octo partivm orationis constrvctione libellus D. Erasmi Rot. cum Iunij Rabirij commentariis* (Lvgdvni, excvdebat Theobaldvs Paganvs, 1551). 8.vo. Baudrier, IV, p 250. The "qqto" (i.e. "cum commentario") refers to the commentary of Junius Rabirius. I have not seen a copy of this work, but suspect that the commentary may be a separate part of the work since the following item in the inventory appears to be the same book without the commentary. The 1559 Spanish *Index* did not mention the grammatical works of Erasmus.

[228] See the previous note. Baudrier mentions a 1550 edition of this work with no mention of a commentary. Baudrier, VIII, p. 239.

[229] Laguna, Andrés de, d. 1560. This might be *Annotationes in Dioscoridem Anazarbevm, per Andream Lacunam* (Lvgdvni, Apud Gulielmum Rouillium, 1554). 16.mo. Bibliothèque Nationale, Paris. National Library of Medicine. Durling, no. 2704. Baudrier, IX, p. 212.

[230] Cordier, Mathurin. *Maturini Corderii De corrupti sermonis emendatione, & Latine loquendi ratione liber unus* (Lugduni, apud Gulielmum Rouilium, 1545). 8.vo. Baudrier, IX, p. 125. Other octavo editions were produced by Sebastián Gryphius in Lyons in 1540, 1541, 1547; Robert Estienne in Paris in 1541; and the heirs of S. Vincentius in Lyons in 1536. The British Library also owns a very similar title by Robertus Vallensis which was published in Paris in 1534.

1 Dictionarium poeticum[231] in 8° 25		025
3 Donatus de octo partibus[232] in 8° 10		030
1 Decisiones Tholose[233] in 8° 51		051
1 Donat[io Constantini] de primatu Romanae sedis[234] in 4to 34		034
3 Divisiones decem nationum[235] in 8° 25		075
1 Dante[236] pp 25		025
1 Dictionarium Hesichii grece[237] 340		340
2 Dispensarium medicine[238] pp 25		050
		9,432
		4,396
xiii, dcn	xxviii	L. 13,828

(f. 21)

7 Elegantie Valle[239] in 4to el uno falto   85   595
3 Epistole Pauli pp   34   102

---

[231] *Dictionarivm poeticvm apvd Gryphium* (Lugduni, apud [Seb.] Gryphium, 1532, 1535, 1536). 8.vo. Baudrier, VIII, p. 63, 85, 92.

[232] Donatus, Aelius. *Donati De Octo Partibvs Orationis Libellvs*. This work was often reprinted in the sixteenth century. The Junta inventory copies may be from Gryphius' press (Lvgdvni, Apvd Seb. Gryphivm, 1536, 1538, 1543 and 1550). 8.vo. Baudrier, VIII, pp. 93, 112, 176, 240.

[233] Toulouse (Archdiocese). *Deci. capelle Tholose. Decisiones materiarum quotidianarum ... in capella sedis archiepiscopalis Tholose decise* (Venundantur Lugd. per Iacobū Giuncti, 1531, 1538). 8.vo. Baudrier, VI, pp. 141, 177.

[234] Donation of Constantine. This was often reprinted. St. Antoninus' work *De Donatione Constantini* was published in Basileae (?) ca. 1520.

[235] *Diuisiones decem nationum totius christianitatis*. The British Library has three octavo editions printed in Rome, all undated, but from the early 16th century.

[236] Dante Alighieri. *Dante* (Lyone, appresso Guglielmo Rouillio, 1551, 1552). 16.mo. British Library. Bibliothèque Sainte-Geneviève. Baudrier, IX, pp. 186, 196.

[237] Hesychius of Alexandria. Folio editions of his Greek dictionary were published by the Giunta firm in Florence in 1520 and by Aldus Manutius in Venice, 1514. British Library.

[238] Cordus, Valerius, 1515-1544. *Pharmacorum conficiendorum ratio, vulgò vocant dispensatorium* (Parisiis, I. Roigny, 1548). 16.mo. British Library. National Library of Medicine. Durling, no. 1027. Another possibility is the work of Thibault Lespleigney (1496-1550), *Enchiridion, (Dispensarium vulgo vocant) compositorum ab antiquoribus junioribusque archiatris medicamentorum tum copia, tum eruditione cunctis artis Medicae candidatis satisfaciens. Nunc primum et natum et editum* (Lugduni, Apud J. et F. Frellonii, fratres, 1543). 16.mo. National Library of Medicine. Durling, no. 2802. Baudrier, V, p. 189.

[239] Valla, Lorenzo, 1405-1457. Quarto editions of the *De linguae Latinae elegantia libri sex* were published in Paris (Parisiis apud Simonem colinaeum, 1532), Granada (Garnatum, 1536), Venice and Lyons; Liondedeis published an edition in Salamanca in 1520. Palau, 349461, 349462. Maggs, 1046.

INVENTARIO DE LOS LIBROS

1 Enchiridion militis [Christiani Erasmi][240] in 8° Alcala	51		051
1 Erasmi De pueris instituendis[241] in 4to	153		153
1 Epistole Eras[mi][242] faltas	340		340
2 Epigrammata gr[aecorum][243] grandi in 4to	51		102
24 Erasmi Juris in 4to	34		816
18 Epistole Plinii[244] in 8° Gryph[ius]	85		1,530
6 Egloga Virgilii[245] in 4to	25		150
1 Epistole Gregorii[246] in 4to	153		153
1 Erasmi hisperaspistes[247] in 8°	68		068
4 Emblemata Alciati[248] pp	51		204
6 Enchrydio [sic] confessorum in 8°	51		306

---

[240] Erasmus, Desiderius. *Enchiridion militis Christiani Erasmi* (Alcalá de Henares, Miguel de Eguía, 1525). 8.vo. This title appears on the 1559 Spanish *Index* as "Erasmi Roterodami, opera haec quae sequuntur: [item 141] Enchiridion militis Christiani, tam latino quam vulgari sermone." The Spanish translation, "Enquiridion del cavallero Christiano" is also on the Spanish *Index* of 1559. The work is also on *Le Catalogue des livres censurez par la faculté de Theologie de Paris* (1544). De Bujanda, I, p. 176; V, pp. 348, 474-75. Martín Abad, p. 316, no. 142.

[241] Erasmus, Desiderius. *Libellus novvs et elegans D. Erasmi roterodami, De pveris statim ac liberaliter instituendis, cum aliis compluribus* (Basileae, per Hieronymum Frobenium [and others], 1529). 4.to. Houghton Library, Harvard University.

[242] Erasmus, Desiderius. The high cost of this edition makes it likely that this was one of the folio editions produced by Froben in Basel, such as *Des. Erasmi roterodami* Epistolarvm opvs complectens vniversas qvotqvot ipse avtor vnqvam evvlgavit, avt evvlgatas uoluit, quibus praeter nouas aliquot additae sunt & praefationes, quas in diuersos omnis generis scriptores non paucas idem conscripsit ... (Basileae ex officina Frobeniana [1541]). Folio. Harvard University. Other folio editions were published by Froben in 1521, 1529 and 1538. The Portonariis Salamanca inventory contained a copy of the *Epistolae*. See above, p. 15.

[243] Greek Anthology. *Epigrammatum Graecorum libri. vii. annotationibus J. Brodaei illustrati* (Basileae, Apud H. Frobenium & N. Episcopium, 1549). Folio. British Library.

[244] Plinius Caecilius Secundus, Caius. Sebastian Gryphius published octavo editions of his *Epistolarum libri decem* in Lyons in 1537, 1539, 1542, 1547 and 1551. Baudrier, VIII, pp. 102, 124, 161, 211, 249.

[245] Virgilius Maro, Publius. This may be the 1504 quarto edition of *Eclogae Vergilii* by the firm of Filippo Giunta in Florence.

[246] Gregorius I, the Great, Saint. *Epistole ex registro beatissimi Gregorij* (Parrhysijs, Udalrici Gering et Mag. Berchtoldi Rembolt, 1508). 4.to

[247] Erasmus, Desiderius. *Hyperaspistes diatribae adversus Seruum Arbitrium Martini Lutheri.* Several editions were published by Froben in Basel (1526, 1527) and by Hillenium in Antwerp (1526).

[248] Alciati, Andrea. *Emblemata D. A. Alciati, denvo ab ipso avtore recognita* (Lvgdvni, apud Gulielmum Rouillium, 1552). 16.mo. Baudrier, IX, p. 196.

2 Epistole Hieronymi[249] in 4to 238		476
1 Eusebii opera[250] in fol. ale[maña] 680		680
5 Expositio titulor[um][251] viejos in 4to 68		340
4 Epistole Pii pape[252] in 4to 34		136
2 Epistole Petri Venerabilis[253] in fol. 204		408
1 Euthymius Sup[er] Psalmos[254] in 8° pre 170		170
1 Epitome Juris in 8° 85		085
2 Elogia clarorum viror[um][255] in fol. 170		340
10 Epistole Francisci Nigri[256] in 4to 25		250
3 Elegantie Valle[257] in 8° 85		255
1 Emillius Farett De aquirenda possessione[258]	272	272

---

[249] Jerome, Saint. *Opvs epistolarvm divi Evsebii Hieronymi Stridonensis, vna cvm scholiis Erasmi* (Lvgdvni, in typographaria officina Ioannis Crespini, 1528). 4.to in 3 vols. Volume 2 contains the printer's mark of Jacobus Giunta. Baudrier, IV, p. 22.

[250] Eusebius *Pamphili*, bp. of Caesarea. *Opera* (Basileae, per Henrichum Petri, 1548). Folio. 2 volumes bound as one.

[251] Brant, Sebastian, 1458-1521. *Expositio titulorum. Expositiões siue declarationes omnium titulorum iuris* (Lugduni, apud Jacobum Giuncti, 1538). 4.to. Library of Congress. The note that these are from an old edition ("viejos") may be intended to distinguish them from the Giunta firm's 1546 edition which had a slightly different title.

[252] Pius II, Pope, 1405-1464. Pius II, the humanist writer Enea Silvio Piccolomini, was the author of *Epistole τ varii tractatus Pij secūdi pōtificis maximi* (Venūdātur Lugduni, ab Stephano gueynard ... Impresse ... per Iohannem Moyliñ al's de cambray, 1518). 4.to. Bibliothèque Nationale, Paris. Baudrier, XI, p. 245.

[253] Pierre le Vénérable, ca. 1092-1156. *Epistolarum libri VI* (Parisiis, Damianus Hichman, 1522). Folio.

[254] Euthymius Zigabenus. *Commentarij in omnes Psalmos è Græco in Latinam conuersi* (Parisiis, apud Ioannem Foucherium, 1547). 8.vo. Columbia University Library.

[255] Giovio, Paolo. *Elogia veris clarorum virorum imaginibus apposita, quae in Musaeo Joviano Comi spectantur* (Venetiis, Apud M. Tramezinum, 1546). Folio. A folio edition was also produced in Florence by Torrentinus in 1551. Both in British Library.

[256] Negri, Francesco, 1500-1563. *Epistole Francisci Nigri* (Venundantur Parisius a Petro Gandoul, [n.d.]). 4.to. Bibliothèque Nationale, Paris.

[257] Valla, Lorenzo. There are numerous 15th and 16th-century editions of his *De elegantia linguae latinae libri sex*. This may be the Lyons edition of Gryphius (Lugduni, 1538, 1548) of Dolet (Lugduni, Apud Steph. Doletum, 1541) of Paganus (Paganus Lugduni, 1554); or the Paris edition of Stephanus (Parisiis, 1541) or Bogardus (Parisiis, Apud Iacobum Bogardum, 1545).

[258] Ferretti, Emilio, 1489-1552. *In tit. de acquirend. possess., vsucap. l. iii, verbor. obligat., prælectiones* (Lugduni, Apud Mathiam Bonhomme, 1552). Folio. British Library. Baudrier, X, p. 222.

INVENTARIO DE LOS LIBROS

2 Enchridion [sic] Psalmor[um][259] pp Gryph[ius] 51		102
7 Enchrydion eckeii[260] pp 51		357
1 Eusebii historia ecclesiastica[261] in fol. 476		476
4 Epistole ovidii qqto[262] in 4to 85		340
1 Epistole Hieronymi[263] in fol. 510		510
4 Elegantie Augustini Dati[264] in 8° 25		100
1 Epistole Tullii qqto[265] in fol. 306		306
2 Epistole Bembi[266] in 8° 85		170
1 Epistole Ovidii[267] in 8° 34		034
2 Epidemìe Hyppocratis[268] pp 51		102
1 Enchridion Erasmi[269] pp 51		051

---

[259] Campen, Jean de, d. 1538. *Enchiridion Psalmorvm. Eorundem ex ueritate Hebraica uersionem* (Lugd., Seb. Gryphius excvd., 1533). 16.mo. Bibliothèque Nationale, Paris. Folger Shakespeare Library. I believe this is the first edition of this paraphrase of the Psalms. There were later 16.mo editions by Gryphius in 1534, 1536 and 1537. Baudrier, VIII, p. 70, 76, 93, 105. Steelsius produced a 12.mo edition in Antwerp in 1535. British Library (1534 ed.).

[260] Eck, Johann, 1486-1543. *Enchiridion locorvm commvnivm aduersus Lutherum & alios hostes Ecclesiæ* (Lvgdvni, Theobaldus Paganus, 1554 and 1555). 16.mo. Baudrier, IV, pp. 258, 262.

[261] This may be Estienne's edition of Eusebius' *Ecclesiasticae historiae ... lib. X* (Lvtetiae Parisiorvm, ex officina Roberti Stephani, 1544). Folio.

[262] Ovidius Naso, Publius. *Epistole cū cōmēto* (Lugduni, I. Dauid, 1528). 4.to. British Library.

[263] Jerome, Saint. *Liber aepistolarvm* (Lugduñ., I. Mareschal, 1526). Folio. 3 parts. The commentary is by Erasmus. Earlier folio editions were published in Lyons in 1508 and 1513.

[264] Dati, Agostino. *Elegantiarum linguæ Latinæ* (Lugduni, apud heredes Simonis Vincentij, 1539). 8.vo. British Library.

[265] A folio edition of Cicero's *Epistolae familiares*, with the commentary of H. Crescentius and others, was published in Venice by Joannes de Tridino in 1526. Michel de Vascosan published another in Paris in 1534. Jean de Roigny printed a folio edition with the commentary of J. Badius, L. Scoppa and F. Robortelli for Benedictus Prevost in Paris, 1549.

[266] Bembo, Pietro, *cardinal*, 1470-1574. *Petri Bembi Epistolarum* (Lugduni, excudebat Theobaldus Paganus, 1540). 8.vo. Baudrier, VI, p. 190; IX, p. 223. The British Library has a 1538 octavo edition published in Lyons by the heirs of S. Vincent.

[267] Ovidius Naso, Publius. *Heroides Epistolae Ouidij cvm Aulii Sabini Responsionibus* (Lugduni, Apud Seb. Gryphium, 1534). 8.vo. British Library. This includes the commentary of J. B. Egnatius and G. Morillon. Baudrier, VIII, p. 80.

[268] Hippocrates. *Libri epidemiorvm Hippocratis primvs, tertivs, sextvs* (Lvgdvni, apud Gulielmus Rouillium, 1550). 16.mo. Baudrier, IX, p. 180. Bibliothèque Nationale, Paris.

[269] Erasmus, Desiderius. *Enchiridion militis Christiani ... D. Ersasmo ... autore. Cui accessit; De praeparatione ad mortem libellus...* (Lugduni, n.p., n.d.). 16.mo. Bibliothèque Nationale, Paris.

3 Enchridion Erasmi[270] in 8° 51		153
15 Epistole selecte in 4to 10		150
1 Epistole aliquod Budei[271] in 4to 34		034
1 Elucidatorium ecclesiasticum[272] in 8° 170		170
2 Epitome adagiorum Erasmi[273] in 8° 85		170
1 Enarratio rei medice in 4to 34		034
1 Erasmus de matrimonio[274] in 8° 17		017
2 Eras[mus] de misericordia dei[275] in 8° 25		050
		11,308

(f. 22)

1 Erasmus contra Carpium[276] in 4to 34		034
1 Eras[mus] de interdictum esu carnium[277] in 8° 17		017

---

[270] Erasmus, Desiderius. *Enchiridion militis Christiani saluberrimis præceptis refertum* (Lugd., Sebastianvs Gryphivs Germanvs excvdebat, 1529, 1531, 1538, 1541). 8.vo. Bibliothèque Nationale, Paris. Baudrier, VIII, pp. 52, 60, 112, 146.

[271] Josse Badius Ascensius published quarto editions of Guillaume Budé's *Epistolae* and *Epistolae posteriores* in Paris in 1520 and 1522.

[272] Clichtove, Josse van, d. 1543. *Elvcidatorivm ecclesiasticvm, ad officivm ecclesiae pertinentia planius exponens: et quatuor libros complectens... Qvarta aeditio* (Parisiis, Apud Ioannem Roigny, 1548). 2 vols. 8.vo. Colophon at end of vol. 2: Excvdebat Anthonius Iurianus. Harvard University.

[273] Erasmus, Desiderius. *Adagiorum epitome*. There are several octavo editions before 1556, including those of Jan van der Loe in Antwerp (1553), Sebastien Gryphius in Lyons (1544, 1550, 1553), Martinus Gymnicus in Cologne (1545), Michael Hillenius in Antwerp (1527, 1545), Ioannes Gymnicus in Cologne (1537, 1539, 1542), and S. Colinaeus in Paris (1523). This was in the Portonariis inventories of 1547 and 1552. See above, p. 15.

[274] Erasmus, Desiderius. *Christiani matrimonii institutio* (Basileae, apud Joannem Frobenium, 1526). 8.vo. Yale University. Harvard University. British Library. This title is on the Paris *Index* of 1544 and the Spanish *Index* of 1559. De Bujanda, I, p. 179; V, p. 350. Other octavo editions were published in Antwerp (apud M. Hillenium, n.d.) and Cologne (s.i., n.d.).

[275] Erasmus, Desiderius. *De misericordia dei* (Antuerpiae, apud J. Gymnicum, 1540; Basileae, apvd Io. Frob., 1524). 8.vo. The Spanish translation is on the Spanish *Index* of 1559. De Bujanda, V, p. 541.

[276] Erasmus, Desiderius. *Apologia adversus rhapsodias calumniosarum querimoniarum Alberti Pii, quondam Carporum principis* (Basileae, in off. Frobeniana, 1531). 8.vo. Bibliothèque Nationale, Paris. See also footnote 193. I have not found a quarto edition of this work.

[277] Erasmus, Desiderius. *De interdictum esu carnium*. Froben published an octavo edition of this in Basel (1522). Other editions: Strasbourg (Argentorati, in aedibus Knoblouchi, 1522), Cologne, (Coloniae, Io. Soter, 1522) and Paris (Lvteciae, Impensis Cōradi Resch, 1523). De Bujanda, I, p. 177; V, p. 350.

INVENTARIO DE LOS LIBROS

1 Eras[mus] de recta pronuntiatione²⁷⁸ in 8° 34		034
1 Epistole manardi²⁷⁹ in 8° Lion 187		<u>187</u>
		272
		<u>11,308</u>
/ xi,dlxxx /		L. 11,580

1 Fortalitium fidei²⁸⁰ falto dela mentado 8°		----
1 Fabule Esopi²⁸¹ in 8° faltos		----
1 Faventinus in prognostica Hyppocratis²⁸²	204	204
15 Flosculus sacramentorum²⁸³ in 8°	17	255
2 Figure biblie²⁸⁴ in 8° el uno falto	34	068
1 Foroliviensis de novo orbe²⁸⁵ in fol.	136	136
8 Fabule esopi in 8° miles	51	408

---

²⁷⁸ Erasmus, Desiderius. *De recta Latini Graeciqve sermonis pronuntiatione*. Octavo editions were published in Paris (Parisiis, ex officina S. Colinaei, 1528; Parisiis, ex officina R. Stephani, 1538; Lvtetiæ, ex officina Rob. Stephani, 1547), Basel (Basileae, in officina Frobeniana, 1528), and Lyons (Lvgdvni, S. Gryphivs excvd., 1531).

²⁷⁹ Manardi, Giovanni, 1462-1536. *Io. Manardi Ferrariensis medici Epistolarum medicinalium*. Perhaps the 1532 edition by Gryphius (Baudrier, VIII, p. 64) or the 1549 edition by Godefridi & Marcelli Beringorum, fratrum, both octavos printed in Lyons. National Library of Medicine. Durling, no. 2913, 2918.

²⁸⁰ Espina, Alfonso de, bp. of Orense. *Fortalitium fidei contra Judeos: Sarracenos: aliosq[ue] christiane fidei inimicos* [Lugduni] Venūdātur a Stephano gueynard, [1511]. 8.vo. S. Gueynard published another edition in Lyons in 1525. Palau, 82477. British Library. Baudrier, XI, p. 256.

²⁸¹ Baudrier (V, pp. 17, 178; VIII, pp. 122, 130, 183, 267) lists octavo editions of Aesop's fables published in Lyons in 1539, 1540, 1542, 1544 and 1554. The British Library has octavo editions published in Lyons in 1535 (Lugduni, I. Giunta); and in 1539 and 1554 (Lugduni, apud S. Gryphium).

²⁸² Vittori, Benedetto, d. 1561. *In Hippocratis Prognostica commentarii. His accessit Theoricae latitudinum medicinae liber* (Florentiae, apud Laurentium Torrentinum, 1551). Folio. National Library of Medicine. Durling, no. 4661.

²⁸³ The library of the University of Oviedo has a copy of Pedro Fernández de Villegas' *Flosculus sacramentorū* (Salamanca, Juan de Junta, 1546). 8.vo. Biblioteca Universitaria, Oviedo. Ruíz Fidalgo, no. 138. The Biblioteca Pública de Toledo lists a 1543 printing of this, also by Juan de Junta. 8.vos. The first edition was published by Melgar in Burgos, 1526. Maggs, 1104.

²⁸⁴ Rampegolo, Antonio. *Figure biblie clarissimi viri fratris Anthonij de Rampegolis, ordinis Sancti Augustini*. Editions were published in Paris by François Regnault in 1506 and 1508; Jehan Petit in 1513, 1518; and in Lyons by V. de Portonariis in 1530 and by Rovillius in 1554.

²⁸⁵ Anghiera, Pietro Martyre d', 1455-1526. *Ioannes ruffus foroliuiensis Archiepūs Cosentinⁱ : legatⁱ apo. ad lectorē de orbe nouo* (Cōpluto, in contubernio Arnaldi Guillelmi, 1516). Folio. Library of Congress. Newberry Library. New York Public Library. Martín Abad, p.246, no. 49A. This is the first edition.

1 Faber sup[er] epistolas Pauli[286] in fol. 204		204
1 Faber sup[er] instituta[287] in 8° Lion 170		170
2 Flores poetarum[288] in 8° ale[maña] 153		306
1 Fulgo de dictis et factis memorab[ilibus][289] in 8° 187		187
1 Formalitates Scoti[290] in fol. 68		068
2 Figuerettus in Plinium[291] in fol. 51		102
2 Flores ultimarum voluntatum[292] in 4to 34		068
4 Flores Avicenne[293] in 8° 51		204
1 Faber sup[er] Evangelia[294] in fol. ale[maña] 476		476

---

[286] Le Fèvre, Jacques, d'Étaples. *Epistolae diui Pauli apostoli* (Venetiis, 1533). This appears on the Spanish *Index* of 1559 under "Iacobi Fabri Stapulensis ... et epistolas Pauli". De Bujanda, V, p. 379.

[287] Ibid. *Super institutionibus ... in quatuor libros Institutionum d. Iustiniani imperatoris lectura* (Lugduni, Jacobus Giunta, 1540, 1543). Folio. Baudrier, VI, pp. 188, 204.

[288] The British Library has incunable editions of this title published in Leipzig and in Cologne, but both are in 4.to.

[289] See footnote 296.

[290] Antonius Trombeta, Bp. of Urbino, is the author of a commentary on Duns, Joannes Scotus, *Magistri Antonii Trombete in tractatū formalitatum Scoti sententia* (Venice, 1504). Folio. British Library. The Giunta firm of Venice published a folio edition in 1525, *Formalitates Scoti*, which includes both Trombeta's commentary and that of Antonio de Fantis. Camerini, I, p. 223.

[291] Figueretus, Martinus. *Joāni Serenissimo Lusitanorum Regi M. F. S. D.* [Fol. 1:] Cōmentū super prologū naturalis historie Plinii cōpositū per M. F. (Ulyxbone, 1529). Folio. British Library.

[292] Rolandinus de Passageriis, d. 1300. *Flores ultimarum voluntatum, non sine sudore collecti* (Lugduni, per Antonium Blanchard, 1524). 4.to. Bibliothèque Nationale, Paris. Baudrier, V, p. 96. This is a work to assist notaries in the preparation of last wills and testaments.

[293] Avicenna. *Flores Avicenne collecti super quinq[ue] canonibus quos edidit in medicina* (Lugd. Per Gilbertum de Villiers, impensis Bartholomei Trot, 1514). 8.vo. British Library. The National Library of Medicine owns this and another edition published in Lyons (Impressi per Claudium Davost alias de Troys, expensis Bartholomei Trot, 1508). Durling, no. 411, 412.

[294] Le Fèvre d'Étaples, Jacques. *Commentarii initiatorii in Evangelia* (Basileae, in aedibus A. Cratandri, 1523; Coloniae, Excusum expensis M. Godefridi Hittorpij, 1532?; Coloniae, Ex officina Euchariana, 1541). Folio. British Library. Princeton Theological Seminary. Cornell University. Andover-Harvard Theological. This work appears in the Spanish *Index* of 1559, under the heading "Iacobi Fabri Stapulensis: In evangelia". De Bujanda, V, p. 379. The Bibliothèque Nationale, Paris, and the Newberry Library also have copies of the folio edition from the press of Simon de Colines in Paris (Meldis, impensis S. Colinaei, 1522).

INVENTARIO DE LOS LIBROS

1 Fuchii practica[295] in 8° Lion 85		085
2 Fulgo de dictis factisque memorabilibus[296] fol. 238		476
1 Firmamentum ordinis Sancti Franciscini[297] 204		204
17 Formalitates Castrovol[298] in 4to 6		102
2 Flores ultimarum voluntatum[299] in 8° 51		102
2 Fiametta del Boccatio[300] in 8° 34		068
1 Formulare Instrumentor[um][301] in 8° 34		034
1 Faventinus de morbo gallico[302] 102		102
8 Flores legum[303] in 8° 12		096
2 Formulare advocator[um][304] in 8° 34		068
2 Floriani Campegii opuscula Symphoriani[305] 34		034

---

[295] Fuchs, Leonhart. Several of the editions of medical works of Fuchs are on the Spanish *Index* of 1559. De Bujanda, V, p. 400-01. The edition in the inventory may be his *De sanandis totivs humani corporis malis. libri quinque* (Lvgdvni, Apud Ioannem Frellonium, 1547, 1551). 8.vo. Baudrier, V, p. 208, 204. G. Rovilius also published this work in Lyon under the title *De curandi ratione libri XIII* (Lugduni, Apud Guliel. Rovillii, & Antonii Constantini, 1548). 8.vo. National Library of Medicine. Durling, no. 1690, 1691

[296] Fregoso, Battista, 1453-1504. *De dictis factisque memorabilibus collectanea* (Mediolani, I. Ferrarius impressit, 1509). Folio. Library of Congress. Newberry Library.

[297] Holy Name College Library (Washington, D.C.) has a copy of *Firmamenta trium ordinum Beatissimi Patris ... Francisci* [Parisiis, Franciscus Regnault, Johannis Petit et Johannis Frellon, 1512].

[298] Pedro, *de Castrovol*. [*Tractatus formalitatum*] (n.p., 1468). 4.to. The text begins: Incipiunt formalitates de nouo cōpilate [...]. University of Texas. Hain-Copinger, 1482. The work contains only 19 leaves. The question which comes to mind is the large number of copies in the inventory, almost a century after printing.

[299] Rolandinus de Passageriis. An octavo edition was published by the Giunti firm of Lyons in 1550. Baudrier, VI, p. 269. See above, footnote 292.

[300] Boccaccio, Giovanni. This is a selection from his *Novelas*, which was condemned in the Portuguese part of the Spanish *Index* of 1559. De Bujanda, V, pp. 509-10. See footnote ?.

[301] Formularium instrumentorum. *Formulare instrumentorū nec non artis notariatus. Nouiter impressum atq[ue] cum summa diligentia castigatum* (Venetijs, in officina Luce Antonij Iunte, 1536). 8.vo. Library of Congress.

[302] Vittori, Benedetto (or Victorius, Benedictus), d. 1561. *De morbo gallico liber* (Florentiae, Laurentius Torrentinus, 1551). 18 cms. Lilly Library, University of Indiana. National Library of Medicine. Durling, no. 4653.

[303] *Flores legū, aut congeries auctoritatum juris civilis.* The British Library has octavo editions by Jehan Petit in Paris [1500?] and 1517 and a 1515 edition by Berthold Rembolt. The University of Chicago has an octavo edition printed in Strassburg in 1496.

[304] Formularium procuratorum. *Formulare Aduocatorum et Procuratorum Romanae Curie* (Lugduni, per Simonem biuilaqua, 1518). 8.vo. Biblioteca Nacional, Madrid.

[305] Champier, Symphorien, 1472-1539. [?]

1 Formularium contractuum[306] in 4to 34   034

/ iiij,ccxcv /   L. 4,295

(f. 23)

49 Gramatica clenardi per Vaseum[307] in 8°   51   2,499
1 Gabriel sup[er] sñas[308] in 4to falto   ----
9 Gramatica nebrissensis[309] in 8°   51   459
4 Gesta Romanorum[310] in 8°   51   204
1 Gramatica Consentini[311] in 4to   25   025
1 Grego[rius] in sumulas Petri Hispani in fol. ligat.   102   102
4 Gabriel sup[er] Cano[n] misse[312] in 4to   153   612
3 Gregorius sup[er] Ezechielem[313] in 8°   102   306
2 Gramatica hebraica[314] in 8°   170   340
6 Gramatica del ciego in 8°   12   072

---

[306] A quarto edition of the *Formularium diuersorum contractuum* was published in Venice by Luc' Antonio Giunta in 1523. University of Pennsylvania. Camerini, I, p. 212.

[307] Juan de Junta published Nicolas Clenardo's (or Cleynaerts') *Institvtiones grammaticae Latinæ ... per Ioannem Vasæum Brugensem auctæ & recognitæ* (Salmanticae, [ca. 1551]). 8.vo. Biblioteca Universitaria, Salamanca. *Index Aureliensis*, 141.309.

[308] Biel, Gabriel. *Gabriel Biel super primũ librum Sententiarum* (in Lugduneñ. emporio, V. de Portonariis [and Jac. Giunta]; arte et industria Ioannis Crespin, 1532). 4.to. British Library. Baudrier, VI, p. 147.

[309] The Latin grammar of Elio Antonio de Nebrija (or Lebrija), *Aelii Antonii Nebrissensis introductiones ... ab Humberto Montemoretano redditae* (Lugduni, Haeredes Iacobi Iuntae, 1549). 8.vo.

[310] The *Gesta Romanorum* was often reprinted in the 15th and 16th centuries. Several octavo editions were published in Paris by Jean Petit.

[311] Consentius, Publius. *P. Consentij... de re grammatica breuissima institutio*. I have not located an edition.

[312] Biel, Gabriel. *Gabriel Biel sup[er] canone misse cum additionibus* (Lugduni ĩ officina Dominici Uerardi, 1541). 4.to. Quarto editions of this work were produced in Lyons by the Giunta firm and by Jean Crespin in 1527 (Baudrier, IV, pp. 32, 405; VI, p. 124) and in Toledo by Villaquirán in 1523 (Pérez Pastor, *Toledo*, p. 49, no. 94). A folio edition was printed by Johannes Clein in Lyons in 1517.

[313] Gregorius I, the Great, Saint. *Homeliae diui Gregorii super ezechielem* (Parrhisiis, Johannis petit, 1511; or Lugduni, S. Beuilaqua, 1515). 8.vos. British Library.

[314] Zamora, Alonso de. *Introductiones artis grammatice hebraice* (In Academia Complutensi, in aedibus Michaelis de Eguia, 1526). 8.vo. Maggs, 1115. Biblioteca Nacional, Madrid. British Library. Houghton Library, Harvard University. Palau, 379023. Rhodes, p. 7. Martín Abad, p. 329, no. 159.

Inventario de los libros

1 Gramatica Prisciani[315]	in fol.	153	153
6 Gomez de ratione medendi[316]	in 4to	25	150
12 Gentilis de peste[317]	in 4to	25	300
5 Gumiel de quantitate syllabarum[318]	in 4to	25	125
2 Gramatica Lascaris[319]	in 4to	170	340
4 Gramatica Eduardi Lusitani	in 4to	34	136
1 Gramatica de Spauterii[320]	in 8°	51	051
1 Guiliaudus in epistolas Pauli[321]	in 8° pre	136	136
1 Gometius sup[er] Bto.	in 8°	119	119
2 Gometius in reg. Cancellarie[322]	in 8°	187	374
2 Gribaldus de ratione studendi[323]	in 8°	51	102
4 Gramatica Cornelii Valerii[324]	in 4to	34	136
2 Gerson de Imitatione Christi[325]	pp.	34	068

---

[315] Priscianus. This may be one of the folio editions of Priscianus' *Institutiones grămatice* (Paris, Typ. Badiana, 1516). Other Paris editions in 1517 by O. Senant and 1527, no printer named.

[316] Gómez, Jorge. *De ratione minuendi sanguinem in morbo laterali* (Toleti, ex officina Ioannis de Ayala, 1539). 4.to. National Library of Medicine. Palau, 103581. Pérez Pastor, *Toledo*, p. 76, no. 182. Durling, no. 2134.

[317] Gentilis Fulginas. *Consilium contra pestilentiam* (n.p., after 1500?). National Library of Medicine. Durling, no. 2046.

[318] Gomiel, Pedro de. *Petri Gomiel opusculū quibusdam regulis deseruiens: quae de quantitate syllabarū a Gramaticis traductor* (Salmantice, 1493). 4.to. Palau, 104531. I have not found a copy of this work. The British Library possesses a facsimile edition.

[319] Lascaris, Constantino, 1434-1501? This is probably the quarto edition of *Graecae institutiones* (Venetiis, in aedibus B. Zanetti, 1537). Legrand, III, no. 359. Bibliothèque Nationale, Paris.

[320] Despautère, Jean, ca. 1460-1520. Editions in octavo of his Latin grammar, *Grammaticae prima pars* were published in Paris by Josse Badius Ascensius in 1512 and 1522.

[321] Guilliaud, Claude, 1493-1551. *In canonicas apostolorvm septem epistolas, collatio* (Parisiis, apud Audoënum Paruum, 1548). 8.vo. Harvard University.

[322] Gómez, Luís, bp., d. 1542. *Commentaria ... in regulas Cancellariae Iudicales* (Lugduni, Ioannes et Franciscus Frellonii, 1545). 8.vo. Palau, 103615. Baudrier, V, 200. Other possible editions include those published in Paris in 1545, 1546, 1552, 1554, and 1555.

[323] Gribaldi, Matteo, d. 1564. *De methodo ac ratione studendi libri tres* (Lugduni, apud Antonium Vincentium, 1541; [and:] Lugduni, apud Theobaldum Paganum, 1543; S. Gryphius, 1544). 8.vo. Baudrier, VIII, p. 188.

[324] Valerius, Cornelius. *Grammaticarum institutionum libri IV*. The Library of Congress has a quarto copy published in 1557 (Lutetiae, apud, F. Morellum) but I have not found an earlier edition.

[325] Imitatio Christi. *Ioannis Gersonis ... De Imitatione Christi Libelli IIII* (Lugduni, apud Theobaldum Paganum, 1545, 1554, 1555). 16.mo. Baudrier, IV, pp. 260, 263.

1 Gramatica Linacri[326] in 8° Gryph[ius] 85		085
1 Galeni ars medicinalis[327] in fol. 85		085
1 Galeni opuscula[328] in 8° 34		034
1 Galen. de alimentis[329] pp 20		020
2 Galen. de defferentiis febrium[330] pp 12		024
1 Galen. de morbor[um] sympto[matum].[331] pp 25		025
4 Galen. de locis affectis[332] pp 30		120
1 Galen. de crisibus[333] pp 12		012
1 Gramatica Diomedis[334] in fol. 51		051
2 Gramatica Aldi[335] in 4to 51		102
2 Gramatica Prisciani[336] in 4to 102		204

---

[326] Seb. Gryphius published Thomas Linacre's *Rudimenta grammatices Thomae Limacri [sic] ex Anglico sermone in Latinum versa* in octavo in Lyons in 1548, 1552 and 1559. Robert Stephanus published octavo editions in Paris in 1533, 1540 and 1550.

[327] Galenus. There are several surviving editions of Galen's *Ars medicinalis*. This may be the 1550 edition (Parisiis, Ex officina typographica Lodovici Begatti). 24 cm. National Library of Medicine. Durling, no. 1853.

[328] Galenus. *Aliquot opuscula nunc primum Venetorum opera inventa et excusa* (Lugduni, apud Gulielmum Rovilium, 1550). 8.vo. National Library of Medicine. Durling, no. 1816.

[329] Galenus. *De elementis libri dvo, Victore Trincavelio interprete* (Lvgdvni, apud Gulielmum Rovillium, 1548, 1550). 16.mo. Baudrier, IX, pp. 142, 171. National Library of Medicine. Durling, no. 1881, 1882.

[330] Galenus. *De differentiis febrium* (Lvgdvni, apud Gulielmum Rovillium, 1548, 1550). 16.mo. Baudrier, IX, pp. 142, 171. National Library of Medicine (1548 ed.). Durling, no. 1878.

[331] Galenus. *De morborvm et symptomatvm differentiis et cavsis libri sex* (Lvgdvni, apud Gulielmum Rovillium, 1550). 16.mo. Baudrier, IX, p. 171. National Library of Medicine. Durling, no. 1818.

[332] Galenus. *De locorvm affectorvm notitia libri sex* (Lugduni, apud Gulielmum Rovillium, 1547, 1549). 16.mo. Baudrier, IX, p. 151. National Library of Medicine. Durling, no. 1892, 1893.

[333] Galenus. *De crisibvs libri tres* (Lugduni, apud Gulielmum Rovillium, 1547 and 1549). 16.mo. Baudrier, IX, pp. 132, 151. National Library of Medicine. Durling, no. 1869, 1871.

[334] Diomedes, *the Grammarian. Diomedis ... de Arte grāmatica opus Vtilissimum* (Pisauri, per Hieronymum Soncinum, 1511). Folio. British Library.

[335] The Latin grammar of Aldus Manutius, *Institutionum grammaticarum libri quatuor*, was published by the Giunta firm in Florence (1519); by Melchor Sessa (1521) and the Manutius firm (1523) in Venice; and by the Estiennes in Paris (1527 and 1531).

[336] Priscianus. Quarto editions of his grammatical works were published in Florence (Florentiae, haeredes Philippi Iuntae, 1525), Paris (In typographia Badiana, 1527), Venice (Venetiis, In aedibus Aldi et Andreae Asvlani, 1527) and Basel (Basileae, apud N. Bryling, 1554).

3 Gramatica Marinei Siculi[337] in 4to 25   075
2 Guliel. Rubio sup[er] sñas[338] in fol. 1,020   2,040
1 Gramatica hebraica Xantis pag.[339] in 4to 136   136
1 Gentilis de fulginio[340] in fol. una   170   170
1 Galeottus de homine[341] in 4to 51   051
10 Gramatica hebraica de Martynes[342]   34   340
18 Grobianus et grobiana[343] in 8°   51   408
1 Gramatica del Busto[344] in 8°   17   <u>017</u>
                                                10,808

(f. 24)

3 Gramatica Donati[345] in 4to 25   075

---

[337] Marineo, Lucio, *Siculus*, 1444?-1536. *Grāmatica breuis ac perutilis* (Compluti excudebat Michael de Eguia, 1532). 8.vo. British Library. Rhodes, p. 127. Martín Abad, p. 411, no. 247. I do not know of a quarto edition of this grammar.

[338] Rubio, Guillermo de. *Disputatorum in quatuor libros Magistri Sententiarum tomus prior super primum et secundum diligenter ab jodoco Badio Ascensio impressus* (Parrhisios, Vaenunduntur in aedibus dicti Ascensii, 1518). Folio. 2 vols. Biblioteca Nacional, Madrid.

[339] Pagnino, Santi, 1470-1541. *Hebraicas institutiones ... grāmatices hebraicae facultatis ...* (Lugduni, p[ro] Antoniũ du Ry, impēsis reuerēdissi do. Frāci. d. Claromōte epi. cardīalis auxita Auenioñ., 1526). 4.to. The work was also published by Estienne in 1549 and 1556 and by S. Gryphius in 1548.

[340] Gentilis Fulginas. *Questiones & tractatus extravagantes ... Gentilis de Fulgineo, noviter ... collecti* (Venetiis, cura heredum Octaviani Scoti & sociorum, 1520). Folio. National Library of Medicine. Durling, no. 2048.

[341] Marzio, Galeotto *Galeottus Martij ... de homine libri dvo. Georgii Mervlae alexandrini in Galeotvm annotationes. Cum indicibus utrobiq[ue] contentorū...* (Basileae, Apud J. Frobenium, 1517). 4.to. British Library. Bibliothèque Nationale, Paris. National Library of Medicine.

[342] Martínez, Martinus. *Institutiones in linguam sanctam* (Parisiis, Apud J. Bogardum, 1548). 8.vo. British Library. Bibliothèque Nationale, Paris.

[343] Dedekind, Friedrich, d. 1598. *Grobianvs et Grobiana. De morvm simplicitate, libri tres* (Franc[ofurti] apud C. Egen[olph, 1549]). 8.vo. Bibliothèque Nationale, Paris. Egenolph also published this in 1554, 1564, 1575, and 1584.

[344] Busto, Bernabé de. *Introductiones grammaticas: breues τ compēdiosas* (Salamanca, [Gonsalvo de Castañeda? Juan de Junta?] 1533). 8.vo. Palau, 37839. British Library. Rhodes, p. 37. Ruíz Fidalgo, no. 32.

[345] Donatus, Aelius. *Aelii Donati Commentarii grammatici tres. Ars prima, ars secunda. De barbarismo, solœcismo, metaplasmo, tropis* (Parisiis, ex officina Rob. Stephani typographi regii, 1543). 4.to. The work was also published in 1510 and 1525 by the Venetian firm of the Giunti (Venetijs, in ędibus nobilis viri lucę antonij Jūta, 1525). Camerini, I, p. 144, 221.

SIXTEENTH CENTURY SPANISH BOOKSTORE

39 Glosa del Cyfuentes[346] in fol. 68		2,652
1 Gramatica greca Gaze[347] in 8° 68		068
1 Gramatica greca Humelbergii[348] 8° 34		034
		2,829
		10,808
/ xiij,dcxxxvij /		L.13,637
1 Hore romane in 8° Caragoca faltas		----
12 Hore conceptionis pp Segovie 6		072
1 Hore romane pp Caragoca[349] 51		051
1 Hore romane pp una 51		051
1 Hyppoliti opera consilijs[350] in 8° 204		204
2 Horatius[351] pp Gryph[ius] 30		060
2 Hiero. pes. in primam partem Sancti Thome 102		204
2 Hieremias Trevir integri Galeni[352] pp 30		060
2 Hiere[mias] Trevir de temperamentis[353] pp 34		068
2 Historie plantarum in 8° ale[maña] 51		102
4 Herodianus histo[riae][354] in 8° Florencie 51		204
5 Hortulus anime[355] pp 34		170

---

[346] Cifuentes, Miguel de. *Glosa de Cifuentes* (Salmāticae, Joannis de Junta, 1546). Folio. British Library. Bibliothèque Nationale, Paris.

[347] Gaza, Theodorus. Probably *Introductionis grammaticae libri quatuor*. Octavo editions were published in Florence (Florentiae, in aedibus P. Iuntae, 1515, 1526) Other octavo editions in Cologne in 1525, and Paris in 1529, 1534, 1536-40 and 1542.

[348] Hummelberger, Michael. *Epitome grammaticæ græcæ* (Basileae, apud Ioan. Heruagium, 1532). 8.vo. British Library.

[349] *Horae b'tae marie virginis* (Cesaraugustae, expensis Georgij Coci, 1517). Palau, 116135.

[350] Marsiliis, Hippolytus de, 1451-1529. *Cōsiliorum criminalium volumina duo* (Lugduni, apud Jacobum Giunta, 1545). 8.vo. Harvard Law School Library.

[351] Horatius Flaccus, Quintus. *Opera* (Lugduni, Seb. Gryphius, 1545, 1551). 16.mo. Baudrier, VIII, pp. 198, 255.

[352] Dryvêre, Jérémie de, 1504-1554. *Novi et integri commentarii in omnes Galeni libros* (Lugduni, apud Gulielmum Rovilium, 1547). 16.mo. National Library of Medicine. Durling, no. 1229.

[353] Dryvêre, Jérémie de, 1504-1554. *Hieremiae Thriveri Brachelii Novi et Integri Commentarii In omnes Galeni De temperamentis libros* (Lugduni, apud Godefridum & Marcellum Beringos, 1547). 16.mo. National Library of Medicine. Durling, no. 1226. Baudrier, III, p. 44.

[354] Herodianus. *Historiae*. The Latin text was published in Florence by the Giunti in March, 1517 (i.e. 1518).

[355] *Hortulus animæ* (Lugduni, apud Theobaldum Paganum, 1546, 1553). 16.mo. Baudrier, IV, pp. 234, 410. This devotional work is on the 1559 Spanish *Index*. De Bujanda, p. 372.

1 Horologiographia munsteri[356] in 4to	102	102
2 Hyppocratis opera[357] in 8° pre	187	374
15 Hore romane latine[358] in 8° grande	85	1,275
2 Hore hierosolimitane pp	25	050
1 Homeri opera grece[359] in 8°	340	340
1 Hymni mirandulani[360] in fol.	102	102
1 Hugo sup[er] psalmos[361] in fol. pre	272	272
1 Hiere[mias] Trevir in aphorismos[362] in 4to	272	544
6 Hymni et orationes in 4to	85	510
17 Hore predicator[um] pp	34	578
4 Hore Marie Virginis in metro 8°	51	204
1 Historia Scholastica[363] in 8°	51	051
2 Historia tripertita[364] in 8°	34	068
9 Hore Romane pp Lisbone	51	459
1 Hore Romane pp v^a faltas	---	----

---

[356] Münster, Sebastian. *Horologiographia, post priorem aeditionem per Sebast. Munsterium* (Basileae, excudebat H. Petrus, 1533). 4.to. Bibliothèque Nationale, Paris. All of the works of were condemned on the Spanish *Index* of 1559. De Bujanda, p. 435.

[357] Hippocrates. *Opera omnia* (Lugduni, S. Gabiano, 1535). 8.vo. British Library. Other Latin editions of the complete works of Hippocrates were published in Basel (In officina And. Cratandri, 1526) and in Lyons (Ant. Vincentius, 1555). A partial edition of the works was published in Lyons (de Gabiano, 1555). Other editions combined some of the works of Hippocrates with those of Galen.

[358] A number of works with the generic title "Ho. rom." are on the Spanish *Index* of 1559. De Bujanda, pp. 372-377. The Junta firm's ties to the Giunta firm of Venice might indicate that this was one of their editions, but it may also be the work of Juan de Brocar mentioned by Palau (Compluti, 1544). Palau, 116138.

[359] The Giunti firm in Florence published a two-volume octavo edition of the works of Homer in Greek in 1519 and the Giunti firm in Venice reprinted it in 1537. Antonio Francini was the editor.

[360] Pico della Mirandola, Giovanni Francesco, 1470-1573. *Joannis Francisci Pici Mirandulani Hymni heroici tres: Ad sanctissimam Trinitatem, Ad Christum et Ad virginem Mariam* (Argentorati, In libraria Officina Mathiae Schureri, 1511). Folio. Bibliothèque Nationale, Paris. British Library.

[361] Hugo de Sancto Charo. *Domini Hugonis cardinalis Postilla, ... in Dauiticum psalterium* (Parisiis, tipis Petri Vidovei, impensis Johānnis Parvi [et al]). Folio. Bibliothèque Nationale, Paris.

[362] Dryvêre, Jérémie de, 1504-1554. *Hieremiae Thriveri Bracheli Commentarii in VII libros Aphorismorum Hippocratis* (Lugduni, apud haeredes Jacobi Juntae, 1551). 4.to. National Library of Medicine. Baudrier, VI, p. 273. Durling, no. 1221.

[363] Petrus, *Comestor*. *Scolastica historia* (Lugduni, I. Crespin, 1526; N. Petit et H. Penet, 1534). 8.vo. British Library.

[364] Cassiodorus Senator, Flavius Magnus, ca. 487 - ca. 580. *Historia tripertita ... de regimine ecclesie primitiue* (Lugduni, Ueneunt apud Iacobū Giuncti, 1526, 1534, 1545). Baudrier, VI, pp. 122, 157.

1 Hore Romane in 8° Lion gp. [Gryphius?] 119		119
1 Hyppocratis aphorismi[365] pp 34		034
3 Hiere[mias] Trevir de medicor[um] sectis[366] in 8°	25	075
		L. 6,403

(f. 25)

4 Index op[eru]m Aristo[teles] in fol. 408		1,632
1 Index op[eru]m Tostati in fol. 1020		1,020
12 Ioannes Clemens in predicamenta[367] in fol. 85		1,020
1 Introductio Vives ad sapientiam[368] in 8°	25	025
1 Institutiones[369] in 8° Lion	136	136
17 Joannes Climachiis de schala paradisi[370]	51	867
6 Iuvenalis qqto.[371] in 4to	85	510
1 Irinei opera[372] in fol. ale[maña]	153	153
7 Iustinus histo[ricus][373] in 8° Florencie	68	476

---

[365] Hippocrates. *Aphorismi Hippocratis Graece et Latine* (Lvgdvni, apud Gulielmum Rouillium, 1549). 16.mo. Baudrier, IX, p. 150.

[366] Dryvêre, Jérémie de, 1504-1554. *De duabus hodie medicorum sectis ac de diversa ipsarum methodo ad studiosos medicina nuper oratio* (Antuerpiae, apud Martinum Nutium, 1544). 8.vo. National Library of Medicine. Durling, no. 1224.1.

[367] Clemente, Juan. *Liber super praedicamenta Arist. cū eorumdē perutili & familiari textus explanatiōe* (Compluti, excudebat Ioannes Brocarius, 1538). Folio. There may have been another folio edition in Alcalá de Henares in 1544. Palau, 55623. Martín Abad, p. 451, no. 287 and p. 519, no. 347.

[368] Vives, Juan Luis, 1492-1540. *Introductio ad sapientiam.* Editions in 1527 (Parisiis, Apud Simonem Colinaeum), 1530 (Antuerpie, apud M. Caesarem) 1531 (Antuerpie, Excudebat Michael Hellenius) and 1551 (Methymnae Campi, ex typographia Guillelmi de Millis).

[369] Cleynaerts, Nicolaus, 1495-1542. *Institutiones absolutissimae in graecam lingvam* (Lugduni, apud Seb. Gryphium, 1543, 1548, 1553). 8.vo. British Library. Baudrier, VIII, p. 179, 223, 265). The author's *Grammaticae institutiones graecae* was also published in Lyons by Dolet in 1541 and by Rovilius in 1546.

[370] Joannes Climacus, Saint, 6th cent. *Scala paradisi.* I have not identified this edition, but the number of copies indicates a probable date of late 1540s-early 1550s.

[371] Juvenalis, Decimus Junius. *Iuuenalis familiare commentum* (Lugd. S. Vincent, 1523). 4.to. British Library.

[372] Irenaeus, Saint, Bp. of Lyons. Froben published Erasmus' edition of the *Opus eruditissimum divi Irenaei* ... (Basel, 1526, 1528, 1534, 1548). Folio. British Library. University of Chicago.

[373] Justinus, Marcus Justinus. *Externae historiae.* Octavo editions of Justinus were published in Florence by Filippo Giunta in February, 1510 (i.e. 1511) and by his heirs in 1525.

INVENTARIO DE LOS LIBROS

4 Itinerarium proviniciarum[374]	in 8°	25	100
1 Institutiones Teophili[375]	pp	68	068
1 Iustinus historicus[376]	in 4to	34	034
1 Iacobus de Valencia[377]	in 4to	306	306
1 Iosephus de antiquitatibus[378]	in 8°	238	238
22 Interpretationes nominum hebraicor[um][379]	in 4to	[ed: 17]	
			374
			L. 6,959

/ vi,dcccclix /

236 Luinus Lemnius[380]	in 8°	34	8,024
1 Licier de primagenitura in fol.		68	068
1 Ludolphus sup[er] psalmos[381]	in 4to	68	068

---

[374] *Itinerarium Antonini. Itinerarium prouinciarum omniū* (Lugduni, haeredes S. Vincentij, [1550?]). 8.vo. British Library. It was also printed by the heirs of Filippo Giunta of Florence as part of the 1526 edition of Pomponius Mela.

[375] Theophilus, antecessor, trans. Theophilus' paraphrase of the Institutes of Justinian was translated into Latin by Conradus Clauserus. This was on the Toledo, Seville and Valencia re-editions of the Louvain *Index*. De Bujanda, V, 271. I have not located a small-format edition of this translation.

[376] Justinus, Marcus Justinus. Quarto editions of Justinus were published in Paris (Jean Petit, 1520? and Bogardus, 1544) and Basel (s.n.i., 1543?).

[377] Pérez de Valencia, Jaime, 1408-1490. *D. Iacobi Perez de Valentia Christopolitani episcopi longe Reuerendi: et ordinis diui Augustii obseruantissimi: ac Theologi vt doctissimi ita pientissimi: diunie plane expositiones: in Centum et quinquaginta psalmos Dauidicos... Cantica ferialia in biblijs contenta. Cantica euangelica. Benedictus. Magnificat. Nūc dimittis. Gloria in excelsis. Canticum Ambrosij et Augustini Te deum laudamus. Cantica canticorum. Premissis. Questionibus τ earum subtillissimis resolutionibus contra iudeos fidei nostre aduersarios. Adiedtum est muperrime Symbolum Athanasij cum aurea eiusdem Expositione.* ... (Lugduni, sūptu honesti viri Iacobi. q. Francisci de Giunta... in edib. Martini Lescuyer chalcographi, 1533). 4.to. Baudrier, VI, p. 151. The Giunta firm published earlier quarto editions in 1521, 1525 and 1526.

[378] Josephus, Flavius. Gryphius published octavo editions of the works in three volumes in 1528, 1539, 1546 and 1555. Volume 2 has the title *De antiquitatibus Ivdaeorvm libri X*. Baudrier, VIII, p. 203.

[379] *Interpretationes nominum hebraicorum.* This short work was intended as a supplement to be bound with editions of the Latin Bible. It is found in several editions in the British Library and in one copy owned by the New York Public Library.

[380] Lemnius, Levinus. *L. L. libelli tres perelegantes ac festivi* (Antwerpiae, apud Martinum Nutium, 1554). 8.vo. Bibliothèque Nationale, Paris. National Library of Medicine. Durling, no. 2764.

[381] Ludolphus de Saxonia, 14th cent. *In psalterio expositio.* Folio editions were published in Paris (Udalricus Hering, 1506; and Bertholdus Rembolt, 1514) and in Lyons (Johannes Moylin, 1518).

1 Lumbricis curatio[382] pp 20		020
1 Lombardus sup[er] epistolas Pauli[383] in 8° pre	187	187
2 Lanfrancus de Corpore Christi[384] in 8°	68	136
4 Lucanus[385] in 8° 25		100
1 Lucubrationes Valle[386] in 8° 119		119
5 Legenda sanctor[um][387] in 4to 85		425
1 Legenda divi Francisci in 8° 85		085
7 Lucerna fratrum minor[um] in 4to 25		175
2 Lucubrationes Chrysostomi[388] in fol. 238		476
1 Luciani opera[389] in fol. Lion 272		272
1 Latomus adversus hereses[390] in fol. 272		<u>272</u>
		L. 10,427

(f. 26)

1 Le cose vulgari de Bruno[391] in 8°   34   034

---

[382] Gabuccini, Girolamo, 16th cent. *De lumbricis alvvm occvpantibus, ac de ratione curandi eos* (Lvgdvni, apud Guliel. Rouil., 1549). 16.mo. National Library of Medicine. Baudrier, IX, p. 154. Durling, no. 1743.

[383] Petrus Lombardus, bp. of Paris, 12th cent. *In omnes D. Pauli Apost. Epistolas Collectanea* (Parisiis, Apud Nicolaum du chemin, 1543). 8.vo. Yale University. An earlier octavo edition was published in Paris (Parisiis, Apud Ioannem Parvum, 1538). Huntingdon Library, San Marino.

[384] Costerus, Joannes, *of Louvain*. ed. *De veritate corporis et sanguinis Domini Nostri Iesv Christi in evcharistiae sacramento* ... (Lovanii, apud Petrum Phalesium, 1550). 8.vo. The first work is "D. Lanfranci contra Berengarium."

[385] Jacobo Cromberger produced an octavo edition of Lucanus' *Pharsalia* in Seville, 1528. Biblioteca Nacional, Lisbon. Griffin, Appendix One, no. 283.

[386] Valla, Lorenzo. *Lucubrationes aliquot ... ad Linguae Latinae restaurationem spectantes* (Lugduni, 1532). 8.vo. British Library. Baudrier also cites a 1531 edition (VIII, p. 57).

[387] Jacobus de Voragine. *Legenda sanctorum. Opvs avrevm qvod legenda sanctorum vulgo nuncupatur* (Lugduni, apud Iacobum Giunta, 1540). 4.to. University of Minnesota. Baudrier, VI, p. 189.

[388] Chrysostomus, Joannes, Saint. *Divi Ioannis Chrysostomi ... & divi Athanasii lucubrationes aliquot non minus elegantes quam utiles* (Basileae, Apud Ioan. Frobenium, 1527). Folio. Biblioteca Nacional, Madrid.

[389] Lucian. *Luciani Samosatensis opera, quæ quidem extant, omnia, è græco sermone in latinum ... translata* (Lugduni, Apud Ioannem Frellonium, 1549). Folio. Bibliothèque Nationale, Paris. Another folio edition was published in Lyons in 1546 by Michael Vascosanus and Ioannes Roigny. Baudrier, V, p. 215.

[390] Latomus, Jacobus, 1475-1544, *J. Latomi ... opera, quæ præcipue aduersus horum temporum haereses ... conscripsit* (Lovanii, 1550). Folio. British Library.

[391] Bruni, Giovanni, 1476-1540. *Le cose uolgari* (Milano, A. Vimercato, 1519). 8.vo. British Library. An earlier octavo edition was published in Venice in 1506.

INVENTARIO DE LOS LIBROS

1 Luciani opuscula aliquot[392] in 8º 51		051
1 Logica coronel[393] in 4to 51		051
1 Lucanus[394] pp 20		020
1 Luciani opera grece[395] 408		408
1 Lexicon grecum in 4to 204		204
2 Lucanus qqto.[396] in fol. 119		238
		1,006
		10,427
/ xj,cmxxxiii /		L. 11,433
1 Missale toletanum[397] in 4to 306		306
1 Macrobius in fol.[398] ale[maña] falto	68	068
3 Missale del Cyruelo[399] in fol. 340		1,020
11 Meditationes Augustini[400] pp Alcala	34	374

---

[392] Lucian. Octavo editions of Erasmus' translation, *Opuscula quaedam* were published in Lyons (Lugduni, Seb. Gryphius Germ. excvd., 1528) and Florence, *Luciani opuscula, Erasmo Roterodamo interprete* (Florentiae, per haeredes Ph. Iuntae, 1519). British Library. Bodleian Library. Baudrier, VIII, p. 49.

[393] Coronel, Antonio. *Quaestiones Logicae*. I have not found a quarto edition of this work.

[394] Lucanus, Marcus Annaeus. The relatively low price and the "pp" indicates that this copy was in small format, such as the 16.mo editions of *Ciuilis belli libri X* published by Sebastian Gryphius in Lyons in 1546 and 1547 or by Simon de Colines in Paris in 1543. Bibliothèque Nationale, Paris. See also footnote 385.

[395] Lucian. This may be the Giunti firm's edition of the Greek text, *Luciani Opera* (Florentiae, sumptu Philippi Iuntae, 1517). Folio. Bibliothèque Nationale, Paris.

[396] Lucanus, Marcus Annaeus. Early sixteenth-century folio editions of the *Pharsalia* of Lucanus were published in Venice (1505, 1511 and 1520), Paris (1506, 1514), Milan (1508, 1525) and Lyons (1519) with the commentaries of Omnibono and Sulpitius.

[397] Juan de Brocar published a quarto edition of the *Missale secundum ... ordinem ... ecclesiae Toletanae* in Alcalá de Henares in 1539. Palau, 173125. Martín Abad, p. 459, no. 295. This may also be the Burgos, 1512 edition (Burgis in officina Frederici ex basilea ... Arnaldus guillelmus brocarius faciendum curauit, 1512). 4.to. Palau, 173121.

[398] Macrobius, Ambrosius Aurelius Theodosius. Folio editions of Macrobius' *In Somnium Scipionis libri duo* from German-speaking territory were published in Cologne (apud Eucharium Ceruicornum, 1521 and 1526) and Basel (ex officina I. Hervagii, 1535).

[399] Ciruelo, Pedro de. *Expositio libri missalis peregregia: nuper edita ex officina ... Petri Cirueli* (In vniuersitate Cōpluteñ., in aedibus Michaelis de Eguia, 1528). Folio. Biblioteca Nacional, Madrid. Harvard Univ. Library. *Catálogo colectivo*, C, 1992.

[400] Augustinus, Aurelius, Saint, bp. of Hippo. *Meditationes, Soliloquio* (Alcalá de Henares, Ex officina Ioannis Brocarii, 1554). 16.mo. Biblioteca Nacional, Madrid. Martín Abad, p. 637, no. 476.

626 Maldo[nati] de senectute[401]	in 8°	25	15,650
885 Maldo[nati] Vite sanctorum[402]	in 8°	34	30,090
58 Maldo[nati] de Civilitate morum	in 8°	17	986
105 Maldo[nati] parenesis[403]	in 8°	12	1,260
226 Maldonati hispaniola[404]	in 8°	20	4,520
2 Macer de virtutibus herbarum[405]	in 8°	30	060
135 Maldonati pastor bonus[406]	in 8°	12	1,620
1 Mesue p. Sylvium[407]	in fol. pre	238	238
2 Mayoris opuscula	in 4to	136	272
1 Missale roma[num][408]	in 4to porta	340	340
8 Minorita de quantitate Syllabarum	in 4to	34	272

---

[401] Maldonado, Juan, 1534-1583. *Opvscvla quaedam docta simul, & elegantia De senectvte Christiana. Paradoxa. Pastor bonus. Lvdvs chartarum, Tridunus, & alii quidam. Geniale ivdicium, siue Bacchanalia.* (Bvrgis, Excvdebat Ioannes Giunta, 1549). 8.vo. Biblioteca Nacional, Madrid. Biblioteca Universitaria, Salamanca. *Catálogo colectivo*, M, 236. Palau, 147698. Bataillon, p. LXXXII, no. 866 or 867.

[402] Maldonado, Juan. *Vitæ sanctorvm* (Venundantur Burgis, apud Lucam de Cañete, 1548; and [Burgos] Venduntur apud Ioannem de Giunta, 1550). Both 8.vo. British Library. Biblioteca Nacional, Madrid. See Dennis Rhodes, "Juan Maldonado and the press in Burgos," *Gutenberg Jahrbuch* 1988, 141-45. The large number of copies may indicate that Juan de Junta was responsible for the financing of both editions. The work was published earlier in Alcalá de Henares (Compluti, in aedibus Michaelis de Eguia, 1537). 8.vo. Martín Abad, p. 444, no. 282.

[403] Maldonado, Juan. *Paraenesis ad politiores literas aduersus gramaticorum uulgum* (Burgos, [Juan de Junta] 1529). 8.vo. Biblioteca Universitaria, Zaragoza. *Catálogo colectivo*, M, 237. Palau, 147695.

[404] Maldonado, Juan. *Ioannis Maldonati Hispaniola nunc deniq[ue] per ipsum autorem restituta atq[ue] detersa: Scholiisq[ue] locis aliquot illustrata* (Bvrgis, in officina Ioannis Iuntae, 1535). 8.vo. University of Pennsylvania. Biblioteca Nacional, Madrid. Palau, 147697. Bataillon, p. LXXXII, no. 865. *Catálogo colectivo*, M, 234.

[405] Macer Floridus, 12th century. *Aemilius Macer De herbarum virtutibus* (Basileae, [Apud Joannem Fabrum Emmeum, 1527]). 8.vo. National Library of Medicine. Durling, no. 2891. This work on medical botany was published in Basel (1517, 1527, 1559), Freiburg (1530) and Venice (1547).

[406] Maldonado, Juan. *Pastor bonus* (Burgis, Excvdebat Ioannes Giunta, 1549). 8.vo. Biblioteca Nacional, Madrid. Palau, 147698.

[407] Yuhanna ibn Mesawayh or Mesuë. *Opera cum commentariis Variorum et alia plura.* The Giunta firm of Venice published the commentary of Jacobo Sylvio (i.e. Jacques Dubois) on Mesuë in folio editions in 1527 and 1549. Camerini, I, p. 233, 373. The Bibliothèque Nationale, Paris, has folio editions dated 1541 (no printer or place) and a Lyons edition (Lugduni, industria ... Stephani Baland. ... sumptibus ... Vincentij de Portonarijs, 1515). The National Library of Medicine has *Universales Joannis Mesue ... Canones, cum Jacobi Sylvii annotationibus* (Basileae, Apud Henrichum Petrum, 1545). Folio. Durling, no. 1097. Baudrier, V, p. 412.

[408] This may be the 1543 quarto edition of the pre-Tridentine missal published in Lyons by Hugues (I) de la Porte. British Library.

2 Missale Carmelitanum[409] in 8° una 153		306
1 Marcellus de verborum proprieta[te][410] in 8° 51		051
1 Macrobius[411] in fol. pre 51		051
1 Martialis[412] pp 30		030
1 Manipulus medicinar[um][413] in fol. 68		068
1 Marsilius de Santa Sophia[414] in 4to 136		136
1 Manuale romanum in fol. 204		204
1 Missale de Astorga[415] in fol. 272		272
2 Mesue p. Sylvium[416] in 8° 85		170
2 Missale del Calice in 4to 187		374
6 Marineus siculus[417] in fol. 119		714
5 Musica del Cyruelo in fol. 17		085

---

[409] The Giunta firm of Venice published octavo editions of *Missale secundum ordinem fratrum Carmelitarum* in 1504 and 1509. Weale, no. 1886, 1887.

[410] Nonius Marcellus. I have not identified this edition.

[411] Macrobius, Ambrosius Aurelius Theodosius. *En tibi lector candidissime Macrobius [Somnium Scipionis Saturnaliorum libri]* (Venetiis per Augustinum de Zannis de Portesio ad instantia Do. Lucam Antonium de Giunta, 1513). Folio. British Library. Yale University. Camerini, I, p. 152. The Bibliothèque Nationale, Paris, has folio editions from Basel (ex officina J. Hervagi, 1535) and Paris (in aedibus Jodoci Badii Ascensii, 1524).

[412] Martialis, Marcus Valerius. *M. V. Martialis epigrammaton libri XIIII* (Lugduni, apud S. Gryphium, 1546, 1548, 1553). 16.mo. Baudrier, VIII, p. 207, 226, 266. Other small-format editions of Martial were published in Paris by S. Colines in 1533, 1540 and 1544.

[413] Sepulveda, Fernando de. *Manipulus Medicinarum: in quo cōtinentur omnes Medicina tam simplices quam composita* (Salamanca, Porras & Liondedei, 1523). Folio. Maggs Bros. *Catalogue no. 495*, 966. Palau, 309305. The British Library also has a 1550 folio edition (Uallisole, apud Ioan. de Villaquiran). Palau, 309306. Rhodes, p. 180. This is a book of recipes for the use of doctors and apothecaries.

[414] Sancta Sophia, Marsilius de, d. 1405. *Opus aureum, signa, causas et curas febrium cōplectens* (Lugduni, 1517). 4.to. British Library. National Library of Medicine. Durling, 2972.

[415] Weale lists two folio missals for Astorga: In regali civitate Legionensi, per Ioannem Legionsem, 1523; [and:] In ciuitate asturiceñ. Impensis Augustini de paz, 1546). Weale, p. 16.

[416] Yuhanna ibn Mesawayh or Mesuë. *Ioannis Mesvae Damasceni, de re medica libri tres. Iacobo Sylvio medico interprete* (Lugduni, apud Ioan. Tornaesium & Gulielmum Gazeium, 1548). 8.vo. Biblioteca Nacional, Madrid. National Library of Medicine. Durling, no. 3143. Octavo editions of Sylvio's commentary on Mesuë were also published in Lyons by Rovilius in 1548 and 1550. Baudrier, IX, pp. 145, 176. *Catálogo colectivo*, M, 1562.

[417] Marineo, Lucio, Siculo, 1444?-1536. This may be his *Opus de rebus Hispaniae memorabilibus* ... which was published in folio edition in Alcalá de Henares (Compluti, Michaelem de Eguia, 1530 and 1533). Bibliothèque Nationale, Paris. Bodleian Library, Oxford. Palau, 152133, 152134. Martín Abad, pp. 392, 393, no. 229A-B.

1 Martianus capella[418] in fol.	102	102
1 Margarita doctor[um] in 8°	25	025
1 Mayor sup[er] 4to Sententiarum[419] in fol.	170	170
1 Margarita philosophica[420] in 4to ale[maña]	340	<u>340</u>
		L. 60,174

(f. 27)

1 Mayro[nis] sup[er] sñas[421] in fol.	306	306
1 Manuale predicator[um] in 8°	34	034
8 Manipulus curator[um][422] in 8° Alcala	60	480
2 Missale carmelitanum[423] gs. vna	510	1,020
4 Missale romanum[424] in 4to	170	680
1 Missale salamantinum[425] in 4to	374	374
2 Missale romanum in 8°	153	306
2 Missale romanum de novis in 4to	340	680
1 Moralia Gregorii[426] in 8°	170	170

---

[418] Capella, Martianus Mineus Felix. *De nuptiis Philologiae et Mercurii libri ii* (Basileae, H. Petrus, 1532). Folio. British Library. For a listing of the editions of this work, see *Rara Arithmetica*, p. 66.

[419] Major, Joannes, Scotus. *Quartus sentētiarū* [of Petrus Lombardus] ([Paris] I. Badii, 1516, 1519). Folio. British Library.

[420] Reisch, Gregor, d. 1525. *Margarita philosophica*. Quarto editions of this title were published in Basel (M. Furterii et J. Scoti, 1508, 1517; Henricvs Petrus, 1535), Strassburg (J. Schotti, 1504 [i.e. 1505]), and Freiburg (per Joannē Schottū, 1503, 1504). *Rara Arithmetica*, pp. 82-84. There are later editions with the title *Margarita philosophica nova*.

[421] Franciscus, de Mayronis. *Franciscus de mayronis in sententias [Petri Lombardi]* (Uenetijs mandato τ expensis ... Luceantonij de giunta, 1519). Folio. Camerini, I, p. 185. The British Library has another folio edition, *Scripta in quatuor libros Sentētiarum* (Venetijs, Impensa heredum O. Scoti & sociorum, 1520).

[422] Guido de Monte Rocherio, 14th century. *Manipulus curatorum* (Alcalá de Henares, Juan de Brocar, 1545). 8.vo. Palau, 177733. Martín Abad, p. 523, no. 354. This title, and its Spanish translation, are on the Spanish *Index* of 1559. De Bujanda, V, pp. 408-09, 507.

[423] This may be the folio edition by the Giunta firm of Venice (Venetiis, arte τ impensis luce antonij de giūta, 1514). Weale, p. 319.

[424] The heirs of Lucantonio Giunta produced quarto editions of the *Missale Romanum* in Venice in 1540, 1546 and 1552. Camerini, I, p. 324, 361, 394.

[425] *Missale ad vsum alme ecclesie Salmāticēsis* (Salmāticeñ., in edibus Ioannis iunte, 1533). 4.to. Biblioteca Universitaria, Salamanca. Palau, 173098. Ruíz Fidalgo, no. 81.

[426] Editions of the work of St. Gregory I, the Great on the book of Job were published in Lyons by Antonius du Ry Lugdunus (1530) and Jacobus Giunta (1543). Baudrier, VI, pp. 135, 204.

INVENTARIO DE LOS LIBROS

4 Magister Sententiar[um][427] in 8° 68	272
2 Missale romanum[428] in fol. Lion 476	952
2 Missale predicator[um][429] in 8° 153	306
1 Missale carthusianum[430] in fol. 306	306
1 Musa Paulina[431] in 8° 102	102
2 Macrobius[432] in 8° 68	136
2 Martialis[433] in 8° 51	102
3 Martialis in 8° Florencie 51	153
2 Macrobius in 8° Florencie[434] 51	102
2 Machavello de re militari in 8° 34	068
3 Musa de Syrupis[435] in 8° 34	102
510 Missale burgense[436] in fol. 680	346,800

---

[427] Magistris, Joannes de, 15th century. *Textus magistri sentētiarum in quattuor sectus libros partiales* (Venundatur Lugduni a Vincentio de portonariis, 1525). 8.vo. Another octavo edition was printed for de Portonariis by J. Moylin in 1527. Baudrier, V, pp. 427, 30.

[428] This may be Rovilius' edition (Lyons, 1550) which appears on the Toledo, Seville and Valencia editions of the 1551 *Catalogvs Librorvm reprobatorvm* and on the 1559 Spanish *Index*. De Bujanda, V, p. 237, 411.

[429] *Missale predicato[rum] cū omnibus ... missis epistolas et euāgelia* ([Venice], luceantonij de giūta, 1506, 1512, 1521, 1522, 1526). 8.vo. Camerini, I, pp. 131, 152, 197, 200, 228.

[430] This may be the 1517 Lyons edition: *Missale secūdū ordinē Carthusiensiū* (Lugduñ., Symonē beuelaqua, 1517). Folio. British Library. Baudrier, II, 22. Weale, 1733.

[431] New Testament. Epistles. *Musa Paulina Aluari Gomez* ... [Gómez de Ciudad Real, Álvaro, 1488?-1536]. (Compluti, in aedibus Michaelis de Eguia, 1529). 8.vo. Biblioteca Nacional, Madrid. British Library. Harvard University. Palau, 103914. Rhodes, p. 30. Martín Abad, p. 378, no. 213.

[432] Gryphius published octavo editions of Macrobius' *In Somnium Scipionis libri II* in Lyons in 1532, 1538, 1542, 1548, 1550 and 1556. Baudrier, VIII, p. 65 and seq. Other editions were published by Filippo Giunta in Florence in 1515, and the Manutius firm in Venice in 1528.

[433] Martialis, Marcus Valerius. *Epigrammaton libri XIIII* (Lugduni, Apud S. Gryphium, 1535, 1553). 8.vo. British Library. Baudrier, VIII, pp. 87, 266.

[434] Filippo Giunti published Macrobius' *Interpretatio in Somnium Scipionis. Saturnaliorum libri septem* in Florence (July, 1515). 8.vo. British Library. Bibliothèque Nationale, Paris.

[435] Brasavola, Antonio Musa. *Examen omnium syruporum quorum publicus usus est... Omnia ab authore recognita...* (Lugduni, Apud Joannem & Franciscum Frellonios, 1544). 8.vo. Another octavo edition was published in Lyons in 1540. National Library of Medicine. Durling, no. 685. Baudrier, V, p. 193. This work on medical potions saw several editions.

[436] *Missale secundum cōsuetudinem Burgeñ. ecclesie* (Burgis, Apud egregium typographū Iohannē de Iunta, 1546). Folio. Academia de la Historia, Madrid. British Library. Palau, 173014. Rhodes, p. 113.

SIXTEENTH CENTURY SPANISH BOOKSTORE

1 Missale hieronymi[437] in 4to 204		204
1 Margarita decreti[438] in 8° 34		034
10 Missale burgense[439] de pergamino 3750		37,500
1 Mayor in sumulas Petri Hispani[440] ligat. 102		102
1 Modus legendi abreviaturas[441] in 8° 8		008
1 Manuale burgense[442] in 4to de pergamino 750		750
		392,049
/ cmlii,ccxxiii /		60,174
		L. 452,223

3 Novum Testamentum[443] pp 68		204
2 Novum Testamentum[444] pp Ant[uerpie] 68		136
2 Novum Testamentum Eras[mi][445] in 8° 102		240
6 Novum Testa[mentum] cum annota. Isidori in 8° 153		918
4 Nicolai Propositi dispensarium[446] in 4to 68		272

---

[437] *Missale romanum consuetudinem fratrum ordinis Sancti Hieronymi* (Caesaraugustae, Georgius Coci Theutonicus, 1543). 4.to. Museo Lázaro Galdiano, Madrid. Palau, 173059.

[438] Martinus Polonus, 13th cent. *Margarita decreti seu tabula Martiniana* (Parrhisiis [device of Marnef on title page] 1513. 8.vo. Columbia University. British Library.

[439] See footnote 436.

[440] Major, John, 1469-1550. *In Petri hyspani summulas commentaria* (Venetiis, Lazarus de Soardis, 1506). Philadelphia College of Physicians.

[441] *Modus legendi abbreuiaturas passim in ivre tam ciuili quam pontificis occurentes* (Lvgdvni, Excudebant Ioannes et Franciscus Frellonii, 1544; Godefridus & Marcellus Beringi, 1552). 8.vo. Baudrier, V, p. 501 and III, p. 52. The British Library has an earlier octavo edition from Paris (Venundatur a B. Rembolt et a G. de Marnef, 1514).

[442] Could this be the 1497 Zaragoza edition? Palau, 150039.

[443] Small-format editions of the Latin New Testament were published by C. Froschauer in Zurich and by Froben in Basel (1524). Froben may be the publisher of the 1549 Basel edition. Both Basel editions are the translation of Erasmus.

[444] This may be one of several editions of the New Testament which are found on the Toledo edition of the 1551 *Index* and the Spanish *Index* of 1559. De Bujanda, V, pp. 237, 418. There are several small-format (16.mo or 12.mo) editions of the Latin New Testament published in Antwerp before 1556: M. Hillenius, 1526, M[artin de] K[eyser], 1527 (Tr. Desiderius Erasmus) 1537 and in 1540; I. Richard, 1542, I. Richard, 1543 (Erasmus version), I. Batman, 1545, I. Gymnicus, 1552 and I. Steelsius, 1555.

[445] Editions of Erasmus' revision of the Vulgate N. T. were published prior to the date of this inventory in Lyons (by Gryphius, 1546, 1549, 1550, 1551, 1552, 1555; by Frellonius, 1553; by Paganus, 1550; and by Rovilius, 1551); in Basel (1550, 1553, 1555) and others in Geneva, Antwerp and Paris.

[446] Prévost, Nicole, 15th cent. *Dispensarium magistri Nicolai Praepositi ad aromatarios; Platearius de simplici medicina* (Lugduñ., C. Tupin, N. Petit et H. Penet imprim.). 4.to. British Library. There are Paris and Lyons editions. Baudrier, VII, p. 185. Bibliothèque Nationale, Paris. The author is also cited Praepositi, Nicolaus.

3 Nestor vocabulista[447] in fol. ale[maña] 136	408
1 Novus orbis[448] in fol. ale[maña] 408	408
3 Naveros de propositionibus[449] in fol. 85	255
1 Novella de regulis juris in 8° 85	085
1 Nisseni Vita mosaica[450] in 4to 17	017
1 Nonius poeta grece[451] 5 in 8° 51	<u>051</u>
	2,958

(f. 28)

26 Navis stultifera[452] in 4to 10	260
	<u>2,958</u>
/ iij,ccxviij /	L. 3,218
52 officium de nomine Jesu in 8° 2	104
41 officium plagarum[453] in 8° 2	082
7 ordinarium misse[454] in 8° in 2bus 34	

---

[447] [Dionysius], Nestor, fl. 1400. *Vocabula suis locis & scdm alphabeti ordinem collocata* (Strassburg, I. Prüss, 1507). Folio. Houghton Library, Harvard University. Bibliothèque Nationale, Paris.

[448] Editions of the *Novus orbis regionum* from the German-speaking areas were published in Basel in 1532, 1537 and 1555 and in Strasburg in 1534. This is an account of the discovery and exploration of the New World.

[449] Naveros, Jacobus. *Dilucidariũ propositionm exponibilium Doctoris Iacobi Naueros* ([Compluti. Miguel de Eguía.] 1535). Folio. Martín Abad, p. 433, no. 270. Biblioteca Universitaria, Barcelona.

[450] Gregory, *of Nazianzus, Saint. Gregorii Nyseni ... Mystica Mosaicæ uitæ enarratio ... Georgio Trapezontio interprete* (Basileae, in aedibus Andreæ Cratandri, 1521). 4.to. British Library. Legrand, 3, p. 266.

[451] Nonnus Panopolitanus. This is probably the paraphrase of the Gospel of John by Nonnus, of Panoplis. The edition may be that of Iohannes Bogardus, Νοννου ποιητου πανοπολιτου μεταβολη του κατα 'Ιωαννην αγιου Ευαγγελιου (εν τη των Παρισίων, 1541). 8.vo. British Library.

[452] Brant, Sebastian, 1458-1521. *Navis stultifera*. This is a Latin translation of *Das Narrenschiff* or Ship of fools. Jodocus Badius Ascensius published quarto editions in Paris in 1505, 1506, 1507, 1513 and 1515.

[453] Catholic Church. Liturgy and ritual. Office, Five Wounds of the Lord. *Officium quinque plagarum D. N. Iesu Christi. Feria VI. post cineres duplex majus* (Mexici ex nova Typographia Matritensi, n.d.). 18.5 cms. Clements Library, Univ. of Michigan. This is the only edition I have found for this office. It would be remarkable if this inventory item did in fact come from Mexico.

[454] Burchard, Johann, bp. of Orta and Città Castellana, d. 1506. *Ordinarivm Missae, ex diversis Sctōrũ patrũ decretis:* ([Salamanca, Juan de Junta] 1547). 8.vo. Also published by Juan de Brocar (Compluti, Apud Ioannem Brocarium, 1548). 8.vo. Martín Abad, p. 547, no. 375.

2 opuscula bertrucii medici[455] in 4to	51	102
1 Ovidii metamorph[osis][456] in 8° falto		
3 officium hebdomade sancte0[457] pp	34	102
1 opera de Marco Rosigliada[458]	51	051
2 opera de Vigo[459] in 8°	102	204
9 ordinarium misse[460] in 8°	34	306
4 ordo divini officii de mercede in 8°	34	136
1 officina textoris[461] in 8°	187	187
2 ordinarium fratrum predicator[um] in fol.	136	272
4 Ovidii amatoria[462] in 8°	51	204
1 Ovidius de arte amandi[463] in 8°	25	025
1 Ovidii amatoria[464] pp	34	034

---

[455] Bertrucius, Nicolaus, d. 1347. Perhaps the 1509 or 1518 Lyons edition: *Nusquam antea impressum Collectorium totius fere medicine Bertrucii Bononiensis* (Lugd., per Claudium Davost alias de Troys, 1509; Lugduni, Impressum in edibus Jacobi Myt, sumptu Bartholomei Trot, 1518). Both 4.to. Bibliothèque Nationale, Paris. National Library of Medicine. Durling, nos. 563, 564.

[456] Ovidius Naso, Publius. The British Library has copies of the three-volume octavo editions of the *Metamorphoseon libri XV* published in Lyons by Seb, Gryphius (Lugduni, Apud S. Gryphium, 1536, 34, 39) and in Paris by Simon de Colines (Parisiis, Apud S. Colinaeum, 1537, 36, 36).

[457] *Officium Hebdomadae sancte* (Venetijs, apud heredes Lucantonij Iunte, 1549 1552, 1555). 16.mo, 12.mo. Camerini, I, p. 374, 397, 408.

[458] Rosiglia, Marco. *Opera del dignissimo doctore medico & poeta maestro Marcho Rosiglia da fuligno: Cioe sonetti: Capituli: Egloghe: Strabotti: & due p̄diche damore* (Venice, Nicolo Zopino, 1515). 8.vo. British Library.

[459] Vigo, Giovanni de. *Opera Domini Io. de Vigo in chyrurgia excellentissimi. Additur chyrurgia Mariani sancti Barolitani Ioannis de Vigo discipuli* (Lugduni, Per Jacobum Giuncti, 1538). 8.vo. National Library of Medicine. Durling, no. 4613. Baudrier, VI, p. 181. The Giunta firm of Lyons also produced this work in octavo editions in 1525 and 1530.

[460] See footnote 454.

[461] Tixier, Jean, seigneur de Ravisy, d. 1524. *Officinae Ioannis Ravisii Textor epitome* (Lugduni, Apud Seb. Gryphivm, 1541 and 1551). 8.vo. Baudrier, VIII, pp. 153, 255. Princeton Univ.

[462] Ovidius Naso, Publius. *Ars amatoria*. The Bibliothèque Nationale, Paris, has a 16.mo edition published in Lyons by S. Gryphius in 1550. Gryphius also published this work in 1534, 1536, and 1540. Baudrier, VIII, pp. 80, 99, 140.

[463] Ovidius Naso, Publius. *P. Oui. Naso de arte amandi τ remedio amoris* (Lugd. a Guil. Boulle, 1531). 8.vo. Baudrier, IV, p. 23. The Bibliothèque Nationale, Paris, also has octavo editions by Aldus Manutius (1502, 1515).

[464] Ovidius Naso, Publius. *Pub. Ovidii Nasonis Amatoria* (Lugduni, apud Seb. Gryphium, 1550). 16.mo. Bibliothèque Nationale, Paris. Baudrier, VIII, p. 245.

2 Ovidius de fastis qqto.[465] in fol.	204	408
1 orationes Longolij[466] in 8°	85	085
2 opuscula Plutarchi[467] in fol. pre	136	272
1 Ovidius de fastis sine qto.[468]	51	051
6 opus aureum sup[er] evangelia[469] in 8°	68	408
2 Ovidius de ponto qqto.[470] in fol.	51	102
1 opera Pomponati[471] in fol.	153	153
1 orationes Tullij qqto. Beroaldi[472] in fol.	272	272
8 ordo divini officij in 8°	34	272
2 Ossune dominicale[473] in 8°	238	476

---

[465] Ovidius Naso, Publius. *P. Ovidii Nasonis ... Fastorum libri VI ... cum commentariis Ant. Constantii* (Basileae, per J. Hervagium, 1550). Folio. This is the third part of Hervagius' edition of the works of Ovid. Folio editions of the *Fasti* were also published in the 16th century in Venice (opera & impensa Ioannis Tacuini de Tridino, 1502, 1508 and 1520), Paris (G. de Gourmont [1520?]) and Milan (Per Magistrum Leonardum Pachel, 1510). These have the commentary of Antonio Constantino. Bibliothèque Nationale, Paris.

[466] Longolius, Christophorus, 1488-1522. Octavo editions of the *Orationes* were published in Florence (per haeredes Philippi Iuntae, 1524), Paris (Jod. Badius, 1526, 1533), Lyons (Gryphius, 1542), and Venice ([1518?], 1539).

[467] Plutarch. *Opuscula quæ quidem extant omnia* (Basileæ, In officina And. Cratandri, 1530). Folio. Other possibilities include *Ethica, seu moralia opuscula* (Parisiis, M. Vascosanus, 1544), and *Opuscula argutissima & ingeniosissima* (Parisiis, Venundantur ab Ioanne Paruo & Iodoco Badio, 1514). Folio editions of Sagundino's translation weres published in Paris (In officina Ascensiana, 1521) and Basel (Apvd Mich. Isingrinivm, 1541, 1552, 1554). British Library. New York Public Library. Newberry Library. University of Chicago. Legrand, 3, p. 399.

[468] See footnote 465.

[469] *Aurea Rosa super euangelia* (in inclyta vrbe Lugd. Impensisq. honesti viri Iacobi. de Giūcta Florentini, 1545). 8.vo. Baudrier, VI, p. 209. There were earlier editions in 1528 and 1533. Baudrier, VI, pp. 129, 148.

[470] Ovidius Naso, Publius. This is one of the parts of the Hervagius folio edition in Basel. See footnote ?.

[471] Pomponazzi, Pietro, 1462-1524. *P. Pomponatii Mantuani Tractatus ... mere peripatetici. De intensione τ remissione formarum ac de parvitate τ magnitudine. De reactione. De modo agendi primarum qualitatum. De immortalitate animae. Apologiae libri tres. Contradictoris tractatus doctissimus. Defensorium autoris. Approbationes rationum defensorii per fratre* (Venetiis, Sumptibus heredū O. Scoti τ sociorū, 1525). Folio. British Library.

[472] Cicero, Marcus Tullius. *In omnes M. Tullii Ciceronis orationes*. Trans. Philippus Beroaldus. (Venetiis, apud Aldi filios, 1552). Folio. British Library, 11396.i.3

[473] Osuna, Francisco de. See footnote 213.

2 Ossune quadragesimale[474] in 8°	85	170
1 Ossune trilogium de passione[475]	51	051
4 Ortys de ornatu anime[476] in 4to	51	204
1 Orantius[477] in fol.	510	510
1 opus regale[478] in 8°	85	085
1 Osorius de nobilitate[479] in 4to	51	051
1 orationes Isocratis[480] in 8°	68	068
1 orationes Aristidis grece[481] in fol.	306	306
2 Ovidius de fastis in 8° Florencie[482]	faltos	068
2 Ortys quadragesimale[483] in 4to	306	612
1 observationes lingue latine in 8°	136	<u>136</u>
		L. 6,807

/ vi,dcccvii /

f. 29)

---

[474] Osuna, Francisco de. *Pars occidentalis in accommodas hisce temporibus Evangeliorum Quadragesimalium expositiōes* (Antuerpiae, Simone Cocus, 1536). 8.vo. Palau, 206851. Other octavo editions: Parisiis, in officina Petri Gualtherot, 1546; Parisiis, apud Vicentium Gualtherot, 1549; Parisiis, Bogard, 1552.

[475] Osuna, Francisco de. *Trilogium evangelicum Primum Christi Passionem* (Antuerpiam, Simon Cocus, 1535). 8.vo. Bibliothèque Nationale, Paris. Palau, 206857.

[476] Ortiz, Francisco, d. 1547. *De ornatu animae liber unicus* (Compluti, Excudebat Ioannes Brocarius, 1549). 4.to. British Library. Biblioteca Nacional, Madrid. Palau, 205624. Rhodes, p. 144. Martín Abad, p. 557, no. 382A-B.

[477] Orantes, Francisco. I have not identified this work.

[478] Vivaldus, Joannes Ludovicus. *Opus regale ſ quo continentur infrascripta opuscula* (Lugduni ab Stephano Gueynard, 1512). 8.vo. British Library. Baudrier, XI, pp. 216, 229.

[479] Osorio, Jeronymo, bp. of Silves, 1506-1580, *De nobilitate civili et Christiana*. Several editions have survived. This may be the quarto edition of 1542 (Lisbon, apud L. Rodericum) or that of 1552 (Florentiae, Laurentium Torrentium).

[480] Isocrates. Octavo editions of the *Orationes* of Isocrates were published in Paris (Lutetiae, Ex officina M. Vascosani, 1553), Venice (apud haeredes Petri Rauani, 1549), in Basel (apud Andream Cratandrum, 1529) and in Venice (Manutius, 1513).

[481] Aristides, Aelius. Λόγοι. A Greek edition of Aristides was published in folio by Filippo Giunta in Florence in 1517 (Florentiæ, sumptibus P. Iuntæ). British Library.

[482] Ovidius Naso, Publius. *Fastorum lib. VI* (Florentiae, per haeredes Philippi Iuntae, 1525). 8.vo. Biblioteca Marucelliana, Florence.

[483] Ortiz, Francisco. *Tomus i [-ii] Homiliarum super nouem versus psalmi L. per totam quadragesimam ...* (Compluti, Ioannes Brocarius, 1549). 4.to. 2 vol. Biblioteca Nacional, Madrid. British Library. Palau, 205625. Martín Abad, p. 553, no. 379 A,B.

INVENTARIO DE LOS LIBROS

1 Paraphrasis in Vallam[484] in 8° Lion	25		025
62 psalterium burgense in 8°	34		2,176
1 paraphrasis Erasmi[485] in fol. falto	750		750
4 psalterium romanum in 4to	34		136
9 paradoxa herbonii[486] in 8°	25		225
1 Pala[cios] Rub[ios] de obtentione reg. Navarre[487] in fol.	85		085
1 psalterium romanum[488] in 8° una	34		034
1 Persius falto in 8°			----
8 psalterium roma[num] pp numero /8/	25		200
2 psalterium cisterciense in 8°	51		102
6 psalterium ymperiale pp	68		408
3 Pictorius de sanitate tuenda[489] in 8°	68		204
16 psalterium romanum[490] in 8°	34		544
1 psalterium Reyneri[491] in 8°	68		068
1 practica Serapionis[492] in fol. una	340		340

---

[484] Erasmus, Desiderius. *Paraphrasis ... inscripta D. Erasmo Roteradamo ... in Elegantiarum libros Laurentij Vallæ* (Lvgdvni, excvdebat Theobaldvs Paganvs, 1551). 8.vo. Also published by Gryphius in 1533, 1535, 1537, 1538, 1540, 1541, 1542, 1543, [and 1550 ?]. Baudrier, IV, p. 251; VIII, p. 72, 87, 107, 119, 140, 153, 168, 181, 245.

[485] Erasmus, Deisderius. *Paraphrases in Novum Testamentum* (Basileae, in officina Io. Frobenii, 1523). 2 vols. Folio. Froben reprinted the work in 1524, 1535, 1541, 1548, 1556 and 1557. The work is on the Paris *Catalogue* of 1544. De Bujanda, I, p. 178.

[486] Herborn, Nikolaus, 1480-1535. *Paradoxa seu theologice assertiones* (Salmanticę, [Gonzalo de Castañeda,] 1534). 8.vo. British Library. Rhodes, p. 96. Ruíz Fidalgo, no. 40.

[487] López de Palacios Rubios, Juan. *De iusticia et iure obtētionis ac retētionis regnis Nauarre* (Burgos, Fadrique de Basilea, 1517?). Folio. This work deals with the justice of Ferdinand's claim to rule the kingdom of Navarre. Maggs, 708 (with illus.).

[488] The Giunti firm of Venice published octavo editions of the Roman Psalter in 1538, 1547 and 1552.

[489] Pictorius, Georg, 1500 (ca.)-1569. *Tuendae sanitatis ratio Vii. dialogis conscripta* (Basileae, H. Petri, 1554). 8.vo. British Library. National Library of Medicine. Durling, no. 3634.

[490] See footnote 488.

[491] Snoy, Reinier, ca. 1477-1537, trans. *Psalterium paraphrasibvs illustratum ... Raynerio Snoygoudano authore* (Parisiis, apud Ioannem Ruellium, 1545; or Lugduni, Apud I. & F. Frellaeos, 1538 and 1542). All 8.vo. British Library. The work was first published in Antwerp by hillenius in 1535. The Spanish translation was condemned on the 1559 Spanish *Index*. Bujanda, V, p. 528.

[492] ibn Serapion, fl. ca. 1070? There are several possible folio editions. This may be *Serapionis medici arabis celeberrimi practica* (Venetiis apud Ivntas, 1550). Folio. National Library of Medicine. Durling, no. 4779. Camerini, I, p. 381.

1 Petrus martyr de novo orbe[493] in fol.		102	102
1 processionarium cisterciense[494] in 8°		102	102
11 philippica Tullii[495] in 8°	40		440
1 practica Carrerii[496] in 8°		119	119
1 Pepin confiteor[497] in 8°	68		068
2 Picta poesis[498] in 8°	34		068
1 Papo[n] in consuetu[dines] Borbonias[499] in fol.		340	340
1 phisica de Soto[500] in fol.		204	204
1 Pontanus de prudentia[501] in 8° Florencie		34	034
2 Pontanus in Ptolomei sententias[502] in 8°		34	068
1 Prudentius[503] in 8°	51		051
1 Polyanthea[504] in fol. ale[maña] de novis		408	408

---

[493] Anghiera, Pietro Martyre d', 1455-1526. *De orbe novo decades octo* (Compluti in aedibus Michaelis de Eguia, 1530; or cōpluto, in contubernio Arnaldi Guillelmi, 1516). Both folio. British Library. Newberry Library. Palau, 12588. Norton, 45 A. Rhodes, p. 10.

[494] *Processionarius secūdum ordinē Cisterciensem nouiter impressus* (Cæsaraugustæ: opera τ impensis Bartholomei a Nagera, 1550). 8.vo. British Library. Rhodes, p. 114.

[495] Cicero, Marcus Tullius. *M. T. Ciceronis Philippicae* (Florentiae, opera & sumptu Philippi Iuntae, 1515). 8.vo. Biblioteca Nazionale, Florence. University of Michigan, Ann Arbor. It is surprising that this number of copies would have survived unsold until 1556. I have not found an octavo edition after 1515.

[496] Carerio, Luigi, fl. 1560. *Ludovici Careri practica nova causarum criminalium* (Lugduni, G. Rovilius, 1550). 8.vo. Baudrier, IX, p. 181 (he had not seen a copy).

[497] Pepin, Guillaume. *Opusculum ... super confiteor novissime pereūdem recognitum et emendatum* (Luthetie, Jean Petit, 1524, 1530; and Paris, Apud C. Chevallonium, 1519, 1534). 8.vo. British Library. Bibliothèque Nationale, Paris.

[498] Aneau, Barthélemy, 1505 (ca.)-1561. *Picta poesis. Ut pictura poesis erit.* (Lugduni, Excudebat Mathias Bonhomme, 1552). Harvard Univ. Library. Baudrier, X, p. 227.

[499] Papon, Jean. *Ioannis Paponis ... in Burbonias consuetudinis commentaria* (Lugduni, apud I. Tornaesium, 1550). Folio. British Library. Bibliothèque Nationale, Paris.

[500] Soto, Domingo de. *Super octo libros physicorum Aristotelis* (Salmanticae, Joannes Giunte, [1545?]). Folio. This is in two volumes, *Commentaria* and *Qvestiones*. Biblioteca Universitaria, Salamanca. Ruíz Fidalgo, no. 128.

[501] Pontanus, Joannes Jovianus. *De prudentia* (Florentiæ, opera et impensa Philippi Giuntæ, 1508; per haeredes P. Iuntae, 1520). 8.vo. British Library. Newberry Library.

[502] Ibid. *Io. Ioviani Pontani commentariorum in centum Claudij Ptolemæi sententias libri duo* (Basileae, apud And. Cratandrum, 1531). 4.to. British Library. Newberry Library.

[503] Prudentius Clemens, Aurelius, 348 - ca. 410. Octavo editions of his works were published by Caesar in Antwerp (1536, 1540), and by Cratandrum in Basel (1527). British Library.

[504] Nani Mirabelli, Domenico, fl. 1500. *Polyanthea, opvs svavissimvs floribvs exornatvm* (Salingiaci, excudebat Ioannes Soter, 1539). Folio. The inventory note "de novis" was probably intended to distinguish this from an earlier folio edition published in Basel (A. Petri, 1512). British Library. University of Iowa.

INVENTARIO DE LOS LIBROS

1 promptuarium juris[505]	gs. pre	850	850
1 Petrus Cyruelo in Aristo[teles] logicam in fol.		170	170
15 Petrus Muñoz sup[er] threnos in 4to	17		255
2 Putaneus de med. purgantium[506] in 4to		51	102
1 Polybus de victus ratione[507] in fol.	34		034
8 Precationes dominice[508] pp.	25		<u>200</u>
			8,912

(f. 30)

1 pandecte medicine[509] in fol.	170		170
32 proverbia Salomonis[510] in 4to	12		384
18 partes orationis in 4to	17		306
1 philosophia Petri Aspinosa[511] in fol.	204		204
1 phisica coronel[512] in fol.	85		085
78 psalmi penitentiales pp	4		242
9 prognostica Antonii Torquati[513] in 8°	17		153
1 Petrus Coronel in predicamenta[514]	34		034

---

[505] Harmenopoulos, Konstantinos, d. 1380? *Promptvarivm ivris civilis, latine redditum per Ioannem Mercervm* (Lugduni, Apud Mathiam Bonhomme, 1556). 4.to. Harvard Law School Library. Bibliothèque Nationale, Paris. Baudrier, X, p. 248.

[506] Dupuis, Guillaume. *De medicamentorum quomodocunque purgantium facultatibus ... libri duo ... avthore Gvilielmo Pvteano Medico Gratianopolitano* (Lugduni, Apud Mathiam Bonhomme, 1552). 4.to. British Library. Bibliothèque Nationale, Paris. National Library of Medicine. Baudrier, X, p. 223.

[507] Polybus. *De Salubri victus ratione privatorum Guinterio Johanne Andernaco interprete* (Basel, A. & C. Wechel, 1528). Folio. Bibliothèque Nationale, Paris. University of North Carolina, Chapel Hill.

[508] *Dominicae Precationis Explanatio* (Lugduni, Apud Seb. Gryphium, 1546). 16.mo. Baudrier, VIII, p. 203. Earlier editions in 1543, 1541, 1540, 1530.

[509] Silvaticus, Mattheus. Folio editions of his *Pandectae medicinae* were published by Lucantonio Giunta (Venice, 1524) and by Theobaldus Paganus for Jacobus Giunta (Lyons, 1534, 1541). Camerini, I, p. 219. National Library of Medicine. Bibliothèque Nationale, Paris. Baudrier, VI, pp. 157, 194, IX, p. 225. Durling, no. 4209.

[510] *Proverbia Salomonis*. This title was published in Lyon by the heirs of S. Vincent, 1537.

[511] I have not identified this work, but Petrus a Spinosa was "Artium magister ... Salmanticensis gymnasij ... ."

[512] Coronel, Luis. *Physice perscrutationes egregij interpretis magistri Ludouici coronel, hispani* (Lugduni, in edibus Jac. Giunti, 1530). Folio. Bibliothèque Nationale, Paris. Baudrier, VI, p. 136.

[513] Octavo editions of Antonius Torquatus' *Prognosticon de euersione Europae & aliae quaedam* were published by Martinus Nutius in Antwerp, in 1544 and 1552. British Library.

[514] I have not identified this author. The subject appears to be the Organon of Aristotle. The author may be related to Antonio Coronel, who also wrote on Aristotle.

1 Petrus Crinitus[515] in fol. 136		136
6 practica Philonii[516] in 8° 102		612
5 practica Lanfranci[517] in 8° 34		170
2 practica Petri Jacobi[518] in 4to 34		068
1 processionale Hieronymi[519] in 8° de perga. 204		204
2 processionale romanum[520] in 8° 85		170
6 Persius qqto.[521] in 8° 34		204
2 postille de lyra sup[er] psalmos[522] in 4to 85		170
2 psalterium carmelitanum in 8° 51		102
1 psalterium romanum cum hymnis in fol. 272		272
3 Pepin dominicale[523] in 8° Lion 153		459
2 Pepin quadragesimale[524] in 8° 153		306

---

[515] Crinitus, Petrus. Either *Commentarii de honesta disciplina* (Florentie, Impressum opera & impensa Philippi de Giunta, 1504) or *De poetis Latinis* (Florentiæ, per Philippum Iuntam, 1505). Both folios. British Library.

[516] Philonius is a pseud. for Balescon de Tarente, fl. 1380-1418. An octavo edition of his *Aureum ac perutile opus practice medicine* was printed by Jacobus Myt and published by Scipion de Gabiano in Lyons in 1535. National Library of Medicine. Durling, no. 4477. Baudrier, VII, p. 181.

[517] Oriano, Lanfrancus de. *Praxis ivdicaria Lanfranci de Oriano cvm Benedicti Vadii, & Celsi Hugonis annotationibus* (Lvgdvni, apud Hæredes Iacobi Giuntæ, 1550). 8.vo. Earlier editions of the *Practica* were published in Lyons in 1528, 1534 and 1538. Baudrier, VI, pp. 161, 182, 269.

[518] Petrus Jacobus a Montepessulano. *Practica Petri Jacobi* (Lugduni, Apud Iacobum Giuncti, 1535, 1539). 4.to. Baudrier, VI, pp. 166, 184.

[519] The British Library has a copy of *Liber processionarius secundum consuetudinem ordinis sancti ... Hieronymi* (Excussum in alma cōpluti vniuersitate: in aedibus Michaelis de Eguia, 1526), but it is a quarto. I have not identified a likely octavo edition. Like the copy in the inventory, the British Library copy is printed on vellum. Rhodes, p. 115.

[520] *Processionale Romanu* (Uenetijs p. Luc. antoniū d' Giūta, 1513). 8.vo. Camerini, I, p. 154.

[521] Persius Flaccus, Aulus. Octavo editions of the *Satyrae sex* with the commentary of J. Murmelius and H. Buschius were published in Paris in 1546 and in Cologne (Colonię, Ex ędibus E. Ceruicorni, 1534). An edition with the commentary of Jod. Badius was published in Lyons in 1506. British Library.

[522] Nicolaus, de Lyra. *Postilla venerabilis fratris Nicolai de Lyra super psalterium* (urbe Parisiēsi, per vdalricū gering, 1483). 4.to. Hain, 10378. British Library IA. 39133.

[523] Pepin, Guillaume. *Sermonum dominicalium totius anni* (Parrhisijs, in aedibus C. Chevallonii, 1529). 8.vo. An earlier edition was published in 1526. British Library. I have not identified a Lyons edition.

[524] Pepin, Guillaume. *Sermones quadragesimales fratris Gulielmi Pepin* (Parisiis, in aedibus Ambrosii Girault, 1540). 8.vo. The British Library also has an earlier octavo edition (Parisius, C. Chevallon, 1517). A 1518 octavo edition of the *Sermones* also by C. Chevallon, covers the epistle readings.

5 precationes biblie[525] pp 51		255
10 precationes Psalor[um] pp 51		510
1 Plinius g[aiu]s. Frob[en][526] 750		750
1 Primasius in epistolas Pauli[527] in 8°	114	114
1 Primasius in apocalypsin[528] in 8°	51	051
1 Plautus[529] in 8° 68		068
1 Pomponius Mela[530] in 8° Florencie	51	051
1 Petrus de Aliaco sup[er] sñas[531]	51	051
1 Propugnaculum ecclesie[532] in 8°	51	051
1 Prosperi opera in fol.[533] 272		272

---

[525] *Precationes Biblicæ Sanctorum Patrũ, Illustriumq. virorum, & mulierum vtriusq. Testamenti* (Lugduni, Apud Ioannem & Franciscum Frellaeos, 1538). 16.mo. The British Library has a 1545 edition of this, also in 16.mo. Baudrier, V, pp. 177, 199. The Antwerp edition was condemned by the Spanish *Index* of 1559 under the entry "Praecationes Biblicae Sanctorum Patrum, Antverpiae per Ioannem Crinitum et Martinum Caesarem". No copy of the Antwerp edition is known. De Bujanda, V, p. 429.

[526] Plinius Caecilius Secundus, Caius, ca.61-113. This may be Froben's edition of the *Epistolarum libri decem* (Basileae, per H. Froben. & N. Episcopivm, 1552) or his edition of *Historia mundi libri XXXVII* of Plinius Secundus, Caius (Basileae, 1525, 1530, 1535, 1539, 1545, 1549, 1554-1555). All folio.

[527] Primasius, bp. of Hadrumetum, fl. 551. *Primasii Uticensis in Africa episcopi, in omnes D. Pauli Epistolas cõmentarij perbreues ac docti* (Parisiis, 1543). 8.vo. British Library. The Bibliothèque Nationale, Paris, has a 1537 edition by Seb. Gryphius in Lyon. Baudrier, VIII, p. 107.

[528] Ibid. *Primasii Vticensis ... Commentariorum libri quinque in Apocalypsim Ioannis Evangelistae* (Basileæ, R. Winter, 1544). 8.vo. British Library. Another octavo edition of this and the commentary on the epistles was produced earlier in Cologne (Coloniae, ex aedibus Eucharij, 1535). Princeton University. The Bibliothèque Nationale, Paris, has another 1544 edition (Parisiis, apud J. Foucherum, 1544). 8.vo.

[529] Plautus, Titus Maccius. *Comœdiæ omnes* (Florentiæ, per haeredes B. Iunte, 1554). Octavo editions of the comedies of Plautus were published by the Giunti of Florence in 1514, 1522 and 1554, and by Seb. Gryphius of Lyons in 1535, and 1537.

[530] Mela, Pomponius. *Pomponius Mela. Ivlivs Solinvs* (Florentiae, per haeredes Philippi Iuntae, 1519) and Feb. 1526 (i.e. 1527). British Library.

[531] Alliaco, Petrus de. *Questiones super libros sententiarũ* [of Petrus Lombardus] ([Lyons,] N. Wolff, 1500). 4.to. The British Library has two undated octavo editions printed in Paris.

[532] Clichtove, Josse van, d. 1543. *Propugnaculum ecclesie. Aduersus Lutheranos* (Apud Coloniam Agrippinam, in aedibus Hieronis Alopecii, impensa G. Hittorpij, 1526). 8.vo. Harvard University. British Library.

[533] Prosper, Tiro, Aquitanus, St. *Divi Prosperi Aquitanici ... Opera accurata ... recognita* (Lugduni, Apud Seb. Gryphium, 1539). Folio. British Library. Bibliothèque Nationale, Paris. Baudrier, VIII, p. 126.

1 Passagiū terre sancte[534] in 4⁽ᵗᵒ⁾ 51		051
1 Pepin de sanctis[535] in 8° 68		068
1 Pincianus in Senecam[536] in 4⁽ᵗᵒ⁾ 34		034
1 Pomponius Mela cum annota. Pinciani[537] 8° 25		025
1 Prosopopeiia animalium[538] in 4⁽ᵗᵒ⁾ 25		025
1 Preparatio mortis[539] viejo 17		017
2 Panormitanus in clementinas[540] 68		136
1 Palacios Rubios de donationibus[541] in fol. 204		204
1 Posteriora Coronel[542] 68		<u>068</u>
		7,527

---

[534] The Spanish *Index* of 1559 condemns "Passagium terrae sanctae" (item 357). De Bujanda (p. 426) suggests that this may be the *Opus transmarinae peregrinationis ad sepulchrum dominicum in Hierusalem* of Bernhard von Breydenbach, the *Peregrinatio Hierusalem* by Pedro de Urrea or may simply be a generic title for such works. The fact that the inventory contains the exact title indicates that this work did exist even though no copy is now known.

[535] Pepin, Guillaume. *Conciones de sanctis sive de imitatione sanctorum* (Parisiis, Apud Claudium Cheualloniū, ipsius expēsis τ Ioānis Petit, 1528). 8.vo. British Library. Bibliothèque Nationale, Paris. There were other editions in 1536 and 1541.

[536] Nuñez de Guzmán, Fernando, called El Pinciano, 1473-1553. Pinciano's work on Seneca, *In omnia L. Annei Senecæ scripta castigationes*, was first published in Venice in 1536 (Venetiis, Iussu I. A. de Burgo, 1536). 4.to. British Library.

[537] Mela, Pomponius. *Pomponii Melæ. Castigationes in Pomponium Melam geographum* ... (Impressum Salmāticeñ. ex officina eximij uiri Ioannis Iuntæ, 1543). 8.vo. Biblioteca Nacional, Madrid. New York Public Library. Palau, 160076. The text of Pomponius Mela with the commentary of Fernando Nuñez de Guzmán. The title page date is 1543, but the colophon date is March, 1544.

[538] Ursin, Jean. *Prosopopeia animalivm aliqvot: in qua multa de eorum uiribus, natura, proprietatibus praecipuè ad rem medicam pertinētibus continentur* [Commentary J. Olivarius] (Viennæ, Apud Mathiam Bonhomme, 1541). 4.to. Harvard University. British Library. The National Library of Medicine has an octavo edition dated 1552. Durling, no. 4458.

[539] Evia, Francisco de, c. 1520 - c. 1560. *Preparatio mortis. Cōpuesto por un frayle dela ordē de los menores* (1545). 8.vo. British Library. This work is found in the Latin section of the Spanish *Index* of 1559 under "Praeparatio mortis, authore F. Francisco de Evia, latine et hispanice" and in the Spanish section as "Praeparatio mortis, en romance y en latin, hecha por fray Francisco de Evia." De Bujanda, V, pp. 430, 527. The British Library copy and the 1543 edition in the Hispanic Society of America (Sevilla, Juan Cromberger) are both in Spanish and form part of the title *Tractado de un exercicio ... llamado Cruz de Christo*.

[540] Niccolò de' Tudeschi, Abp. 1386-1445. *Apparatus solennis ... Nicolai Siculi ... in Clementinas, de novo correctus cum additionibus* (Parisiis, expensis ... Enguilberti et Johannis de Marnef, 1520). 8.vo. Bibliothèque Nationale, Paris.

[541] López de Palacios Rubios, Juan, d. 1524. Probably his *De donationibus inter virum et uxorem*, but I do not know of an edition earlier than Lyons, 1576. Cf. with footnote 560.

[542] Coronel, Antonio. *Expositio super libros posteriorū Aristotelis insertis questionibus Anthonii Coronel* (Parisius, O. Senant [1510?]). Folio. British Library. Bibliothèque Nationale, Paris.

INVENTARIO DE LOS LIBROS

/ xvi,clxix /   <u>8,912</u>
                                L. 16,169

(f. 31)

2 Quartum Hadriani[543] in 8°	119	238
1 quinque libri minores in 4to	85	085
1 Quintus Curtius[544] pp	51	051
5 Quintus Curtius[545] in 8°	51	255
4 quodlibeta Hadriani[546] in 8°	85	340
1 quadratura Pauli Veneti[547] in fol.	68	068
2 Quintilianus[548] in 8° Florencie	85	170
1 quodlibeta Henrici a Gandauo[549] in fol.	510	<u>510</u>
j,dccxvij		L. 1,717

1 Rationale divinor[um] officiorum[550] viejo in 4to	102	102
1 Repetitio Segure[551] in fol.	340	340

---

[543] Adrian VI, pope. *Hadriani Sexti Pontificis Maximi Quaestiones in Quartum Sententiarum* (Lugduni, Apvd Gvlielmvm Rovilivm, 1546 and 1547). 8.vo. Baudrier, IX, pp. 129, 134.

[544] Curtius Rufus, Quintus. *De rebus gestis Alexandri Magni Macedonum regis Historia* (Lugduni, Apud Seb. Gryphium, 1547). 16.mo. British Library. Bibliothèque Sainte Geneviève, Paris. Baudrier, VIII, p. 216.

[545] Ibid. Ibid. Octavo editions were published in Florence (Sumptu Philippi Iuntae, 1517), Venice (in aedibus Aldi, 1520), Paris (Apud S. Colinaeum, 1533 and 1543), Lyons (Apud Seb. Gryphium, 1541 and 1545) and Basel (Froben, 1545).

[546] Adrian VI, pope. *Hadriani Sexti Pontificis Maximi Quaestiones duodecim Quodlibeticae* (Lvgdvni, Apvd Iacobvm Gionta, 1546, 1547). 8.vo. Baudrier, VI, pp. 217, 220.

[547] Paulus Venetus, d. 1429. *Quadratura magistri Pauli Veneti* (Venetiis, Per Bonetum Locatellum, 1493). Folio. British Library.

[548] Quintilianus, Marcus Fabius. *M. F. Qvintilianvs ... De institutione oratoria* (Florētiæ, opera & sumptu Philippi Iuntæ, 1515). 8.vo. British Library.

[549] Henricus Gandavensis, 1217-1293. *Quodlibeta magistri Henrici Goethals a Gandavo* (Parhisiensis, Venundantur ab Iodoco Badio Ascensio, 1518). Folio. Catholic University of America. Bibliothèque Nationale, Paris.

[550] Durantis, Gulielmus. *Rationale divinorum officiorvm* (Lugduni, apud Iacobvm Givnti, 1539). 4.to. The British Library also has several quarto editions from Lyons printed earlier in the century. See Baudrier, XI, pp. 137, 283, 289-293. Numerous incunable editions exist.

[551] Segura, Diego de, fl. 1520. *Aurea frugifera peneque divina commentaria solennesque repetitiones decem* (Salmanticae, apud Andream de Portonariis, 1547). Folio. Ruíz Fidalgo, no. 158.

1 Robertus Senalis in posteriora[552]	51	051
1 Raulini quadragesimale[553] in 8°	170	170
1 repeticio Benedicti[554] in fol.	510	510
9 regule divi Hieronymi pp	25	225
1 reportata Tartareti[555] in fol.	272	272
1 repertorium Montalvi[556] in fol.	272	272
12 regule sacre scripture in 8°	51	612
2 regule Bernardi Dias de Luco[557] in 8°	51	102
24 Regule predicator[um][558] in 8° Sal[aman]ca	25	600
1 regule cancellarie[559] pp	34	034
1 Repeticio Pala[cios] Rub[ios] de donationibus[560]	238	238
1 rethorica divina Guliel. Paris.[561]	51 ligat.	051
7 Ruardus contra hereses[562] in 4to	102	102

---

[552] Alliaco, Petrus de. *Posteriora cum additiōibus magistri roberti cenalis* (Salmantice per Laurentium de lyhom de deis, 1518). Folio. British Library.

[553] Raulin, Jean, 1443-1514. *Opus sermonū quadragesimaliū* (in emporio Lugduneñ., I. Clein, 1518). 8.vo. British Library.

[554] Benoît, Guillaume, fl. 1514. *Repetitio Capituli, Raynuntius de testamentis ...* (Lugduni, apud Antonium Vincentium, 1544). Folio. This is a two volume work on the canon law of wills and inheritances.

[555] Tartaretus, Petrus, 15th cent. *Reportata sup[er] libros ethicorum Aristotelis edita a m̃ro ñro Tartareto in Universitate parisiensi* [n.p., 1501]. Folio.

[556] Díaz de Montalvo, Alonso. *Repertorium notabilium questionum* [Lyons? J. Siber? 1485?]. Folio. British Library.

[557] Díaz de Lugo, Bernardo. *Regulae iuris, cum suis ampliationibus, & Restrictionibus, ex variis codicibus excerptæ* (Lugduni, apud Gulielmum Rouillium, 1554). 8.vo. Baudrier, IX, p. 215.

[558] Augustinians. *Regvla beati Avgvstini et constitntiones (sic) ordinis Fratrum Praedicatorum, cum aliis opusculis* (Salmanticae, in aedibvs Ioannis Ivntae, 1543). 8.vo. Biblioteca Nacional, Lisbon. Palau, 289418.

[559] Catholic Church. Cancellaria Apostolica. *Regulae cancellariae apostolicae, Innocentij octavi, Iulij secundi ac Clementis septimi cum commentarijs & scholijs* (Lugduni, Apvd Antonivm Vincentivm, 1545). 12 cm. Library of Congress.

[560] López de Palacios Rubios, Juan, d. 1524. *Repetitio rubricae et capituli per vestras de donationibus inter virum et uxorem* (Valladolid, per Jacobū de Gomiel, 1503; Salamanca, 1523). Folio.

[561] Guilelmus Parisiensis, a Dominican, professor of theology. *Rhetorica diuina. Libri sancti Effrem de cōpunctione cordis ...* (Basileae, J. Froben, 1492?). 8.vo. British Library.

[562] Tapper, Ruard, 1487-1559. *Declaratio articulorvm a veneranda Facvltate theologiae Lovaniensis, aduersus nostri temporis Haereses* (Lugduni, apud Mauricium Roy et Ludouicum Pesnot, 1554). 4.to. Bibliothèque Nationale, Paris. Baudrier, IV, 306.

INVENTARIO DE LOS LIBROS

1 regule cancellarie[563] in 8°	51	051
64 repeticio Urzurro[564] in fol.	51	<u>3,264</u>
/ vj,dccccxcvj /		L. 6,996

(f. 32)

1 sermones patavini[565] in 3bus 8° pre	408	408
1 speculum Galeni[566] in 8°	68	068
1 scholia Manutii in epistolas Tullii[567] in 8°	17	017
1 Sedullii carmen pascale cum aliis[568] in 4to	153	153
1 Sermones Dormi Secure[569] in 8° falto		068
1 Summa angelica[570] in 8° falta		---

---

[563] Catholic Church. Cancellaria Apostolica. *Regulae cancellariae. Liber aureus practicis ipsis vtilissim. regulas cancellarie ap[osto]lice Innocētij .viii. nuperrime castigatas ... quibus ordinatim subiecte sunt regule Căcellarie Iulij ii. cū huberrimis glossematibus. Itē regule apostolice Clementis vii.* (Lugduni, in officina Guillermi Boulle ... impresse per Benedictū Bonynum, 1534). 8.vo. Harvard Law School. Newberry Library. Bibliothèque Nationale, Paris. Baudrier, IV, p. 27.

[564] Urzurrum, Michael de. *Repetitio valde subtilis* ... (Burgensi, per Alfonsum de melgar, 1521). Folio.

[565] Antonio da Padova, Saint. Jodocus Badius published a three-volume octavo edition of the *Sermones* in Paris in 1520-1521. British Library.

[566] Champier, Symphorien. *Speculum Galeni. Epithome Galeni: sive Galenus abreviatus* ([Lyons, Symon Vincent, 1512; Lugduni, Joannes de Jonvelle dictus Piston, 1517). Both 8.vo. National Library of Medicine. Durling, no. 945, 946. Legrand, 3, pp. 183, 235.

[567] Cicero, Marcus Tullius. It is not certain which of the works of Cicero's letters this is, but the Manutius firm published several octavo editions. This may be *Familiares epistolae ... Pauli Manutij scholia* (Venetijs, Apud Aldi filios, 1548). 8.vo. British Library.

[568] Sedulius, Coelius. *Sedulii Paschale cum Aelii Antonii Nebrissensis interpretatione nuper excusum* (Granatam, Sancho de Nebrija, 1553). Other quarto editions: Compluti, Michaelis de Eguia, 1524 and 1531; Caesaraugustae, Georgii Coci, 1529; Toleti, arnaldi guillelmi brocarij, 1516 1nd 1520; Lugduni, Mareschal τ Chaussard, 1512).

[569] Johannes de Verdena. *Sermones dormi secure. Sermones dominicales per totum annum cum singularibus expositionibus Evangeliorum* (Parisiis, Apur Ambrosium Girault, 1538). 8.vo. 2 pts. Biblioteca Nacional, Madrid. There is also another undated Lyons edition in octavo from the press of the heirs of Simon Vincent and a 1515 Lyons edition from the firm of Huguetan and Balet. Baudrier, XI, p. 307.

[570] Angelus Carletus, de Clavasio, 1411-1495? *Summa Angelica de casibus conscientiae* (Lugduni, apud Jacobum Giuncti, 1534). 4.to. Baudrier, VI, p. 161. There were numerous editions in Venice, Strassburg and Lyons.

1 Scotus sup[er] sñas⁵⁷¹ in 8° faltos	408
1 Sermones Quintini⁵⁷² in 8° 25	025
1 Strebeus in particiones orato. Tullii⁵⁷³ in 8° 60	060
1 Singularia doctor[um] in 4ᵗᵒ 85	085
3 Sermones Jordani⁵⁷⁴ in 4ᵗᵒ 204	612
2 Sylve morales in 4ᵗᵒ ligat. 85	170
1 Salustius⁵⁷⁵ pp 25	025
1 Salustius⁵⁷⁶ in 8° Lion 34	034
3 Solinus⁵⁷⁷ in 8° Lion 34	102
4 Ser[mones] Berlette⁵⁷⁸ in 8° 68	272
2 Ser[mones] laosana in 8° 8	136
1 Symon [Fidati] de Cassia sup[er] evangelia⁵⁷⁹ in fol. 442	442
1 Secunda 2e Sancti Thome qqto.⁵⁸⁰ in fol. 476	476
1 Scriptum Sancti Thome in 8° 612	612

---

⁵⁷¹ Duns, Joannes, Scotus, 1265?-1308? *Questiones quodlibetales ex quattuor Sentētiarū voluminibus a Joāne duns Sco.* (Lugduni, Impresse per Jacobum Myt, sumptu Jacobi Giunta, 1520). 8.vo. New York Public Library. Baudrier, VI, p. 100.

⁵⁷² The author is probably Jean Quintin, 1500-1561, but I have not identified this title.

⁵⁷³ Strebée, Jacques Louis, d. ca. 1550. *De partitione oratoria M. T. Ciceronis dialogus Iacobi Lodoici Strebaei, ac Georgii Vallae...commentariis, illustratus* (Lugduni, Apud Seb. Gryphium, 1554, 1545, 1536). 8.vo. Biblioteca Nacional, Madrid. There is also an octavo edition produced in Lyons in 1546 by T. Paganus.

⁵⁷⁴ Jordan *von Quendlinburg* (d. 1380). *Opvs sermonvm* (Venundantur Parisius in officina Damiani Hichman 1521). 4.to. Yale University. The work was printed by Jean du Pré.

⁵⁷⁵ Sallustius Crispus, Caius. *De L. Sergij Catilinæ coniuratione, ac Bello Iugurthino historiæ* (Lvgdvni, Apvd Seb. Gryphivm, 1547, 1551). 16.mo. Baudrier, VIII, p. 211, 248.

⁵⁷⁶ ibid. *De L. Sergij Catilinæ coniuratione, ac Bello Iugurthino historiæ* ([Lyons], Apud Gryphium, 1545, 1546, 1549, 1555). 8.vo. Baudrier, VIII, pp. 193, 201, 229, 274.

⁵⁷⁷ Solinus, Caius Julius. *Polyhistor* (Lvgdvni, Apvd Seb. Gryphivm, 1537, 1538). 8.vo. Baudrier, VIII, p. 101, 110. Another octavo edition was published in Lyons by the heirs of S. Vincent in 1539.

⁵⁷⁸ Gabriel of Barletta. Octavo editions of his *Sermones* were published in Paris (per J. Seurre, 1507; C. Chevallon, 1516; A. Girault, 1527), Lyons (Lugduni, S. Beuelaqua, 1516) Rouen (Rothomagi, G. Bernard, 1515) and Brescia (Brixie, L. Britannici, 1521). Baudrier, II, p. 18.

⁵⁷⁹ Simone Fidati, *da Cascia*, d. 1348. *Expositio super totum corpus evangeliorum.* Folio editions were published in Strassburg (c. 1486), Florence (1496), Basel (1517), Cologne (1540).

⁵⁸⁰ The Giunti firm of Venice published the three parts of the *Summa theologica* of St. Thomas Aquinas in a folio edition in 1522-23. Camerini, I, p. 203.

1 Summa rosella[581] in fol.	238	238
2 Sacrarum orationes pp	85	170
1 Silius Italicus qqto[582] in fol.	102	102
1 Summa sylvestrina[583] in 4to	375	375
1 Summa consilior[um][584] in 4to	238	238
1 Summa tabiena[585] in 4to	238	238
1 Similia sacre scripture[586] in 8°	102	102
1 Supplementum cronicor[um] in fol.	510	510
1 Sonsinatis sup[er] sñas[587] in 8°	85	085
1 Summa rolandina[588] in 4to	119	119
1 Summa Astensis[589] in 4to	272	272
1 Strabo de situ orbis[590] in fol.	102	102
		6,724

---

[581] Trovamala, Baptista. *Summa Roselle De casibus conscientiae* (Impressum Argentine, apud Ioannem Knoblouch, 1516). Folio. British Library. Law School Library, Univ. of California, Berkeley.

[582] Silius Italicus, Caius. *Quae hoc libro contineatur Silij italici Vita ex Petro Crinito & Petro Marso. Secundi belli punici compendium ex marso. Silij italici vatis ... Libri decem & septē cum ... cōmentarijs* (Parrhisijs, ex aedibus Nicolai de pratis, impensis Poncii probi & Francisci regnault, 1512). Folio. British Library. Biblioteca Nacional, Madrid.

[583] Mazzolini da Prierio, Sylvestro. *Sylvestrinae Svmmae, qvae svmma svmmarvm merito* (Lvgdvni, apvd Gvlielmvm Rovillivm, 1552). 4.to. Baudrier, IX, p. 201. The British Library has a 1533 edition printed in Lyons by I. Moylin for Iacobus Giunta.

[584] Carranza de Miranda, Bartolomé. *Summa Conciliorum et Pontificum a Petro vsq; ad Paulū tertium, succincta complectens omnia, quæ alibi sparsim tradita sunt ... Nunc denuo ... recognita, & aucta* (Salmanticæ, Apud A. de Portonariis, 1549). Another edition was published in 1551. 4.to. British Library. Rhodes, p. 42.

[585] Cagnazzo, Giovanni, d. 1521. *Summa summarum, qvæ tabienae dicitur...* (Bononię, B. Hectoris, 1517). 4.to. British Library.

[586] Alardus Amstelredamus, 1491?-1544. *Selectae aliqvot similitvdines sive collationes, tum ex biblijs sacris, tum ex ueterum orthodoxorum commētarijs* (Cologne, 1539). 8.vo. or *Similitudines sive collationes ex Biblijs sacris & veterū Orthodoxorū commentarijs* (Lugduni, Excudebant Ioannes & Franciscus Frellonii, fratres, 1543). 8.vo. Biblioteca Nacional, Madrid. *Catálogo colectivo*, A, 1120. Baudrier, V, p. 193.

[587] Barbo, Paolo, d. 1494. *Clarissimi...Pauli Soncinatis...diuinum Epitoma, quaestionum in quatuor libros Sententiarum a...Ioanne Capreolo Tholosano disputatarum* (Lugduni, per Ioannem Crespinum, 1528). 8.vo. Biblioteca Nacional, Madrid. *Catálogo colectivo*, A, 1120.

[588] Rolandinus de Passageriis, d. 1300. *Summa artis notariae* (Venetiis, 1489). 4.to. Yale Law Library.

[589] Astesanus, de Ast. *Summa Astensis* (Lugduni, S. Gueynard, 1519). 4.to. British Library. Baudrier, XI, p. 250.

[590] Strabo. *De situ orbis* (Venetiis, A. Philippo Pincio, 1510). Folio. British Library. There are several earlier folio editions in the British Library.

(f. 33)

3 Speculum sapientie[591] in 8° 25		075
1 summa Petri Dolose in 8° 170		170
1 Sedullius in epistolas Pauli[592] in fol. 136		136
1 Sermones Augustini[593] in 4to 272		272
1 summa Amarcani in fol. 204		204
2 secunda 2e Sancti Thome[594] sine qto. 170		340
3 sermones de missa in 8° 34		102
3 Siliceus de nomine Jesu[595] 8° 40		120
1 Suetonius qqto.[596] in fol. 612		612
3 secreta mulierum[597] in 8° 10		030
2 Savonarola de symplicitate vite[598] 8° 34		068
9 speculum ecclesie[599] in 8° 25		225
1 sermones Godschalfi[600] in fol. 340		340

---

[591] *Speculum sapientiae*. The supposed author is St. Cyrillus, bp. of Jerusalem or St. Cyrillus of Thessalonica. This may be the ca. 1500 edition of Jean Petit in Paris, that of Arnaldus Guillermus de Brocario in Logroño in 1503, or the 1505? edition of C. de Zyrichzee in Cologne. All octavos. British Library.

[592] Sedulius Scotus, 9th cent. *Sedulii Scotti ... in omnes Epistolas Pauli Collectaneum* (Basileæ, per H. Petrum, 1528). Folio. British Library.

[593] Augustine, Saint. *Sermones* (Lugduni, I. Mareschal, 1520). 2 parts. 4.to. British Library.

[594] See footnote 580.

[595] Martinus Silicaeus, Joannes Blasius, Cardinal, 1486-1557. *De diuino nomine Iesus* (Toleti, Joanes Ferrarius, 1550). 8.vo. Palau, 313097. He lists another edition in Toledo in 1551. Palau, 313098.

[596] Suetonius Tranquillus, Caius. *Duodecim Caesares*. A folio edition of the text was produced with the commentary of Erasmus (Lugduni, 1548). Earlier folio editions were produced in Basel (Basileae, apud J. Frobenium, 1518; Per H. Frobenium et N. Episcopium, 1533) and in Cologne (Coloniae, in aedibus Eucharii Cervicorni, 1527). British Library.

[597] Albertus, Magnus, Bp. of Ratisbon. *Secreta mulierum τ virorum* (Parisiis? Nicolas Roussel? 1513?). 8.vo. National Library of Medicine. Durling, no. 98.

[598] Savonarola, Girolamo. *Opuscula, De simplicitate vitæ Christianę* (Compluti, in aedibus Michaelis de Eguia, 1530). 8.vo. Biblioteca Nacional, Madrid. Martín Abad, p. 402, no. 236.

[599] Hugo de Sancto Charo, Cardinal, d. 1263. *Speculum sacerdotum ecclesie* (Compluti, Excudebat Ioannes Brocarius, 1546). 8.vo. San Lorenzo El Escorial. Martín Abad, p. 534, no. 361.

[600] Godschalk, Jean, 1507?-1571. *Latini sermonis observationes*. I have not located a folio edition.

INVENTARIO DE LOS LIBROS

1 sermones Sancti Aporta[601] 204		204
2 sermones Petri Apalude[602] in 8° 25		050
16 sermo[nes] abbatis ab Aguilar in 4to 10		160
1 Sutor de detractatione biblie[603] in fol. 85		085
1 Seysellus de statu ecclesie[604] in fol. 238		238
1 sermones Patavini[605] in 4to 153		153
2 ser[mones] quadrag[esimales] Herborn[606] in 8° 85		170
2 sermones Guarici[607] in 8° 51		102
1 Strabotti de Francesco Ciei[608] in 8° 25		025
1 Sulpitii opera diversa[609] in 4to 68		068
1 scripta Ioannis de monte regio[610] in 4to 51		051
1 Sutoris vita carthusianor[um][611] in 4to 102		102
4 sententie juris selecte in 8° 10		040
1 Seysellus de divina providentia[612] in 4to 51		051

---

[601] Porta, Sancho. *Sermones estiuales de tempore venerabilis Santij porta* (Lugd. opera τ industria Iohannis Cleyn, 1513). 4.to. Baudrier, XII, p. 285. or *Sermones festiuitatum beatissime virginis Marie* (Valentie industria τ opa Ioannis Ioffre, 1512). Folio. British Library. Rhodes, p. 159.

[602] Petrus de Palude, patriarch of Jerusalem, d. 1342. Perhaps the *Aurei et perutiles Sermones Domini Petri de Palude ... vulgo intitulati: omnes quidem resurgemus* (Lugduni, s.i., 1517). 8.vo. Biblioteca Nacional, Madrid. *Catálogo colectivo*, L, 136.

[603] Cousturier, Pierre, d. 1537. This may be his *De tralatione Bibliae et novarum reprobatione interpretationum Petri Sutoris doctoris theologi* (Parisiis, apud Ioannem Paruum, 1525). Folio. British Library. This work deals with Erasmus' translation of the New Testament.

[604] Seyssel, Claude de, 1450?-1520. I have not been able to identify this title.

[605] Antonio da Padova, Saint. I have not identified a quarto edition. See footnote 565.

[606] Herborn, Nikolaus, 1480?-1535. Herborn published attacks on Lutheranism. I have not found a copy of this work.

[607] Guerricus, Abbot of Igny, d. ca. 1157. *Sermones D. Gverrici ... per Ioannem Gaigneium ... ante aliquot annos in lucem editi* (Lutetiae Parisiorum, Per N. Diuitem, 1547). 8.vo. University of Chicago. The British Library also has an octavo edition, *Sermones antiqui* (Parisiis, Apud G. Cheualloniū, 1539).

[608] Cei, Francesco. *Sonecti, capituli, canzone, sextine, stanze et strambocti ... in laude de Clitia* (Firenze, per Philippo di Giunta, 1514). 8.vo. Biblioteca Nacional, Madrid. The Giunta firm also published this in 1503. Biblioteca Nazionale, Florence.

[609] Sulpitius, Joannes, Verulanus, 15th cent.

[610] Mueller, Johannes Regiomontanus, 1436-1476. *Scripta clarissimi mathematici M. Ioannis Regiomontani ... Obseruationes motuum solis, ac stellarum* (Norimbergae, Apud Ioannnem Montanum & Vlricum Neuber, 1544). 4.to. Harvard University. Columbia University.

[611] Cousturier, Pierre, d. 1537.

[612] See footnote 604.

21 Synonymor[um] sylva⁶¹³ in 8°   34   714
1 Salustius⁶¹⁴ in 4ᵗᵒ qqto.   85   085
                                                  4,992
        / xj,dccxvi /   6,724
                                              L. 11,716

2 Tritenhemius de scripto[ribus] ecclesiasticis⁶¹⁵ in 4ᵗᵒ   136   272
14 Terentius⁶¹⁶ in 8° Milis   42   588
1 Tracta[tus] de sponsionibus⁶¹⁷ pp   34   034
1 Tergitus in fol.   51   051
1 Triumphus Christi⁶¹⁸ falto in fol.   ----
2 Terentius qqto.⁶¹⁹ in 4ᵗᵒ   68   136
1 Terentianus maurus⁶²⁰ in 4ᵗᵒ   85   085
1 Terentius⁶²¹ pp   30   030
                                                  1,196

(f. 34)

4 Textus phisicor[um] Aristo[telis] abreviatus⁶²² in 8°   34   136

---

[613] Pelegromius, Simon, 1507?-1572. *Synonimorum sylva Simonis Pelegromij opera atqz labore in vsvm eorum qui compositioni student epistolari congesta* (Bvrgis, Excudebat Ioannes à Iunta, 1555). 8.vo. Biblioteca Nacional, Madrid. *Catálogo colectivo*, P, 884.

[614] *Opera Sallustiana.* Quarto editions of the commentary of Jodocus Badius on the works of Sallust were published in Lyons in 1508, 1517 and 1523. British Library.

[615] Trithemius, Johannes, 1462-1516. *De scriptorib[us] eccl'iasticis* (Parrhisi[us] Venūdatur a B. Rembolt, ubi impressus ē, et a I. Paruo, 1512). 4.to. British Library.

[616] Terentius, Publius, afer. *Pvb. Terentii Aphri Comoediae sex* ([Medina del Campo] Ex typographia Guillelmi de Millis, 1552). 8.vo. Pérez Pastor *Medina del Campo*, p. 83, no. 94.

[617] Giganti, Girolamo. *Tractatus de pensionibus ecclesiasticis, Hieronymo Gigante ... autore* (Lugduni, apud Gulielmum Rouillium, 1548). 16.mo. Harvard Law School. I think this must be the item in the inventory in spite of the spelling "sponsionibus."

[618] Christophorus, de Sancto Antonio. *Triumphus Christi contra infideles* (Salmantice, Alfonso de Porres τ Laurentij Lion de deis, 1524). Folio. British Library. Rhodes, p. 52. This may also be: Tovar, Luis de. *Triūphus xp̄i* (Valladolid en la emprenta de mæstre Nicolas Tierri, 1534). Folio. British Library. Rhodes, p. 206.

[619] Terentius, Publius, afer. *Pvblii Terentij Aphri comicorū latinorū principis comœdiæ: cum cōmētarijs famatissimorū oratorū* (Lugduni, 1535). Baudrier, VI, p. 166.

[620] Terentianus Maurus. *De litteris, syllabis, pedibus et metris ... .* There are several possible editions. This may be the 1531 quarto edition of Simon Colines in Paris. British Library.

[621] Terentius, Publius, afer. *P. Terentii Afri Comoediae, Multo maiore, quam hactenus unquam, uigilantia repurgatae* (Lvgdvni, Apvd Seb. Gryphivm, 1550). 16.mo. Baudrier, VIII, p. 245.

[622] Aristoteles. *Textus abbreuiatus Aristotelis super octo libris phisicorum.* The British Library has a folio incunable with this title, but I have not found an octavo edition.

1 Treio sup[er] epistolas Pauli[623] in fol.	272		272
1 Tabula de lyra sup[er] bibliam[624] in fol.	51		051
1 Titus livius livius[625] in 8°	408		408
1 Theophilactus sup[er] epistolas Pauli[626] in 8°		119	119
7 Tragedie Senece[627] in 8°	51		357
1 Titelman Philosophia[628] in 8°	85		085
1 Titelman dialectica[629] in 8°	85		085
3 Theologia mystica[630] pp	51		153
1 Tracta[tus] sacerdotalis[631] in 8°	85		085

---

[623] Trejo, Guterrius de. The British Library has a copy of his *In sacrosancta Iesu Christi quattuor Euangelia ... commentarij* (Hispali, excudebat P. de Luxan, 1554). Folio. I have not found a copy of his commentary "Super epistolas Pauli."

[624] Nicolaus, de Lyra. I cannot identify this title.

[625] Livius, Titus. *T. Livii ... Decades tres cum dimidia...Annotationes Beati Rhenani et Sigismundi Gelenii* (Lugduni, apud haeredes S. Vincentii, 1537). 2 vols. in 1. 8.vo. Bibliothèque Nationale, Paris. The *Catalogue générale des livres imprimés* indicates that the complete edition consisted of 4 volumes. There are prefaces by Erasmus and Gelenius. Another of several possibilities is the 5-volume octavo edition of S. Gryphius which was published in Lyons in 1554. Baudrier, VIII, p. 272-273. The high price of the inventory copy lends weight to the supposition that it was a large, perhaps multi-volume edition.

[626] Theophylactus, Abp. of Okhrid, fl. 1078. *In omnes Diui Pauli Apostoli epistolas enarrationes* (Parisiis, apud I. Bogardum, 1542, 1548). 8.vo. British Library.

[627] Seneca, Lucius Annaeus. *Tragoediae decem* (Compluti, in aedibus Ioannis Brocarii, 1552). 8.vo. Biblioteca General de Navarra, Pamplona. Martín Abad, p. 587, no. 410.

[628] Tittelmans, Franciscus, 1502-1537. *Compendium naturalis philosophiae.* Rovilius published editions in Lyons in 1545, 1558 and 1564.

[629] Tittelmans, Franciscus. *Compendium dialecticae ... ad libros logicorum Aristotelis.* The Bibliothèque Nationale, Paris, has two octavo editions (Parisiis, ex officina P. Calvarini, 1539, 1548). This work was published in several Lyons editions. His *Dialecticae considerationis* on the Organum of Aristotle also saw several editions in Antwerp, Paris and Lyons, by J. Roigny, G. Rovilius, and F. Regnault.

[630] Herp, Hendrik, d. 1477. The "Theologia mystica Henrici Herpii" is on the Spanish *Index* of 1559. The Spanish version is condemned as well as the Latin. De Bujanda, V, pp 442-443. I do not know of a surviving small-format ("pp") edition in Latin; Juan de Brocar however published a Spanish translation of this in 12.mo under the title *Espejo de perfecion* (Alcalá de Henares, Juan de Brocar, 1551). De Bujanda, V, pp. 544. See footnote 819.

[631] Nicolaus de Plove. *Tractatus sacerdotalis vtilissimus domini Nicolai de Ploue ... De sacramentis et diuinis officijs: De expositione Misse. De dicendis horis canonicis. De sententia excommunicationis & suspensionis. De interdicto ecclesiastico. De irregularitate. Super additū est in fine huius tractatus Cōfessionale beati Thomi de Aquino* (Parisiis, Ex officina Ambrosij Girault, 1540). 8.vo. Yale University. (The "Confessionale" of St. Thomas is lacking in this copy.)

2 Tyraquellus de utroque retractu[632] in 4to	374	748
4 Turrequremata sup[er] psalmos[633] in 8°	85	340
11 Thomas Roca[634] in fol.	34	374
3 Triumphus Christi[635] in fol.	170	510
2 Tracta[tus] de conversione paganor[um] in fol.	85	170
1 Thomas sup[er] posteriora[636] in fol. una	102	102
8 Tractatus de Frias[637] in 4to	85	680
1 Theophilact[us] sup[er] epistolas Pauli[638] in fol.	204	204
1 Titus Livius in fol.[639] una de primis	476	476
1 Titus Livius in fol. una de novis	476	476
9 Tracta[tus] sylogismorum Enzinas[640] in 8°	51	459
4 Textus de Spauterii[641] in 8°	34	136
6 Titi Livii decas prima[642] in 8°	17	102

---

[632] Tiraqueau, Andre, 1488-1558. *De vtroqve retractv, mvnicipali, et conventionali, commentarii dvo.* I haven't found a 4.to edition.

[633] Torquemada, Juan de, *cardinal*, 1388-1468. *Expositio super toto psalterio.* There are many editions of this work, principally before 1500.

[634] Rocha, Thomas. *Thome Rocha gottolani ... f libros tres Augustini nimphi* (Burgeñ. per Alphonsum de melgar, 1523). Folio. British Library.

[635] See footnote 618.

[636] The Giunti firm of Venice published a folio edition of St. Thomas Aquinas' commentary on Aristotle's *Perihermenias* and *Posteriorum analyticorum* in 1553. Camerini, I, p. 400.

[637] Juan de Junta published Martinus de Frías' *Tractatus perutilis* in Burgos [1528? and 1550] and the same work under the title *Tractatus breuis ... de arte & modo audiendi confessiones ...* in 1529. The 1550 edition also contains the Spanish translation of the last section of the work, "Modus & ordo visitandi," with a separate title, *Tratado del modo y estilo que en la visitacion ordinaria se ha de tener.*

[638] Theophylactus, Abp. of Okhrid. *In omnes Divi Pauli Apostoli Epistolas enarrationes.* Folio editions of this work were published in Basel (Apvd And. Cratand., 1540) and Paris (Iodoco Badio Ascensio & Ioanni Roigny, 1534). Houghton Library, Harvard University. Columbia University Library.

[639] Among the likely folio editions of Livy we might cite the Lyons edition of J. Frellonius (1553) and A. Vincentius (1554), the Paris editions of J. Parvus and Josse Badius (1511, 1513, 1516, 1531), M. Vascosanus (1543) and A. Parvus (1543, 1552), and the Basel editions of Hervagius (1539, 1543, 1549, 1555) and J. Froben (1531, 1535). British Library. Bibliothèque Nationale, Paris.

[640] Enzinas, Ferdinandus de. *Tractatvs sillogismorvm* (Parrisiis, Brunello, 1528). University of California, Los Angeles.

[641] Despautère, Jean, ca. 1460-1520. *Contextus vniversae grammatices Despavterianae prime partis, syntaxeos, artis uersificatoriae, & figurarum* (Lvgdvni, apvd Seb. Gryphivm, 1536). 8.vo. Baudrier, VIII, p. 91.

[642] Livius, Titus. *T. Liuii Patauini Historici, ab vrbe condita decadis prime* (Salmantice, in edibus Joannis Junte, 1533). 8.vo. Biblioteca Capitular y Colombina, Seville. Palau, 139137. Ruíz Fidalgo, no. 82.

3 Tesaurus Spirituales pp	22		075
1 Tractatus de bannitis[643] in 8°	68		068
1 Tracta[tus] de prescriptionibus[644] in 8°	85		085
4 Titelman de mysterio fidei[645] pp	51		204
1 Tractatus de vera contritione 8°	34		034
1 Titelman sup[er] ecclesiasten[646] pp	68		068
1 Titelman sup[er] Job[647] in 8°	85		085
1 Theodoretus ad Timotheum[648] in 4to	25		025
1 termini chlichtovei[649] in 8°	51		051
26 Termini Gasparis Lap. in 4to	25		650
1 Topica cantiuncule[650] in fol.	85		085
1 Tracta[tus] de synodo[651] in 8°	25		025

---

[643] Nellus, *a Sancto Geminiano*. *Tractatus insignis de Bannitis* (Lvgdvni, Apud Hæredes Iacobi Giuntæ, 1550). 8.vo. Baudrier, VI, p. 266.

[644] Balbi, Giovanni, d. 1295. *Tractatus de praescriptionibus Tractatus secundus et perutilis profunde: subtilisq[ue]: ac quotidiane materie ois prescriptiois: tā ciuilis q[uam] canonice...* (Lugduni per Benedictū Bonyn, 1532). 8.vo. Bibliothèque Nationale, Paris. Baudrier, V, p. 441.

[645] Tittelmans, Franciscus. *Svmma Mysteriorvm Christianæ Fidei. Ex authoritate diuinarum scripturarum veteris & noui Testamenti, congesta* (Lugduni, apud Theobaldum Paganum, 1547). 16.mo. Baudrier, IV, p. 238. The Bibliothèque Nationale, Paris, has another 16.mo edition (Lugduni, sub scuto coloniensi, 1546). Baudrier, V, p. 207.

[646] Tittelmans, Franciscus. *Commentarii in Ecclesiasten Salomonis* (Lugduni, apud Gulielmum Rouillium, 1555). 16.mo. Baudrier, IX, p. 219. Rovillius also published an edition in 16.mo in 1553. Bibliothèque Nationale, Paris. Baudrier, IX, p. 204. The British Library has a 1549 edition of this in 16.mo printed in Paris (Parisiis, Ioannes Dauid), and the Bibliothèque Nationale, Paris another (Parisiis, ex typogr. P. Galteri, 1552).

[647] Tittelmans, Franciscus. *Elucidatio in librum D. Iob*. The Bibliothèque Nationale, Paris, has octavo editions published in Antwerp (Antuerpiae, in aedibus J. Steelsii, 1547), Paris (Parisiis, apud J. Roigny, 1547; Parisiis, apud H. et D. de Marnef, 1550) and Lyon (Lugduni, apud G. Rovilium, 1554).

[648] This may be Priscianus, Theodorus, fl. 5th cent. *Ad Timotheum fratrem, Phaenomenon euporiston* (Basileae, In officina Frobeniana, 1532). 4.to. National Library of Medicine. Durling, no. 3763.

[649] Clichtove, Josse van, d. 1543. *Introductiones. In terminos. In artium diuisionem. In suppositiones. In prædicabilia. ...* (Parisiis, apud Simonem Colinaeum, 1525). 8.vo. Yale University. Other editions were published in Paris by Stephanus in 1505, 1517 and 1520.

[650] Cantiuncula, Claudius. *Topica legalia quibus adjecimus [other works]* (Basileae, Apud Hieronymum Curionem, 1545). Folio. British Library. Biblioteca Universitaria, Barcelona. *Catálogo colectivo*, C, 418.

[651] Botteo, Enrico. *Tractatus de Synodo episcopi et de statutis episcopi synodalibus Henrici de Bottis Bressiani* (Lugduni per Ioannē dauid al's la mouche, 1529). 8.vo. Baudrier, V, p. 457. Yale University. Bibliothèque Nationale, Paris.

1 Tracta[tus] de episcopo⁶⁵² in 8°   25   025
1 Theocritus grece⁶⁵³ in 8°   51   051
1 Tragedie Sophoclis grece qqto.⁶⁵⁴ in 4ᵗᵒ   85   085
1 Theosophia arborei⁶⁵⁵ in fol.   680   680
1 Titus Livius⁶⁵⁶ in 8° Florencie   408   408
                                                                   9,232
       / x,cmxxviij /   1,196
                                                                L. 10,428

(f. 35)

45 Virues de matrimonio regis Anglie⁶⁵⁷ 8°   10   450
43 Viaje del principe⁶⁵⁸ in 8°   34   1,462
 7 Vocabularium ecclesiasticum⁶⁵⁹ in 4ᵗᵒ   85   595

---

⁶⁵² Bertachini, Giovanni, c. 1448-1497. *Tractatus de episcopo* (Lugduni per Benedictu Bōnyn, 1533). 8.vo. Catholic University of America. Bibliothèque Nationale, Paris. Baudrier, V, p. 448.

⁶⁵³ Theocritus. The Giunti firm of Florence published Greek editions of the Idylls in 1540, and the Bucolica in 1515.

⁶⁵⁴ Sophocles. *Sophoclis Tragoediæ septem. Cum interpretationibus vetustis* [Antonio Francini, comm.] (Florentiæ, per hæredes P. Iuntæ, 1522; apud Iunctam, 1547). 4.to. British Library. These are the Greek texts of the tragedies.

⁶⁵⁵ Arboreus, Joannes, 16th cent. *Primus (Secundus...) tomus Theosophiae Joannis Arborei...complectens sanam et difficilimorum locorum cum Veteris tum Novi Testamenti expositionem* (Parisiis, apud Simonem Colinaeum, 1540). Folio. Three vols. British Library. Bibliothèque Nationale, Paris. The *Tertius tomus* was published in 1553 (Parisiis, apud J. de Roigny. Folio. Bibliothèque Nationale, Paris.

⁶⁵⁶ Livius, Titus. The Giunta firm published the *Decades* in Florence (per heredes Philippi Iuntae, 1522; [and] in aedibus Bernardi Iuntae, 1532). 8.vo. British Library. University of Chicago.

⁶⁵⁷ Ruíz de Virués, Alonso, bp., d. 1545. *Tractatus de matrimonio Reg. Angliæ* (Salmanticæ [Gonsalvo de Castañeda?] 1530). 8.vo. British Library. Rhodes, p. 218. Ruíz Fidalgo, no. 25. Ruíz de Virués, chaplain to the court of Emperor Charles V and Abbot of San Zoilo (Benedictine), was an early supporter of Erasmus. In 1537 he was brought before the Inquisition on charges of Lutheranism. The case is described by Manuel Serrano y Sanz in *Revista de Archivos* (December, 1901; January, 1902; June, 1902).

⁶⁵⁸ Álvarez, Vicente. *Relacion del camino y buĕ viaje que hizo el Principe de España Don Phelipe nuestro señor, año ... de 1548 años: que passo de España en Italia* (Medina del Campo, Guillermo de Millis, 1551). 8.vo. Biblioteca Nacional, Madrid. Pérez Pastor, *Medina del Campo*, p. 71, no. 75. *Catálogo colectivo*, A, 1074.

⁶⁵⁹ Fernández de Santaella, Rodrigo, 1444-1509. *Vocabvlarivm Ecclesiasticvm* (Methymnae Campi, Excudebat Guillelmus de Millis, 1551, 1555). 4.to. The work was also published in quarto editions by Cromberger in Seville in 1515, in Alcalá de Henares by Juan Varela in 1533, in Zaragoza by Coci in 1538 and in Alcalá de Henares by Miguel de Eguía in 1527 and 1529, by Brocar in 1539, and in Salamanca by Pedro de Castro. Pérez Pastor, *Medina del Campo*, p. 131, no. 119. Griffin, Appendix One, no. 111. Martín Abad, no. 192, 214, 314. Rhodes, p. 78. Ruíz Fidalgo, no. 159.

19 Virgilius[660] in 8° Ant[uerpie]	68	1,292
1 Winton de eucharistia[661] in 8°	51	051
1 Vitruvius[662] in 8° Florencie	68	068
1 Vita Thome Cantuariensis falto	---	----
1 Vocabularium Nebrissensis[663] in fol. Stelle	408	408
18 Vite divi Pauli heremite[664] in 4to	10	180
19 Valerius Probus[665] in 4to	10	190
1 Virgilius qqto. Nebrissensis[666]	170	170
1 Waldensis contra Witclevistas[667] in fol.	306	306
1 Vocabularium juris[668] in 8°	51	153
1 Viridarum poetarum[669] in 8°	85	085
1 Vite beate Marie in fol.	153	153

---

[660] Virgilius Maro, Publius. Octavo editions of the *Bucolica* were published in Antwerp in 1541 (Apud M. Hillenium) and 1544 (Apud I. Steelsium). British Library.

[661] Gardiner, Stephen (pseud. Winton), bp. of Winchester, 1483?-1555. *Confvtatio cavillationvm ... sacrosanctum Evcharistivm sacramentvm* (Lovanii, Apud Petrum Colonaeum, 1554). 8.vo. Union Theological Seminary. Bibliothèque Nationale, Paris.

[662] Vitruvius Pollio, Marcus. *Vitruuius iterum et Frontinus à Iocundo reuisi* (Florentiæ, sumptibus Philippi de Giunta) or *De architectura libri decem, additis I. Frontini de aqueductibus libris* (Florentiæ, per haeredes Philippi Iuntæ, 1522). Both 8.vo. British Library.

[663] Nebrija, Elio Antonio de. This may be *Dictionarium Latinohispanicum* (Antverpiae, In aedib. Ioannis Steelij, 1553). Folio. Hispanic Society of America. This is Nebrija's Latin-Spanish dictionary which was first published in 1492.

[664] This work is by St. Hieronymus. I have not been able to identify this edition.

[665] Probus, Marcus Valerius. *De literis antiquis opusculum* (Basel, V. Curio, 1522?). 4.to. British Library. There are several surviving 4.to editions of his *De interpretandis Romanorum litteris* but none that I know of was published close enough to the date of the inventory to account for the number of copies.

[666] Nebrija, Elio Antonio de. His translation and commentary on Vergil's complete works was published in Granada: *Pvblii Vergilii Maronis Partheniae Mantuani opera ... Ælii Antonii Nebrissensis ... in eadem Ecphrases ad modum familiares* (Granada, Sancho de Nebrija, 1545-1546). Yale University. Palau, 370400.

[667] Netter, Thomas, 1375 (ca.)- 1430. *Tomus primus Doctrinalis fidei Ecclesie Catholicae contra Witclevistas & Hussitas eorumque sectatores* ([Parisiis], impressore J. Badio, 1532). Folio. Bibliothèque Nationale, Paris. The Newberry Library has a 1523 edition by Regnault, and the Bibliothèque Nationale, Paris also has the 1520 edition of Josse Badius Ascensius.

[668] Nebrija, Elio Antonio de. *Vocabularius utriusque iuris difficillimas quasque voces iuxta receptos iuris interpretes edifferens* (Lugduni, impensis Jacobi q. Francisci de Giunta, 1533). 8.vo. Baudrier, VI, p. 153. Another possibility is the 1533 edition (Lugduni, reimpressum apud Benedictum Bōnyn [for Vincentius Portonariis]) or the 1538 (Parisijs, ex officina viduae C. Cheuallonij). 8.vo. British Library.

[669] There are several possible octavo editions of the popular anthology of Latin poetry *Viridarium illustrium poetarum flores* compiled by Octavianus Mirandula, fl. 1507.

1 Universalia Scoti[670] in fol. una	119	119
1 Villalobos in Plinium[671] in fol.	102	102
2 Virgilius[672] in 8° Lion el uno viejo	70	140
4 Virtutum vitior[um]que exempla[673] pp	51	204
1 Varro de lingua latina[674] in 8°	34	034
1 Valerius maximus[675] pp una	34	034
3 Virgilius[676] pp	51	153
4 Virues contra Lutherum[677] in 4to	153	612
1 Vitruvius de modo studendi[678] in 8°	85	085
1 Vite et sentencie de philosophi in 8°	17	017
1 Vegetii mulo medicina[679] in 4to	25	025

---

[670] Duns, Joannes, Scotus, 1265?-1308? *Universalia Scoti. Questiones Scoti super Uniuersalia Porphyrij: necnon Aristotelis Predicamenta ac Perihermenias* ... (Impresse Venetys mādato sumptibus heredū nobilis viri quōdam dñi Octauiani Scoti, 1520). Folio. University of California, Berkeley.

[671] López de Villalobos, Francisco, 1473-1549. *Glossa literalis in primum et secundum naturalis historiae libros* (Compluti, Michaelis de Guia, 1524). Folio.

[672] Virgilius Maro, Publius. The "old" copy may be the ca. 1520 or 1521 Lyons octavo edition and the other the 1544 edition of the *Opera* by Sebastien Gryphius. Baudrier, VIII, p. 191. The British Library also has octavo editions from Lyons published in 1540 (Apud Steph. Doletum) and 1543 (Apud S. Gryphium).

[673] Nicolas de Hannappes, Patriarch of Jerusalem. *Virtvtvm vitiorvmqve exempla, ex vtrvsqve legis promptvario decerpta* (Lugdvni, apud Gulielmum Rouillium, 1547). 16.mo. Baudrier, IX, p. 141. The Biblioteca Nacional, Madrid, has a 1553 edition by Rovilius which is described as a 12.mo and the American Antiquarian Society another (Antuerpiae, 1544) in 24.mo.

[674] Varro, Marcus Terentius. *De lingua latina*. There are several possible octavo editions. This may be that of S. Gryphius (Lugduni, 1535) or of B. Westheimer (Basel, 1536).

[675] Valerius Maximus. *Valerii Maximi Dictorvm factorvmque memorabilium exempla* (Lugduni, apud S. Gryphium, 1547, 1550). 16.mo. Bibliothèque Nationale, Paris. Another edition in 16.mo was published by S. Colinaeus (Parisiis, Ex officina S. Colinæi, 1543). British Library. Baudrier, VIII, p. 218, 246.

[676] Small-format editions of the works of Virgil were published in Lyons in 1546 and 1555 by Gryphius (Lugduni, Apud S. Gryphium) and by Paganus (Lugduni, Apud T. Paganum, 1548). Baudrier, VIII, p. 208, 281.

[677] Ruíz de Virués, Alonso, bp., d. 1545. *Disputationes viginti adversus Lutherana dogmata per Philippum Melanchtonem defensa*. This may be the Cologne edition (Melchior Novesianus, 1545) or the Antwerp edition (Joannes Crinitus, 1541). Bataillon, CI, no. 1121.

[678] Roscius, Lucius Vitruvius, 16th cent. *De docendi studendique modo, ac de claris puerorum moribus* (Basileae, ex officina Roberti Winter, 1541). 8.vo. Harvard University. British Library.

[679] Vegetius Renatus, Flavius. *Artis veterinariae, sive mulomedicinae libri quatuor, jam primum typis in lucem aediti* (Basileae, Johannes Faber Emmeus, 1528). 4.to. Bibliothèque Nationale, Paris. National Library of Medicine. Durling, no. 4563.

INVENTARIO DE LOS LIBROS

3 Vocabularium 7 linguarum[680] in 8° 17		051
2 Vives de corruptis disciplinis[681] in 8° 119		238
2 Villalobos de principiis in fol. 102		<u>204</u>
		L. 7,581

/ vii,dlxxxj /

(f. 36)

1 Xenophontis opera grece[682] in fol. 408		408
1 Xodar de 7 vbis. domini[683] in fol. 51		<u>051</u>
		L. 469

,cccclxix

Libros de romance

47 Abecedario spiritual lib[ro] 3o[684] in 4to 85		3,995
36 Abecedario spiritual lib[ro] 2o[685] in 4to 85		3,060
1 Arte de Consento[686] in fol. 187		187
8 Apoptheg[mata] de Thamara[687] in 8° 95		760

---

[680] Calepino, Ambrogio, 1436-1511. Several editions of his *Dictionarum linguarum septem* were published in the 16th and 17th centuries, but I have not found an octavo edition before 1556.

[681] Vives, Juan Luis, 1492-1540. *De disciplinis libri XX* (Cologne, apud Ioannem Gymnicum, 1536). 8.vo. Newberry Library. Yale University. Gymnicus issued an earlier edition in 1532, and Frellonius issued another in Lyons in 1551. The title of the first volume of the work is "De corruptis artibus libri septem."

[682] Xenophon. [Works]. Folio editions of the works in the Greek text were published by the Giunti in Florence in 1516 and 1527. British Library.

[683] Jodar, Juan de. *Obra deuotissima intitulada De septem Verbis* (Seuilla, por Bartholome Perez, 1532). Biblioteca Nacional, Madrid. Palau, 124667. *Catálogo colectivo*, J, 325.

[684] Juan de Junta published editions of Francisco de Osuna's *Tercera parte del libro llamado Abecedario spiritual* in Burgos in 1544 and 1555. 4.tos. Palau, 206823, 206824.

[685] Juan de Junta published Osuna's *Segunda parte del libro llamado abecedario spiritual* in Burgos, in 1539, 1545 and 1555. 4.tos. Palau, 206818-206820.

[686] Consentius, grammarian. This item might be a Spanish translation of his *Ars de barbarismis et metaplasmis*, but I have not found such an edition in folio.

[687] Erasmus, Desiderius. *Libro de Apophthegmas* (in the Spanish translation of Francisco de Thámara) (Enuers, Martín Nucio, 1549; Çaragoça, por Esteuan de Nagera, 1552). 8.vo. Palau, 80369, 80370. Bataillon, LI, no. 459, 460. See below for the translation by Juan de Jarava. Both Thámara and Jarava were supporters of Erasmian ideals.

8 Abecedario espiritual lib[ro] 1o[688] in 4to 85		680
6 Abecedario spiritual lib[ro] 4to[689] in 4[to] 85		510
5 Abecedario spiritual libro 5to[690] in 4[to] 85		425
4 Apophtegmata de Jarava[691] in 4[to] 85		340
109 Arte de Canto llano[692] in 8° Alcala y Salamanca	14	1,526
4 Aviso de Cacadores[693] in 4[to] Alcala	34	136
2 Apocalypis ro[man]ce in fol. 187		374
3 Aparejo de bien morir[694] in 8° 10		030
8 Aviso de curas[695] in 8° 51		408
11 Aviso de curas[696] in 4[to] 51		561

---

[688] Osuna, Francisco de. *Primera parte del libro llamado Abecedario spiritual* (Burgos, en casa d' juã de jūta, 1537; or Medina del Campo, Pedro de Castro, 1544). 4.tos. Palau, 206814-15.

[689] Juan de Junta published Francisco de Osuna's *Ley de amor y quarta parte del abecedario spiritual* in Burgos in 1536 and 1542. 4.tos. Palau, 206828-29

[690] Osuna, Francisco de. *Quinta parte del abecedario spiritual* (Burgos, Juan de Junta, 1542 and 1554). 4.tos. Palau, 206832, 206832-II.

[691] Erasmus, Desiderius. Editions of translations of Erasmus' *Apophthegmata* by Juan de Jarava and Francisco de Thámara were published in Antwerp in 1549. Jarava's was published under the title *Libro de vidas y dichos graciosos, agudos y sentenciosos de muchos varones griegos y romanos ... traduzidos en Romance Castellano por J. Jarava* (Anvers, en casa de Iuan Steelsio, 1549; re-issued in 1552). 8.vo. Biblioteca Nacional, Madrid. Bataillon, op. cit., p. LI, no. 457, 458. Bonilla, pp. 483-497. Palau, 80367, 80368 note. I do not know of a quarto edition of Jarava's translation.

[692] Miguel de Eguía published an octavo edition of *Arte de cãto llano y puesta y reducida nueuamente en su entera perficion* by Juan Martínez in Alcalá de Henares in 1532. Martín Abad, p. 409, no. 244. Ruíz Fidalgo does not list a Salamanca edition.

[693] Núñez de Avendaño, Pedro. *Auiso de caçadores, y de caça* (Alcalá de Henares, en casa de Ioan de Brocar, 1543). 4.to. British Library. Hispanic Society of America. National Library of Medicine. Biblioteca Nacional, Madrid. Palau, 197084. Penney, p. 388. Rhodes, p. 141. Martín Abad, p. 511, no. 339. Durling, no. 3369.

[694] Erasmus, Desiderius. *Preparacion y aparejo para bien morir* (Anvers, En casa de Martin Nucio, 1555). 8.vo. British Library. Hispanic Society of America. Bonilla, pp. 480-482. Penney, p. 186. Juan de Junta also published an octavo edition of this work in Burgos in 1535. Bataillon, p. LV, no. 508. The Bayerische Staatsbibliothek, Munich, has a copy of this rare edition and Dr. Hermann Hauke has been kind enough to send me several photocopies from the work.

[695] Díaz de Lugo, Juan Bernardo. *Aviso de curas* (Alcalá de Henares, En casa de Joan de Brocar, 1551). 8.vo. Biblioteca Nacional, Madrid. Harvard Univ. (incomp.) Martín Abad, p. 573-75, no. 394A-B.

[696] Ibid. *Aviso de curas ... Agora nueuamẽte añadido* (Alcalá de Henares, en casa de Ioã de Brocar, 1543, 1545). 4.to. British Library. Hispanic Society of America. Rhodes, p. 65. Martín Abad, pp. 509, 523 no. 337, 353. Pérez Pastor, *Imprenta en Medina*, p. 68, no. 72, cites a 1550 quarto edition published in Medina del Campo by "Pedro de Castro ... a costa de Guillermo de Millis." Palau, 72621, 72622.

INVENTARIO DE LOS LIBROS

12 Arcipreste de Talavera[697]	in 8°	25	300
3 Aviso de penitentes	in 8°	12	036
1 Abecedario spiritual lib[ro] 6to[698]	in 4to	85	085
36 Aphorismos de Venero[699]	in 8°	4	144
30 Arte de servir a Dios[700]	in 8°	20	600
13 Arte de canto[701]	in 4to	14	182
89 Aranzeles[702]	in fol.	51	4,539
9 Arte de amystad[703]	in 4to	51	459
2 Arte de bien morir[704]	in 4to	25	050
1 Aparejo de bien morir[705]	in 4to	25	025
8 Andria de Terentio[706]	in 4to	10	080

---

[697] Martínez de Toledo, Alfonso, *archpriest of Talavera*. *El arcipreste de Talavera habla de los vicios de las malas mujeres y complexiones de los hombres*. The Hispanic Society of America has folio editions published in Toledo by Hagenbach (1500) and by Brocar (1518). Palau, 156104, 156106. The inventory copy is probably the 1547 octavo edition by Andrés de Burgos in Seville. Palau, 156108.

[698] Osuna, Francisco de. *Sexta parte del Abecedario espitritual ... q. trata sobre las llagas de Jesu Christo* (Medina del cāpo, en la imprēta de Matheo y Francisco del Canto, 1554). 4.to. Biblioteca, Universidad de Salamanca. Pérez Pastor, *Medina del Campo*, p. 125, no. 109. Palau, 206833.

[699] Venero, Alonso de. I have not been able to find a copy of this work.

[700] Madrid, Alonso de. *Arte para servir a Dios* (Burgos, 1530 and Salamanca, 1546). Both by Juan de Junta. The number of copies may however point to the edition by Brocar in Alcalá de Henares in 1555. Martín Abad, p. 644, no. 483. Palau (146630) reports a 1545 Salamanca edition, but no copy is known, and Bécares Botas reports a rare 1549 Seville edition by Jacome Cromberger now in the Biblioteca Universitaria, Barcelona. Bécares Botas, *La librería de Benito Boyer*, p. 224.

[701] Juan de Junta published quarto editions of Gonçalo Martínez de Bizcargui's *Arte de canto llano y contrapunto y canto de organo* in Burgos in 1528, 1535 and 1543. Biblioteca Nacional, Madrid. Library of Congress. Palau, 154824. *Catálogo colectivo*, M, 844.

[702] *Aranzel. Quaderno delas ordenancas hechas por sus altezas cerca de la ordē judicial τ aranzeles delos derechos que las justicias y escriuanos del reyno han de llevar por razon de sus officios y como lo han de usar*. This is probably the edition of Juan de Junta's associate Juan de Cánova in Salamanca, 1554. Palau, 14723. Juan de Junta published earlier folio editions of this in Burgos, in 1538 (Palau, 203133; Gil Ayuso, 78), and in Salamanca, 1544 (Palau, 242557; Gil Ayuso, 112). British Library. Biblioteca Nacional, Madrid.

[703] Cicero. *Libro llamado Arte de Amistad, con maravillosas ejemplos, agora nuevamente recopilado, ... traducido ... por Fray Angel Cornejo* (Medina del Campo, por Pedro de Castro, 1548). 4.to. Pérez Pastor, *Medina del Campo*, p. 51. no. 59. Palau, 54345.

[704] Fernández de Santaella, Rodrigo, 1444-1509. *Arte de bien morir* ([Seville, Jacobo Cromberger, ca. 1511-1515]). 4.to. Palau, 89769. Griffin, Appendix One, no. 121.

[705] See footnote 694. I have not found a quarto edition.

[706] Terentius, Publius, afer. *Andria*. I have not identified a quarto-size Spanish edition of this work before 1556.

1 Appiano Alexandrino[707] in fol.   102   102
11 Arithmetica de Tejeda[708] in 4to   51   561
1 Albeyteria[709] in 4to   34   034
18 Arithmetica de Gutierres[710] in 4to   8   144
1 Assolanos de P[ier]o Bembi[711]   pp   51   051
2 Angela de Fulginio[712] in 4to el uno enqua[dernado]   51   102
2 Annota del Pastoral   34   <u>068</u>
                                                              L. 20,564

/ xx,dlxiiij /
(f. 37)

2 Baculo de n[uest]ra peregrinacion in 8°   6   012
1 Batalla de perros in 8°   8   008
1 Buen plazer[713] in 8°   17   017
5 Batalla de dos[714] in fol.   68   340
6 Boetio de Consolacion[715] in 4to   25   150

---

[707] Appianus, of Alexandria. *Historia de todas las guerras civiles que uvo entre los romanos* (Alcalá de Henares, en casa de Miguel de Eguia, 1536). Folio. Biblioteca Nacional, Madrid. *Catálogo colectivo*, A, 1871. Palau, 13811.

[708] Texeda, Gaspar de. *Suma de arithmetica* (Valladolid, en la officina de Francisco Fer-nandez de cordoua, 1546). 4.to. British Library. Rhodes, p. 203. *Rara Arithmetica*, p. 240.

[709] Dieç, Manuel. *Libro de Albeyteria nueuamēte corregido y emendado* (Salamanca, Juan de Junta, 1544). 4.to. The Junta firm also published a quarto edition in Burgos in 1530. Biblioteca de Catalunya, Barcelona. National Library of Medicine. Durling, 1124. Palau, 73711 note.

[710] Gutiérrez de Gualda, Juan. *Arte breue y muy prouechosa de cuēta Castellana y Arismetica dōde se muestran las cinco reglas de guarismo por la cuēta castellana. y reglas de memoria* (Toledo, por Fernando de santa catalina, 1539). 4.to. Palau, 111616. Pérez Pastor, *Toledo*, p. 76, no. 184.

[711] Bembo, Pietro. *Los Asolanos. Nuevamente traduzidos de lengua Toscana...* (Salamanca, en casa de Andrea de Portonariis, 1551). 12.mo. Hispanic Society of America. Penney, p. 56. Palau, 27065.

[712] Angela, of Foligno, 1248?-1300.

[713] Hurtado de Mendoza, Juan. *Buen plazer trobado en treze discātes de quarta rima Castellana segun imitacion de trobas Francesas* (Alcala en casa de Ioan de Brocar, 1550). 8.vo. British Library. Hispanic Society of America. Rhodes, p. 100. Martín Abad, p. 563, no. 387. Palau, 117284.

[714] Puteo, Paris de (or Paride del Pozzo). The Hispanic Society of America owns a copy of his *Libro llamado batalla de dos* (Seville, Dominico de Robertis, 1544). It is a Spanish translation of *De re militari*. British Library. Palau, 234605. Rhodes, p. 160.

[715] Boethius, Anicius Manlius Severinus. *Libro de Boecio seuerino intitulado de la consolaciō de la philosophia* (Medina del Campo, por Pedro de Castro ... a costa de juan de Espinosa, 1542). 4.to. Palau, 31223. Pérez Pastor, *Medina del Campo*, p. 16, no. 25.

INVENTARIO DE LOS LIBROS

  4 Bonaventura de la pureza de la conscientia[716] 8° 15   060
  1 Bonaventura de la Vida de N[uest]ro Señor[717] in 4to 34   <u>034</u>
    / dcxxj /   L. 621

  35 Confessionario de Segura[718] in 4to 60   2,100
533 Computus[719] in 4to 6   3,198
  9 Cronica del Peru[720] in 8° 68   612
  1 Cronica de Florian de Campo[721] falto -- 306
17 Convite del Sacramento[722] in 4to 51   867
  1 Comedia Salvagia[723] in 4to 10   010
20 Cronica del rey Don Alonso[724] in fol. 170 3,400
15 Cartillas de pergamino in 4to 34   510
  1 Cavallero determinado[725] in 8° Miles 30 030
20 Colirio spiritual pp 8   160

---

[716] Bonaventura, *Saint, Cardinal. Tratado de la pureza de la conciencia* ([Seville, Jacobo Cromberger, ca. 1516-1520]). 8.vo. The Biblioteca Colombina of Seville has a copy of this work. Palau, 290257. Griffin, Appendix One, no. 208.

[717] Bonaventura, Saint. *Comiença el tractado d'l Seraphico doctor sanct Buenauentura, en la contemplacion de la vida de nuestro señor Iesu Christo* ([Zaragoza] en la casa de A. Millan, 1556). 8.vo. British Library. A Spanish translation of *Meditationes vitae Christi*.

[718] Segura, Juan de. *Confessionario: assi vtil para los confessores y para saberse los penitētes examinar y confessar* (Burgos, en casa de Juan de Junta, 1555). 4.to. Biblioteca, Universidad de Salamanca. Hispanic Society of America. Penney, p. 511. Palau, 141973.

[719] Juan de Junta published a short work on the church calendar by Hierónymo de Valencia, *Arte del Computo nueuamente compuesta* (Burgos, 1539). 4.to. British Library. Palau, 348141. Rhodes, p. 210.

[720] Cieza de León, Pedro. *Parte primera de la chronica del Peru*. Octavo editions were produced in Antwerp in 1554 by the firms of Joannes Steelsius and Martin Nutius. British Library. Bibliothèque Nationale, Paris. Palau, 54647, 54648.

[721] See footnote 755.

[722] Osuna, Francisco de. *Gracioso cōbite delas gracias del sancto sacramēto del altar* (Burgos, en casa de Juā de junta, 1537 and 1543). 4.to. National Library of Prague (1543 ed.). Kašpar (1983), 302. British Library. Biblioteca Univ., Valencia. Palau, 206836, 206837. Maggs, 697. Maggs, 698 (with illus.). Rhodes, p. 145. The work was also published by Juan Cromberger (Sevilla, 1544).

[723] Villegas Selvago, Alonso de, b. 1534. *Comedia llamada Seluagia* (Toledo, en casa de Ioan Ferrer, 1544). 4.to. British Library. Pérez Pastor, *Toledo*, p. 110, no. 275. Rhodes, p. 216.

[724] *Chronica del muy esclarecido principe, y rey don Alonso*. The Hispanic Society of America owns two folio editions (Valladolid, a costa y en casa d' Sebastiā Martinez, 1551 [and 1554]). Palau, 64895, 64896.

[725] La Marche, Olivier de, 1426?-1502. *Discursos de la vida humana y aventuras del Caballero determinado* (Medina del Campo, por Guillermo de Millis, 1555). 8.vo.

62 Contemptus mundi[726] in 8° Burgos	30		1,860
2 Cronica del rey Don Rodrigo[727] in fol.	204		408
179 Cruz de Christo[728] pp	17		3,043
18 Confessionario de Via	6		128
14 Cronica de las Yndias libro primo[729] in 8°	85 no	4	340
9 Cronica de las Yndias in 2bus in 8°	170		1,530
15 Confessionario del Vita Christi in 8°	8		120
50 Confessionario del Tostado[730] in 8°	25		1,250
24 Celestina claudina[731] in 4to	25		600
6 Cesares de mondonedo[732] in fol.	153		918
7 Contemptus mundi[733] in 8° Alcala	30		210
24 Carcel de amor[734] in 8°	10		240

---

[726] Imitatio Christi. *Contēptus mundi, nueuamente romançado, con su tabla. Van añadidos cien Problemas de la oracion* (Burgos, en casa de Juan de Junta, 1555). 8.vo. Biblioteca Nacional, Madrid. *Catálogo colectivo*, I, 124.

[727] Corral, Pedro del. *La Cronica del Rey dō Rodrigo con la destruycion de España y como los moros la ganaron* (Toledo, en casa de Iuan Ferrer [at end:] a costa del Señor Juan de Espinosa mercader de libros, 1549). Folio. Pérez Pastor, *Toledo*, p. 94, no. 235. There are earlier editions in Seville by, J. Cromberger in 1511; by an unnamed printer in 1522, 1526, and 1527; an edition in Valladolid by Thierry in 1527; and an incunable with no attribution of place or publisher ((s.l., s.i., 1499). Palau, 65008. Griffin, Appendix One, no. 63.

[728] Bonaventura, Saint. *Cruz de Christo* (Sevilla, en casa de Juan Cromberger, 1543, 1545; Medina del Campo, en casa de Guillermo de Millis, 1553). 8.vo. Pérez Pastor, *Medina del Campo*, p. 86, no. 98. Maggs, 116. Griffin, Appendix One, no. 498, 511.

[729] Fernández de Oviedo y Valdés, Gonzalo. *Coronica delas Indias*. I have not located an octavo edition. See footnote 735.

[730] Tostado, Alonso, bp., d. 1455. *Cōfessional del Tostado. Nuevamente impresso* (Medina del Campo, por Pedro de Castro, 1544). 8.vo. Biblioteca Nacional, Madrid. Pérez Pastor, *Medina del Campo*, p. 42, no. 48. Palau, 146757. *Catálogo colectivo*, T, 1436.

[731] Fernández, Sebastián. *Tragedia muy sentida y graciosa llamada la madre Claudina Madre de Parmeno y maestra de Celestina* (Toledo, en casa de Fernando de santa Cathalina, 1548). 4.to. British Library. Rhodes, p. 77. Not in Pérez Pastor, *Toledo*.

[732] Guevara, Antonio de, bp. of Mondoñedo. *Vida de los césares* (Valladolid, por industria d'l honrado varon impressor de libros juā de villaquiran, 1545). Folio. Another folio edition in 1539. Palau, 110328, 110330.

[733] Imitatio Christi. *Libro de la Imitaciō de Christo: llamado Cōtemptus Mundi. Nueuamente romançada cō su tabla* (Alcalá de Henares, en casa de Juan Brocar, 1548, 1555). 8.vos. Palau, 127375 (with erroneous date), 127385; Rhodes, p. 104. Martín Abad, nos. 374, 487.

[734] San Pedro, Diego de. *Carcel de amor por Hernando de sant Pedro* (Medina del cāpo, por Pedro de Castro, 1547). 8.vo. Pérez Pastor, *Medina del Campo*, p. 48, no. 56. The British Library has a copy of this work published in Burgos, 1526 (no printer) which is probably from the press of Alonso de Melgar or Juan de Junta, and another published in 1496 from the press of Fadrique de Basilea in Burgos. Whinnom, p. 40, F7.

INVENTARIO DE LOS LIBROS

5 Cronica de las Yndias[735] in fol. de las viejas 170		850
5 Cavallero de la + [Cruz][736] in fol. 85		425
1 Consuelo de la viejes[737] in 4to 10		010
15 Colloquios de Mejia[738] in 8° 34		<u>510</u>
	L.	23,635

(f. 38)

10 Cronica de los frayles de S. Hieronymo[739] in fol. 85		850
28 Celestina[740] pp 17		476
3 Celestina 2da[741] in 4to 25		075
2 Celestina primera[742] in 4to 25		050

---

[735] Fernández de Oviedo y Valdés, Gonzalo. *Coronica delas Indias* (Salamanca, Juan de Junta, 1547). Folio. Palau, 89529. The Cromberger firm of Seville also published a folio edition in 1535. Palau, 89528. Griffin, Appendix One, no. 384.

[736] Salazar, Alonso de (possible author). *Libro del inuēcible cauallero Lepolemo hijo del Emp[er]ador de Alemaña: y de los hechos que fizo llamādose el cauallero de la Cruz* (Seuilla, en casa de Juan cromberger, 1534). Folio. British Library. Another edition was published in 1542. Biblioteca Nacional, Lisbon. Palau, 135975. Eisenberg, p. 72. Griffin, Appendix One, no. 364, 464. Palau also lists folio editions from Valencia (1521, 1525) and Seville (Dominico d' Robertis, 1548).

[737] *Consuelo de la vejez* (Salamanca, en casa de Juan de jūta, 1544). 4.to. Biblioteca Nacional, Madrid. Palau, 60413. *Catálogo colectivo*, C, 2863.

[738] Mejía, Pedro, 1496?-1552? *Colloquios o Dialogos* ([Sevilla?] s.i., [1547?]; and Çaragoça, en casa de Bartholomé de Nagera, 1547). 8.vo. The British Library has other octavo editions of this work published in Seville (por Domenico d' Robertis, 1547 [and:] por Christoual aluarez, 1551) and in Antwerp (en casa de Martin Nucio, 1547). Rhodes, p. 134. Palau, 167364-167368.

[739] Vega, Pedro de la. *Cronica de los frayles de la orden del bienauenturado sant Hieronymo* (Alcalá de Henares en casa de Iuan de Brocar, 1539). Folio. British Library. Rhodes, p. 213.

[740] Rojas, Fernando de. *Tragicomedia de Calisto y Melibea* (Antwerp, En casa de Martin Nucio, 1550). 12.mo. Biblioteca Nacional, Madrid. *Catálogo colectivo*, R, 1248. Palau does not list this edition, but cites another 12.mo produced by M. Nucio in 1545. Palau, 51149.

[741] Silva, Feliciano de. *Segunda comedia de Celestina* (Medina del campo, en casa de Pedro touās enel coral de boeys, 1534). 4.to. British Library. Pérez Pastor, *Medina del Campo*, p. 5, no. 12. Rhodes, p. 181. Ruíz Fidalgo, no. 52. Tovans is the printer who sold a press to Juan de Junta and Alexandro de Cánova in Salamanca in 1532.

[742] Rojas, Fernando de. *Tragicomedia de Calisto y Melibea* (Burgos, por Juan de Junta, 1531). 4.to. No copy known. Palau, 51142. Other later quarto editions were published in Seville by the Cromberger firm in 1535 and 1550); in Toledo (en casa de Juan de ayala, 1538); and in Salamanca (por Pedro de castro, 1540). Griffin, Appendix One, nos. 385, 541. Several of these are in the Biblioteca Nacional, Madrid.

4 Christopathia[743] in 4[to] 34		136
3 Cortesano[744] in 4[to] 85		255
12 Cyruelo contra pestilencia[745] in 4[to] 17		204
8 Castilio inexpugnable[746] in fol. 51		408
2 Cayda de principis[747] in fol. 136		272
6 Contempla[ciones] Sobre el psalmo miserere[748] in 8°	10	060
2 Comentario de Marco Polo veneciano[749] in fol. 17		034
14 Coronacion de Juan de Mena[750] in fol. 4to	10	140
9 Carlo magno[751] in fol. 20		180
4 Camino del Cielo[752] in 4to 51		204

---

[743] Quirós, Juan de. *Christo. Pathia Obra de Ivan de Qviros* (Toledo, en casa de Iuan ferrer, 1552). 4.to. British Library. Biblioteca Nacional, Madrid. Rhodes, p. 161. Pérez Pastor, *Toledo*, p. 103, no. 260. Palau, 245596.

[744] Castiglione, Baldassare. *Libro llamado el cortesano* ([Seville, Jacobo Cromberger] 1549). 4.to. Palau, 47960. Griffin notes that this translation by Juan Boscán was published by Cromberger in 1542, 1549 and a late-1540s undated edition. Griffin, Appendix One, nos. 468, 533, 536. The work was also published in a quarto edition in Toledo in 1539 by an unnamed publisher. Pérez Pastor, *Toledo*, p. 75, no. 181. Palau, 47960. Palau, 47957, cites a Salamanca edition (Salamāca por Pedro Touans. Acosta del ... guillermo d' Milles, 1540).

[745] Ciruelo, Pedro. *Hexameron theologal sobre el regimiento medicinal contra la pestilencia* (Alcalá de Henares, Arnao Guillem de Brocar, 1519). 4.to. National Library of Medicine. Palau, 54926. *Catálogo colectivo*, C, 1974. Martín Abad, p. 266, no. 78. Durling, no. 963.

[746] Arredondo y Alvarado, Gonzalo de. *Castillo inexpugnable defensorio d'la fe. y concionatorio admirable para vencer a todos enemigos espirituales y corporales* (Burgos, por Juan de junta, 1528). Folio. Biblioteca Nacional, Madrid. Hispanic Society of America. Penney, p. 41. *Catálogo colectivo*, A, 2639. Palau, 17361.

[747] Boccaccio, Giovanni. *Libro llamado cayda de principes* (Alcalá de Henares, en casa de Juan Brocar, 1552). Folio. Hispanic Society of America. Palau, 31165. Maggs, 96 (with illus.). Martín Abad, p. 584, no. 407.

[748] *Contemplaciones sobre el psalmo miserere*. This may be the work which the Spanish *Index* of 1559 mistakenly attributed to Erasmus, "Exposicion sobre el psalmo, Miserere mei, Deus, y cum invocarem, del mesmo Erasmo." De Bujanda thinks that this resulted from a confusion with a work by Savonarola (De Bujanda, V, pp. 476-77).

[749] Polo, Marco. *Comentario de Marco Polo veneciano* (Logroño, en casa d' Miguel de eguia, 1529). Palau, 151208 note. Folio. British Library. Rhodes, p. 158.

[750] Folio editions of Juan de Mena's *La coronacion* were published in Salamanca (?) (1499). Seville (1512, 1520, 1528, 1534), Valladolid (1536, 1540) and Toledo (1547). Palau, 162683 et seq.

[751] *Hystoria del Emperador carlo magno y d'los doze pares de Francia* ... (Salamanca, por Juā de junta, 1544). Folio. British Library. Rhodes, p. 98. This is a translation of "Conqueste du grant roy Charlemagne des Espaignes."

[752] Alarcón, Luis de. *Camino del cielo en que se demuestra como se busca y halla Dios*. The British Library has an octavo edition (Alcalá de Henares, en casa de Ioan de Brocar, 1547). Palau, 4649. Palau says a quarto edition was published in Granada in 1550, but apparently he had not seen it.

3 Centiloquio[753] in 8° de problemas 8	024
7 Constitutiones de S. Benitto de Valladolid[754] 25	175
1 Cronica de Florian do Campo nueva[755] 510	510
2 Cronica de Florian do Campo viejas[756] 340	680
12 Confessionario del Cyruelo[757] in 8° 12	144
5 Cathechismo[758] in 8° 17	085
1 Cordial de las 4 cosas postrimeras[759] in 4.to 51	051
1 Cordial del anima[760] in 4.to 17	017

---

[753] Ruescas, Agustín de. *Dialogo en verso, intituladoCentiloquio de problemas: en el qual se introduzē dos philosophos, el vno Pamphilo llamado, que cient philosophicas pregūtas propone* ... (Alcalá de Henares, Juan de Brocar, 1546, 1548). 8.vo. British Library. Salvá, 2151. Maggs, 320 (with illus.). Rhodes, p. 172. Martín Abad, p. 535, 552, no. 362, 384.

[754] *Constituciones de la Congregacion de san Benito de Ualladolid. 1546.* (eñl monesterio y colegio de sant vicēte de salamāca, por Iuā de iūta impressor, 1546). 4.to. Biblioteca Nacional, Madrid. *Catálogo colectivo*, C, 2703. Palau, 59824.

[755] The "nueva" edition of Florián de Ocampo's *Coronica general de España* is probably that of de Millis: *Hispania vincit. Los Cinco Libros primeros de la Cronica General* (Medina del Campo, Guillermo de Millis, 1553). Folio. Pérez Pastor, *Medina del Campo*, p. 97, no. 101. Maggs, 300. Palau, 198378. Penney, p. 158. Rhodes, p. 143.

[756] Ibid. The old edition referred to ("viejas") is probably one of the Zamora editions (1541 and 1543).

[757] Juan de Junta published at least two editions in Burgos of Pedro Ciruelo's *Arte para biē cōfessar* (1527, 1536 and probably the unsigned Burgos editions of 1532 and 1541. It was also published in Alcalá de Henares, 1526 and 1532 by Miguel de Eguía. Pedro de Castro published the *Confesionario* in Salamanca in 1538 and 1546, and in Medina del Campo in 1544 and 1548. Pérez Pastor cites Toledo editions in octavo by Remon de Petras in 1524 and 1525 and an unverified 1551 edition, *Arte de bien confesar*. Since the inventory of Juan de Ayala contained 314 copies of "Confisionario del Ciruelo," it is possible that the 1551 edition may have been Ayala's. Palau, 54907-54910. Martín Abad, no. 176, 246. Ruíz Fidalgo, no. 54. Pérez Pastor, *Medina del Campo*, p. 35, no. 36; p. 52, no. 60. Pérez Pastor, *Toledo*, p. 50, no. 98; p. 51, no. 103; and p. 99, no. 248.

[758] Ponce de la Fuente, Constantino, d. 1559. *Catecismo Christiano, compuesto por el doctor Constantino* (Sevilla, 1547). De Bujanda, V, no. 450. Guerrero García, p. 237, no. 9, 2°. This work was condemned on the Spanish *Index* of 1559. No copy seems to have survived. The only known copy of the second edition, an octavo printed in Antwerp by Guillaume Simon in 1556, is found in the Bibliothèque Royale Albert Ier, Brussels. The author was an admirer of Erasmus. Bataillon, pp. 522-540.

[759] Denis le Chartreux. *Cordial de las 4 cosas postrimeras: es a saber d'la muerte: del juyzio final: dela pena infernal: y la gloria celestial* (Alcalá de Henares, por Miguel de Eguía, 1526). 4.to. Biblioteca Serrano Morales, Valencia. Palau, 74001. Martín Abad, p. 335, no. 166.

[760] Denis le Chartreux. *Cordial del Anima* ("empremptada en ... Ualencia," 1495). Folio. Palau, 74002. Palau says that the only known copy is in the Biblioteca Pública de Palma de Mallorca.

4 Conquista de Rodas⁷⁶¹ in fol. 51		204
34 Cancionero Spiritual⁷⁶² in 4ᵗᵒ 15		510
3 Cartas de Rua⁷⁶³ in 8° 10		030
1 Cronica del rey Don Guiliermo⁷⁶⁴ 68		068
2 Contemplaciones del Cyruelo⁷⁶⁵ in 4ᵗᵒ 51		102
3 Contemplaciones del Cyruelo⁷⁶⁶ in fol. 51		153
1 Comentarios de Cesar⁷⁶⁷ in fol. 51		051
4 Cronica de Carion⁷⁶⁸ in 8° la una falto 60		240
4 Confessiones de S. Augustin⁷⁶⁹ in 8° 85		340
11 Carcel de amor⁷⁷⁰ in 4ᵗᵒ 10		110

---

⁷⁶¹ Fontanus, Jacobus. *La muy lamĕtable cŏquista y cruĕta batalla d' Rhodas* (Valladolid, juan de villaquiran, 1549). Folio. The same title was published earlier in Seville: Caoursin, Gulielmus. *La muy lamentable conquista y cruenta batalla de Rhodas* (Sevilla, en casa de Iuan Varela, 1526). British Library. Palau, 59384, 93416. Rhodes, p. 80, 164.

⁷⁶² *Cancionero espiritual en el qual se tratan muchas y muy excelētes obras sobre la concepcion de la gloriosissima virgē nuestra señora sancta Maria: y de las letras de su nōbre todo en metros diferentes. por vn religioso d'la orden del biē auĕturado sant. Hieronymo* (Valladolid, por Juan de Villaquiran, 1549). 4.to. British Library. Hispanic Society of America. Penney, p. 88. Palau, 41966.

⁷⁶³ Rhua, Pedro de. *Cartas de Rhua lector en Soria, sobre las obras del ... Obispo de Mondoñedo* (Burgos, en casa de Juan de Junta, 1549). 8.vo. British Library. Bibliothèque Nationale, Paris. Palau, 266027. *Catálogo colectivo*, R, 1538.

⁷⁶⁴ *Chronica del rey dō Guiliermo rey de Inglaterra τ duque de Angeos* (Toledo, s.i., 1526). Folio. Biblioteca Nacional, Madrid. Pérez Pastor, *Toledo*, p. 59, no. 127. Palau, 65002. *Catálogo colectivo*, C, 3683.

⁷⁶⁵ Ciruelo, Pedro. *Contemplaciones muy deuotas sobre los mysterios sacratissimos de la Passion de nuestro redemptor Jesu Christo* (Alcalá de Henares, en casa de Juan Brocar, 1543). 4.to. Abadía de Montserrat. Palau 54948. Martín Abad, p. 513, no. 340.

⁷⁶⁶ Ibid. This is the folio edition of the above work, published by Brocar (Alcalá de Henares, en casa de Joan de Brocar, 1547). Palau, 54999. Martín Abad, p. 539, no. 366.

⁷⁶⁷ Caesar, Caius Julius. *Comentarios de Cesar* (Alcalá de Henares, en casa de Miguel de Eguia, 1529). Folio. Palau, 54138. Martín Abad, p. 377, no. 212.

⁷⁶⁸ Carion, Johann. *Suma y compendio de todas chrónicas del mundo* (Medina del Campo, Guillermo de Millis, 1553). This is a translation of *Chronica Ioannis Carionis conversa ex Germanico in Latinum a doctissimo viro Hermanno Bono*, which was published first in Germany in 1537. There are two Latin editions of the same date and an Italian edition of 1543. All translations and the original are prohibited by the 1559 Spanish *Index*. De Bujanda, V, pp. 334, 469.

⁷⁶⁹ Octavo editions of the *Confessiones* of St. Augustine were published in Salamanca in 1551 and 1554 by Andreas de Portonariis.

⁷⁷⁰ See footnote 734.

5 Cortes de Vall[adol]id año 1548[771]	68		340
37 Capitulos de Toledo año 1539[772]	25		925
6 Cortes de Madrid[773]	17		102
83 Cortes de Valladolid año 1523[774]	31		4,233
30 Capitulo de Corregidores[775] in fol.	17		510
1 Confessionario del Hieronymo	34		034
3 Centiloquio de Problemas[776]	8		024
9 Constantinus sup[er] beatus vir[777] in 8°	34		306
10 Celestina tercera[778] in 4to	25		250
1 Comedia petrea[779] in 4to	8		008

---

[771] Spain. Laws. *Las Cortes de Valladolid del Anno M.D.XLVIII* (Valladolid, por Francisco Fernandez de Cordoua, 1549). Folio. British Library. Harvard Law School. Palau, 63147, 235094. Rhodes, p. 190.

[772] Spain. Laws. *Capitulos nuevamēte concedidos por la S.C.C.M. del Emperador y rey nuestro señor en las cortes que tuuo y celebro en la ciudad de Toledo el año passado de M.D. y XXXIX* (Medina del Campo, Pedro de Castro, 1545). Folio. Harvard Law School Library. Pérez Pastor, *Medina del Campo*, p. 41, no. 46. Palau, 63128 note.

[773] Spain. Laws. *Las cortes de Madrid. Quaderno de las leyes y prematicas reales... de Madrid de M.D.xxviii.* Folio. Editions were published in Toledo in 1528 and in Alcalá de Henares (en casa de Joan de Brocar, 1540 and 1546). Harvard Law School Library. Palau, 63093-63095. Martín Abad, no. 307, 356.

[774] Spain. Laws. *Quaderno de las cortes: que en Valladolid tuuo su magestad del Emperador y rey nuestro señor el año de .1523. años.* Folio. Editions of the 1523 Cortes de Valladolid were published by Juan de Junta in Burgos, 1529 and 1535. Biblioteca Nacional, Madrid. Harvard Law School. Maggs, 794. Palau, 63141, 63142. Gil Ayuso, 55, 68.

[775] Spain. Laws. *Capitulos de Corregidores. Capitulos hechos por el Rey τ la Reyna nŕos señores. Enlos quales contienē las cosas q̃ an de guardar τ cõplir los gouernadores: assistētes: corregidores: juezes de residēcia τ alcaldes de las ciudades villas τ lugares de sus reynos τ señorios* (Salamanca, Juan de Junta, 1545). Folio. Biblioteca Pública, Toledo. Palau, 43295. Gil Ayuso, 114. Ruíz Fidalgo, 119. Another folio edition was printed in Burgos in 1527, probably by Juan de Junta. Palau, 43294. Gil Ayuso, 37.

[776] See footnote 753.

[777] Ponce de la Fuente, Constantino, d. 1559. *Exposicion del primer Psalmo de David cuyo principio es Beatus vir, dividida en seys sermones* (Sevilla, [Juan de Leon], 1546). 8.vo. Bayerische Staatsbibliothek, München. Biblioteca del Palacio, Madrid. *Catálogo colectivo*, P, 2490. De Bujanda, V, p. 462. This work was condemned by the Spanish *Index* of 1559. It is quite rare. Palau, 230917, gives 1548 as the date of this work.

[778] Gómez de Toledo, Gaspar. *Tercera parte de la tragicomedia de Celestina* (Toledo, en casa de Hernãdo de santa catalina, 1539). 4.to. Biblioteca Nacional, Madrid. *Catálogo colectivo*, G, 1216. Pérez Pastor, *Toledo*, p. 76, no. 183. There is also an earlier edition, *Tercera parte de la tragico-comedia de Celestina* (Medina del Campo, por Gaspar Gomez, 1536). 4.to. Pérez Pastor, *Medina del Campo*, p. 11, no. 19 (copying Brunet).

[779] Álvarez de Ayllón, Pedro. *Comedia de Preteo y Tibalda llamada disputa y remedio de amor en la qual se tratan subtiles sentencias por quatro pastores* [Toledo, en casa de Juan Ferrer, 1553]). 4.to. Hispanic Society of America. Penney, p. 21. Pérez Pastor, *Toledo*, p. 105, no. 264.

5 Coplas sobre el psalmo miserere 10 050
                                       13,620

(f. 39)

6 Comedia Florinea[780] in 4to 51   306
1 Conquista de Ultramar[781] viejo falto --   ----
23 Cortes de Segovia[782] a[ñ]° 1534 51   1,173
1 Confessionale del arcobispo florentino[783] in 4to 30   030
1 Contemptus mundi[784] in 8° falto --   ----
2 Confessionario de Cherubin[785] in 8° 15   030
                                                                 1,539
/ xxxviij,dccxciiij /   L. 38,794   13,620
                                                                23,635

---

[780] Rodríguez Florián, Juan. *Comedia llamada Florinea que tracta de los amores del buen duque Floriano, cō la linda y muy casta y generosa Belisea* (Medina del Campo, en casa de Guillermo de Millis, tras la iglesia mayor, 1554). Pérez Pastor, *Medina del Campo*, p. 128-30, no. 114, 115. Salvá, 1380 (with illus.). Maggs, 881. Palau, 273970. Penney, p. 477. *Catálogo colectivo*, R, 1205. First edition. The Maggs Catalogue says that the work is imitative of the Celestina. "Little is known of Juan Rodríguez Florián, ... a sixteenth-century writer ... and resident of Valladolid, where he is believed to have been born." Hispanic Society of America. Biblioteca Serrano Morales, Valencia.

[781] *La gran conquista de vltramar* (Salamanca por Hans giesser, 1503). 2 vols. Folio. British Library. Rhodes, p. 90.

[782] Spain. Laws. *Quadernos de las cortes ... d'Segouia ... de M.D.xxxij. Juntamente con las cortes ... de Madrid ... de M.D.xxxiiij* (Salamanca, en casa de Juan de Junta, 1550). Folio. Palau, 242696. Gil Ayuso, 138. It is probable that the dates of the two Cortes were thus conflated by the compiler of the inventory. Harvard Law School owns a 1535 edition printed in Alcalá de Henares by Miguel de Eguía. Maggs catalogue (795). Palau, 63119.

[783] Antoninus, Saint, Abp. of Florence, 1389-1459. *Summa de confession llamada Defecerunt: compuesta por Fray Antonino Arçobispo de Florencia* (Seuilla, Juan Cromberger, 1534, 1537). Both 4.to. British Library. Rhodes, p. 11. Griffin, Appendix One, no. 366 and 404. Other quarto editions were published in Seville by Andres de Burgos in 1544 and by Pedro de Castro in Medina del Campo in 1550. Biblioteca Nacional, Madrid. Pérez Pastor, *Medina del Campo*, p. 67, no. 70. *Catálogo colectivo*, A, 1640.

[784] Imitatio Christi. *Tractado intitulado Contemptus mundi* (Seuilla, enla emprenta de Jacome Cröberger, 1542, 1547). 8.vos. Griffin, Appendix One, nos. 469, 515. The Junta firm also printed this work in 1555 and had a large mumber of copies in the inventory. See footnote 726.

[785] Florencia, Cherubino de. *Cōfessionario ... traduzido de la lengua Toscana* (Salamanca, por Juan de Junta Impressor, 1546). 8.vo. Palau, 92330. Ruíz Fidalgo, no. 137. The only copy I know of is in the Colleción Massó, Bueo (Pontevedra).

33 Deseoso[786] in 4to 85		2,805
2 Don Cristalian de Spaña[787] 306		612
318 Desafio del rey de Francia[788] in 4to 6		1,908
12 Dichos de philosophos[789] in 4to 11		132
3 Doctrinal de Confessores[790] in 4to 51		153
1 Don Polindo[791] falto in fol. 85		085
17 Dichado dela Vida humana[792] in 4to 17		289
2 Dos dialogo Spiritual in 8° 17		034
1 Demandas y respuestas in 8° 4		004
23 Dialogos de Mejia[793] in 8° 34		782
3 Dialogos de Mejia[794] in 8° Ant[uerpie] 40		120

---

[786] *Spill de la vida religiosa. Tratado llamado el Desseoso y por otro nombre espejo de religiosos* (Burgos, en casa de Juan de Junta, 1548 and 1554). 4.to. Biblioteca Nacional, Madrid. Hispanic Society of America. This is a translation of "Spill de la vida religiosa," written in Catalan and first published in Valencia in 1529 "by a devout priest, who humbly hides his identity." Maggs, 1036. Palau, 321569, 321570.

[787] Cristalián. *Comiença la hystoria de ... Cristalian de España* (Valladolid, en casa de Iuan de Villaquiran, 1545). Folio. Biblioteca Nacional, Lisbon. Bibliothèque Nationale, Paris. Bayerische Staatsbibliothek, Munich. British Library. Eisenberg, p. 60. Rhodes, p. 60. The authorship of this work is attributed to Beatriz Bernal or her daughter Juana Gatos.

[788] *El desafio de los reyes de Francia y Inglaterra* (Burgos, por Juan de Junta impressor de libros, 1528). 4.to. Biblioteca Nacional, Madrid. Palau, 70656. *Catálogo colectivo*, D, 359. If this is indeed the edition in question, it appears strange that so many copies should have remained unsold almost thirty years after publication.

[789] Díaz, Hernando. *La vida y excelentes dichos delos mas sabios Filosofos que vuo eneste mundo* (Seuilla, en casa d' Cromberger, 1541, 1535). 4.to. British Library. Rhodes, p. 64. Griffin, Appendix One, no. 446, 387. An earlier edition was published in Toledo in 1527. Pérez Pastor, *Toledo*, p. 62, no. 139.

[790] Castillo de Villasante, Diego del. *Tratado que se llama Doctrinal de confessores* (Alcalá de Henares, En casa de Juan de Brocar, 1552). 4.to. Hispanic Society of America. Martín Abad, p. 577, no. 399.

[791] Polindo. *Historia del inuencible cauallero don Polindo hijo del rey Paciano Rey de Numidia τ d'las marauillosas hazañas y estrañas auenturas q̃ andãdo por el mundo acabo: por amor de la princesa Belisia fija del rey naupilio rey de Macedonia* (Toledo, [Miguel de Eguía], 1526). Folio. British Library. Biblioteca Nacional, Lisbon. Pérez Pastor, *Toledo*, p. 60, no. 132. Palau, 230331. Eisenberg, p. 86. Rhodes, p. 158.

[792] Cessolis, Jacobus de. *Dechado de la Vida Humana. Moralmẽte sacado del Iuego del Axedrez*. [Xerxes, pseud.]. (Ualladolid, en la officina de Francisco fernandez d'Cordoua, 1549). 4.to. British Library. Rhodes, p. 219. Palau, 54222.

[793] See footnote 738.

[794] See footnote 738.

2 Don Chyrongilio[795] in fol. 136		272
2 Don Clarian de Spaña libro primo[796] in fol. 170		340
2 Don Clarian de Spaña libro 2.do [797] in fol. 170		340
11 Despertamiento del animo in Dios[798] in 8° 25		275
1 Declaracion del decalogo in 8° Caragoca 34		034
9 De quatuor novissimis[799] in 4.to rro[man]ce 34		306
12 Declaracion sobre los 7 peccados mortales 8° 6		072
13 Declaracion del pater noster[800] in 8° 12		156
2 Don Felisbian[801] in fol. 68		136
2 Don Roselao de Grecia[802] in fol. 102		204

---

[795] Vargas, Bernardo de. *Los quatro libros del valeroso caballero don Cirongilio de Tracia* (Seville, Jácome Cromberger, 1545). Folio. British Library. Biblioteca Nacional, Madrid. Bibliothèque Nationale, Paris. Biblioteca de Catalunya. Griffin, Appendix One, no. 500. Eisenberg, p. 54. Rhodes, p. 141

[796] Velázquez de Castillo, Gabriel. *Libro primero del inuencible cauallero Don Clariã de landanis* (Medina del Campo, en casa de Pedro de Castro, 1542). Folio. Biblioteca Nacional, Madrid. There were also folio editions in Seville (Jacobo Cromberger, 1527) and Toledo (Villaquirán, 1518). Pérez Pastor, *Medina del Campo*, p. 18, no. 27. Eisenberg, p. 55-56. Griffin, Appendix One, no. 271. Palau, 55249-55251.

[797] Clarian de Landanis. *El segundo libro del muy valiēte ... don Clarian de landanis* (Seuilla [Juan Cromberger] 1535). Folio. British Library. Eisenberg, p. 56. By an unknown calling himself "Álvaro, fisico."

[798] Vives, Juan Luis. *Comentarios para despertamiento del anima en dios. Y preparacion del anima para orar* (Burgos, en casa de Juan de Junta, 1539). 8.vo. Biblioteca Nacional, Madrid. Palau, 371683. *Catálogo colectivo*, V, 1306.

[799] Denis le Chartreux. *Libro de quatuor nouissimis que quiere dezir de los quatro postreros trances que compuso en Latin el religioso y bienauenturado varon Dionysio Rikel monge Cartuxano* (Toledo, en casa de Juan de Ayala a costa de juan de Medina librero, 1548). 4.to. Pérez Pastor, *Toledo*, p. 92, no. 230. This work is on the 1551 *Index* of Toledo and the 1559 Spanish *Index*. De Bujanda, V, pp. 255, 472.

[800] Erasmus, Desiderius. *Declaracion del pater noster dividida en siete peticiones* (Anvers, Joannes de Grave, 1549). 16.mo. This is on the Spanish *Index* of 1559. Bataillon, p. LIX, no. 567, 568. De Bujanda, V, p. 476. Palau, 80366. Bonilla (p. 479) cites an octavo edition from Logroño, 1528.

[801] Philesbián de Candaria. *Libro primero del muy noble y esforçado cauallero don Philesbian de Candaria: hijo del noble rey don Felinis de ungria e de la reyna Florisena* (Medina del Campo? 1542). Eisenberg, p. 86. Palau, 224695.

[802] Espejo de Caballerías. *Don Roselao de Grecia. Tercera parte de espejo de cauallerias: enel qual se cuētā los famosos hechos del infante don Roserin: y el fin q̃ ouo en los amores dela princesa Florimena. Dōde vereys el alto principio y hazañosos hechos en armas de dō Roselao de Grecia su hijo. 1547.* (Toledo en casa de Juan de Ayala/ a costa de Diego lopes mercader de libros, 1547). Folio. Chapin Library, Williams College, Williamstown. Eisenberg, p. 61. Mr. W. G. Hammond was very kind to send me photocopies of the title page and colophon of this, the first edition, of the third part.

2 Declaracion de instrumentos[803] in 4to 51		102
9 Doctrina cordis[804] in 4to 34		306
3 Discursos de Machavello[805] in 8° 85		255
1 Differentias de Vanegas[806] in 4to libro primo	102	102
2 Dialogo entre penitente y confessor[807] 8° 10		020
6 Demonstracion de la incarnacion in 4to 12		072
6 Don Seraphino de Fermo[808] in 4to Miles 119		714
1 Don Florisel de Niquea[809] 2da parte 170		170
3 Despertador del anima[810] in 4to el uno roto 30		090
10 Despertador del anima in 8° 25		250

---

[803] Bermudo, Juan. *Comiença el libro primero de la Declaraciõ de instrumẽtos musicales* (Ossuna, por Juan de Leõ, 1549). 4.to. Hispanic Society of America. Maggs, 87 (with illus.). Penney, p. 59. Palau, 2811. The British Library has a folio edition of this published in 1555. Rhodes, p. 26.

[804] Bonaventura, Saint, Cardinal, ca. 1217-1274. *Doctrina cordis d'l serafico dotor Sant Bonaventura* (Baeza, 1551). Houghton Library, Harvard. The British Library also has a quarto edition published in Toledo in 1510 by Juan Varela de Salamanca. *Catálogo colectivo*, B, 2715.

[805] Macchiavelli, Niccolò. *Los discursos* (Medina del Campo, por Guillermo de Millis, 1552 and 1555). 8.vo. Hispanic Society of America. Penney, p. 324. Pérez Pastor, *Medina del Campo*, p. 81, no. 91; p. 132, no. 120. Palau, 150605, 150606.

[806] Vanegas de Busto, Alejo. *Primera parte de las diferencias de libros q̃ ay en el uniuerso* (Toledo, en casa de Iuã de Ayala, 1540, 1546). Quarto. British Library. Rhodes, p. 212. Pérez Pastor, *Toledo*, p. 78, no. 187 and p. 88, no. 219.

[807] *Saludable y deuoto dialogo entre vn penitente y un cõfessor* (Sevilla, por Christoual aluarez, 1550). 8.vo. Biblioteca Nacional, Madrid. *Catálogo colectivo*, D, 627.

[808] Serafino, da Fermo. *Las obras spiritvales de Don Seraphino d' Fermo* (Medina del Campo, en casa de Guillermo de Millis, 1554). 4.to. British Library. The work was also published by Juan de Cánova in 1554. It is surprising that the title in the inventory is the one by Guillermo de Millis, and that there were no remaining copies of the Junta edition (Salamanca, en casa de Iuan de Iũta, 1552) for sale. The work is condemned on the Spanish *Index* of 1559. Biblioteca Nacional, Madrid. De Bujanda, V, pp. 539-41. Maggs, 366. Palau, 87739, 87741.

[809] Silva, Feliciano de. *La Cronica de los muy valientes y esforçados y invencibles cavalleros dõ Florisel de Niquea: y el fuerte Anaxartes: hijos del muy excelẽte principe Amadis de Grecia* (Valladolid, a costa de Juan Despinosa librero, y de maestro Nicolas Tierri impressor, 1532; and Seuilla, enlas casas de Jacome Cromberger, 1546). Folio. This is Book X of the series of chronicles of the deeds of Amadís, de Gaula. Salvá, 1515. Maggs, 981. Rhodes, p. 9. Griffin, Appendix One, no. 507. Palau, 10495.

[810] Raymundus de Sabunde, 15th cent. *Despertador del alma*. On the Spanish *Index* of 1559. De Bujanda, V, p. 473. There are editions from Seville (no printer, 1544, in 8.vo) and Toledo (Juan de Ayala, 1552).

5 Directorio delas obras canonicas[811] in 8°	25	125
35 Deliberacion en causa delos pobres de Soto[812] 4[to]	34	1,190
14 Doctrina Christiana de Jimenes[813] in 8° Ant[uerpie]	40	560
1 Deliberacion en causa delos pobres del Benedictino	34	034
2 De la celestial hierarchia[814] in fol.	17	034
		13,083

(f. 40)

14 Description del reyno de Galicia in 4[to]	34	476
1 Dante escritto de mano	---	----
12 Doctrina de religiosos[815] in 4[to]	85	1,020
		1,496
xiiij,dlxxix		13,083
	L.	14,579

139 Epistolas y evangelios[816] in 8° Burgos	68	9,452
2 Epistolas y evangelios[817] in 8° Alcala	68	136

---

[811] The Biblioteca Nacional, Madrid has an octavo lacking its title page, whose second leaf reads: "Siguese el primer directorio: que es para orar y meditar... Directorio para las horas canonicas... Directorio de confession... Directorio para comulgar... Declaracion del pater noster... Declaracion del credo...(Caragoça, en casa de George Coci, 1539). 8.vo. *Catálogo colectivo*, D, 1217.

[812] Soto, Domingo de. *Deliberacion en la causa de los pobres* (Salamanca, en officina de Juā de Jūta, 1545). 4.to. Biblioteca Nacional, Madrid. British Library. Houghton Library, Harvard University. Palau, 320084. *Catálogo colectivo*, S, 1643.

[813] See footnote ?.

[814] *Comienca el libro de la Celestial Jerarquia y inffernal labirintho metrifficado en metro castellano.* (Pamplona or Logroño, por Arnaldo Guillen de Brocar, ca. 1500). The Hispanic Society of America has another, with no place or printer, ca. 1521). Folio. Penney, p. 121.

[815] Humbert de Romans. *Dotrina de religiosos: cōpuesto por el maestro fray Huberto de romanis quinto maestro general de la ordē de los predicadores* (Salamanca, por Juan de Junta, 1546). 4.to. Biblioteca Nacional, Madrid. Hispanic Society of America. British Library. Penney, p. 264. *Catálogo colectivo*, H, 1011. Rhodes, p. 99. Palau, 116964.

[816] Montesino, Ambrosio de, bp., d. 1514. *Evāgelios epistolas; leciones y prophecias que la sancta yglesia cāta en la missa por todo el año* (Burgos, en casa Juan de Junta, 1555). 8.vo. Bibliothèque Nationale, Paris. Palau, 84802. The printing of this work only one year before the inventory accounts for the large number of copies still unsold or undistributed. Bataillon (p. 556) notes that this work, in the revision of Ambrosio de Montesino, was frequently reprinted in the sixteenth century. The Inquisition was more open to partial editions of the Bible than to the full text.

[817] Martín Abad (no. 503) notes that he has not been able to locate a copy of this Alcalá de Henares edition.

7 Epistolas de Ortys[818] in fol. 136		952
16 Espejo de perfection[819] in 8° 25		400
50 Exposicion de la passion in 8° 6		300
32 Erasmus del nombre Jhs.[820] in 8° 4		128
239 Excellencias de la fe[821] in 4to 51		12,189
128 Eneydos de Virgilio[822] in 4to 10		1,280
6 Epistolas y evangelios[823] in fol. 170		1,020
5 Espejo de consolacion 4ta parte[824] in fol. 153		765
5 Epistolas de Mondonedo lib[ro] prim[er]o[825] in fol. 136		680
5 Epistolas de Mondonedo lib[ro] 2do [826] in fol. 136		680

---

[818] Ortiz, Francisco. *Epistolas familiares* (Alcala de Henares, en casa del señor Iuan Brocar, 1551). Folio. British Library. Houghton Library, Harvard. Hispanic Society of America. Maggs, 694. Palau, 205626. Rhodes, p. 144. Martín Abad, p. 576, no. 396; p. 598, no. 425.

[819] Herp, Hendrik, d. 1477. *Espejo de perfeciō ... con otro libro llamado Memorial de la vida de nuestro Redemptor Iesu Christo* (Alcalá de Henares, en casa de Joan de Brocar, 1551). 8.vo. Biblioteca Nacional, Lisbon. This work is condemned by the Spanish *Index* of 1559. De Bujanda, V, p. 544. Martín Abad, p. 569, no. 390. (Martín Abad describes this as an octavo, and De Bujanda as a 12.mo).

[820] I have found no work by Erasmus resembling this title. Pérez Pastor (*Toledo*, p. 97, no. 243 and p. 99, no. 251) cites a similar title, *Del divino nombre de Iesus ...* , a translation of the Latin work *De diuino nomine Iesus, per nomē tetragrammaton significato* by Juan Martínez Guijeño or Guijarro (also known as Juan Martínez Siliceo), Archbishop of Toledo. (Toledo, 1551). 8.vo.

[821] Maluenda, Luis de. *Tratado llamado excelencias de la fe* (Burgos, en casa de Juā de jūta, 1537). 4.to. British Library. Palau, 84930, 339593. *Catálogo colectivo*, T, 1515.

[822] Virgilius Maro, Publius. *Los doze libros de la Eneida de Vergilio* (Toledo, en casa de Iuan de Ayala). 4.to. Biblioteca Nacional, Madrid. Hispanic Society of America. Pérez Pastor, *Toledo*, p. 111, no. 279. Penney, p. 602. The Spanish translation of the Aeneid is by Gregorio Hernández de Velasco.

[823] Montesino, Ambrosio de, bp., d. 1514. *Epistolas y evangelios por todo el año* (Seuilla, enlas casas de Jacome Crōberger, 1549; Toledo, Juan Ferrer, 1549; Toledo, en casa de Juan de villaquiran τ Juan de ayala, 1535). Folios. Griffin, Appendix One, no. 534. Pérez Pastor, *Toledo*, p. 69, no. 164.

[824] Dueñas, Juan de. *Quarta parte del espejo de consolacion* (Valladolid, por Iuā de Villaquirā, a costa de Iuā de espinosa, 1551). Folio. British Library. Biblioteca Pública, Palma de Mallorca. *Catálogo colectivo*, D, 1597.

[825] Guevara, Antonio de. *Libro primero de las epistolas* (Alcalá de Henares, Juan Brocar, 1551). Folio. There were also folio editions in Valladolid (por Juan de Villaquiran, 1544, 1549) and Zaragoza (en casa de george coci a espensas de Pedro bernuz y Bartholome de nagera, 1543). Folio. British Library. Biblioteca Nacional, Madrid. *Catálogo colectivo*, G, 1800.

[826] Guevara, Antonio de. *Segunda parte de las epistolas* (Valladolid, por industria del honrrado varō juan de Villaquiran, 1545). Folio. British Library. Palau, 110212. Other folio editions of the second part were published in Valladollid in 1542 and 1549, and Zaragoza, 1543. Rhodes, p. 91-92.

6 Enchrydio de los tienpos[827] in 8°	51		306
164 Espejo de illustres personas[828] in 8°	10		1,640
5 Espejo de Consolacion in fol. lib[ro] primo[829]	153		765
3 Espejo de Consolacion in fol. lib[ro] 2do[830]	153		459
3 Eras[mo] dela misericordia de Dios[831] in 8°	12		036
6 Exposi[cio] del pater noster de arcobis[po] de Sevilla[832] in 4to	25		150
1 Espejo de consolacion lib[ro] 3o[833] in fol.	153		153
3 Enchrydio de Erasmo[834] in 8° rro[man]ce	51		153
1 Estylo de escrivir cartas de yciar[835] in 4to	51		051

---

[827] Juan de Junta published Alonso de Venero's *Enchiridion de los tiempos*, in Burgos, 1529 and 1540, and in Salamanca in 1543 and 1545. 8.vo. Biblioteca Nacional, Madrid. *Catálogo colectivo*, V, 554-557.

[828] Alonso de Madrid. *Espejo de illustres personas* (Burgos, [Juan de Junta?], 1527 and 1544). 8.vo. Palau, 146621, 146629. The Cromberger firm also published octavo editions of this title in 1539, 1542 and 1549. Griffin, Appendix One, nos. 427, 456, 528.

[829] Dueñas, Juan de. *Espejo de consolacion: parte primera* (Burgos, por Juan de Junta...a costa del señor Juan de Espinosa, 1546). Folio. Biblioteca Nacional, Madrid. Hispanic Society of America. Penney, p. 179. Palau, 76516. *Catálogo colectivo*, D, 1576.

[830] Dueñas, Juan de. *Segvnda parte del Espeio de consolacion* (Burgos, en casa de Juã de Junta...a costa de Juã despinosa mercader, 1549). Folio. Biblioteca Nacional, Madrid. Palau, 76523 (note). *Catálogo colectivo*, D, 1578.

[831] Erasmus, Desiderius. *Sermon de Desiderio Erasmo... dela grādeza y muchedumbre delas misericordias de Dios nuestro Señor* (Logroño, [Miguel de Eguía] 1528). Bayerische Staatsbibliothek. Another edition was published in Antwerp in 1549 by Joannes de Grave. The Spanish translation of the work is on the Spanish *Index* of 1559. De Bujanda, V, p. 541. Bataillon, p. LIX, no. 568, 569 and plate XII.

[832] Deza, Diego de, abp. of Seville, 1443-1523. *Exposicion del Pater Noster: dirigida a la muy christianissima y muy poderosa reyna doña Isabel de Castilla* (Alcalá de Henares, por Miguel de Guia, 1524). 4.to. Biblioteca Nacional, Madrid. Palau 71535. Guerrero, no. 2. Martín Abad, p. 309, no. 132. Deza served as Inquisitor General of Spain. See also Bataillon, *Erasmo y España*, pp. 29-34.

[833] Dueñas, Juan de. *Tercera parte del Espejo de consolacion* (Valladolid, por Juã de Villaquirã a costa dele señor Juan de Espinosa, 1550). Hispanic Society of America. Penney, p. 179. Palau, 76528.

[834] Erasmus, Desiderius. *Enchiridion o manual del cauallero christiano en romance. Una carta del autor a su Magestad. El sermon del Niño Jesus* (Anvers, Martin Nucio, 1555). 8.vo. On the 1559 Spanish *Index*. Palau, 80339. De Bujanda, V, p. 474. Earlier editions were published in Seville (Gregorio de la Torre y Juan Canalla), Lisbon (Luís Rodriguez, 1541), Alcalá de Henares (Miguel de Eguía, 1533), [Alcalá de Henares or Logroño] (Miguel de Eguía, 1529), and Seville (Jacobo Cromberger, 1528). Bonilla, pp. 420-421. Bataillon, LVI, no. 518-530. See also footnote 240.

[835] Yciar, Juan de. *Nuevo Estilo de escreuir cartas mensageras* (Zaragoça, por Agustín Millan, 1552). 4.to. There was an earlier quarto edition in Zaragoza: *Cosa nueva. Este es el estilo de escrivir cartas mēsageras* (Çaragoça, por Bartholome de Nagera, 1547). 4.to. British Library. Palau, 117830, 117831. Yciar, or Iciar, was an early Spanish calligrapher.

INVENTARIO DE LOS LIBROS

38 Emblemas de la justicia[836] in 8° 10		380
1 Espejo del anima[837] in 4to 85		085
4 Exercitio de la Vida Spiritual[838] in 4to / 8° 25		100
15 Epistolas y evangelios in 8° Miles 68		1.020
6 Estymulo de amor[839] in 4to 34		204
2 Epistolas de Mondonedo libro primo[840] in 8° 85		170
2 Epistolas de Mondonedo libro 2do in 8° 85		170
8 Estymulo de humildad in 4to 25		200
5 Elegancias romancadas[841] in 4to 25		125
1 Espejo de bien vivir in 8° 10		010
1 El momo[842] in fol. 51		051
8 Escala espiritual[843] in 8° 34		272
7 Expos[icio] del pater noster de Savonarola[844] 4to 25		175

---

[836] Alciati, Andrea. *Los emblemas* (Lyon, Guilielmo Rouillio, 1549). 8.vo. British Library. Hispanic Society of America. Penney, p. 15.

[837] Evia, Francisco de. *Espejo del anima, agora de nueuo collegido de la Sagrada Escriptura y de lo que han escrito los santos doctores* (Valladolid, Francisco Fernández de Córdova, 1550). Palau, 84827.

[838] Cisneros, Garsías de, 1455-1510. The Hispanic Society of America has a 1571 Salamanca edition entitled *Compendium breue de exercicios spirituales Sacados d'un libro llamado Exercitario de vida spiritual* produced for Simon de Portonariis by Pedro Laso. The British Library has an octavo edition of this work, lacking the title page, produced by J. Luschner in Montserrat in 1500. The copy in the Junta inventory must have been produced between the two dates. The makers of the inventory were apparently unsure of the format.

[839] Bonaventura, St. [Supposititious works.] *Estimulo de amor de sant buēauētura. Nueuamēte impsso τ corregido* (Logroño, en casa de miguel de Eguia, 1529). 4.to. British Library. The British Library also has a 1551 edition from Baeça. Could this be a Spanish translation of *Stimulus amoris* which is attributed to St. Bernard, Abbot of Clairvaux?

[840] Guevara, Antonio de. *Libro primero de las Epistolas familiares*. I have not located an octavo edition.

[841] Nebrija, Antonio de. *Elegancias romançadas por el maestro Antonio de Nebrija* (Alcalá de Henares, per Michaelem de Eguia, 1526). 4.to. Martín Abad, p. 335, no. 167. An earlier edition was published by Arnao Guillén de Brocar in Alcalá de Henares, ca. 1517, and by Fadrique de Basilea [?] in Burgos [?], ca. 1495.

[842] Alberti, Leon Baptista. *El Momo. La moral τ muy graciosa historia del Momo: compuesta en Latin por el docto varon Leon Baptista Alberto florentin. Trasladada en Castellano por Augustin de Almaçan ... medico d' su Magestad.* (Alcalá de Henares, Joan de Mey, Flandro, 1553). Folio. British Library. Hispanic Society of America. Maggs Bros. *Catalogue no. 495*, 22. Penney, p. 12. Rhodes, p. 3. Martín Abad, p. 607, no. 437.

[843] John Climacus, Saint. *Escala espiritual* (Alcalá de Henares, En casa de Juan de Mey Flandro, 1553). 8.vo. Biblioteca Nacional, Lisbon. Martín Abad, p. 623, no. 454.

[844] Savonarola, Girolamo. *Exposicion del Pater noster*. An octavo edition was produced in Antwerp (Anvers, Martinus Nutius, [1550]), but I have not located a quarto edition. On the Spanish *Index* of 1559. De Bujanda, V, p. 477.

SIXTEENTH CENTURY SPANISH BOOKSTORE

2 Espejo de Cavalleria libro 2do[845] in fol. 85		170
2 Espejo del principe Christiano[846] in fol. 170		340
		35,187

(f. 41)

1 Epistolas de Sancta Catalina de Siena[847] in fol.	170		170
1 Erasmo sobre el pater noster[848] 25			025
1 Egloga real in 4to 12			012
8 Exercitio del verdadero christiano 10			080
4 Espejo de la vida in 4to 15			060
			347
xxxv,cmxxxiiij			35,187
			L. 35,434

2 Flos sanctor[um][849] in fol. Toledo	204	408
4 Florambel de Lucea[850] in fol.	119	476
2 Felis magno[851] in fol.	85	170

---

[845] López de Santa Catalina, Pedro? *Libro segundo de espejo de cauallerias q̃ trata los amores de dõ Roldã cõ Angelica la bella y las estrañas auēturas q̃ acabo el infante dõ roserin hijo d'l rey dõ rugiero y brãdamõte* (Seuilla, en casa de Iacome Cromberger, 1549). Folio. The first part was published by Cromberger in Seville in 1545 and 1551; the second part in Toledo, 1527 and in Seville 1533, 1536 and 1549. Bayerische Staatsbibliothek, Munich. Bibliothèque Nationale, Paris. Palau, 82336 note. Griffin, Appendix One, no. 358, 523. Eisenberg, p. 61.

[846] Monzón, Francisco de. *Libro primero d'l espejo del prĩcipe christiano: que trata como se ha d'criar vn principe o niño generoso desde su tierna niñez* (Impreso en lisboa ẽ casa de Luis Rodriguez, 1544). Folio. British Library. Biblioteca Nacional, Madrid. Palau, 179984. Bataillon, LXXXVIII, no. 947.

[847] Caterina *da Siena, Saint,* 1347-1380. *Obra de las epistolas y oraciones de la bienauenturada virgen sancta catherina de Sena ... traduzidas d'l toscano* (Alcalá de Henares, A. de Brocar, 1512). Folio. Palau, 297779

[848] Erasmus, Desiderius. See footnote 800.

[849] *Flos sanctorum. A honor y alabança de nro. señor jhu xpo* (Toledo, 1511). Folio. Palau, 92886 note. Pérez Pastor, *Toledo*, p. 34, no. 51.

[850] Florambel de Lucea. *La prmera [sic] parte dela coronica del inuencible cauallero Florambel de Lncea [sic]: hijo del esforçado Rey Florineo de Escocia* (Sevilla, Antõ Aluarez, 1548). Folio. British Library. Rhodes, p. 79. Palau, 92312.

[851] Felix, *Magno. Los quatro libros del muy noble τ valeroso cauallero Felix magno hijo d'l rey falangris de la grã bretaña ...* (Seville, en casa de Sebastian Trugillo impressor de libros, 1549). Folio. 2 vols. British Library. Biblioteca de Catalunya, Barcelona. Palau, 87525. Eisenberg, p. 68. Rhodes, p. 75. Eisenberg lists earlier editions from Seville (1543) and Barcelona (1531).

INVENTARIO DE LOS LIBROS

6 Fuero real[852] in 4.to 306	1,836
2 Fasciculus mirrhe[853] in 8° Ant[uerpie] 60	120
194 Forma libellandi[854] in fol. 17	3,291
1 Fuente de vida[855] in 8° 4	004
7 Flores de Consolacion in 8° 25	175
	L. 6,480

/ vj,cmlxxx /

14 Guia del Cielo[856] in fol. 153	2,142
1 Guerra de Milan in fol. 102	102
5 Guerra de Alemana[857] in 8° 25	125
1 Guido[858] in fol. 187	187
	L. 2,556

---

[852] Laws, statutes. *Fuero real de España ... Glosado por ... Alonso díaz de Mõtaluo. Assimesmo por vn sabio doctor de la vniversidad de Salamanca addicionado y concordado con las Siete Partidas.* Folio editions were published by Juan de Junta in Burgos in 1533 and 1541; perhaps by him in Salamanca in 1543 and 1544; and by Pedro de Castro in Medina del Campo in 1544. British Library. Bibliothèque Nationale, Paris. Harvard Law School Library.

[853] *Fasciculus mirrhe, el qual tracta de la passion de nuestro redemptor Iesu Christo.* This may be the 1553 edition (Antwerp, Martinus Nutius). 8.vo. Biblioteca Nacional, Madrid. Hispanic Society of America. *Catálogo colectivo*, F, 128. Penney, p. 197. The Junta firm also produced editions in 1528 (Salamanca [Juan de Junta?]) and 1543 (Salamanca, por Juan de Junta impressor de libros). Biblioteca Nacional, Lisbon. British Library. It is on the Spanish *Index* of 1559. De Bujanda, V, p. 479-480. Palau, 86881.

[854] Infante, Juan, 15th cent. *Forma libellandi*. Folio. Editions of this work of Juan Infante were published by Juan de Junta in Burgos (1529 and 1536) and in Salamanca (1543). British Library. Biblioteca Nacional, Madrid. Biblioteca Universitaria, Oviedo. Palau, 119232, 119233, 119235. *Catálogo colectivo*, I, 176, 178, 179.

[855] Bernabé de Palma. *Fuente de vida ... por un frayle de la Orden de sant Francisco* (Burgos, Juan de Junta? 1528). 8.vo. Palau, 95261, note. No copy of this edition seems to have survived.

[856] León, Pablo de. *Libro llamado Guia del cielo el qual trata de los vicios y virtudes, sacado de la secundae sancto Thomas* (Alcala de Henares, en casa de Iuan de Brocar, 1553). Folio. British Library. Rhodes, p. 110. Martín Abad, p. 611, no. 440. Juan de Ayala published an edition in Toledo in 1549. Pérez Pastor, *Toledo*, p. 93, no. 233. Palau, 135519.

[857] Ávila y Zúñiga, Luis de. *Commentarios de la Guerra de Alemaña hecha por el Emperador Carlos I° en los años de 1547-1548* (Toledo, por Juan de Ayala, 1549). 8.vo. Pérez Pastor, *Toledo*, p. 93, no. 233. Other octavo editions were printed in Antwerp by Steelsio in 1549 and 1550. The British Library and the Hispanic Society of America also have a 1548 edition (Venetia, a instancia de Thomas de Çornoça, 1548). Penney, p. 45. Rhodes, p. 21.

[858] Guy de Chauliac, c. 1300-1368. *Guido de Caulhiaco: cirurgiano y maestro en mediciina* (Sevilla, Jacobo Cromberger, ca. 1518-1520). Folio. National Library of Medicine. Durling, 2246. Griffin, Appendix One, no. 215.

/ ij,dl /

1 Horas pp rromance[859]	51	051
1 Horas dela passion in 8° faltas	--	----
124 Horas in 8° ro[man]ce de Burgos[860]	80	9,920
4 Horas in 8° Sal[aman]ca rromance[861]	85	340
3 Henrique de Vihuela[862] in fol.	476	1,428
1 Horas de Sevilla[863] in 8° faltas	---	----
1 Horas pp 16 faltas	---	----
100 Horas pp 32 las 2 faltas	17	1,700
3 Horas pp 16 faltas	---	----
2 Hugo de Celso[864] in fol.	408	816
3 Horas Roma[nas] ro[man]ce in 8° Caragoca[865]	85	255
2 Horas pp 16	51	102
2 Historia de la tomada de orã in fol.	25	050
10 Horas de la passion pp	25	250

---

[859] A number of Spanish translations of the *Horas Romanas* are on the Spanish *Index* of 1559, including the name of printer and date and place of publication, but it is impossible to sort out these in the Junta inventory because of the paucity of information. Item 506 on the *Index* singles out the edition of Juan de Junta in Salamanca for condemnation. De Bujanda, V, pp. 489-495. It is not surprising that several of the inventory editions are in small format, either 16.mo or 32.mo.

[860] The Spanish *Index* of 1559 (item 505) condemned "Ho. Ro. en romance, en Burgos, por Alonso de Melgar, año de 1519." De Bujanda, V, p. 493. Palau, 116148. Palau cites an edition of Juan de Junta, [Horas de nuestra señora segun el uso Romano] printed in Burgos in 1551, which, judging from the number of copies in the inventory, is probably the work represented here, but no copy is presently known.

[861] The Spanish *Index* of 1559 (item 506) condemned "Ho. Ro. en romance, por Ioan de Iunta, en Salamanca, año de 1542, 1551." De Bujanda, V, p. 493. Palau, 116152 note.

[862] Enríquez de Valderrávano, Enrique. *Libro de musica de vihuela entitulado Silva de Sirenas* (Valladolid, por Francisco Fernandez de Cordoua, 1547). Folio. British Library. Rhodes, p. 69. Palau, 79860.

[863] A 1537 edition from the presss of Juan Cromberger, *Horas de nr̃a señora romanas en romance con las quatro passiones*, has survived in the Hispanic Society of America. Penney, p. 111. The Spanish *Index* of 1559 banned Cromberger's editions of 1528, 1538, 1542 and 1550, none of which are now known. The *Index* also banned the Seville editions of Dominico de Robertis (1541 and 1550), Juan Varela (1531 and 1539) and Gregorio de la Torre (1556). De Bujanda, V, p. 490-491.

[864] Descousu, Celse Hugues. This is probably the *Reportorio Universal de todas las leyes destos Reynos de Castilla ... por el doctor Hugo de Celso* (Medina del Campo, por Iuan Maria de Terranova y Iacome de Liarcari, 1553). Folio. Harvard Law School Library. *Catálogo colectivo*, C. 1443. There are also folio editions of 1538 and 1547 from Valladolid in the British Library. Rhodes, p. 63.

[865] The Spanish *Index* of 1559 bans the Spanish translation of the *Ho[rae] Roma[nae]* from the press of Pedro Bernuz and Bartholome de Nagera (1542, 1547, 1552, 1554 and 1556). De Bujanda, V, p. 491-92.

2 Hierarchia celestial[866] in fol.   17   <u>034</u>
                                                                        L. 14,946

                           xiiij,dcmxlvj
(f. 42)

2 Instruction del anima in 4.to   40   080
41 Introduction de Vives rro[man]ce[867]   25   1,025
13 Institutiones de Taulero[868] in 8°   25   325
1 Intonario in fol. Sal[aman]ca   17   017
1 Instruction Christiana[869] in 4.to   102   102
1 Iustino historico[870] in fol.   85   085
3 Instruction de la vida Christiana[871]   17   051
11 Instruction de guerra in 4.to   12   132
15 Iardin de Donzellas[872]   12   180
5 Iardin del alma[873] in 4.to   51   255

---

[866] See footnote 814.

[867] Vives, Juan Luis. *Introduction ala sabiduria ... Todo nueuamente traduzido en castellano* (Anuers en casa de Iuan Steelsio, 1551). 8.vo. British Library. Rhodes, p. 218. This is a translation of his *Introductio ad sapientiam*. (See footnote 368).

[868] Tauler, Johann. *Instituciones y doctrina del excelente Theologo Fray Iuã Taulero* (Coimbra, 1551). 8.vo. Palau, 328257.

[869] Segura, Juan de. *Libro de Instrucion Christiana y de exercicios spirituales y Preparaciõ para la missa y sancta comuniõ* (Burgos, en casa de Juan de Junta, 1554). 4.to. Hispanic Society of America. Biblioteca Nacional, Madrid. Palau, 141972. Bataillon, LXXX, no. 836. Guerrero, no. 19. Penney, p. 511. *Catálogo colectivo*, L, 1229.

[870] Justinus, Marcus Justinus. *Justino clarissimo abreviador de la historia general del famoso y excelente historiador Trogo Pompeyo* (Alcalá de Henares, Juan de Brocar, 1540). Folio. British Library. Martín Abad, p. 467, no. 306. Palau, 126806. "Iustino historiador, en romance" is on the Spanish *Index* of 1559. De Bujanda, V, pp. 498-99. The translator is Jorge de Bustamente.

[871] García de Villalpando, Antonio. *Instruccion de la vida christiana compuesta para la de los moriscos nueuamente convertidos de orden del Cardenal Arzobispo Ximenez, por su Visitador general y Canonigo de Toledo el Doctor ...* ([Toledo], por Pedro Hagembach Aleman, [1500]). 4.to. Pérez Pastor, *Toledo*, p. 17. (Pérez Pastor had not seen a copy.) One would suppose that the inventory copies were of a later edition.

[872] Martín, de Córdoba. *Iardin delas nobles donzellas* ([Medina del Campo] P.C. [Pedro de Castro] a costa de Iuã de espinosa, 1542). 4.to. Biblioteca Nacional, Madrid. British Library. Pérez Pastor, *Medina del Campo*, p. 18, no. 128. Rhodes, p. 128. Palau, 61878 note.

[873] Díaz Tanco de Frexenal, Vasco. *Jardin del Alma Xp̃iana do se tractan las significaciones de la missa y de las horas canonicas. Y delas nueue ordenes ecclesiasticas ...* (Valladolid, en casa de Iuan de Caruajal, 1552). 4.to. Salvá, 3881. Maggs, 326 (with illus.). Penney, p. 171. Rhodes, p. 66. Palau, 72905.

6 Institutiones ymperiales[874] in 8° rro[man]ce	85	510
3 Informacion de la tierra sancta[875] in 4to	51	153
9 Instruction o refugio del alma[876] in 4to	40	360
6 Itinerario de Luys Patreyo[877] in fol.	25	150
11 Iuego de damas pp	25	<u>275</u>
		L. 3,700

/ iij,dcc /

9 Luzero de la vida de Xp̄o[878] in fol.	85	765
8 Libro de la verdad de la fe[879] in 4to	68	544
40 Leche de la fe[880] in fol.	238	9,520
104 Luz de religiosos[881] in 8°	3	312

---

[874] Justinian I, Emperor of the East. *Las Instituciones Imperiales (o principios del Derecho Civil)* (Tolosa, por Guion de Bodauila, 1551). 16.mo. This is a Spanish translation of the code of Justinian by Bernardino Daza. British Library. Palau, 126758.

[875] Aranda, Antonio de. *Uerdadera ỹformacion de la Tierra Santa* ... . (Alcalá de Henares, en casa de Miguel de Eguya, 1533); (Toledo, en casa de Juã de Ayala, 1537); (Alcalá de Henares, en casa de Juan d'Brocar, 1539); (Sevilla, por Juã crōberger, 1539); (Toledo, en casa de Fernando de sancta catalina, 1545); (Toledo en casa de Iuan ferrer. A costa de Diego Perez mercader de libros, 1550/1551). 4.to. Academia de la Historia, Madrid. Biblioteca Pública, Toledo. Griffin, Appendix One, no. 429. Pérez Pastor, *Toledo*, p. 72, no. 169; p. 83, no. 205; p. 99, no. 247. Palau, 14902-14905.

[876] López de Stuniga, Diego de. *Instruction y refugio del anima y conciencia escrupolosa y tenerosa de Dios* (Salamanca, Juan de Junta, 1552). 4.to. Biblioteca Nacional, Madrid. Palau, 381567.

[877] Varthema, Ludovico de, 15th cent. *Itinerario del venerable varon miser Luis patricio romano: enel qual cuēta mucha parte del a ethiopia Egipto: y entrãbas Arabias: Siria y la India. Buelto de latin en romance por Christoual de arcos clerigo* (Sevilla, Jacobo Crōberger, 1520). Folio. Hispanic Society of America. This is an account of a journey to Syria, Egypt, Persia, India, Ethiopia et al.

[878] The *Index* of 1559 condemns the *Luzero de la vida christiana* of Pedro Ximénez de Prexano. De Bujanda, V, pp. 506-07. Juan Varela published an edition in Seville in 1515, the Crombergers published editions in the same city in 1524, 1528 and 1543, and Juan Ferrer in Toledo in 1555. Griffin, Appendix One, nos. 248, 281, 482. Could this be the same work?

[879] Soares, João. *Libro de la verdad de la fe* (Alcalá de Henares, en casa de Juan de Brocar, 1545). 4.to. Biblioteca Nacional, Lisbon. This work by Soares, bishop of Coimbra, is on the Spanish *Index* of 1559. De Bujanda, V, p. 504. Martín Abad, p. 521, no. 352.

[880] *Tratado llamado leche de la fe*. This work of Luis de Maluenda was published by Juan de Junta in Burgos, 1545. It is on the *Index* of 1559. Bayerische Staatsbibliothek, München. Palau, 147978. De Bujanda, V, p. 504.

[881] *Luz de religiosos* ([Seville, Jacobo Cromberger, 1510-11]). 8.vo. Palau, 45684; Griffin, Appendix One, no. 70. The verso of the title page reads: "Carta de vn religiosissimo e doctissimo varõ frayle, de la ordē de sāto domingo: embiada a doña magdalena cōdessa de la mirãdola que q[ue]ria entrar en la religion. E fue buelta de ytaliano en nuestro castellano." Palau dates this ca. 1525.

32 Leyes del estylo[882] in fol. 68		5,576
4 Lectiones de Job de Jarava[883] pp Ant[uerpie] 12		048
31 Lux bella in Musica[884] in 4to 10		310
5 Lumbre del alma[885] in 4to o 8° 10		050
2 Lucano[886] in fol. 85		170
1 Lengua de Erasmo[887] in 8° 34		034
1 Lengua de Erasmo[888] in 4to 34		034
1 Libro de Vihuela de Luys de Milan[889] 204		204

---

[882] *Leyes del estylo*. Editions of this title were published by Juan de Junta's associate Canova in 1554. There is an edition without indication of publisher, date or place which is thought to be Salamanca, Juan de Junta, c. 1540.

[883] *Las liciones de Job con los nueve psalmos, que con ellas se cantan en las horas de los finados. Trasladadas de latin en lengua castellana por Hernando Jarava* (Anvers, Martinus Nutius, 1550). 12.mo. This work is on the Spanish *Index* of 1559. De Bujanda, V, p. 502-03. An earlier edition was published by Nutius in 1540.

[884] Durán, Domingo Marcos. *Tractado dela musica llamado Lux bella* (Seuilla, J. Cromberger, 1518). 4.to. A slim work of 14 leaves, which accounts for its low price. Library of Congress. Griffin, Appendix One, no. 181.

[885] Cazalla, Juan de. *Libro llamado lumbre del alma*. 8.vo. De Bujanda relates the hypothesis of Justo Cuervo and Marcel Bataillon that the condemnation of "Obra impressa en Valladolid por maestro Nicolas Tierry, año de 1528, en romance," refers to this title. The inventory copy is probably the octavo edition Cromberger published in Seville in 1542. Biblioteca Nacional, Lisbon. De Bujanda, V, pp. 511-12. Griffin, Appendix One, no. 461. Palau, 50720, 50721.

[886] Lucanus, Marcus Annaeus. The Hispanic Society of America has an undated, unsigned copy of the Spanish translation of Lucanus' Pharsalia by Martín Lasso de Oropesa: *La historia que escrivio en latin el poeta Lucano* (n.p., ca. 1530?). Folio. Penney, p. 319. The British Library apparently has another copy, but dates it c. 1540 and assigns it to the press of Joannes Crinitus in Antwerp. Rhodes, p. 121.

[887] Erasmus, Desiderius. This appears on the 1559 Spanish *Index*, listed with the works of Erasmus, as "Lingua, tam latino quam vulgari sermone" and again as "Lengua de Erasmo, en romance y latin y en qualquier lengua vulgar." De Bujanda, V, pp. 349, 501-02. The probable edition is that of M. Nucio in Antwerp in 1550: *La lengua de Erasmo nueuamente Romançada por muy elegante estilo*. Biblioteca Nacional, Madrid. Bonilla, pp. 475-479. Bataillon, no. 543-551.

[888] Ibid. The quarto edition of the previous item may be one of the Seville editions of the Cromberger firm (1533, 1535, 1542, 1543/44), the Toledo edition of Juan de Ayala and Juan de Villaquirán (1533), the Lyons, 1538 edition (Lvgdvni, apvd Seb. Gryphivm) or the Basel, 1547 edition (Basileae, apvd H. Frobenium et N. Episcopium). Biblioteca Nacional, Madrid. Bayerische Staatsbibliothek, Munich. British Library. Griffin, Appendix One, no. 356, 376, 465, 492. Bonilla, pp. 471-475.

[889] Milán, Luis de. *Libro de musica de vihuela de mano. Intitulado El maestro* (Valencia, por Francisco Dias Romano, 1536). Folio. Biblioteca Nacional, Madrid. British Library. Rhodes, p. 135. Palau, 169131.

2 Libro de pestilencia⁸⁹⁰ in fol.   34   068
12 Laborintho (sic) de amor in 4ᵗᵒ   17   204
 3 Loores del monte Calvario⁸⁹¹ in 4ᵗᵒ   119   357
 2 La Circe⁸⁹² in 8°   34   068
 7 Libro de suertes⁸⁹³ in fol.   34   238
11 Loores de n[uest]ra Señora⁸⁹⁴ in 4ᵗᵒ   85   935
 1 La vida de la Madalena⁸⁹⁵ in 4ᵗᵒ   85   085
 3 Libro de la verdad de la fe⁸⁹⁶ in fol.   136   408
 1 Lucidante⁸⁹⁷ in fol.   68   068
16 Las fiestas q. se hizierō a Julio Tercio⁸⁹⁸ in 4ᵗᵒ   2   032

---

⁸⁹⁰ Lobera de Ávila, Luis. *Libro de pestilencia curativo y preservativo: y de fiebres pestilenciales, con la cura de todos los accidentes dellas, y de las otras fiebres, y habla de phlebotomia, ventosas, sanguisuelas: y de las diez y nueve enfermedades subitas que son utilissimas* (Alcalá de Henares? Juan de Brocar? 1542?). Folio. National Library of Medicine. Durling, no. 2830.

⁸⁹¹ Aranda, Antonio de. *Loores del dignissimo lugar del Calvario: en que se relata todo lo que nuestro redemptor Iesus hizo y dixo en el ... .* (Alcala de Henares en casa de Joā de Brocar [1551]). 4.to. Palau, 14910. Hispanic Society of America. Martín Abad, p. 567, no. 389.

⁸⁹² Gelli, Giovanni Battista, 1498-1563. *La Circe.* I do not know of a Spanish edition or translation, but Italian editions were produced in 1550 in Florence (Torrentino) and Venice (Bindoni) and a French translation was published in Lyons in 1550 by Guillaume Rouille. All are octavos.

⁸⁹³ Spirito, Lorenzo, d. 1496. *Libro del juego de las suertes* (Valencia, Joan Joffre, 1528). Folio. Biblioteca Nacional, Madrid. This work of is the Spanish translation of his *Libro della ventura*. It is on the Spanish *Index* of 1559. De Bujanda, V, pp. 504-05.

⁸⁹⁴ Aranda, Antonio de. *Loores de la Virgen nuestra Señora ... sobre la exposicion de las siete palabras.* (Alcala de Henares. En casa de Juan de Brocar, que santa gloria aya, [1552]). Palau, 14911. Martín Abad, p. 595, no. 420.

⁸⁹⁵ *Historia dela bendita Magdalena, sacada largamēte delos euāgelios τ otras p[ar]tes: por mādado dela muy alta τ catholica gran reyna doña Ysabel* (Toledo, Arnaldus Guillem de Brocar, 1521). 4.to. British Library. Maggs, 467 (with illus.). Rhodes, p. 130. Pérez Pastor (*Medina del Campo*, p. 5, no. 13) cites *Vida de Santa Maria Magdalena* (Medina del Campo, 1534) from the catalogue of the library of Cristobal Colón.

⁸⁹⁶ Soares, João, 1507?-1572. *Libro de la verdad de la fe* (Lisboa, Luis Rodríguez, 1543). Folio. Biblioteca Nacional, Lisbon. This work is on the Spanish *Index* of 1559. De Bujanda, V, p. 504.

⁸⁹⁷ *Libro primero de la crónica del valeroso caballero Lucidante de Tracia* (Salamanca, 1534). Folio. Palau, 143428. Palau says that the only known exemplar had disappeared from the Biblioteca Colombina of Seville.

⁸⁹⁸ *Las fiestas que se hizierō en Roma en la election de nuestro muy sancto padre Iulio papa tercero con el sumptuoso aparato de su coronacion y la solemnidad con que se abriō la puera sancta* (Medina del Campo, Pedro de Castro, 1550). 4.to. Hispanic Society of America. Palau, 91219. Penney, p. 482.

INVENTARIO DE LOS LIBROS

3 Libro de la verdad de la fe[899] in fol. 136		408
1 Lucidante[900] in fol. 68		068
16 Las fiestas q. se hizieron a Julio Tercio[901] in 4to	2	032
8 Libro de Cosina[902] in 4to 51		408
5 Los triumphos de Petrarcha[903] in 4to Miles	153	765
103 Leyes de Toro[904] in fol. 17		1,751
158 Leyes de abogados y procuradores[905] in fol. 17		<u>2,686</u>
		L. 25,640

(f. 43)

17 Leyes de hermandad[906] in fol. 17		289
2 Libros de Vihuela de Mudarra[907]	136	272

---

[899] Soares, João, 1507?-1572. *Libro de la verdad de la fe* (Lisboa, Luis Rodríquez, 1543). Folio. Biblioteca Nacional, Lisbon. This work is on the Spanish *Index* of 1559. De Bujanda, V, p. 504.

[900] *Libro primero de la crónica del valeroso caballero Lucidante de Tracia* (Salamanca, 1534). Folio. Palau, 143428. Palau says that the only known exemplar had disappeared from the Biblioteca Colombina of Seville.

[901] *Las fiestas que se hizierõ en Roma en la election de nuestro muy sancto padre Iulio papa tercero con el sumptuoso aparato de su coronacion y la solemnidad con que se abrió la puerta sancta* (Medina del Campo, Pedro de Castro, 1550). 4.to. Hispanic Society of America. Palau, 91219. Penney, p. 482.

[902] Nola, Roberto de. *Libro d' cozina* ([Seville, Juan Cromberger, 1538]). 4.to. British Library. Griffin, Appendix One, no. 422. Griffin observes that there is also a 1543 edition of this title in the Biblioteca Nacional, Madrid, but that it is not by the Cromberger press as Palau had affirmed. The work was also produced in a quarto edition in Toledo in 1525. Pérez Pastor, *Toledo*, p. 54, no. 109.

[903] Petrarca, Francesco. *Los trivmphos de Francisco de Petrarcha ahora nueuamente traduzidos en lengua Castellana, en la medida, y numero de versos, que tienẽ en el Toscano, y con nueva glosa* [trans. by Hernando de Hozes] (Vendense en Medina del Campo, en casa de Guillermo de Millis, 1554). 4.to. British Library. Biblioteca Nacional, Madrid. Pérez Pastor, *Medina del Campo*, p. 127, no. 113. Rhodes, p. 155. Palau, 224258, 224259.

[904] *Leyes de Toro*. Juan de Junta published folio editions in Burgos in 1531, 1538 and 1541; and in Salamanca in 1544 and 1546. Palau, 137417, 137421-22, 137426-27. Harvard Law School Library. See also footnote 188.

[905] *Leyes de los abogados y procuradores* (Salamanca, en casa de Juan de Junta, 1550). Folio. Biblioteca del Palacio, Madrid. Bibliothèque Nationale, Paris. Palau, 137413, 137450. Gil Ayuso, 141.

[906] *Leyes de hermandad*. Unsigned editions of this were published in Burgos (1527), and Salamanca (1540), both probably from the Junta press. Both folio. Biblioteca Nacional, Madrid. Biblioteca del Palacio, Madrid. Gil Ayuso, 41, 89. Palau, 137451, 137452. *Catálogo colectivo*, L, 651, 652.

[907] Mudarra, Alonso, ca. 1506-1580. *Tres libros de Mvsica en cifras para vihvela* (Sevilla, en casa de Iuan de Leõ, 1546). Oblong 8.vo. Biblioteca Nacional, Madrid. *Catálogo colectivo*, M, 2230. Palau, 184036.

SIXTEENTH CENTURY SPANISH BOOKSTORE

2 Libros de Vihuela de Narvays[908] in 4to	204		408
4 Luz del alma[909] in 4to	51		204
2 Las 4 enfermedades[910] in fol.	102		<u>204</u>
			1,377
			<u>25,640</u>
/ xxvij,xvij /			L. 27,017
8 Manual de doctrina Christiana de Ximenes[911] 8°	51		408
6 Manual de doct[rina] Christiana de Ximenes 8° Portugal[912]	51		306
5 Meditationes de S. Augustin[913] pp Ant[uerpie]	34		170
27 Medicina spiritual preservativa	20		540
10 Memorial de amor sancto[914] in 4to numero 10	68		680
6 Memorial de la vida de Christo in 8°	12		072

---

[908] Narváez, Luís de. *Los seys libros del delphin de musica de cifras para tañer Vihuela* (Valladolid, por Diego Hernãdez de Cordoua, 1538). oblong 4.to. Biblioteca Nacional, Madrid. British Library. Rhodes, p. 140. Palau, 187732.

[909] Meneses, Felipe de. *Luz del alma Christiana, contra la ceguedad & ignorancia en lo que pertenece a la fe y la ley de Dios y de la yglesia* (Medina del Campo, por Guillermo de Millis, 1556). 4.to. Biblioteca Nacional, Madrid. Biblioteca Universitaria, Salamanca. British Library. This is the third edition. The first edition was produced in Valladolid by Francisco Fernández de Córdoba in 1554, and the second edition in Seville by Martín Montesdoca in 1555. Pérez Pastor, *Medina del Campo*, p. 136, no. 128. Palau, 164443, 164444. Guerrero, no. 17. Rhodes, p. 132.

[910] Lobera de Ávila, Luis. *Libro delas quatro enfermedades cortesanos q̃ son Catarro. Gota arthetica Sciatica. Mal de piedra y d'Riñones τ Hijada. E mal de buas* (Toledo, en casa de Iuan de ayala, 1544). Folio. Biblioteca Nacional, Madrid. National Library of Medicine. Durling, no. 2831. Pérez Pastor, *Toledo*, p. 82, no. 202. Palau, 139424.

[911] Jiménez, Diego. *Enchiridion, o Manual de Doctrina christiana* (Antwerp, en casa de Martin Nucio, 1554). Biblioteca Nacional, Madrid. Palau, 124058. Guerrero, no. 15. Bataillon, p. CXV, no. 1324. The Spanish *Index* of 1559 condemned the "Manual de Doctrina Christiana, el qual esta impresso en principio de unas horas de nuestra señora en romance impressas en Medina del campo por Matheo del Canto, año de 1556 o de otra qualquiera impression... ." De Bujanda (V, p. 508). De Bujanda comments that the author is unknown, but this entry in the Junta inventory assigns authorship to Jiménez.

[912] This is the same title printed in Portugal (Lisbona, Germano Gallarde, 1552). Palau, 124058 note. Hispanic Society of America. Penney, p. 283.

[913] Augustinus, Aurelius, Saint. *Libro de las meditaciones y soliloquios y manual* (Anvers, Martin Nucio, 1550). 12.mo. Hispanic Society of America. Penney, p. 43.

[914] Orozco, Alonso de. *Comiença el libro llamado memorial d'amor sancto, hecho por vn religioso d'la hordẽ...d'... sancto Augustin... en el q̃l se tracta la manera como se a d'traer ñro redẽptor Jesu xpo. en el coraçõ siempre presente: por memoria continua de amor* (Seuilla ẽ casa de Antõ Iuarez, 1545). 4.to. Biblioteca Nacional, Madrid. Palau, 204437.

5 Marco Aurelio[915] in 8° 51		255
4 Muestra de la pena y gloria[916] in 8°	10	040
12 Milagros de la pena de Francia in 4to	25	300
2 Mar de historias[917] in fol. 68		136
10 Meditationes de S. Anselmo[918] in 4to	10	100
2 Morales de S. Gregorio[919] in fol. 544		1,088
2 Monte Calva[rio] o Siette palabras de Mondonedo[920] 8° Ant[uerpie]	85	170
3 Monte Calvario[921] in fol. 85		255
17 Meditationes de S. Augustin[922] in 8° 34		578

---

[915] Guevara, Antonio de. *Libro aureo de Marco Aurelio, emperador, y eloquentissimo orador*. This historical novel pretends to be a translation from an ancient manuscript (Maggs). It was much reprinted in the 16th century. Maggs, 438, describes editions by Juan Cromberger (Seville, 1533) and Sebastian Martinez (Alcalá de Henares, 1566). Rhodes (p. 92-93) lists British Library copies from Valladolid, Antwerp, Alcalá de Henares, Seville, Venice, Rome, and Madrid. It is most probably one of the octavo edtions of Cromberger (Seville, 1533, 1540, 1549). Griffin, Appendix One, no. 348, 434, 524.

[916] Mejía, Pedro. *Muestra de la pena y gloria perpetua: con que se alcança la bienauenturança: juntamēte con la declaraciō d'l pater noster. Apuntado por el mangifico señor Pedro Mexia vezino de la cibdad de Toledo* (Toledo en casa de Juan de Ayala, 1550). Small 8.vo. Biblioteca Nacional, Madrid. Palau, 167390. Pérez Pastor, *Toledo*, p. 998, no. 244.

[917] Pérez de Guzmán, Fernando. *Mar de istorias* (Valladolid por Diego de gumiel, 1512). Folio. British Library. Rhodes, p. 151. Palau, 221018.

[918] Anselm, Saint. *Meditaciones de San Anselmo* (Toledo, s.i., 1504). 4.to. Biblioteca Nacional, Madrid. *Catálogo colectivo*, A, 1573.

[919] Gregorius, I, the Great, Saint, pope, 540 (ca.)-604. *Los Morales de Sant Gregorio papa* (Sevilla, ca. 1530). Folio. Maggs, 434. The British Library has copies of the 1527 edition (Seuilla por Iacobo chromberger) and the 1534 edition (Seuilla, en casa del jurado Iuan varela d'salamanca). Rhodes, pp. 27-28.

[920] Guevara, Antonio de. *Libro llamado Monte Calvario* (Antwerp, en casa de Martin Nucio, 1550). 8.vo. British Library (2nd part). Palau, 110368.

[921] A folio edition of the two-volume *Libro llamado Monte caluario* was published by Villaquirán in Valladolid in 1545 and 1546; and in 1551 and 1552 Sebastián Martínez published it. Maggs, 447. The British Library has copies printed by Nutius (Envers, 1550) and Valladolid (1545, 1546). Rhodes, p. 93.

[922] Augustinus, Aurelius, Saint, bp. of Hippo. *Las meditaciones, Soliloquios y Manual del bienauēturado sant Augustin Obispo de Hypponia* (Medina del Campo, en la imprenta de Francisco del Canto, 1553). 8.vo. Pérez Pastor, *Medina del Campo*, p. 84, no. 95. Griffin describes two octavo edtions of this work printed by the Cromberger firm, one a very rare copy in the Biblioteca Pública de Évora (Siuilla enlas casas de Jacome Crōberger, 1546) and the other in 1550 (Seuilla enlas casas de Jacome Cromberger, 1550). (Griffin, Appendix One, no. 505, 543).

15 Mysterios de la missa[923] in 4to 20		300
4 Manual Christiano pp 45		180
12 Memorial de la Passion in 8° 25		300
13 Medidas del Romano[924] in 4to 34		442
2 Morgante libro primo[925] in fol. 119		238
10 Milagros de S. Isidoro in 4to 51		510
1 Milagros de Nuestra Señora de Monserate in 4to 68		068
5 Menordano in medicina[926] in fol. 25		125
2 Marco Aurelio[927] pp 51		102
1 Marco Aurelio in 8° Ant[uerpie][928] 187		187
3 Milagros del Sancto Crucifixo de Burgos[929] 34		102
4 Medicina Sevillana[930] in 4to 34		136
~~4 Muestra dela pena y gloria in 8°~~[931]		~~040~~

---

[923] Hernando de Talavera, Abp. of Granada, 1428?-1507. *Libro que trata de los sacratísimos misterios de la misa* (Seuilla, Juã Cröberger, 1541). 4.to. Biblioteca Pública, Évora. Griffin, Appendix One, no. 454.

[924] Sagredo, Diego de. *Medidas d'l Romano Vitruuio* (Toledo, en casa de Juan de Ayala, 1549). 4.to. Pérez Pastor, *Toledo*, p. 96, no. 240. There were earlier editions in Lisbon in 1541 and 1542. Palau, 284924 and 284925.

[925] Pulci, Luigi. *Libro primero de Morgante, Roldan y Reynaldos* (Sevilla, Juan Canalla, 1552). The British Library has another edition, *Libro del esforçado Morgãte* (Valēcia por Frãcisco diaz Romano, 1533). Folio. This is a translation of the Italian work, *Morgante maggiore*. Palau, 242098.

[926] Chirino de Cuenca, Alonso. *Tractado llamado menor daño de medicina* (Sevilla, Juan Cromberger, 1538). Folio. Salvá, 2695. Maggs, 237 (with illus.). Griffin, Appendix One, no. 412. There is a title page woodcut of Sts. Cosmas and Damian, physicians martyred ca. 303. The British Library has editions from Toledo (Hagenbach successor, 1505) and Seville (en las casas de Iacome Cröberger, 1547). Griffin, Appendix One, no. 509. All folios. Other Seville editions were published in 1505 (Penney, p. 133), and 1542(?) and 1550/1551 (Griffin, Appendix One, no. 466, 538). The National Library of Medicine has a 1513 folio edition published in Toledo. Durling, no. 958. Pérez Pastor, *Toledo*, p. 37, no. 61.

[927] Guevara, Antonio de. See footnote 912.

[928] Guevara, Antonio de. Antwerp editions of *Libro aureo de Marco Aurelio* were published by Ioannes Grapheus (1529), Iuan Steelsio (1545 and 1550), Martin Nucio (1550). Only Nucio's is in octavo. British Library. See also footnote 912.

[929] *Hystoria de como fue hallada la ymagen del sancto Crucifixo ... con algunos de sus miraglos* (Burgos, Juan de Junta, 1554). 8.vo. Biblioteca Nacional, Madrid. Palau, 115079. *Catálogo colectivo*, H, 506. The colophon reads " ... milagros del sancto Crucifixo de sancto Augustin de Burgos ... ."

[930] Juan, *de Aviñón, fl. 1358-1419. Seuillana medicina. Que trata el modo conservativo y curativo de los que abitan en la muy insigne ciudad de Sevilla* (Seuilla, en casa de Andres de Burgos, 1545). 4.to. The National Library of Medicine (Bethesda) and the British Library have copies. Rhodes, p. 106. Durling, no. 2637.

[931] See footnote 913.

INVENTARIO DE LOS LIBROS

/ vij,dcclxxxviij /   L. 7,788

5 Novellas de Boccatio[932] in fol. 153	765
7 Notas de Roque de huerta[933] 119	833
5 Norte de los estados[934] in 4to 51	255
4 Norte de Confessores in 8° 10	040
3 Natura angelica[935] in fol. 68	204

L. 2,097

/ ij,xcvij /

(f. 44)

9 obras de Savonarola[936] in 8° 51	459
2 officio del angel custodio[937] in 8° 6	012
3 Orlando Furioso[938] in 4to Ant[uerpie] 204	612

---

[932] Boccaccio, Giovanni. *Las cientnouellas de micer Iuan Bocacio ... Agora nueuamente impressas: corregidas y enmendadas* (Medina del Campo, por Pedro de Castro impressor: a costa de Iuã de espinosa, 1543). Folio. British Library. Huntingdon Library, San Marino. Other folio editions: Toledo, Juan de Villaquiran, 1524 (Pérez Pastor, *Toledo*, p. 50); Valladolid, Diego Fernández de Córdoba, 1539; Valladolid, Juan de Villaquiran, 1550. This work is on the Spanish *Index* of 1559. De Bujanda, V, pp. 509-10.

[933] Huerta, Roque de. *Recopilacion de notas de escripturas publicas.* (Salamanca, por Juan de Junta, 1551). Folio. Harvard Law School. Biblioteca Nacional, Madrid. Palau, 116656. This is a manual for notaries, giving models for contracts.

[934] Osuna, Francisco de. *Norte delos estados: En que se da regla de bivir alos Mãcebos: y alos Casados* (Burgos en casa de Juã de Junta, 1541). 4.to. Biblioteca Nacional, Madrid. Hispanic Society of America. Palau, 206841. Penney, p. 399. *Catálogo colectivo*, F, 1026. The Bibliothèque Nationale, Paris, also has a quarto edition published in Seville in 1531.

[935] Ximenes, Francesch, ca. 1340 - ca. 1409. *La natura angelica* (Burgos, Fadrique de Basilea, 1516). Folio. This may also be the folio edition of Miguel de Eguía, *La natura angelica: nuevamente impressa: emendada: e corregida* (Alcalá de Henares, en las casas de Miguel de Eguia, 1527). Folio. British Library. Columbia University. Boston Public Library. Hispanic Society of America. Penney, p. 194. Rhodes, p. 219. Palau, 85189, 85190.

[936] Savonarola, Girolamo. *Las obras que se hallan romançadas* (Anuers, en casa de Martin Nucio, c. 1549). 8.vo. The British Library and the Hispanic Society of America have copies. Penney, p. 507. Rhodes, p. 178.

[937] Griffin has described a slight octavo work printed in Seville by Juan Cromberger in 1535, *Officium angeli custodis*, but that work appears to be in Latin. Is it possible that the Cromberger press also issued a Spanish version, or that the Latin work was simply placed with the Spanish books? Griffin, Appendix One, no. 381.

[938] Ariosto, Ludovico. *Orlando Furioso*. Either the 1549 or the 1554 Antwerp edition in quarto from the press of Martín Nucio. The Spanish translation is by J. de Urrea. The British Library has a copy of the 1549 edition. Rhodes, p. 17. Palau, 16596, 16600.

5 Obras de Servantes[939] in 4to 51		255
2 obras de Horozco[940] in fol. 272		544
4 ordenancas del adelantamiento[941] in fol. 25		100
2 obras del duque de Gandia[942] in 8° 34		068
12 Orlando [Furioso][943] in 4to Toledo 170		2,040
9 oratorio del Toledano in 8° 10		090
1 oratorio de religiosos[944] in fol. 102		510
2 obras de Xenophon[945] in fol. 238		476
5 obras de Mena[946] in 8° Ant[uerpie] 102		510

---

[939] Cervantes de Salazar, Francisco. *Obras q̃ Francisco Ceruantes ha hecho, glosado, y traduzido. La primera es vn Dialogo de la dignidad del hombre... La segunda es el Appologia de la ociosidad y el trabajo, intitulado Labricio Poriundo, donde se trata con marauilloso estilo delos grandes males de la ociosidad, y por el contrario de los prouechos y bienes del trabajo* (Alcalá de Henares, en casa de Iuã de Brocar, 1546). 4.to. British Library. Biblioteca Nacional, Madrid. University of Illinois, Urbana. Martín Abad, p. 531, no. 359. Palau, 54065.

[940] Orozco, Alonso de. *Recopilacion de todas las obras que ha escrito el muy reuerẽdo padre fray Alõso d' Orozco* (Valladolid, en casa de Sebastian Martinez impressor, 1554). Folio. Palau, 204419, 204420.

[941] Spain. Laws. *Ordenanças cerca de los que han de hazer y guardar los alcaldes, & juezes de residencia de los tres adelantamientos de Burgos, y Leon, y Palencia, y los escriuanos, y abogados, y otros officiales, que siguen sus audiencias* (Medina del Campo, por Guillermo de Millis, 1555). Folio. Biblioteca Nacional, Madrid. Harvard Law School Library. Pérez Pastor, *Medina del Campo*, p. 134, no. 122. *Catálogo colectivo*, O, 285. Palau, 202562. An earlier edition was published by Brocar (Alcalá de Henares, en casa de Joan de Brocar, 1543). Folio. Palau, 202561.

[942] Francisco de Borja, Saint, 4. duque de Gandia. *Segunda parte de las obras* (Medina del Campo, Guillermo de Millis, 1552). 8.vo. Hispanic Society of America. Penney, p. 71. Another edition was published in Antwerp by Martín Nucio in 1556.

[943] Ariosto, Ludovico. *Orlando Furioso. De Lvdivico Ariosto nueuamente traduzido de beruo ad berbum del vulgar Toscano en el nuestro Castellano, por Hernando Alcocer* (Toledo, por Iuan Ferrer impressor, impressor de libros, 1550). 4.to. British Library. Rhodes, p. 18. Pérez Pastor, *Toledo*, p. 97, no. 242. Palau, 16598.

[944] Guevara, Antonio de, bp., d. 1545? *Oratorio de religiosos y exercicio de virtuosos* (Valladolid, Juan de Villaquiran, 1546; [and:] Caragoça, en casa de George Coci, 1543). Both folio. British Library. Maggs, 448. Rhodes, p. 93. Palau, 110336-110338. The first edition was published in Vallladolid by Villaquirán in 1542.

[945] Xenophon. *Las obras de Xenophon trasladadas de Griego en Castellano por ... Diego Gracian* (Salamanca, por Juan de Junta, 1552). Folio. British Library. Hispanic Society of America. Legrand, 141. Penney, p. 609. Rhodes, p. 218.

[946] Mena, Juan de. *Todas las obras del famosissimo poeta Ivan de Mena, glosadas por Fernan Nuñez* (Anvers, en casa de Martin Nucio, 1552). 8.vo. British Library. Palau, 162700.

INVENTARIO DE LOS LIBROS

651 ordenancas del Calçado de Burgos[947] 12	7,812
2 obras de Juan de Mena[948] in fol. 102	204
	L. 13,692

/ xiii,dcxcii /

151 Perla preciosa[949] pp 8	1,208
2 Processo Iudiciario in 4to 102	204
4 Problemas de Villalobos[950] in fol. 85	340
4 Problemas de la oration pp 6	024
20 Problemas de Jarava[951] in 8° 034	680
19 Prag[matica] de Cassa y Pesca[952] in fol. 20	380
8 Prag[matica] de brocados[953] 10	080

---

[947] Burgos. Laws. *Ordenanças que hablan cerca del Calçado y Corambre: hechas por la muy noble y mas leal ciudad de Burgos cabeça de Castilla* ([Burgos?] s.i., [1552?]). Folio. Biblioteca Nacional, Madrid. *Catálogo colectivo*, O, 287. Palau, 202753.

[948] Mena, Juan de. *Copilacion d' todas las obras del famosissimo poeta Juã de mena* (Toledo, en casa de Fernando de sancta catalina defunto, 1547). Folio. Pérez Pastor, *Toledo*, p. 91, no. 228. Maggs, 604 (with illus.). Other folio editions of the works of Juan de Mena were published in Seville by Varela (1528, 1534), and in Valladolid by Villaquirán (1536). Palau, 162695-162698.

[949] *Perla preciosa*. This small work is on the Spanish *Index* of 1559. The fairly large number of copies in the Junta inventory raises questions about whether the Junta firm financed the printing. If a copy could be found it would be interesting to examine the type founts to see if there are any similarities to Junta material. De Bujanda, V, p. 524.

[950] López de Villalobos, Francisco, 1473-1549. *Libro intitulado los problemas de Villalobos que tracta de cuerpos naturales y morales. Y dos dialogos de medicina. Y el tractado de las tres grandes. Y una cancion. Y la comedia de Amphytrion.* This was published in folio editions in Zamora (1543), Zaragoza (1544), and Sevilla (1550). British Library. National Library of Medicine. Rhodes, p. 120. Durling, no. 2858.

[951] Jarava, Juan de. *Problemas, o Preguntas problematicas, ansi de Amor, como naturales, y acerca del Vino: bueltas nuevamente de Latin en lengua Castellana, y un dialogo de Luciano, quae se dize Icaro Menippo* (Alcalá de Henares, en casa de Juan de Brocar, 1546). 8.vo. British Library. Palau, 123114. Rhodes, p. 102. Martín Abad, p. 531, no. 359. The Maggs catalogue says that this was intended for the amusement of students at the University of Alcalá. It includes a composition entitled *Alabança de la Pulga* ("In praise of the Flea").

[952] Spain. Laws. *Las prematicas y Ordenanças: que sus Magestades ordenaron eneste año de mill τ quinientos y cinquenta y dos dela orden que se ha de tener de aqui adelante en la Caça y Pesca* (Alcalá de Henares, en casa de Joan de Brocar defūto que sancta gloria aya, 1553). Folio. Palau, 235131. Palau also lists a 1552 edition of this which does not bear the name of printer or place of publication. Harvard Law School Library. Palau, 235127.

[953] Spain. Laws. *Las Prematicas y Ordenanças que sus Magestades ordenaron sobre trages, Brocados, Oro y Sedas* (Medina del Campo, por Francisco del Campo, a costa de Juan de medina, 1552). Folio. Pérez Pastor, *Medina del Campo*, p. 82, no. 92. Palau, 235126. Palau (235123) lists another edition with no name of publisher or place, dated 1552.

2 Pastoral de s. Gregorio[954] 17		034
2 Plutarcho contra las riquezas[955] 6		012
1 Perla preciosa[956] in 8° 8		008
5 Psalmi cum hymnis in 8° 51		255
14 Prag[maticas] del Reyno[957] in fol. 204		2,856
13 Psalmos in Prosa[958] in 8° 34		442
9 Paradoxas contra el Comun paresier[959] in 8°	34	306
5 Proverbios de Seneca[960] in fol. 85		425
4 Propaladia[961] in 4to 51		204

---

[954] Gregorius I, the Great, Saint, pope, ca.540-604. *Treynta y seys amonestaciones del Pastoral ... traduzidas d'latin en romāce* (Caragoça, por Diego hernādez, 1547). 8.vo. British Library. Rhodes, p. 91. *Catálogo colectivo*, G, 1547.

[955] Plutarch. *Contra la condicia delas riquezas* (Valladolid, Fernando de Cordoba, 1538). Palau, 229185.

[956] *Perla preciosa aora nuevamente impressa, en la ciudad de Baeça con otras oraciones.* Condemned, see footnote 946, 953. An octavo copy has survived in the Biblioteca Nacional, Madrid (R.34742). De Bujanda, V, p. 524. Palau mentions an octavo edition produced in Baeça in 1551.

[957] Spain. Laws. *Las pragmaticas del reyno. Recopilaciō de algūas bulas* .... Folio editions were published in Seville (por Iuan Varela, 1520), Valladolid (Juan de Villaquirán, 1540) and Toledo (en casa de Hernando de santa catalina, 1545; [and:] en casa de Juan ferrer, 1550). This may also be the compilation by Diego Pérez, *Pragmaticas y leyes hechas y recopiladas por mandado de los muy altos ... Principes* (Medina del cāpo, por Pedro de Castro, 1549). Folio. Pérez Pastor, *Medina del Campo*, p. 53, no. 68.

[958] This may be *Psalterio de Dauid, con las Paraphrases y breues declaraciones de Raynerio Snoy Goudano, agora nueuamente traduzido en lengua Castellana* (Anuers, en casa de Iuan Steelsio, 1555). 8.vo. British Library. Rhodes, p. 28.

[959] This is probably the work of Ortensio Lando condemned in the Spanish *Index* of 1559 under the heading "Paradoxas o sentencias fuera del comun parecer, traduzidas de italiano en castellano." See Paul Grendler, *Critics of the Italian world (1530-1560)* (Milwaukee, 1969), p. 226 and Brunet, *Manuel*, IV, col. 362. De Bujanda, V, pp. 523-24.

[960] Seneca (pseud.) *Proverbios de Seneca. Introduction por el doctor Pero Diaz de Toledo* ... (Medina del Campo, Adrian Ghemart, 1555 [on title page]; Guillermo de Millis, 1552 [colophon]). Folio, in red and black. Maggs, 961 (with illus.). The British Library also has earlier folio editions by Jacobo Cromberger (Sevilla, 1528 and 1535). Maggs, 961 (with illus.). Rhodes, pp. 179-80. Griffin, Appendix One, nos. 286, 386.

[961] Torres Naharro, Bartholomé de. *Propaladia de Bartolome de torres Naharro. Cōtienēse enla Propaladia. Tres lamentaciones Comedia calamita. de amor Comedia Aquilana. Una satira. Dialogo d'l nascimiēto Onze capitulos.* ... (Seuilla: en casa de Juan cromberger [1534]). 4.to. Hispanic Society of America. The author was a sympathizer of Erasmus and a proponent of church reform. This work is on the Spanish *Index* of 1559. A listing of the works of Torres Naharro is found in Joseph E. Gillet, *Propalladia and other works of Bartolomé de Torres Naharro*, 4 vols. (Bryn Mawr, Pa., 1943-61). There are three Spanish editions by the Cromberger press and one by Andrés de Burgos in Seville, another in Toledo (no copy known) and one by Nutius in Antwerp (12.mo), all before 1550. De Bujanda, V, pp. 525-26. Griffin, Appendix One, no. 202, 264, 374. Pérez Pastor, *Toledo*, p. 71.

INVENTARIO DE LOS LIBROS

1 Propaladia⁹⁶² in fol.	51	051
1 Proverbios de Ynygo Lopez⁹⁶³ in fol.	10	010
11 Philosophia moral en coplas⁹⁶⁴ in fol.	25	275
1 Preguntas del Almirante libro primo⁹⁶⁵	85	085
24 Psalmos de Jarava⁹⁶⁶ in 8vo	34	<u>816</u>
	L.	8,695

(f. 45)

1 Preguntas del Almirante libro 2ᵈᵒ ⁹⁶⁷	85	085
1 Palmerin de Inglaterra libro 2ᵈᵒ ⁹⁶⁸ in fol.	68	068

---

[962] Ibid. ibid. ([Sevilla] por Jacobo cromberger [?] aleman y Juan cromberger [1526]). Folio. Biblioteca de Catalunya, Barcelona. See footnote 958. Griffin, Appendix One, no. 264, 202.

[963] López de Mendoza, Iñigo, *Marquis de Santillana*. *Prouerbios de dõ Iñigo lopez de mendoça*. A folio edition was published in Toledo by Gaspar de Ávila in 1525 and by Juan de Ayala in 1537. Pérez Pastor, *Toledo*, p. 53, no. 107; p. 72, no. 170. Other folio editions were printed in Seville by Juan Varela in 1526 and by the Crombergers in 1509, 1512, 1516, 1519, 1530, 1533, 1538 and 1549. Griffin, Appendix One, nos. 39, 79, 154, 187, 309, 347, 418 and 519.

[964] Castilla, Francisco de. *De los tratados de philosophia moral en coplas* (Sevilla, en casa de Andres d' Burgos, 1546). Folio. Biblioteca Nacional, Madrid. *Catálogo colectivo*, C, 1059. Palau, 47983.

[965] Escobar, Luis de. *Las qvatrocientas respvestas a otras tātas preguntas, q̃ el yllustrissimo señor dõ Fradrique enrriquez: Almirante de Castilla y otras personas ... embiaron*. Two parts. Nucio produced editions in Antwerp in 1546 [?], 1550 [?] and Francisco de Cordoua printed others in Valladolid in 1545 (first edition) and 1550. Two Zaragoza editions were produced in 1545 (Caragoça, por Diego Hernādez; [and:] Caragoça, en casa de Jorge Coci). Hispanic Society of America. Palau, 81064-81068.

[966] Jarava, Hernando de, trans. *Lo que en este libro esta traduzido de latin en lengua castellana con una breve exposicion es lo siguiente: Los siete psalmos penitenciales. Los quinze psalmos del canticungrado. Las lamentaciones de jeremias. Lo qual todo la muy poderoso y christianissima señora Leoñor Reyna de Francia mando ansi traduzir y componer* (enueres, en casa de Martin Nucio, 1543). 8.vo. British Library. The Spanish *Index* of 1559 condemns "Psalmos penitenciales y el Canticum grado y las lamentaciones, romançadas por el Maestro Iarava, o qualquier otro autor, o sin el." De Bujanda, V, p. 529. Rhodes, p. 28. Palau, 68776.

[967] See footnote 962.

[968] Moraes, Francisco de. *Libro segundo del muy esforçado Cavallero Palmerin de inglaterra hijo del rey dõ Duardos enel qual se prosiguen y han fin los ;muy dulces amores que tuvo con la Ynfanta Polinarda* (Toledo, en casa de Fernando de santa Catalina defunto, a costa de Diego Ferrer mercader de libros, 1548). Folio. British Library. Biblioteca de Catalunya, Barcelona. Österreichische Nationalbibliothek, Vienna. Rhodes, p. 147. Pérez Pastor, *Toledo*, p. 91, no. 229. Palau, 210451. Eisenberg, p. 83-84. The first volume was published in 1547. The colophon in vol. 2 reads "A costa de Diego Ferrer mercader de libros."

SIXTEENTH CENTURY SPANISH BOOKSTORE

137 Prag[matica] del pan[969] in fol. 2		274
19 Pragma[tica] de los panos[970] 34		646
4 Pragma[tica] de Valladolid año 1548[971] 51		204
100 Pragma[tica] de las lanas[972] in fol. 12		1,200
73 Pragma[tica] de los herederos[973] 12		876
127 Prag[matica] de ladrones[974] 8		1,016
3 Pragma[tica] de arrendadores 17		051
18 Prag[matica] de telas de oro y plata 10		180
176 Prag[matica] de lanas y panos[975] 25		4,400
23 Prag[matica] de bonetes panos y sombrero[976] 25		575

---

[969] Spain. Laws. *Pregmatica del pan* [Alcalá de Henares, Juan de Brocar, 1539?]. Folio. Biblioteca Nacional, Madrid. Martín Abad, p. 465, no. 301. If Martín Abad is correct in his estimate of the date, the inventory copy is probably a later edition, judging by the large number of copies. Palau, 235085.

[970] Spain. Laws. This may be *La pregmatica d'los paños* (Valladolid, a costa de Francisco Lopez, 1549). Folio. Palau, 235097.

[971] Spain. Laws. *Las Pragmaticas y Capitulos que su Magestad del Emperador y Rey nuestro señor hizo en las cortes que se hicie con don Phelipe ... en Valladolid ... en 1548* (Valladolid, por Francisco Fernandez de Cordova, 1549). Folio. Biblioteca Nacional, Madrid. *Catálogo colectivo*, P, 2886. Palau, 235094.

[972] Spain. Laws. *Las Prematicas ... de como se han de comprar las lanas y a que son obligados los que las compraren y sacaren del reyno* (Alcalá de Henares, en casa de Juan de Brocar que santa gloria aya, [1552]). Folio. Martín Abad, pp. 579-80, no. 401, 402. Palau, 235114-235116.

[973] I have not found a law relating to *herederos* and wonder if this could have been mistaken for *herradores*? There are copies in the Biblioteca Nacional, Madrid, of *Pragmatica, y aranzel nueuamente hecho ... por donde los herradores de las ciudades ...* (s.l., s.i., 1556) and an earlier edition, *Prematica y aranzel ... por dõde los herradores ...* (s.l., si.i, 1531?). Folio. *Catálogo colectivo*, P, 2770, 2771. Palau, 235080, 235089, 235092, 235132-II.

[974] Spain. Laws. *La prematica que su Magestad ha mãdado hazer este año de MDLii de la pena que han de auer los ladrones y rufianes y vagamundos y para que sean castigados los bolgazones ansi hombres como mugeres y los esclauos de qualquier edad ...* (Alcalá de Henares, en casa de Iuan de Brocar defuncto, 1552, 1553). Folio. Hispanic Society of America. Harvard Law School Library. Martín Abad, pp. 594, 608, nos. 419, 439. Palau, 235124, 235125.

[975] Spain. Laws. *Leyes, ordenanças prematicas y declaraciones delas ordenãças antiguas q̃ hablã del obraje delas lanas τ paños* (Salamanca, [Juan de Junta] 1543). Folio. Biblioteca Nacional, Madrid. British Library. Rhodes, p. 184. *Catálogo colectivo*, L, 663. Palau, 137442.

[976] Spain. Laws. *Ordenanças sobre el obraje delos paños. Lanas: Bonetes: τ sombreros. Nueuamente hechas. De como se han de hazer, teñir y vender assi los paños estrangeros como los que en estos reynos se hizieren* (Alcalá de Henares en casa de Juan d'Brocar, 1552). Folio. Indiana University. An earlier edition was done in Toledo by Juan de Ayala, 1544. Biblioteca Nacional, Madrid. Pérez Pastor, *Toledo*, p. 83.

INVENTARIO DE LOS LIBROS

  40 Prag[matica] de Valladolid de vestido año 1547   6   240
  18 Prag[matica] de Valladolid año 1537[977]   68   1,224
  36 Prefacios in fol.   10   360
  13 Prefacios toledanos   10   130
    4 Prag[matica] de obrase de panos[978]   25   100
  35 Papelones de Flandres   14   490
100 Papelones d'España   10   1,000
  50 Prag[matica] de oro y brocados[979]   10   <u>500</u>
                                                              13,619
              / xx,cccxiiij /   <u>8,695</u>
                                                         L. 22,314

    5 Questiones del Tostado[980] in 8°   68   340
  84 Questiones del Tostado[981] in fol.   85   7,140
    4 Questiones del Templo[982] in 8°   34   136

---

[977] Spain. Laws. *Las Pregmaticas y Capitulos que su Magestad del Emperador y Rey nuestro señor hizo en las cortes de Valladolid el año de [1537]. Con la declaracion que sobre las trages y sedas hizo* (Medina del Campo, por Pedro de Castro, 1545). Folio. Archivo Histórico Nacional, Madrid. Harvard Law School Library. Pérez Pastor, *Medina del Campo*, p. 42, no. 49. *Catálogo colectivo*, P, 2885. There are also earlier editions in Valladolid (Diego Fernández de Córdova) and Cuenca (Guillermo Reymon), both in 1538. Biblioteca del Palacio, Madrid. Harvard Law School Library.

[978] Spain. Laws. *La pregmatica del obraje de los paños* (Alcalá de Henares, en casa de Juan de Brocar defunto, 1552; [and:] Toledo, en casa de Juan de Ayala para Salzedo librero vezino de Alcala, 1552) or *Leyes, ordenanças prematicas y declaraciones delas ordenãças antiguas q̃ hablã del obraje delas lanas τ paños* (Salamanca [Juan de Junta?] 1543). All folio. Palau, 235086, 235102, 235103, 235104, 235128, 235129.

[979] Spain. Laws. *Las pregmaticas y ordenanças que sus Magestades ordenaron sobre los trajes: brocados: oros: y sedas* (Alcalá de Henares, en casa de Juan de Brocar, 1552). Folio. British Library. Rhodes, p. 190. Palau, 235126. The British Library has another impression of this by Brocar, and another edition by Francisco del Canto in Medina del Campo.

[980] Tostado, Alonso. *Las XIIII Questiones del Tostado, a las quatro dellas por marauilloso estilo recopila toda la sagrada escriptura* (En Anvers, a costa de Martin Nucio, 1551). 8.vo. *Catálogo colectivo*, T, 1439.

[981] Tostado, Alonso. *Libro intitulado las catorze questiones del Tostado*, Burgos, [Juan de Junta?] 1545. Folio. Biblioteca Nacional, Madrid. Hispanic Society of America. British Library. Palau, 146767. Penney, p. 564. Rhodes, p. 206

[982] Vergara, Juan de. *Tratado de las ocho questiones del tẽplo* (Toledo, en casa de Ioan Ferrer, 1552). 8.vo. British Library. Rhodes, p. 215. Vergara was a leading Spanish pro-Erasmian and was tried for heresy by the Office of the Inquisition in Toledo in the early 1530s. For a brief account of his accusation, arrest and imprisonment by the Inquisition, see Henry Charles Lea, *A History of the Inquisition in Spain* (New York, 1906-07; reprint New York, 1966), vol. 3, pp. 416-418.

15 Question y carcel de amor[983] 51		765
1 Quadragesimal de Gabriel Vaca[984] in fol. 119		119
4 Quaderno de alcavalas[985] 51		204
7 Quaderno de leyes[986] 51		357
8 Querella de la paz[987] in 8° 25		200
1 Question de amor[988] in 4to 25		025
		L. 9,286

/ ix,cclxxxvj /

---

[983] *Question de amor. Y carcel de amor* (Enueres, en el unicornio doro por industria de Martin Nucio, 1546). 8.vo. Palau, 243462. The anonymous *Questión de amor* is bound with the *Carcel de amor* of Diego de San Pedro in several editions. This may also be the edition produced in Paris (en casa de Hernando Caldera y Claudio Caldera, 1548); in Zaragoza (?) ([Stevan G. de Nagera?] 1551) or the later Antwerp edition (Martin Nucio, 1556). Hispanic Society of America. Penney, p. 160. Palau, 243463-243466. The first known edition is that of Diego de Gumiel in Valencia, 1513. British Library. Whinnom, p. 69.

[984] Vaca, Gabriel. *Libro muy prouechosso para todo fiel christiano. Intitulado Sermonario Quadragesimal Medicinal* (Valladolid, en cassa d' Sebastiã Martinez, 1553). Folio. Biblioteca Nacional, Madrid. *Catálogo colectivo*, V, 2.

[985] Spain. Laws. *Quaderno de alcavalas*. This may be the 1554 Salamanca edition by Cánova or the earlier Junta edition (Salamāca, por Juan de Junta impressor de libros, 1543). The Junta firm also published an edition in Burgos, 1529. Folio. Biblioteca Nacional, Madrid. Library of Congress. Gil Ayuso, nos. 56, 102. Palau, 65529, 242547, 242549.

[986] Spain. Laws. *Quaderno d'las leyes y prematicas reales fechas en las cortes ... de Madrid* (Alcalá de Henares, en casa de Juan de Brocar, 1546). Folio. British Library. Hispanic Society of America. Martín Abad, p. 524, no. 356. This could also be *Quaderno de las leyes y nueuas decisiones hechas y ordenadas en la ciudad de Toro sobre las dudas de derecho...* (Medina del Campo, por Pedro de Castro, 1546). Folio. Harvard Law School Library.

[987] Erasmus, Desiderius. *Tractado de las querellas de la Paz, compuesto por Erasmo Roterodamo varón doctissimo. Con otros dos tractados que escrivió el Papa Pío ...* (Alcalá de Henares, en casa de Miguel de Eguia, 1529). 8.vo. Bibliothèque Nationale, Paris. Bibliothèque Mazarine, Paris. Bayerische Staatsbibliothek, Munich. Bataillon, p. LIX, no. 575. Palau, 80357. Martín Abad, p. 373, no. 208. This is on the Spanish *Index* of 1559 under "Querella de la paz, de Erasmo, en romance." De Bujanda, V, p. 531. The number of copies in the inventory seems high for a publication of this date, but I have not identified a later octavo edition.

[988] *Questión de amor*. Quarto editions of this work were printed in Alcalá de Henares (en casa de Juan de Brocar, 1540), Lisbon (Luys Rodríguez, 1540), Medina del Campo (por Pedro de Castro, a costa de Juan de Espinosa mercader, 1544) and Zaragoza (en casa de George coci por Pedro Bernuz, 1548). Martín Abad, p. 471, no. 310. Palau, 243458, 243460, 243461.

47 Refranes glosados[989] in 8° 5		235
12 Reglas de S. Augustin in 8° 17		204
19 Repertorio de tienpos[990] in 8° 17		323
7 Regla de la confradia de nombre de Dios 2		014
12 Regimiento de salud[991] in fol. 85		1,020
4 Regimiento del alma[992] pp 10		040
5 Rromances de Sevilla pp 51		255
2 Rromances pp 51		102
47 Repertorio de Caminos[993] pp 8		<u>376</u>
	L.	2,569

(f. 46)

38 Reprobacion de astrologia judiciaria[994] 8° 17		646
8 Relacion de las yndias in 4to 25		200

---

[989] The British Library owns copies of two editions of *Refranes glosados*: [Burgos? c. 1530, Juan de Junta] and [Burgos, Juan de Junta?] 1541. The work was earlier published by Alonso de Melgar in 1524. Rhodes, p. 162. Palau, 253484 note, and 253485.

[990] Li, Andrés de. *Repertorio d'los tiempos: el mas copioso que hasta agora se ha impresso* (Toledo, en casa de Fernādo de santa catherina imprensor de libros, 1546). 8.vo. Pérez Pastor, *Toledo*, p. 87, no. 216. Latassa and Palau cite an edition of this work published by Juan de Junta in Burgos, 1531 but no copy of that edition appears to have survived. Griffin describes a 1510, and a ca. 1514 edition by Jacobo Cromberger and a 1529 edition by Juan Cromberger in Seville. Griffin, Appendix One, nos. 51, 109, 308. Maggs, 917, describes another work of the same title by Sancho de Salaya, *Repertorio de tiempos nuevamente corregido* (Granada, 1542). The British Library has an octavo edition of Juan Alemany, *Lunario: o repertorio de los tiempos* (Valencia, en casa de Iuā Nauarro, 1553). Rhodes, p. 5.

[991] Lobera de Ávila, Luis. *Libro del regimiento de la salud, y de la esterilidad de los hombres y mugeres, de las enfermedades de los niños...* (Valladolid, en casa de Sebastian martinez, 1551). Folio. British Library. Rhodes, p. 116. Palau, 139429.

[992] I have not found a small-format copy of this work. See footnote 993.

[993] Villuga, Pedro Juan. *Repertorio de todos los caminos de España* (Medina del Campo por Pedro de Castro, a costa de Juan de Spinosa, 1545). 16.mo. British Library. Hispanic Society of America. Penney, p. 601. See also Alberto Marcos Martín, *Auge y declive de un nucleo mercantil y financieor de Castilla la vieja* (Valladolid: Univ. de Valladolid, 1978), pp. 19-20.

[994] Savonarola, Girolamo. *Reprobacion de la astrologia judiciaria o divinatoria* (Salamanca, en la officina de Juan de Junta, 1546). 8.vo. Biblioteca Nacional, Madrid. British Library. Palau, 261762. Rhodes, p. 163.

8 Repertorio de Cortes[995] in fol.	85			680
126 Resmas y una mano de menudencia		476		60,000
4 Regimiento del alma[996] in 8º	10			040
				61,566
/ lx,cxxxv /				2,569
				L. 64,135
24 Soliloquios de Bernal Dias[997] pp	10			240
8 Superstitiones de Cyruelo[998] in 4to	34			272
4 Soliloquios de Bernal Dias[999] in 8º	15			060
1 Sergas de Esplandian[1000] in fol.	68			068
2 Sphera[1001] in rro[man]ce in 4to	51			102
15 Sermones de la passion in 8º	15			225

---

[995] Spain. Laws. *Repertorio de todas las prematicas y capitulos de cortes hechos por su Magestad desde el año de mil y quinientos y veynte y tres hasta el año de [1544]* (Medina del Campo, por Pedro de Castro, a costa de Guillelmo de Miles y Ioan Pedro, 1547). An updated edition was published in 1551. Folio. Biblioteca Nacional, Madrid. Pérez Pastor, *Medina del Campo*, p. 44, no. 55; p. 72, no. 78. *Catálogo colectivo*, R, 674, 675. Palau, 235100. The compiler of this work was Andrés Martínez de Burgos.

[996] Horozco, Alonso de. *Regimiento del alma. Compuesto por vn padre de la orden de sant Augustin dela prouincia de España de la obseruancia* (Valladolid: en casa d'Sebastiã Martinez, 1551). 8.vo. British Library. Rhodes, p. 144.

[997] Díaz del Castillo, Bernal, 1496-1584. No copy seems to have survived.

[998] Ciruelo, Pedro. *Reprouacion delas supersticiones y hechizerias. Libro ... el qual compuso y escrivio el Reverendo maestro Ciruelo ... y agora de nuevo lo ha revisto y corregido: y aun le ha añadido algunas mejorias. Con sus acotaciones por las margenes* (Sevilla, Andres de Burgos, 1547). 4.to. National Library of Medicine. Durling, no. 964. Other quarto editions were published by Pedro de Castro (Salamanca, 1538, 1539, 1541 and 1547); by Pedro Tovans (Salamanca, 1540); by Juan de Brocar (Alcalá de Henares, 1547); and by Juan de Cánova (Salamanca, 1556). Ruiz Fidalgo, nos. 53, 57, 66, 72, 77. Martín Abad, p. 543, no. 369. This is a condemnation of black magic, necromancy, divination, the occult.

[999] See footnote 994.

[1000] Juan de Junta published a folio edition of *Las sergas de Esplandian hijo de Amadis de gaula* (Book V of *Amadís*) in Burgos, 1526. Biblioteca de Catalunya, Barcelona. Eisenberg, p. 43.

[1001] Sacro Bosco, Johannes de. *Tractado de la Sphera qve compvso el doctor Ioannes de Sacrobvsto con muchas additiones. Agora nueuamente traduzido de Latin en lengua Castellana por el Bachiller Hieronymo de Chaves* (Seville, Juan de Leon, 1545). 4.to. British Library. Maggs, 966 (with illus.). Rhodes, p. 173.

3 Sylenos de Erasmo[1002] in [blank] 10		030
21 Sueno de Feliciano[1003] in 4 ^{to} 2		042
1 Summa de Virtudes in 4 ^{to} 15		015
3 Solis mundo in fol. 170		510
2 Salustio in fol. 25		050
12 Salustio[1004] in 4 ^{to} 25		300
1 Summa de geographia[1005] in fol. 51		051
15 Sosiego del anima[1006] in 4 ^{to} 10		150
5 Siette Psalmos con glosa[1007] in 8° 25		125
8 Summa de philosophia natural[1008] in 4 ^{to} 25		200
1 Summa de illustres varones[1009] in fol. 375		375
2 Sylva de varia lection[1010] in fol. 153		306

[1002] Erasmus, Desiderius. *Silenos de Alcibiades compuestos por ... doctor Erasmo.* This is on the Spanish *Index* of 1559. De Bujanda, V, pp. 541-42. It may be the octavo edition of Martín Nucio (En Anvers, en casa de Martin Nucio, 1555). An earlier quarto edition was produced by Jorge Costilla (Valencia, 1529). Biblioteca Nacional, Madrid. Hispanic Society of America. Penney, p. 186. Palau, 80358, 80358 note. Bonilla, pp. 460-462.

[1003] Silva, Feliciano de. *Sueño de Feliciano de Silua enel qual le fueron representadas las excelencias del amor* ([Salamanca, Juan de Junta?] 1544). 4.to. British Library. Rhodes, p. 182. Ruíz Fidalgo, no. 182. Palau, 313281.

[1004] Sallustius Crispus, Caius. *Salustio Cathilinario τ Jugurgurta. Cõ glosa en romance. Nueuamente impresso* (Medina del Cāpo, por Pedro de Castro a costa de Juan de Espinosa, 1548). 4.to. Pérez Pastor, *Medina del Campo*, p. 53, no. 65.

[1005] Fernández de Enciso, Martín. *Suma de geografía q̄ trata de todas las partidas τ prouincias del mundo* (Seuilla, por Juã crōberger, 1519, 1530). Folios. British Library. Hispanic Society of America. Rhodes, p. 77. Griffin, Appendix One, no. 195, 313. Palau, 88433, 88434.

[1006] Fuensalida, Francisco de. *Breue summa llamada Sossiego y descanso del anima* (Alcalá de Henares, en casa d'Ioan de Brocar, 1541). 4.to. British Library. Biblioteca Nacional, Madrid. Martín Abad, p. 487, no. 325. Palau, 95254.

[1007] See footnote 963.

[1008] Fuentes, Alonso de. *Summa de philosophia natural, enla qual assi mismo se tracta de astrulugia y astronomia, e otras sciencias* (Seuilla en casa de Iuã de Leõ, 1547). 4.to. British Library. Rhodes, p. 83. Palau, 95383.

[1009] Sedeño, Juan. *Summa de varones illustres; en la qual se cõtienen muchos dichos, sentēcias, y grandes hazañas y cosas memorables de doscientos emperadores, reyes y capitanes que ha habido en todas las naciones* (Medina del Campo, Diego Fernández de Córdova, 1551). Folio. Philosophical Society of America. Houghton Library, Harvard University. Pérez Pastor, *Medina del Campo*, p. 73, no. 82. Palau, 305688.

[1010] Mejía, Pedro. *Silua de varia lecion* (Valladolid, en casa de Iuan de Villaquirã, 1551). Folio. British Library. Rhodes, p. 134. The Cromberger firm produced folio editions in Seville in 1540, 1542, 1543 and 1548. Griffin, Appendix One, nos. 442, 459, 476 and 516.

3 Sol de Complativos (sic)[1011] in 8° 25		075
7 Sermones de S. Bernardo[1012] in 4to 34		238
2 Sermon de la Madalena[1013] in 8° 20		040
500 Sucesso de Inglaterra 1		500
18 Sermon de Chrisosthomo in 8° 10		180
7 Syliceo sobre el pater noster rro[man]ce[1014] in 8° 40		280
		L. 4,434

/ iiij,cmxxxiiij /

12 Triumphos de Petrarcha[1015] in 4to qqto. 153		1,836
2 Titelman de los mysterios de la missa[1016] 153		306
160 Thesoro de devocion pp 10		1,600
20 Tratado de oracion de Erasmo[1017] in 8° 8		160
17 Thesoro de misericordia[1018] in 4to 68		1,156
10 Tractado de vendemmia in 8° 6		060

[1011] Hugo de Balma, 13th cent. *Sol de contemplatiuos* (Toledo, Juan Varela de Salamanca, 1514). 8.vo. Houghton Library, Harvard University. Palau, 22460.

[1012] Bernard, Saint, abbot of Clairvaux. *Sermones*. Quarto editions of the Sermones were published in Seville by Juan Varela de Salamanca (1515); in Logroño by Arnao Guillen de Brocar (1511) and by Miguel de Eguia (1529); and in Valladolid by Arnao Guillen de Brocar (1519).

[1013] Jiménez, Diego. *Sermon de la Magdalena* (Enveres, Martinus Nutius], 1554). This was printed with the author's *Enchiridion, o manual de Doctrina christiana*. Palau, 124058.

[1014] Martinus Silicaeus, Joannes Blasius, Cardinal, 1486-1557. *Syliceo sobre el pater noster*. 8.vo. I have not found a copy of this.

[1015] See footnote 900. This edition appears to be distinguished from the other quarto by the inclusion of a commentary ("qqto.").

[1016] Tittelmans, Franciscus, 1502-1537. The work in the inventory appears to be a translation of *Tractatus mysteriorum missae* which was published in Lyons in 1550 and in Paris (Parisiis, apud F. Regnault, 1545). I have not found a copy of the Spanish version. Baudrier, IV, p. 247.

[1017] Erasmus, Desiderius. *Tratado de la oracion y forma que todo christiano deve seguir compuesto por Erasmo Rotherodamo*. This appears on the 1559 Spanish *Index*, under the heading "Modus orandi Deum, tam latino quam vulgari sermone" and, in the Spanish books section, under "Manera de orar de Erasmo, en romance y en latin y en otra qualquier lengua vulgar." De Bujanda, pp. 348, 507-08. The Spanish translation is probably the 1546 edition of Andrés de Burgos of Seville. Sebastian Gryphius published a Latin edition in Lyons in 1529 and Froben in Basel in 1524. De Bujanda notes that the only known copy of the Spanish edition (in the Bayerische Staatsbibliothek, München), was destroyed during World War II.

[1018] Toro, Gabriel de. *Thesoro de misericordia diuina y humana* (Salamanca, por Juan de Junta, impressor de libros, 1548). 4.to. Palau, 334676. Hispanic Society of America. Biblioteca Nacional, Madrid. British Library. Penney, p. 561. Maggs, 1022. Rhodes, p. 83.

INVENTARIO DE LOS LIBROS

148 Tratado de quentas de Castillo[1019] in 4to   17   2,516
                                                       L. 7,634

(f. 47)

1 Tractado del asino in 4to   10   010
4 Tratado de la vida de Christo[1020] pp 25   100
12 Tratado de censos[1021] in fol.   34   408
15 Tractado de cambios[1022] in 4to   25   375
5 Tebayda comedia[1023] in 4to   25   125
1 Tostado sobre Eusebio[1024] in fol.   1,020   1,020
6 Tractado de Vita Christi in 8°   34   204
23 Tratado de indulgentias[1025] in 8°   10   230
3 Triumphos de Petrarcha[1026] in fol.   153   459

[1019] Castillo de Villasante, Diego del. *Tratado de cuentas* (Salamanca, por Juan de Junta, impressor de libros, 1542 and 1551). 4.to. Biblioteca Nacional, Madrid. British Library. Folger Shakespeare Library. Maggs, 157. Palau, 48068 note, 48069. Rhodes, p. 48.

[1020] The Spanish *Index* of 1559 condemns the "Tractado de la vida de Iesu Christo, con los mysterios del Rosario en metro," a work by Alonso Traspinedo. De Bujanda, V, p. 546, no. 593a. See also Martín Abad, p. 524, no. 355, in connection with a work of similar title by Pedro de la Vega which was condemned in 1598 (Alcalá de Henares [Juan de Brocar] 1545). No surviving copy known.

[1021] Pizarro, Diego. *Tractado sobre los Censos. Tractado mvy necessario y provechoso, a las consciencias, sobre los censos al quitar, & otros* (Vendense en Medina del Campo, en casa de Gulielmo de Milis, 1551). Folio. Biblioteca Nacional, Madrid. *Catálogo colectivo*, P, 1579. This is merely the 1548 edition printed in Guadalupe by Francisco Diaz, with a new title page.

[1022] Saravia de la Calle. *Instrucion de Mercaderes muy provechosa ... Tambien ay otro tractado de Cambios en el qual se tracta de los cambios licitos y reprovados* (Medina del Campo, Pedro de Castro, 1544). 4.to. The Hispanic Society and the British Library have copies of this and the 1547 reprint. Maggs, 955. Penney, p. 506. *Rara Arithmetica*, p. 229. Rhodes, p. 178. First edition.

[1023] *Siguese la comedia llamada Thebayda* (Seville, Andrés de Burgos, 1546). 4.to. Palau, 331378.

[1024] Tostado, Alonso, bp. d. 1455. *Tostado sobre el eusebio*. A two-volume folio edition was published in Salamanca by Hans Gysser in 1506-07. Hispanic Society of America. Penney, p. 565. Palau, 146759-146763.

[1025] This may be *Tratado muy prouechoso ... delas indulgencias, y perdones* by Juan de Argomanas (Salamāca en casa d' Juā de Junta, 1547). 8.vo. Biblioteca de Catalunya, Barcelona. Biblioteca Universitaria, Oviedo. Palau, 16142. *Index Aureliensis*, 107.257.

[1026] Juan Varela printed a folio edition of Petrarch's *Triumphos* in Seville in 1526. British Library. Houghton Library, Harvard University. Palau, 224254. Arnao guillen de Brocar published the first Spanish edition, in folio, in Alcalá de Henares, 1512. British Library. Hispanic Society of America. Palau, 224253.

14 Tratado de re publica[1027] in fol. 10		140
2 Tratado de rieptos[1028] in 4to 6		012
1 Triumpho de los apostolos[1029] in fol. 25		025
9 Triumphos de la +[1030] 25		225
2 Tratado de oracion[1031] de Porras 10		020
12 Theorica de virtudes[1032] in 4to 15		180
2 Tractado de re militari[1033] in fol. 34		068
4 Thesoro de angeles[1034] in 4to 34		136
1 Tesoro de la passion[1035] in fol. 15		015
3 Tesoro de virtudes[1036] in 4to 25		075
1 Tratado del sacramento in 8° 6		006
2 Tullio de officiis rro[man]ce[1037] pp 68		136

[1027] Castrillo, Alonso de, fl. 1521. *Tractado de republica cō otras hystorias* (Burgos, Alonso de Melgar, 1521). Hispanic Society of America. Penney, p. 105. Palau, 48506.

[1028] Valera, Diego de. *Tratado delos rieptos τ desafios ... Cirimonial de principes* ([Valencia: Juan Viñao, c. 1520]). 4.to. British Library. Rhodes, p. 210. Palau, 348608.

[1029] Ludolphus de Saxonia, 14th cent. The University of Oviedo has a copy of *Los doze triumphos de los doze apostolos* (Sevilla, Juan Varela, 1521) which they attribute to Ludolphus de Saxonia. I do not know of another edition of this work. *Catálogo colectivo*, L, 1627.

[1030] Savonarola, Girolamo. *El triumpho de la cruz d' Xp̄o alias la verdad d' la fee* (Valladolid, por Francisco Fernandez de Cordova, 1548). 8.vo. Biblioteca Nacional, Madrid. *Catálogo colectivo*, S, 692, 693.

[1031] Porras, Antonio de. *Tratado de la oraciō q. se diuide en tres partes* (Alcalá de Henares, Por Juan de Brocar, 1552). 4.to. Biblioteca Nacional, Madrid. Biblioteca del Monasterio de San Lorenzo, El Escorial. Palau, 232997. Martín Abad, p. 576, no. 398.

[1032] Castilla, Francisco de. *Theorica de virtudes en coplas y con cōmento* (Zaragoza, por Agostin Millan, 1552). 4.to. Hispanic Society of America. Penney, p. 101. Palau, 47981.

[1033] Salazar, Diego de. *Tratado de re militari* ([Alcalá de Henares] en casa de Miguel de Eguya, 1536). Folio. British Library. Rhodes, p. 173. Martín Abad, p. 437, no. 274. Palau, 286503. This is Machiavelli's *Arte de guerra* with minor changes.

[1034] Evia, Francisco de. *Thesoro de los Angeles* (Astorga, por industria ... Agostin de paz, 1547). 4.to. British Library. The Spanish *Index* of 1559 condemns this devotional work. De Bujanda, V, p. 545. Palau, 84826.

[1035] Li, Andrés de. *Tesoro de la Passion sacratissima de Nuestro Redēptor* (Seuilla, Impressa por Jacobo Cromberger, 1517). Folio. Rosenwald Collection, Library of Congress. Griffin, Appendix One, no. 171. Palau, 137663.

[1036] Isla, Alonso de la. *Libro llamado Thesoro de virtudes muy vtil e copioso* (Medina del Campo, por Pedro de Castro impressor de libros, 1543). 4.to. Hispanic Society of America. Penney, p. 276. Pérez Pastor, *Medina del Campo*, p. 24, no. 34. Palau, 121831.

[1037] Cicero, Marcus Tullius. *Libros de Marco Tulio Ciceron, en que tracta delos Officios ...* (En Anuers, en casa de Iuan Steelsio, [1549?]). 16.mo. British Library. Rhodes, p. 53.

INVENTARIO DE LOS LIBROS

1 Triumphos de Vasco Dias del Fregenal[1038]	68	068
		4,037
/ xi,dclxxj /		7,634
		L.11,671

2 Vidas de Lucullo y Cymō[1039]	in 4to 68	136
6 Vergel de oracion[1040]	in 4to 51	306
1 Via spiritus[1041]	in 4to 51	051
2 Vitoria de Christo	in 4to 34	068
201 Vergel de virginidad[1042]	in 4to 51	10,251
6 Vitoria de sy mesmo[1043]	in 8° 25	150
10 Valerian de Hungaria[1044]	in fol. 272	2,720
3 Vergel de sanidad[1045]	in fol. 85	255

[1038] Díaz Tanco de Fregenal, Vasco. *Los veinte triumphos hechos por Uasco Diaz de Frexenal* (s.l., s.i., n.d.). 4.to. Biblioteca Nacional, Madrid. Hispanic Society of America. Palau, 72899. Penney, p. 171. Rhodes, p. 66. Rhodes assigns the place of printing to Valencia, with a probable date of about 1535.

[1039] Plutarch. *Las vidas de dos illustres varones, Cimon Griego, y Lvcio Lucullo Romano* (Lyons? Juan Frellon?, 1547). 4.to. Biblioteca Serrano Morales, Valencia.

[1040] Orozco, Alonso de. *Comiēca el libro llamado Uergel de oracion y monte de contemplacion* (Seuilla, en casa d' Anton Aluarez, 1548). 4.to. Wagner (1987), no. 291.

[1041] Palma, Bernabé de. *Via espiritus: o dela perfecion del anima* (Salamanca, por Iuan de Iunta impressor y mercader de libros, 1541). 4.to. Biblioteca Nacional, Lisbon. Palau, 137903. Ruíz Fidalgo, no. 91. De Bujanda, V, pp. 549-50. This work of Palma was condemned by the Spanish *Index* of 1559.

[1042] Maluenda, Luis de. *Vergel de virginidad conel Edificio spiritual de la caridad* (Burgos, en casa de Juan de Junta, 1539). 4.to. Palau, 360296. Biblioteca Nacional, Madrid. British Library. Houghton Library, Harvard University. Palau cites another edition [Burgos? c.1532, Juan de Junta?] but no copy is known to exist.

[1043] Cano, Melchor. *Tractado de la victoria de si mismo traduzido de toscano ... Y ansi mismo yna instituciō de fray Domingo de Soto* (Toledo, en casa de Juā de Ayala, 1551, 1553). 8.vo. Pérez Pastor, *Toledo*, p. 100 no. 253; p. 107, no. 268. Palau, 42332 note. Bataillon, p. XL, no. 314. *Catálogo colectivo*, C, 349. The British Library also has an octavo edition published in Valladolid (en casa de Sebastian Martinez, 1550). Rhodes, p. 41.

[1044] Clemente, Dionís. *Cronica del muy alto principe y esforçado cavallero Valerian de Ungria* (Valencia, por Francisco diaz Romano, 1540). Folio. Biblioteca Nacional, Madrid. Bayerische Staatsbibliothek, Munich. Biblioteca de Catalunya, Barcelona. Palau, 348845. *Catálogo colectivo*, C, 3695. Eisenberg, p. 89.

[1045] Lobera de Ávila, Luis. *Vergel de sanidad: que por otro nōbre se llamaua Banquete de caualleros, y orden de biuir ansi en tiempo de sanidad como de enfermedad* ([Alcalá de Henares, en casa de Iuan de Brocar, 1542]). Folio. Three volumes. National Library of Medicine, Bethesda. National Library of Scotland. British Library. Martín Abad, p. 492, no. 327. Durling, no. 2834. Palau, 139416.

12 Visitacion de Santa Ysabel[1046] 12		144
8 Violetta del alma[1047] 34		272
16 Vidas de n[uest]ra Señora[1048] in 8° 25		400
19 Vergel de n[uest]ra Señora[1049] in 8° 51		969
2 Valerio de las histo.[1050] in fol. 51		102
2 Vita y excellencias de S. Juan baptista 17		034
21 Vita beata[1051] in 4to 12		232
17 Vita de S[anta] m[ari]a[1052] 25		425
2 Vellocino dorado[1053] in 4to 5		102

[1046] Morejón, Diego de. *La Visitacion de Nra. Señora a Santa Ysabel con la vida de Santana, trobada por Diego de Morejon* (Valencia, Juan Jofre, c. 1520). 4.to. Maggs, 642. Not in Salvá, Palau.

[1047] Raymundus de Sabunde, 15th cent. *Violeta del anima. Que es summa de la Theologia natural a manera de dialogo* (Valladolid, Por Francisco Fernādez de Cordoua impressor, 1549). 8.vo. Academia das Ciencias, Lisbon (only copy known). This work was condemned by the Spanish *Index* of 1559. Palau, 283945 (reports an expurgated copy in Zaragoza). De Bujanda, V, p. 551-52. It is a translation of an adaptation by Pierre Dorland, *Viola animae*, which was published in Toledo in 1500.

[1048] Pérez, Miguel. *La vida y excelencias y milagros de la sacratissima virgen Maria nuestra Señora*. The Hispanic Society of America has a folio edition (Toledo, Juan de Ayala, 1549) and the Boston Public Library another (Sevilla, Juan varela de salamanca, 1525). The Library of Congress has a quarto edition (Toledo, en casa de Miguel de Eguia, 1526). I have not found an octavo edition. Palau, 219438. Penney, p. 417. Bataillon, p. XCIII, no. 1014, 1015. Pérez Pastor, *Toledo*, p. 96, no. 239. See note on the following work.

[1049] Pérez, Miguel. *Vergel de nuestra Señora* (Seuilla, por Dominico de Robertis, 1542). 4.to. British Library. Rhodes, p. 151. I have not found an octavo edition of this title. The Spanish *Index* of 1559 condemns this title. De Bujanda, V, p. 548 says that another title for this work is "Vida de nuestra señora" (see preceding item on inventory). See no. 600 on the *Index* of 1559. De Bujanda, V, p. 550.

[1050] Pérez de Guzmán, Fernando. *Valerio d'las hystorias escolasticas d'la sagrada escriptura τ d'los hechos despaña cō las batallas cāpales. Copiladas por Fernan perez de Guzman [or rather, by D. Rodríguez de Almela]* (Toledo, en casa de Juan de ayala, 1541). Folio. British Library. Rhodes, p. 151. Pérez Pastor, *Toledo*, p. 79, no. 191.

[1051] Lucena, Juan de. *Tratado de Vita beata* (Medina d'l campo por Pedro de Castro, 1541). 4.to. Pérez Pastor, *Medina del Campo*, p. 12, no. 23. The Biblioteca Nacional, Madrid, apparently has a 1543 edition of this, also by Pedro de Castro.

[1052] *Vita de Santa Maria Magdalena* (Medina del Campo, 1534). 4.to. Pérez Pastor, *Medina del Campo*, p. 5, no. 13. Pérez Pastor did not see this work, but copies Gallardo, citing an entry in the ms. catalogue of the Biblioteca Colombina. The Biblioteca Nacional, Madrid has a quarto edition, *Vida de Santa Maria Magdalena e como sirvio a la virgen Maria nuestra señora* (Burgos, por Fadrique aleman de Basilea, 1514).

[1053] Gómez de Ciudad Real, Álvaro, 1488?-1536. *El vellocino dorado: y la historia de la ordē del Tuson... Assi mismo el sūmario d'los catholicos reyes dō Fernādo y doña Ysabel cō la tomada d'Granada y d'otros pueblos q̄ valerosamēte cōquistarō* (Toledo, en casa d' Juā de Ayala, 1546). 4.to. Biblioteca Nacional, Madrid. Newberry Library. Pérez Pastor, *Toledo*, p. 86, no. 214. Palau, 103918.

INVENTARIO DE LOS LIBROS

/ xvi,dcxviij /   L. 16,618

(f. 48)

Siguen los libros enquadernados

1 Angela de Fulginio[1054] in 4to 68		068
1 Almayn de authoritate ecclesie[1055] in 4to 136		136
7 Artes del Antonio[1056] in 8° entabladas 60		420
3 Artes del Antonio enquadernadas 8° 68		204
1 Arte de canto[1057] in 4to 12		012
1 Arbor consanguinitatis[1058] in 4to 12		012
1 Apocalypsis en rromance 204		204
1 Anto[nius] Andreas in artem vet. Aristo[telis][1059] in fol. 102		102
1 Aristo[telis] physica in fol. p[ergamin]o 136		136
2 Aviso de Curas[1060] in 8° p[ergamin]o 51		102
1 Apuleo del asino de oro[1061] in fol. p[ergamin]o 51		051

[1054] Angela, of Foligno, 1248?-1300.

[1055] Almain, Jacques. *Libellus de auctoritate ecclesie seu sacrorum conciliorum eam representantium... contra Thomam de Vio* (Parrhisiis, Venundantur a Johanne Granion, 1512). 4.to. Biblioteca Nacional, Madrid. Bibliothèque Nationale, Paris. *Catálogo colectivo*, A, 948.

[1056] Nebrija, Elio Antonio de. *De institutio grammatica*. The common name for his Latin grammar was "Arte de Antonio." The royal decree mandating the use of this grammar was included in the 1598 Junta edition stating "We order that from the date of this decree forward, the said *Arte*, newly compiled and arranged, is to be read in the universities, schools and studios of our dominions ... ." See footnote 309.

[1057] See footnote 701. If this is the same edition, it is difficult to explain why the bound copy should sell for less than the unbound copies unless it were a used copy.

[1058] See footnote 206.

[1059] Andreae, Antonius, d. 1320. *Scriptum Antonij Andree In arte veteri & In disuisionibus Boetij cum questionibus eiusdem...*(Venetiis, Octavianus Scotus, 1508). Biblioteca Vaticana. Scotus produced folio editions of this work in 1480 and 1492. British Library. Bibliothèque Nationale, Paris. The British Library also has a 1496 folio edition.

[1060] See footnote 695.

[1061] Apuleius, Lucius. *Lucio Apvleyo del Asno de oro, corregido y añadido* (Medina del Campo, por Pedro de Castro, a costa de Juan de Espinosa, 1543). Folio. Biblioteca Nacional, Madrid. Bibliothèque Nationale, Paris. *Catálogo colectivo*, A, 1974. Pérez Pastor, *Medina del Campo*, p. 23, no. 32. There is also an early folio edition, *Libro de lucio apuleyo del asno de oro. Enel ql trata muchas historias y fabulas alegres* ([Seville, Jacobo Cromberger, ca. 1513]). The only known copy is in the Bibliothèque Sainte Geneviève, Paris. Griffin, Appendix One, no. 97. Palau, 14055.

1 Agricultura[1062] in fol. p[ergamin]o 170		170
1 Aristo[teles] dialectica qqtarijs de Lapide[1063] in fol. 136		136
1 Abecedario Spiritual 4ta parte[1064] in 4ᵗᵒ p[ergamin]o 85		085
1 Ametto del Boccatio[1065] in 8° p[ergamin]° 34		034
1 Albumasar astrologus[1066] ligat. viejo falto ---		----
~~1 Ambro. in epistolas Pauli in 8°~~ [1067] estan escrittos		----
~~1 Almanach perpetuum 4ᵗᵒ ligat.~~ [1068] con los de papel		----
1 Annothomia Caroli Stephani[1069] 680		680
3 Alphabetum hebraicum[1070] in 8° p[ergamin]o 10		030
1 Boscan[1071] ligat. p[ergamin]o 85		085
1 Breviarium romanum de la paloma 136		136
1 Breviarium de S. P[iet̀r]o ligat. 102		102
2 Breviarium predicator[um] viejo pp ligat. 85		170
1 Breviarium romanum cum lectiones viejo 68		068
1 Baptismale mantuani opuscula in 8° 102		102
1 Breviarium predicator[um] pp 102		102
1 Breviarium de la paloma viejo 119		119
1 Breviarium del Calice in 8° 187		187
2 Breviarium de la + [Cruz] in 8° ligat. 170		340
1 Breviarium cisterciense 119		119

[1062] Herrera, Gabriel Alonso de. *Libro de agricultura, que es la labrança* (Toledo, en casa de Juā Ferrer, 1551). Folio. Pérez Pastor, *Toledo*, p. 99, no. 249. There are also other folio editions in Alcalá de Henares (A. Brocar, 1513; M. de Eguía, 1524; Juan de Brocar, 1539), in Logroño (M. de Eguía, 1528), in Toledo (A. Brocar, 1520; Fernādo de santa catalina, 1546) and Zaragoza (G. Coci, 1524).

[1063] Aristoteles. *Libri artis Porphyrij et Aristotelis cū explanatiōe magistris Iohānis de lapide* (apud Basileam, per Ioannē de Amerbach, [1495?]). Folio. British Library.

[1064] See footnote 689.

[1065] Boccaccio, Giovanni. *Ameto* (Firenze, per gli heredi di Philippo di Giunta, 1521, 1529). 8.vo. British Library.

[1066] Abū Ma'shar, 805.

[1067] See footnote 86.

[1068] See footnote 87.

[1069] Estienne, Charles, 1504-1564. This might be his *De dissectione partium corporis humani libri tres, a Carolo Stephano... editi. Una cum figuris, & incisionum declarationibus, a Stephano Riverio chirurgo compositis* (Parisiis, apud Simonem Colinæum, 1545). Folio. British Library. National Library of Medicine. Durling, no. 1391.

[1070] Octavo editions of the *Alphabetum hebraicum* were published in Venice by Aldus Manutius (ca. 1501 and ca. 1540), in Paris by R. Estienne (1539, 1544) and in Lyons by Sébastien Gryphius (c. 1528, re Maittaire, II, p. 567).

[1071] Boscán Almogáver, Juan. *Las obras de Boscan y algvnas de Garcilaso de la Vega*. This popular work was much reprinted in sixteenth-century Spain, France and Italy. Possibly the edition of Pedro de Castro in Medina del Campo in 1544. Pérez Pastor, *Medina del Campo*, p. 31, no. 35. Maggs, 99-101. Penney, p. 72. Rhodes, pp. 34-35. Palau, 33377.

INVENTARIO DE LOS LIBROS

1 Breviarium de la Corona 170	170
1 Breviarium dominicum viejo 102	102
1 Breviarium roma[num]¹⁰⁷² in 4to 272	272
2 Breviarium roma[num] ligat. cum lectiones 153	306
1 Breviarium toletanum viejo 170	170
1 Breviarium romanum de novis 204	204
1 Breviarium segoviense[1073] 136	136
1 Boetius[1074] in 4to, r[oman]ce 68	068
1 Biblia in fol. ligat. vieja 238	238
1 Bruxellensis in summulas Hispani[1075] 51	051
2 Bassolis sup[er] sñas[1076] in fol. 1,020	2,040
1 Boetij opera[1077] in fol. ligat. 306	306
	L. 8,175

(f. 49)

1 Bernardi opera[1078] 918	918
1 Baculus clericalis[1079] ligat. p[ergamin]o 68	068
1 Bernardi opera Junta[1080] 510	510
1 Breviarium de mercede in 8° 175	170
2 Breviarium carmelitanum in 8° 153	306
	1,972
/ x,cxlvij /	8,175

[1072] The Giunti firm of Venice published a quarto edition of the Roman Breviary in 1554. Camerini, I, p. 405.

[1073] *Breviarium secundum ordinationem ecclesie Segobiensis* (Vallisoleti, in officina Nicolai Tyerri, 1527). Folio. Biblioteca Nacional, Madrid. *Catálogo colectivo*, B, 2440.

[1074] Cromberger published quarto editions of Boethius' *La consolacion de la filosofia* (Seville, 1518 and 1521). Griffin, Appendix One, nos. 179, 234.

[1075] Joannes XXI, pope. *Interptatio Georgij Bruxcellēsis in summulas Petri Hyspani vna cū Thome Bricot questionibus additis* (Lugd., P. Mareschal τ B. Chaussard, 1505). 4.to. British Library.

[1076] See footnote 210.

[1077] Boethius, Anicius Manlius Severinus. *Opera omnia* (Basileae, Apud H. Petrum, 1546). Folio. British Library.

[1078] Bernard de Clairvaux, Saint, 1091-1153. Although neither the place of publication nor the format is specified, the high cost indicates that this was probably a folio edition of the complete works such as the 1547 edition by Jean Roigny in Paris.

[1079] See footnote 116.

[1080] Bernard de Clairvaux, Saint, 1091-1153. *Opera omnia* (Lvgdvni, Iacob. Givnti, 1544). Folio (36 cms.). University of Chicago. The Giunti firm of Lyons produced other folio editions in 1538 and 1546. Biblioteca Nacional, Madrid. Biblioteca Universitaria, Salamanca. *Catálogo colectivo*, B, 922, 924, 925.

L. 10,147

1 Cronica de arderique[1081] in fol. p[ergamin]o 102	102
1 Concordantie biblie in 4to 442	442
2 Con.ª montagnana[1082] in 4to 170	340
1 Confessionario del Tostado[1083] viejo 20	020
1 Corporales de darroque[1084] in 4to 17	017
1 Comedia de Nicolao Graffo 34	034
1 Covarubias Sup[er] 4to [1085] 187	187
3 Conde Partinuples[1086] in 4to 17	051
1 Conde Fernand Goncales[1087] en papel 8	008
1 Catullus in 4to 51	051
1 Colloquio espiritual in 8° 51	051
1 Confessionario del Cyruelo[1088] in 8° 34	034
1 Coronel in posteriora[1089] in 8° 17	017

[1081] Arderique. *Libro del esforçado caballero Arderique: en el qual se cuenta el proceso de sus amores: las hazañas muy señaladas* (Valencia, por Juan viñas, 1517). Folio. The only surviving copies are from the edition of 1517. Österreichisches Nationalbibliothek, Vienna. Bibliothèque Mazarine, Paris. Palau, 15768. Eisenberg, p. 52.

[1082] Montagnana, Bartholomaeus. *Consilia Montagnane. Consilia Magistri Bartholomei Montagnane. Tractatus tres de balneis Patavinis. De compositione & dosi medicinarum. Antidotarium eiusdem... Cum tabula consiliorum et numero foliorum recenter addita* ([Lugd., Impressum in edibus Jacobi Myt], 1525). 4.to. National Library of Medicine. Durling, no. 3235.

[1083] Tostado, Alonso, bp., d. 1455. *Confessiõal* (Seuilla por Iuan varela de salamanca, 1518). 4.to. British Library. Rhodes, p. 206. There were also editions in Alcalá de Henares by Arnao Guillén de Brocar in 1516 and 1517. Martín Abad, p. 249, no. 51; p. 256, no. 62.

[1084] Cueva, Gaspar Miguel de la. *Historia del misterio divino del sanctissimo sacramento del altar q̃ esta enlos corporales de Daroca* (Alcalá de Henares, en casa de Juan de Brocar q. sancta gloria aya, 1553). 4.to. Biblioteca Nacional, Madrid. British Library. Hispanic Scoiety of America. *Catálogo colectivo*, C, 3774. Penney, p. 161. Palau, 66141 note.

[1085] See footnote 122.

[1086] *Libro del esforçado cavallero cõde Partinuples* (Burgos, Juan de Junta, 1547). 4.to. Biblioteca Nacional, Madrid. Palau, 212680. The work was also published by Cromberger in Seville in 1519 and by Miguel de Eguía in Toledo in 1526. Griffin, Appendix One, no. 192. Pérez Pastor, *Toledo*, p. 60, no. 133.

[1087] Perhaps *La chronica del noble cauallero el conde fernan gonçalez* (1530) or *La hystoria breue del muy excelẽte cauallero el conde fernã gõçales* (1537 and 1546), all in Burgos by Juan de Junta. The work is attributed to García Moreno. A 1526 quarto edition in Burgos was probably also the work of this press. Salvá, 1601. Maggs, 367. Palau, 87750, 87753, 87754.

[1088] See footnote 757.

[1089] See footnote 542.

6 Contemptus mundi,[1090] ro[man]ce in 8° 45	270
103 Calendarium franciscanor[um] 8° passado no vale nada	----
1 Comentarios de Cesar[1091] in fol. 119	119
1 Carlo magno[1092] in fol. 25	025
1 Cronica del Peru[1093] in 8° 68	068
1 Cassianus de Institutione monasterior[um][1094] 34	034
1 Cronicon Eusebij[1095] in fol. 375	375
1 Congregator Jacobi Dondi[1096] in fol. 306	306
1 Comentarios de Cesar[1097] in 8° toscano 68	068
1 Castrovol economica[1098] in fol. 136	136
1 Corona beate Marie in fol. 85	085
1 Cronica de los frayles de S. Hieronymo 102	102
1 Cano de penitentia[1099] in 4to 85	085
1 Castillo inexpugnabile[1100] in fol. 85	085
1 Cavallero determinado[1101] in 8° 51	051

[1090] Imitatio Christi. *Contemptus mundi*. This is probably the Junta edition printed in Burgos in 1555. See footnote 726.

[1091] Caesar, Caius Julius. *Los commentarios*. Folio editions in Spanish were published in Toledo (por maestre Pedro hagembach, 1498) Alcalá de Henares (Miguel de Eguía, 1529) and Paris (En Paris. Vendese en la ciudad de Anueres, 1549). British Library. Rhodes, p. 38. Palau, 54137, 54138.

[1092] See footnote 751.

[1093] Cieza de León, Pedro. See footnote 720.

[1094] Cassianus, Joannes, ca. 370 - ca. 435. *Opus ... de Institutis cenobiorum*. This is probably one of the Lyons editions (Lugduni, per Jacobum myt, [1525]; or Lugduni, per Simonem Beuilaqua, 1516).

[1095] Eusebius Pamphili, bp. of Caesarea. *Chronicon*. I have not located a folio edition of this work.

[1096] Dondi, Jacopo de, 1295-1359. Probably the *Aggregator*, a work of medieval medicine and prescriptions (Venetiis, apud Ivntas, 1543). Folio. Camerini, I, p. 350.

[1097] Caesar, C. Julius. *I Commentarii ... tradotti in thoscana* (Vinegia, G. Giolito de Ferrari e fratelli, 1554). 8.vo. Newberry Library. The Aldus firm also produced an octavo edition in Italian in 1547.

[1098] Pedro, *de Castrovol*. Edition unidentified. This is probably a commentary on the *Oeconomica* of Aristotle.

[1099] Cano, Melchor. See footnote 169.

[1100] See footnote 746.

[1101] La Marche, Olivier de, 1426 (ca.) - 1502. *El cavallero determinado* (En Anuers, en casa de Iuan Steelsio, 1553, 1555). 8.vo. Hispanic Society of America. Biblioteca Nacional, Madrid. Houghton Library, Harvard University. Penney, p. 294. *Catálogo colectivo*, L, 66. or *Discurso dela vida humana, y auenturas del cauallero determinado* (Anuers, M. Nucio, 1555). 8.vo. British Library.

1 Cronica Gaguini[1102] ligat. 102		102
1 Copie verbor[um][1103] in 8° viejo 25		025
2 Clementinas[1104] viejas y rotas 34		068
1 Cronica Saxonie vieja 68		068
1 Ciceronis rethorica[1105] in fol. 85		085
1 Claudianus poeta[1106] in 4ᵗᵒ 51		<u>051</u>
		3,562

(f. 50)

1 Ciceronis epistole ad Atticum[1107] in 8° 60		060
3 Colloquia Vives[1108] ligat. 34		102
1 Celestina 2ᵈᵃ[1109] in 4ᵗᵒ 25		025
1 Cuellar in aphorismos[1110] ligat. 272		272
1 Cesares de Mondonedo[1111] in fol. p[ergamin]o 170		170
1 Capreolus sup[er] sñas[1112] en 4 Cuerpos ligat.		<u>1,020</u>
		1,646

[1102] Gaguin, Robert, 1433-1501. Perhaps a later edition of *Compendium Roberti Gaguini super francorum gestis* (Parisiis, Impressit Bertholdus Rembolt, impensis Iohannis parui, 1511). 4.to. Newberry Library. The work is a medieval history of France. The French translation has the title *Les croniques de frāce*.

[1103] See footnote 195.

[1104] Covarrubias y Leyva, Diego de, abp., 1512-1577. *Clementinae, si fvriosvs, de homicidio, relectio* (Salmanticae, excudebat Andreas à Portonarijs, 1554). Folio. British Library. Rhodes, p. 60. The description of the inventory copies as "old and torn" probably points to an earlier edition than this. This may also be the work of Joannes, de Imola, *Super Clementinis cōmentaria* which was printed for de Portonariis in Lyons in 1539 and by Regnier for the heirs of Jacobus Giunta in 1551. Both folios.

[1105] Cicero, Marcus Tullius. *[De Inventione Rhetorica]*. Most of the folio editions were produced in Venice in the incunable period.

[1106] See footnote 185.

[1107] Cicero, Marcus Tullius. *M. Tul. Ciceronis Epistolae ad Atticum, Brutum, & Q. Fratrem, ex diversorum exemplarium praecipue Victorii ac Manutii collatione diligentissima castigatae* (Lugduni, Apud Seb. Gryphium, 1543, 1551, 1555). 8.vo. Baudrier, VIII, pp. 180, 279.

[1108] See footnote 196.

[1109] See footnote 741.

[1110] Enrique Cuellar produced a commentary on Hippocrates' *Prognostica* (see footnote 179) but I have not found his work on the *Aphorismos* of Hippocrates.

[1111] See footnote 732.

[1112] Capreolus, Johannes, d. 1444. The 4-volume edition of his work on St. Thomas Aquinas, *Quaestiones in IV libros Sententiarum, seu Libri IV defensionum theologiae Thomae Aquinatis* (Venice, Octavianus Scotus, 1483-84). Folio. Houghton Library, Harvard University. Brown University, Providence. University of California, Los Angeles.

INVENTARIO DE LOS LIBROS

/ v,ccxj /   3,569 [sic]
                                                        L. 5,211

2 Doctrina o manual de Ximenes[1113] 8° 51	102
1 Diurnale predicator[um] 85	085
1 Diurnale de Astorga pp 85	085
3 De conscribendis ep[isto]lis[1114] viejos 45	135
1 Diurnale burgense viejo 51	051
1 Dechado de la vida humana[1115] in 4.to 25	025
2 De fecerunt ro[man]ce[1116] in 4.to 51	102
1 De quantitate syllabarum[1117] in 4.to 17	017
1 Declaratio del pater noster,[1118] ro[man]ce in 4.to 34	034
1 De quatuor novissimis[1119] in 4.to 68	068
1 Deseoso[1120] in 4.to p[ergamin]o 85	085
1 Dynus sup[er] 4ta primi[1121] in fol. p[ergamin]o 238	238
1 Digestum novum[1122] viejo 102	102
1 Decreta augustana in 4.to 17	017
1 De corrupti lati sermo. emendatione[1123] 8° 68	068

[1113] See footnote 908.

[1114] Erasmus, Desiderius. *Opus de conscribendis epistolis* (Parisiis, Apud S. Colineū, 1523). 8.vo. British Library. This may also be the 1531 edition by Gryphius in Lyons. Baudrier, VIII, p. 58.

[1115] Cessolis, Jacobus de. *Dechado de la vida humana. Moralmĕte sacado del Iuego del Axedrez* (Valladolid, en la officina de Francisco fernandez d' Cordoua, 1549). 4.to. British Library. Rhodes, p. 219.

[1116] Antoninus, Saint, Abp. of Florence, 1389-1459. *Summa de confession llamada Defecerunt.* See footnote 783.

[1117] Cordier, Mathurin. *Regulae speciales de syllabarum quantitate, quas Despauterius in carmen non redegit* (Parisiis, Ex typographia Matthaei Davidis, 1551). 4.to. Biblioteca Nacional, Madrid. *Catálogo colectivo*, C, 3015.

[1118] This may be the earlier edition of Erasmus' *Declaracion del Pater noster diuidida en siete peticiones* which Miguel de Eguía published in Logroño in 1528. Bayerische Staatsbibliothek, München. De Bujanda, V, p. 476.

[1119] See footnote 799.

[1120] See footnote 786.

[1121] Garbo, Dino del, d. 1327. *Dynus super quarta primi Cum Tabula. ... Dyni Florentini in quartā Fen primi Auicen.* (Venetiis, Lucantonio Giunta, 1522). British Library. Camerini, I, p. 207.

[1122] Justinian I, Emperor of the East. *Corpus juris civilis. Digestum novum.* There are a number of 15th- and 16th-century editions, published mainly in Lyons.

[1123] Cordier, Mathurin. See footnote 230.

1 Dynus in chyrurgia[1124] in fol. 238	238
1 Dispensarium Prepositi[1125] in fol. 34	034
1 Dialectica Petri Hispani[1126] fol. 102	102
2 Dieta salutis[1127] 34	068
1 Declaracio officij misse in fol. 68	068
	L. 1,724

/ j,dccxxiiij /

1 Ep[isto]le Ortys[1128] entabladas solamente 136	136
1 Ep[isto]le Hieronymi in 4to viejos 170	170
3 Elegantie Valle[1129] in 8° 85	255
2 Ep[isto]le Plinij[1130] in 8° 68	136
1 Estymulo de amor con el convite[1131] 102	102
1 Egloga de Virgilio viejo 25	025
1 Estymulo de amor[1132] in 4to 51	051
1 Ep[isto]le Ovidij in 8° 51	051
1 Eras[mo] de recta pronuntiatione[1133] in 8° 25	025
	L. 951

(f. 51)

1 Erasmus de pueris institutuendis[1134] 8° 34	034
1 Ephemerides viejo in 4to 51	051
1 Ep[isto]le Pauli in 8° 51	051

[1124] Garbo, Dino del, d. 1327. *Dinus in chirurgia cum tractatu eiusdem de ponderibus et mensuris: necnon de emplastris et unguentis. Additi sunt insuper Gentilis de Fulgineo super tractatu de lepra* [and other works] (Venetius, expensis heredum Luciantonij Iunte Florentini, 1544). Folio. Wayne State University Medical School.

[1125] See footnote 446. This may be the folio edition of de Gabiano (Lugduni, 1537).

[1126] Joannes XXI, pope, d. 1277. I assume that this is his commentary on the Organon of Aristotle, but have not identified the edition.

[1127] Bonaventura, *Saint, Cardinal*. [Suppositious works]. *Dieta salutis* (Venetiis, Apud C. Arrivabenum, 1518). 8.vo. Biblioteca Nacional, Madrid.

[1128] Ortiz, Francisco. *Epistolas familiares*. See footnote 818.

[1129] See footnote 257.

[1130] See footnote 244.

[1131] See footnote 839.

[1132] See footnote 839.

[1133] See footnote 278.

[1134] Erasmus, Desiderius. *Ejusdem libellus de ratione studii et pueris instituendis* (Compluti, Michaelis a Eguia, 1529). 8.vo. There was also a 1525 edition. Bataillon, p. LV, no. 513, 514. Palau, 80334. See also footnote 241.

1 Exponibilia de Celaya[1135] in fol. 68		068
1 Epitetha textoris[1136] in fol. 170		170
1 Ep[isto]le Ovidij[1137] in 8° 51		051
1 Ep[isto]las y evangelios[1138] in 8° 68		068
1 Epitome op[eru]m Augustini[1139] in fol. 476		476
1 Ep[isto]le Ovidij qqto.[1140] in fol. 102		102
1 Exemplario[1141] in fol. 25		025
1 Eras[mo] de matrimonio[1142] in 8° 10		010
1 Enchridio psalmor[um][1143] pp 51		051
1 Ep[isto]le divi Pauli in 4to 25		025
1 Egloga real 17		017
1 Ep[isto]le Symachu[1144] in 4to 17		017

[1135] Celaya, Juan de, fl. 1516-1531. *Magna exponibilia*. A commentary on Aristotle's *De generatione et corruptione*. Palau, 51083.

[1136] Tixier, Jean, seigneur de Ravisy, d. 1524. *Epitheta ... ab authore suo recognita ac in nouam formam redacta* (Parrhisiis, Apud E. Chauldiere, 1524). Folio. Newberry Library.

[1137] Ovidius Naso, Publius. Several octavo editions of the *Epistolae heroides* were published in Florence, Lyons and Paris from the 1520s to the 1540s.

[1138] See footnote 816.

[1139] Augustinus, Aurelius, Saint. *Epitome Omnivm Opervm Divi Avrelii Avgvstini ... primum quidem per Iohannem Piscatorium compendiaria quadam via collecta* (Coloniae ex officina Melchioris Nouesiani, 1549). Folio. University of Chicago. British Library.

[1140] Perhaps part of the Hervagius folio edition of Ovid. See footnote 1206.

[1141] *Exemplario contra los engaños y peligros del mundo*. This Spanish translation of *Directorium humanae vite alias parabole antiquorū sapientū* was first printed in Zaragoza in 1493 in a folio edition. Other folio editions were published in Burgos (Fadrique de Basilea, 1498), in Zaragoza (George Coci, 1521) and Seville (Juan Cromberger, 1534, 1537, 1541 and 1546).

[1142] Erasmus, Desiderius. The Spanish *Index* of 1559 condemns the "Christiani matrimonii institutio" of Erasmo. This may be the 1526 edition of the Latin text produced by Johann Froben in Basel, or the Spanish translation published by Juan Joffre in Valencia: *Colloguio d' Erasmo intitulado institucion d'l Matrimonio christiano: traduzido de latin en lengua Castellana: por Diego Morejon*. Bayerische Staatsbibliothek, Munich. De Bujanda, V, p. 350. Bataillon, p. LII, no. 474 and Plate XIV.

[1143] Seb. Gryphius published editions of the *Enchiridion Psalmorum. Eorundem ex ueritate Hebraica uersione, ac Ioannis Campensis è regione paraphrasim* in Lyons in 1533, 1534, 1536, 1537 and 1540. 16.mo. Another 16. mo edition of the same title was published in Paris in 1533 by C. Chevallonius. British Library. Biblioteca Nacional, Madrid. *Catálogo colectivo*, E, 251, 252.

[1144] Symmachus, Quintus Aurelius, d. 405. *Symmachi cons. ro. Fpistolæ (sic) familiares. Item Lavdini equitis hierosolymitani in epistolas Turci magni traductio* (Argentine, p[er] Ioannē Knoblouchū, 1511). 4.to. University of Michigan. British Library. Other quarto editions were published in Strassburg (J. Schotti, 1510) and Venice (B. dei Vitali [1503-1513?]).

1 Espejo de tristes libro 3o[1145]	170	170
1 Espejo de tristes libro 4o[1146]	170	170
1 Espejo de tristes libro 2o[1147]	170	170
3 Epitus[1148] in 4to	6	018
1 Epata in 8°	34	<u>034</u>
		1,778
/ ij,dccxxix /		<u>951</u>
		L. 2,729

1 Fiometa del Boccatio[1149]	51	051
1 Fabulas de Esopo[1150] in toscano	34	034
1 Flosculi lingue latine	34	034
1 Flor de virtudes[1151] in 4to	17	017
1 Falencia Socini[1152] in 8°	68	068

[1145] Dueñas, Juan de. The first part, *Espejo de consolacion: parte primera, en la qual se veran muchas y grandes hystorias de la sagrada escriptura. Para consolacion de los que en esta vida padecen tribulacion*, was published by Juan de Junta in Burgos, 1546, "a costa del señor Juan de Espinosa, mercader de libros vezino de Medina del Campo." The third part was printed in Valladolid by "el honrrado varõ Juã de Villaquirã ... a xxix días del mes de Mayo [1550] ... a costa de Juan de espinosa." Folio. British Library.

[1146] Ibid. The fourth part of *Espejo de consolacion* was also printed by Villaquiran in 1551, "a q̃tro días del mes de Julio ... " Folio. British Library.

[1147] Ibid. The second part was printed in Burgos in 1549 by Juan de Junta "a costa de Juã despinosa mercader de libros vezino de Medina del campo." It was also printed in Medina del Campo in 1546, by Pedro de Castro, and in the same city in 1551 "por Diego Fernandez de Cordoua," in each case at the expense of Juan de Espinosa. All folios. Biblioteca Nacional, Madrid. Hispanic Society of America. British Library. Pérez Pastor, *Medina del Campo*, p. 44, no. 52. Rhodes, p. 69.

[1148] *Las preguntas que el emperador Adriano hizo al infante Epitus* (Burgos, en casa de Juan de Junta, 1540). 4.to. Biblioteca Nacional, Madrid (unique copy?). Palau, 236261. *Catálogo colectivo*, P, 2946. It is on the *Index* of 1559. De Bujanda, V, p. 527.

[1149] Boccaccio, Giovanni. *Libro llamado Fiameta* (Seuilla por Iacobo crõberger, 1523). Folio. British Library. Griffin, Appendix One, no. 243. As a partial edition of the *Decamerone*, this work would have been condemned by the Spanish *Index* of 1559. De Bujanda, V, pp. 509-10.

[1150] Aesop. *Favole d'Isopo* (Venetia, M. Tramezino, 1544). 8.vo. British Library.

[1151] *Flor de virtudes, nueuamẽte Impresso y corregido* (Alcalá de Henares, por Miguel de Eguia, 1526). 4.to. Penney, p. 207. Palau, 92879. Martín Abad, p. 327, no. 156. Hispanic Society of America. Other editions in Zaragoza (Pedro Hardouyn, 1534), Seville (Domenico de robertis, 1534) and Medina del Campo (Pedro de tovans, 1534). This could also be the 1517 Burgos edition of Fadrique de Basilea.

[1152] Soccini, Bartolommeo, 1436-1507. *Fallen. Socini. Regule cũ suis ampliationibus et fallentiis e toto jure delecte* ... (Lugduni, Expensis Iacobi q. Francisci de Giunta, 1533, 1541). 8.vo. British Library. Baudrier, VI, pp. 149, 193.

1 Flosculus Sacramentor[um]¹¹⁵³ in 8° 25		025
1 Formulare advocator[um]¹¹⁵⁴ in 8° 68		068
1 Formulare instumentorum¹¹⁵⁵ in 8° 68		068
1 Flos sanctorum¹¹⁵⁶ in fol. 238		238
1 Flos sanctor[um] en Italiano 187		<u>187</u>
		L. 790

/ ,dccxc /

1 Gra[mmati]ca hebraica in 8° 102		102
1 Gra[mmati]ca greca Gaze¹¹⁵⁷ pp ligat. 25		025
1 Gumel de quantitate syllabarum¹¹⁵⁸ in 4ᵗᵒ 17		017
1 Guerra de Alemana¹¹⁵⁹ in 8° 25		025
1 Gra[mati]ca Maturini Corderi¹¹⁶⁰ in 8° 34		034
1 Gra[mati]ca Prisciani¹¹⁶¹ in fol. 85		<u>085</u>
		L. ,288

(f. 52)

1 Galenus de usu partium¹¹⁶² in fol. 204   204

---

¹¹⁵³ Fernández de Villegas, Pedro. *Flosculus sacramentorū* (Salmanticae, Ioānis iunte, 1546). 8.vo. Biblioteca Universitaria, Oviedo. Palau, 89951.

¹¹⁵⁴ *Formulare Advocatorum et Procuratorum Romane Curie* (Lugduni, per Simonem bivilaqua, 1518). 8.vo. Biblioteca Nacional, Madrid.

¹¹⁵⁵ See footnote 301.

¹¹⁵⁶ *Flos sanctorum*. The 1556 Zaragoza edition of this work (no surviving copy known) is on the *Index* of 1559. De Bujanda, V, p. 480-81. Palau, 92889, lists a 1551 Zaragoza edition by Pedro Bernuz.

¹¹⁵⁷ Gaza, Theodorus. *Theodori Grammatices Libri IIII*. A small-format (15 cm.) edition was published by the house of Aldus in Venice in 1525. Yale University.

¹¹⁵⁸ See footnote 318.

¹¹⁵⁹ See footnote 857.

¹¹⁶⁰ Cordier, Mathurin. This may be his *Comentarius pverorvm de Latinæ Linguæ elegantia & varietate* (Lugduni, Excudebat Ioannes Frellonius, 1551). 8.vo. Palau, 61787. Baudrier, V, p. 221.

¹¹⁶¹ Priscianus. Folio editions of his Latin grammar were published in Paris (in aedibus J. de Marnef, 1520) and Cologne (Eucharius Cervicornus ære & impensa G. Hyttorpij, 1528). British Library.

¹¹⁶² Galenus. *De usu partium corporis humani libri XVII, universo hominum generi apprime necessarii, Nicolao Regio Calabro interprete. Tertio exactiore cura ad Graeci exemplaris veritatem castigati, per Jacobum Sylvium medicum & Martinum Gregorium. Huc accessit ejusdem Jacobi Sylvii brevis Isagoge, partis ususque rationem edisserens* (Parisiis, apud Christianum Wechelum, 1543). Folio. National Library of Medicine. Durling, no. 1949. Wechel also produced a folio edition in 1538.

1 Gabriel sup[er] Canō misse[1163]   170   170
1 Gra[mati]ca Nebrissensis in 4to viejo   51   051
1 Gra[mati]ca Sulpitij[1164] in 4to pvo   51   051
                                                                         476
/ ,dcclxiiij /   288
                                                                         L. 764

10 horas ro[man]ce in 8° Burgos   102   1,020
3 horas pp 16 Caragoca[1165]   102   306
2 horas 16 Caragoca mal enquadernadas   51   ~~102~~ vale
1 horas en ro[man]ce 16   95   475
1 hore predicator[um] 16 ligat.   95   095
1 hymnos y orationes in 4to 102   102
1 Halii filij Abbas[1166] in 4to 170   170
1 hore ro[man]ce portugues p[ergamin]o   51   051
1 Holcot sup[er] sapientiam[1167] in fol. p[ergamin]o   170   170
1 horas viejas su principio   ----
4 horas Delgato ligat.   34   136
1 hore romane lat[ine] in 8° gotico   119   119
1 Horatius cum Juvenale et Persio in 8°   68   068
1 Homeri Ulixea grece[1168]   51   051
                                                                      L. 2,865

/ ij,dccclxv /

1 Jacobus de bello visig[odo] en papel   136   136

[1163] Biel, Gabriel. See footnote ?.

[1164] Sulpitius, Joannes, Verulanus, 15th cent. Perhaps the *Grammatices compendium* (Venetiis, Rauanis, 1525; or Venetiis, de Sabio, 1536).

[1165] *Horas romanas*. Several Zaragoza editions are on the *Index* of 1559. See above, with the unbound books and De Bujanda, V, p. 491-92. The "pp" indicates that this would be a small-format edition.

[1166] Ali ibn al-Abbas, al-Majusi al-Arrajani. The work in question is probably the *Liber totius medicine necessaria cōtinens* (Lugduni, Typis Jacobi Myt, 1523). 4.to. British Library. National Library of Medicine. Durling, no. 168.

[1167] Holkot, Robertus, d. 1349. *Super librū Sapientie rursus recognitus mendisque ac erroribus purgatus quāplurimis ac pulcherrimis annotationibus in marginibus ornatus atque membratim peroptime distinctus* (Uenetijs, expensis heredum Octauiani Scoti, 1509). Folio. Yale University. Massachusetts Historical Society. Biblioteca Vaticana.

[1168] Perhaps vol. 2 of the Greek edition of Homer by the heirs of Filippo Giunti (Florence, 1519) which includes the Batrachomyomachia and the Hymns. Vol. 1 contains the Iliad.

1 Jeronymo Pardo[1169] in fol. 85		085
1 Isagoge Ioannicii[1170] in 4.to 25		025
1 Institutiones oratorie[1171] in 4.to 25		025
1 Iliados Homeri lib[ri] 1,2,3. grece in 8° 34		034
2 Iustinus historicus[1172] in 8° 51		102
1 Ilias Homeri[1173] pp ligat. 68		068
1 Ientacula Caietani[1174] pp 17		017
1 Iuvenalis qqto.[1175] in 4.to 68		068
1 Isagoge Sanctis Pagnini[1176] in fol. 510		510
1 Itinerario escritto de mano viejo ---		----
	L.	1,070

/ j,lxx /

6 libri minores[1177] in 4.to entablados solamente 102   612

[1169] Pardo, Gerónimo, fl. 1500. *Medulla dyalectices* (Parisius, D. Gerlier, 1505). Folio. British Library.

[1170] Articella. *Articella nuperrime impressa cum quamplurimis tractatibus pristine impressioni superadditis*. This may be from the 1515, 1519, or 1525 Lyons edition. Early editions were titled *Liber hysagoge Joannicii*. See also footnote 72.

[1171] Quintilianus, Marcus Fabius. *Institutiones oratoriae* (Venetiis, In Aedibus Aldi, Et Andreae Soceri, 1514). 4.to. Yale University. Folger Shakespeare Library.

[1172] Justinus, Marcus Justinus. *Iustini ex Trogi Pompeii historijs externis libri XLIIII*. Sébastien Gryphius published octavo editions of Justinus in 1538, 1543, 1548, and 1551 in Lyons. Other octavo editions were published in Paris (ex officina Rob. Stephani, 1543; I. Lodoicus Tiletanus, 1543; apud S. Colinaeum, 1530), in Basel (apud Michaelem Isingrinium, 1539), in Cologne (apud Iohan. Gymnicum, 1533).

[1173] The British Library has a copy of Homer's *Ilias* published in 16.mo (Parisiis, Apud Carolam Guillard, 1545).

[1174] Vio, Tomaso de, called Gaetano, *cardinal*. *Novi Testamenti Ientaculis Tractatus* (Salamanca, A. de Portonariis, 1551). Earlier editions were published in Cologne (Colonie, 1526) and Lyon (Lugduni, per Joannem Crespinū. Impēsis Jacobi q. Frācisci de Giūcta, 1530 and 1537). The Lyons Giunta edition included the *Summula Caietana*, a work De Bujanda says was widely distributed in Spain. The *Index* of 1559 condemns the "Summa Gayetana, en romance." De Bujanda, V, p. 542.

[1175] Juvenalis, Decius Junius. *Juvenalis Familiares commentum. Argumēta Satyrarum Juvenalis per Anthoniū Mācinellū τ per Jodocū Ba'[dium]* (Lugduni: Bernardi Rosier τ Johānis Thome, 1512). 4.to. *Catálogo colectivo*, J, 923.

[1176] Pagnino, Santi. *S. P. ucensis ... Isagoge ad sacras Literas liber unicus* (Lugduni, H. à Porta, 1536). Folio. British Library.

[1177] Nebrija, Elio Antonio de. *Libri minores de novo correcti per Antonium Nebrissensem* (Compluti, in aedibus Michaelis de Eguia, 1529). 4.to. Biblioteca Nacional, Madrid. Palau, 50363. Martín Abad, p. 372, no. 207. Another quarto edition was published in Granada in 1545. Columbia University. Fadrique de Basilea produced an earlier edition in Burgos in 1514, and Miguel de Eguía in 1525, 1526 and 1528. Palau, 189304-189311.

4 Luz del alma[1178] pp p[ergamin]o 68		272
1 Loores del monte Calvario[1179] in 4to 187		187
1 Libellus de honesta voluptate[1180] in 4to 102		102
1 Logica Armandi[1181] in 8° 68		068

(f. 53)

1 Lumbricis curatio[1182] pp p[ergamin]o 25		025
1 Lactantius[1183] in fol. 102		102
1 libro de coplas en loor de n[uest]ra Señora en toscano 34		034
1 Logica Pauli Veneti[1184] in fol. 136		136
i,dxxxviij		L. 1,538
4 Maldonati Vite patrum[1185] in 8° 51		204
1 Maldonati Vite patrum viejos 34		034
1 Maldona[ti] de civilitate morum 8° 34		034
1 Meditationes[1186] in 8° 45		045
1 Martialis in 8° 51		051
1 Manuale chori apuntado 8° 85		085
1 Missale carthusianum in 8° 136		136
1 Margarita doctorum in 8° 34		034

[1178] See footnote 906.

[1179] Aranda, Antonio de. See footnote 891.

[1180] Platina, Bartolomeo, 1421-1481. *Platina De honesta volvptate & ualitudine, uel de obsonijs, & arte Coquinaria libri decem* (Strassburg, in officina Ioannis Knoblouch, 1517). 4.to. Another quarto edition was done the same year in Venice by Joannes Tacuinus. The subject matter is Italian cookery. Both in John Crerar Library, Chicago.

[1181] Armandus de Bellovisu, d. 1334? *De declaratione difficilium terminorum tam theologiae quam philosophiae atque logicae* ([Lyons] N. Wolf, 1500). 8.vo. British Library.

[1182] See footnote 382.

[1183] Lactantius, Lucius Caecilius Firmianus. *Institvtionvm libri septem* (Coloniæ, Ex officina typographica Petri Quentl, 1544). Folio. Another folio edition was produced in Basel by A. Cratander and J. Bebelius in 1532. British Library. University of Illinois, Urbana. This is an early work on Christian apologetics.

[1184] Paulus Venetus, d. 1429. *Pauli venetus super libris posteriorum* (Venetijs, Lucantonij de Giunta, 1521). Folio. Camerini, I, p. 196. The author is also known as Paulus Nicolettus.

[1185] Maldonado, Juan. Could this be *Vitae sanctorum*? See footnote 402.

[1186] Cleynaerts, Nicolaus, 1495-1542. *Meditationes Graecanicae in artem grammaticam* (Lugduni, Apud Seb. Gryphium, 1543, 1548, 1552, 1553). 8.vo. Baudrier, VIII, p. 180, 226, 261, 266. The work was also produced in octavo editions in Paris by J. Roigny in 1536 and C. Wechel in 1541; and in Lyons by T. Paganus in 1538 and by S. Dolet in 1541.

1 Musa paulina[1187] in 8° 085	085
1 Mirabilia rome[1188] in 8° 34	034
1 Memorial de amor sancto in 4to 25	025
2 Milagros de la pena de Francia in 4to 68	136
1 Martialis in 8° ligat. viejo 34	034
3 Minorita de quantitate syllabarum in 4to 34	102
1 Metaphora in medicina[1189] in fol. 119	119
2 Mingo Revulgo[1190] ligat. 15	030
1 Maria[no] Barolita in chyrurgia[1191] in 8° 51	051
1 Moria Erasmi[1192] in 8° 34	034
1 Maldo[nati] de felicitate christiana[1193] in 8° 34	034
1 Manupulus curator[um][1194] in 8° 51	051
1 Maldo[nati] parenesis[1195] in 8° 25	025
27 Maldo[nati] de senectute[1196] in 8° 45	1,255
1 Martialis qqto.[1197] in fol. 85	085

[1187] See footnote 431.

[1188] Albertini, Francisco degli. *Mirabilia Rome*. The British Library has a quarto edition of this title published in Lyons in 1520, but I have not found an octavo edition.

[1189] Laredo, Bernardino de, 1482-1545? *Metaphora medicine τ chirurgie: nueuamēte copilada por vn frayle menor de la p[ro]vincia de los Angeles* (Hyspali, Impressa in domo Joannis Varele, 1522 and 1536). Folio. National Library of Medicine. Durling, 2738. Santander Rodríguez, pp. 245-250.

[1190] Mingo Revulgo, pseud. *Coplas de Mingo Revulgo. Glosadas por el famoso Coronista Hernando de Pulgar* (Burgos, en casa de Juan de Junta, 1553). 4°. Biblioteca Nacional, Madrid (unique copy?). Palau, 170285.

[1191] Santo, Mariano, b. ca. 1490. *Compendium in chyrurgia studiosis quibuscunq[ue] ipsam exercere volētibus lōge vtilissimū per marianū sanctum Barolitanū virū undecunq[ue] doctissimum nuperrime editum* (Lugduni, Impensis Jacobi q. Francisci de Giūcta, 1525). 8.vo. Yale Medical School Library.

[1192] Erasmus, Desiderius. This work appears on the *Index* of 1559, with the works of Erasmus, under the heading "Moria, tam latino quam vulgari sermone," and with the Spanish books under the entry "Moria de Erasmo, en romance, y en latin, y en otra qualquier lengua." De Bujanda, pp. 348, 509. Froben and Gryphius published several Latin editions.

[1193] Maldonado, Juan. *Ioannis Maldonati quaedam opuscula nunc primum in lucem edita. De felicitate Christiana. Praxis sive de lectiōe Erasmi.* (Burgis, [Juan de Junta?] 1541). 8.vo. Biblioteca Nacional, Madrid. Bataillon, p. LXXXII, no. 868. *Catálogo colectivo*, M, 235.

[1194] See footnote 422.

[1195] See footnote 403.

[1196] See footnote 401.

[1197] Martialis, Marcus Valerius. *Cornucopiae: opus cōmētariorum quod N. Perottus cornucopiae intitulauit, cum textu Martialis* (Parrhisiis, [B. Rembolt] τ ab I. Paruo, 1514). Folio. Other folio editions were published in Basel (Basileae, Apud A. Cratandrum, 1521; Apud V. Curionem, 1526). British Library. The commentary is by Nicolaus Perottus.

1 Museus poeta grece[1198] in 4to 25	025
2 Mamotrectum biblie[1199] in 4to 102	204
2 Missale burgense[1200] de pergamino ligat. bezerio	7,976
1 Milagros de S. Isidoro in 4to 102	102
1 Maldonati pastor bonus[1201] in 8° 34	034
1 Maldonati opuscula in 8° [25]	025
	L. 11,049

xi,xlix

1 Novum Testamentum Erasmi[1202] viejo 8° 102	102
1 Natura angelica[1203] in fol. 136	272
1 Notas de Roque de huerta[1204] in 8° 153	153
	L. 527

/ ,dxxvij /

(f. 54)

1 Ovidij opera in 2bus ligat. 170	170
1 op[er]a parva in 8° ligat. p[ergamin]o 102	102
1 Ovidij amatoria[1205] in 8° viejo 51	051
1 obras de S. Bonaventura in 8° viejas 34	034
1 origenes sup[er] Mattheum[1206] in 8° 34	034
1 ordenances reales en frances 34	034
1 Oliveros de Castilla[1207] in 4to 17	017
1 Ovidius de fastis in 4to 34	034

[1198] Musaeus. Aldus Manutius published a Greek edition of Musaeus in quarto in Venice about 1497. Other quarto editions: Gilles de Gourmont, [Paris 1507? and 1520?] and André Wechel (Paris, 1555). British Library.

[1199] Marchesinus, Joannes. *Mammotrectus super Bibliam*. Numerous editions, especially before 1500, in Venice, Strassburg, Cologne, Mainz, and Milan.

[1200] See footnote 436.

[1201] See footnote 406.

[1202] Possible early octavo editions of Erasmus' Vulgate include those published in Basel (1516, 1519, 1520, 1521, 1522, 1523, 1527), Paris (1522), and Antwerp (1520).

[1203] See footnote 932.

[1204] See footnote 930.

[1205] See footnote 462.

[1206] Origen wrote commentaries on all of the gospels but I have not located a copy of the work on the Gospel of Matthew.

[1207] Olivier de Castile. *La historia d'los dos nobles Oliveros de castilla y Artus de Algarue* (Burgos, en casa de Juan de Junta, 1554). 4.to. Houghton Library, Harvard University. Palau, 200855. Anninger, 145.

INVENTARIO DE LOS LIBROS

1 ordenancas reales[1208] viejas y faltas	----
2 oratio appologetica in 4to 25	050
1 Ovidij metamorph[osis] qqto.[1209] in fol. 102	102
1 Ovidius de fastis qqto.[1210] in fol. 102	102
1 Occam sup[er] phisicam[1211] in 4to 136	136
1 op[er]a sive rosarium coronell[1212] in fol. 204	204
1 opuscula Plutarchi[1213] in fol. 170	170
1 Orlando[1214] in 4to 170	170
1 oratorio de religiosos[1215] in fol. 170	170
1 orationum Ciceronis p[ars] 3a[1216] pp 68	068
1 orationes Tullij in 8° Florencie[1217] 102	102
1 op[eru]m Politiani thomus 2^{dus} [1218] in 8° 051	051
1 odyssea Homeri[1219] grece ligat. 102	102
4 officio de la Cemana sancta pp 51	<u>204</u>
ij,cvij	L. 2,107
1 Prudentius[1220] in 4to 85	085

[1208] Díaz de Montalvo, Alonso. *Ordenãças reales de Castilla* (Burgos, en casa del Señor Juan de junta: florētino, 1536 and 1541). Folio. Biblioteca Nacional, Madrid. Palau, 203131, 203134.

[1209] This could be the first part of the three-volume folio edition of Ovid produced by Hervagius, *Metamorphoseos libri quindecim cum commentariis Raphaelis Regii* (Basileae, per J. Hervagium, 1543). Folio. Bibliothèque Nationale, Paris. British Library.

[1210] This is the third part of Hervagius' folio edition of Ovid. See footnote 1206.

[1211] Ockham, William, d. ca. 1349.

[1212] Coronel, Antonio. *Prima [-secunda] pars Rosarii magistri Anthonij Coronel* ... (Parisiis, apud Oliveriū Senant, 1512). Folio.

[1213] See footnote 467.

[1214] Ariosto, Lodovico. *Orlando Fvrioso* ... *traduzido en Romance Castellano por don Ieronymo de Vrrea* (a Leon, en casa de Gvlielmo Roville, 1550). 4.to. British Library. Baudrier, IX, p. 177. See also footnote 940.

[1215] See footnote 941.

[1216] Cicero, Marcus Tullius. Sebastién Gryphius issued 3-volume editions of the *Orations* in 16.mo format in Lyons in 1545, 1546, 1550 and 1555. British Library. Bibliothèque Nationale, Paris. Baudrier, VIII, pp. 196, 206, 244, 279.

[1217] Filippo Giunti published the *Orationes* of Cicero in Florence, 1515. 4 vols. 8.vo. Bibliothèque Nationale, Paris.

[1218] Poliziano, Angelo, 1454-1494. *Angeli Politiani opervm tomvs secundus* (Lvgdvni, Sebastianus Gryphius Germanus excudebat, 1528, 1533, 1550). 8.vo. Baudrier, VIII, pp. 46, 68, 236.

[1219] Homer. See footnote 1165.

[1220] Prudentius Clemens, Aurelius, 348 - ca. 410. Brocarius produced an edition of the *Opera* in Logroño in 1512, but I do not know if it is a quarto.

1 Perla y cruz de Christo[1221] pp 34		034
2 Processionarium Romanum ligat. 136		272
1 Practica de Vigo[1222] in 8° 119		119
1 Processionarium toletanum ligat. 204		204
1 Psalterium Jeronimi in 8° 51		051
1 Psalterium Romanum pp Caragoca 51		051
2 Persius qqto.[1223] in 8° 34		068
1 Psalterium romanum in 4to viejo 25		025
1 Previlegium fratrum predicator[um] in 8° 85		085
1 Practica Ferrariensis[1224] in 4to 102		102
1 Pindarus grece[1225] in 8° 34		034
1 Progymnas[mata] rethorices Petrei[1226] in 4to 34		034
1 Passion[1227] en 4to 8		008
1 Philosophia Ioannis de magistris[1228] in fol. 51		051
1 Persius qqto[1229] fol. 51		051

[1221] This may be an edition combining the condemned work *Perla preciosa* (Baeza, s.i., 1551) or *Perla preciosisima* ((Toledo, Ramón de Petras, 1525) and the *Cruz de Christo* of St. Bonaventure. I have not found such an edition.

[1222] Vigo, Giovanni de, fl. 1500. *Opera ... in arte chyrurgia* (Lugduni, excusa per Joannem Moilin de Chābray, impensis ... Jacobi q. Francisci de Giuncta Florētini, 1534). 8.vo. Baudrier, VI, p. 158. British Library. The National Library of Medicine has other octavo editions by the Giunta firm published in 1525, 1530, 1531 and 1538.

[1223] Persius Flaccus, Aulus. *Satyrae sex, Ioanne Murmelio scholiaste cum indice copiosiore & annotatione varietatis quae est in carmine Persiano* (Parisiis, ex officina C. Wecheli, 1546, 1553). 8.vo. Harvard University.

[1224] Ferrari, Giovanni Pietro, fl. 1400. *Practica noua iuris* (Lugduni, in edibus Martini Lescuyer ... impensis Iacobi q. Francisci de Giunta ac sociorum, 1533). 4.to. British Library. Baudrier, VI, p. 152.

[1225] This may be the octavo edition of the Greek text of Pindar published by Cratander (Basileae, per And Crat[andrum] 1526) or by Aldus Manutius (Venetiis, Aldus et Andreas Asulanus, 1513).

[1226] Petreius, Joannes (or Pérez, Juan). *Progymnasmata artis rhetoricae, vna cum annotationibus in Senecæ declamationes* (In celeberrima Complutensi Academia: Ioannes Brocarius, 1539). 4.to. British Library. Biblioteca Nacional, Madrid. Rhodes, p. 155. Martín Abad, p. 455, no. 291.

[1227] San Pedro, Diego de, fl. 1500. *La passion de nuestro redemptor* (Burgos? Juan de Junta? c. 1540). 4.to. British Library. Palau, 293402-II. Rhodes, p. 176. This edition has only twenty leaves and the low price in the inventory suggests that it was a small work.

[1228] Magistris, Joannes de, 15th cent. *Quaestiones super tota philosophia naturali.* There are several incunable editions but the only folio edition I know of is that in the British Library (Parme, D. de Moyllis, 1481).

[1229] Persius Flaccus, Aulus. *Satyrae sex cvm qvinqve commentatoribvs et eorum in singulas satyras argumentis* (Basileae, Frobenius et Episcopus, 1551). Folio. Biblioteca Nacional, Madrid. This may also be the 1523 folio edition of J. Badius Ascensius in Paris.

1 Practica gatenarie[1230]   in 4⁽ᵗᵒ⁾   34   034
1 Progymnasca localia de Caranca[1231]   in 4⁽ᵗᵒ⁾   51   051
                                                    L. 1,359

(f. 55)

1 Parthenice mantuani[1232]   in 4⁽ᵗᵒ⁾   25   025
1 Paraphrasis in elegantias Valle[1233]   25   025
1 Philippica Ciceronis[1234]   in 8°   51   051
1 Psalmos de Jarava[1235]   in 8°   34   034
1 Pala[cios] Rub[ios] in leg. Tauri[1236]   in fol.   306   306
1 Parthenice mantuani qqto.[1237]   in fol.   51   051
1 Petrus Crinitus[1238]   in fol.   102   102
1 Pandecte medicine[1239]   in fol. p[ergamin]o   170   170
1 Pomponius Mela in 4⁽ᵗᵒ⁾   25   025

[1230] Gatinaria, Marcus. *M. Gatinarie de curis egritudinum particularium noni Almansoris practica vberrima. Blasij Astarij de curis febrium libellus utilis. Cesaris Landulphi de curis earundem opusculum. Sebastiani Aquilani tractatus de morbo Gallico celeberrimus. Ejusdē questio de febre sanguinis* (Lugduñi, Impressum per Simonem Bevilaqua, expensis Vincentii de Portonariis, 1506 [i.e. 1516]). 4.to. National Library of Medicine. Baudrier, V, p. 403. Durling, no. 2016.

[1231] Carranza de Miranda, Sancho. *Progymnasmata logicalia* ([Compluti] Per impressorem Arnaldum Guillelmum de Brocario, 1517). 4.to. León, Collegiata de San Isidoro. Martín Abad, p. 255, no. 61

[1232] Baptista *Mantuanus*, 1448-1516. *Parthenice septem: nouiter impresse* (In Complutensi Academia. Per Arnaldum guillelmum de brocario, 1523). 4.to. Folger Shakespeare Library. Martín Abad, p. 293, no. 110. An earlier edition was published by Brocar in 1517. The inventory copy may also have been an edition of the *Prima parthenice* or the ... *secunda,* ... *tertia.*

[1233] Erasmus, Desiderius. See footnote 484.

[1234] See footnote 495.

[1235] See footnote 963.

[1236] López de Palacios Rubios, Juan. *Glosemata: legum Tauri quas vulg⁹ de Toro appellat* (Salmanticensi academia, expensis Johānis de junta calcographi, 1542). Folio. British Library. Hispanic Society of America. Palau, 141670. Penney, p. 101. Rhodes, p. 47.

[1237] Baptista Mantuanus. *Parthenice prima f. Baptiste Mantuani ... Cum ... Sebastiani Murrhonis interpretationib[us]: cumq[ue] ... explanatione Iodoci Badii Ascensii* ([Paris] Veneunt in edibus Francisci Reginaldi ... necno Egidii Gormontii [after 1507]). Folio. Huntington Library. Yale University.

[1238] See footnote 515.

[1239] See footnote 509.

1 Problemmas de Villalobos[1240] in fol.	85	085
1 Philosophia Orbelli[1241] in p[ergamin]o	17	017
1 Processionarium benedictinum in 4to	102	102
1 Petrus de Aliaco[1242] in 4to	25	025
1 Petrus de Argilata[1243] in fol.	85	085
1 Predicamenta in fol. ligat.	85	085
1 Prima parte summe sancti Thome[1244] in fol.	68	068
1 Panis quotidianus in 4to ligat.	136	136
		1,392
/ ij,dcclj /		1,359
		L. 2,751

1 Quintus Curtius[1245] in 8° p[ergamin]o	45	045
1 Quiros sobre la passion[1246] in 4to	51	051
1 Quintilianus[1247] in 8° viejo	119	119
1 Quintus Calaber in Homerum[1248] in 8°	51	051
1 Quintilianus[1249] in fol. ligat.	204	204
1 Quadragesimale Ossune[1250]	85	085

[1240] López de Villalobos, Francisco. *Libro intitulado Los problemas de Villalobos: que tracta de cuerpos naturales y morales. Y dos dialogos de medicina* ... (Caragoça, en casa de George Coci, 1544). Folio. British Library. Other folio editions were published in Zamora (1543) and in Seville (1550).

[1241] Orbelli, Nicolaus de. *Cursus librorum philosophie naturali* and *Sumule philosophie rationalis* (Basileae, 1503) are found bound together.

[1242] See footnote 531.

[1243] Argellata, Petrus de. *Petri de Largelata chirurgie libri sex: novissime post omnes impressiones ubique terrarum excussas* ... *Adjuncta etiam Chirurgia* ... *Albucasis cum cauteriis & instrumentis suis figuraliter appositit* (Venetijs, Mandato & expensis Luceantonii de Giunta, 1531). Folio. National Library of Medicine. British Library. Durling, no. 258. Camerini, I, p. 242.

[1244] Thomas Aquinas, Saint, 1225?-1274. *Prima pars. s. tho. cū cōmē. car. Caietani* (Uenetijs apud heredes Luce antonij Iunte, 1538). Folio. Princeton University. Camerini, I, p. 317. This firm also published an earlier edition in 1521.

[1245] Curtius Rufus, Quintus. *Opera*. The Giunta firm of Florence published octavo editions in 1507 (edited by Luca della Robbia) and 1517 (edited by A. Francinus).

[1246] The author is probably Juan de Quirós, author of *Christopathia*.

[1247] Quintilianus, Marcus Fabius. *M. F. QVINTILIANVS ... de institutione oratoria* (Florētiæ, Sumptu P. Iuntæ, 1515). 8.vo. British Library. Trinity College, Cambridge.

[1248] Quintus, *Smyrnaeus*. *Quinti Calabri derelictorum ab Homero libri quatuordecim* (Antuerpiae, Apud Ioannem Steelsium, 1539). 8.vo. British Library.

[1249] Quintilianus, Marcus Fabius. There are several folio editions of the *Institutiones oratoriae*, including a 1549 edition by Vascosanus in Paris.

[1250] Osuna, Francisco de. See footnote 474.

1 Quodlibeta Sancti Thome[1251] in fol. 102		102
		L. 657

/ ,dclvij /

6 Repertorio de t[iem]pos[1252] in 8° 25		150
1 Rethorica tullij in ro[man]ce 34		034
1 Repeticio Urzurro[1253] 68		068
2 Reyna Sibilla[1254] in 4to 17		034
1 Rey Canamor[1255] ligat. 17		017
1 Reglą siue declamatio d. Augustini 25		025
1 Rethorica Aristo[teles][1256] in 8° 34		034
1 Rationale in 4to novi tab. 238		238
1 Robertus Senalis in posteriora[1257] in 4to 51		051
		L. 651

/ ,dclj /

(f. 56)

1 Sermones Bernardi de Tempore[1258] in 4to 85		085
1 Sermones Liciensis[1259] in fol. 119		119
1 Silius Italicus[1260] in 8° 68		068

[1251] Thomas Aquinas, Saint. *Quodlibeta*. Folio editions were published in Venice in 1501 and 1503, and Cologne in 1501 and 1509.

[1252] See footnote 987.

[1253] See footnote 564.

[1254] *La historia de la reyna Sebilla* (Burgos, en casa de Juan de Junta, 1551 and 1553). 4.to. Biblioteca Nacional, Madrid. Bibliothèque Nationale, Paris. Palau, 115293 note. *Catálogo colectivo*, H, 523, 524.

[1255] *La historia del rey Canamor* (Seuilla, por jacobo cromberger aleman, 1528). 4.to. British Library. Griffin, Appendix One, no. 285. It was later printed by the Junta firm in Burgos in 1562. Griffin notes that the inventory of the Cromberger bookshop in 1529 valued the book at 14 *maravedís*, and the number of copies were 1,501, clearly a large edition.

[1256] Aristoteles. *Rhetorica* (Basileae, Apud Isingriniū, 1546). 8.vo. British Library.

[1257] Alliaco, Petrus de. See footnote 552.

[1258] Bernard *de Clairvaux*, St., 1091-1153. *Sermones de tempore et de sanctis* (Venetijs, Johannem Emericū [for Lucantonio Giunta] 1495). 4.to. British Library. Newberry Library. Library of Congress. Camerini, I, p. 86.

[1259] Caraccioli, Roberto, 1425-1495. A number of editions of his sermons were published before 1500, in Venice, Cologne, Strassburg, Basel, Lyons, Antwerp, Naples, Rome.

[1260] Silius Italicus, Caius. The Giunta firm of Florence published an octavo edition of *Opus de bello punico secundo* in 1515. British Library. Another copy is listed below in the inventory (see footnote 1264) with the note "Florentie" which might mean that this copy could be from the Lyons (Gryphius, 1551) or Paris editions.

1 Ser[mone]s Barlette[1261] in 8° 68		068
1 Sermon de amores[1262] in 4to 10		010
1 Seraphino de Fermo[1263] in 8° 34		034
1 Superstitiones de Cyruelo[1264] in 4to 34		034
1 Sant angela de Fulg[inio][1265] in 4to 51		051
1 Sedullius de Carmine pascali[1266] in 4to 25		025
1 Silius Italicus[1267] in 8° Florencie 68		068
1 Sophismata Bureidan[1268] in 4to 68		068
1 Sumule de Magistris[1269] in 4to 85		085
1 Sermones Dorbelli[1270] in 8° 85		085
1 Sermones Bonaventure[1271] in 8° 68		068
1 Siliceus de nomine Jesu[1272] in 8° 51		051
1 Summa consilior[um][1273] in 4to 238		238
1 Summa roselle[1274] in fol. 238		238
1 Sphera qqto.[1275] in fol. 476		476

[1261] See footnote 578.

[1262] Buen Talante. *Sermon de amores del maestro buĕtalāte* ([Medina del Campo, Pedro del Castro] 1542). 4.to. British Library. Rhodes, pp. 36, 48. The work is also attributed to Christóbal de Castillejo.

[1263] Serafino, da Fermo. De Bujanda lists two 1554 editions of his works, Medina del Campo (Guillermo de Millis) and Salamanca (Juan de Canova); and a 1556 edition, Anvers (Martinus Nutius). I am not sure which of these are octavos. See also footnote 808.

[1264] See footnote 995.

[1265] Angela, of Foligno, 1248?-1300.

[1266] See footnote 568.

[1267] Silius Italicus, Caius. Probably the *De bello punico* published by Filippo Giunti (Florentiæ, opera & sumptu Philippi Iuntæ, 1515). 8.vo. British Library.

[1268] Buridan, Jean, fl. 1328-1358. There are two surviving incunable editions of the *Sophismata* published in Paris.

[1269] Magistris, Joannes de, 15th cent. *Summularum Petri Hispani glossulae* [Venice], Bonetus Locatellus for Octavianus Scotus, 1490.

[1270] Dorbellus, Petrus. *Sermones hortuli conscientie sup[er] Epistolas quadragesime* (Parrhisiis, J. Barbier, 1508). 8.vo. British Library.

[1271] Bonaventura, St. *Sermões quattuor nouissimorum perutiles* ... (Colonie, apud Predicadores [C. van Zierikzee, 1505?]). 8.vo. British Library.

[1272] See footnote 595.

[1273] See footnote 584.

[1274] See footnote 581.

[1275] Sacro Bosco, Johannes de. *Spherae tractatus* (in urbe Uenata, Luce Antonii Iuntae Florentini officina, 1531; or Salamanca, Imprenta de Rodrigo y Gonzalo de Castañeda, 1534). Folio. Camerini, I, p.245. Ruíz Fidalgo, no. 43. The Giunti edition includes other authors' works, and commentary by Luca Gaurico, while the Castañeda edition includes the commentary of Pedro de Espinosa.

INVENTARIO DE LOS LIBROS

1 Summa angelica[1276] in fol. 136	136
1 Salustius qqto. in 4to 85	085
1 Sermones festinales Sanctij Aporte[1277] 102	102
1 Sumule Petri Hispani in 4to 34	034
1 Sylogismi Petri Doltz in fol. 68	068
1 Speculum Cyrilli[1278] viejo 30	030
2 Sotonis deliberacio in causa pauperum[1279] ligat. 20	040
1 Summa de virtudes in 4to 17	017
1 Schala celi[1280] escritto de mano ---	----
1 Sabellici cronice parte 2$^{da[1281]}$ ---	====
	L. 2,383

/ ij,cnlxxxiij /

2 Terentius[1282] in 8° ligat. 68	136
1 Tratado de indulgentijs[1283] 34	034
1 Titus Livius viejo 272	272
2 Treynta preguntas naturales[1284] 51	102

[1276] Angelus Carletus, de Clavasio, 1411-1495? *Summa angelica de casibus conscientiae* ([Strassburg], Impēsis peruidi viri Joānis Knoblouch, 1520). Folio. Andover-Harvard Theological Library. The British Library has several earlier folio editions from Strassburg.

[1277] Porta, Sancho, d. 1429. *Sermones festiuitatum annualium beatissime virginis marie ... emendati per fratrem Alfonsum de Castro ...* (Valentie, industria τ op[er]a Ioannis Ioffre, 1512). Folio. British Library. The University of Chicago has a two-volume edition of Porta's sermons printed in Lyons by Johannis Cleyn in 1516-1517.

[1278] Cyrillus, *Episcopus*. *Speculum sapientiae*. There are several incunable editions. Since the inventory describes the copy as "old" it may be one of the Paris editions (Georgius Mittelhus, 1497; Jehan Petit, 1500?) or that of Logroño (Lugruñij, per Arnaldū guillermū de Brocario, 1503). British Library.

[1279] Soto, Domingo de. See footnote 197.

[1280] Jerome, Saint. [Supposititious works.] A manuscript copy of the *Scala celi*.

[1281] See footnote 149.

[1282] Terentius, Publius, afer. *P. Terentii Afri comoediæ sex, post omnes omnium editiones summa denuò uigilantia recognitae* (Lugduni, apud Seb. Gryphium, 1534, 1546). 8.vo. Library of Congress. Beinecke Library, Yale University. Baudrier, VIII, p. 79, 208. There are numerous other possibilities in octavo, particularly those published in Paris, Basel and Venice.

[1283] See footnote 1022.

[1284] López de Corella, Alonso. *Trezientas preguntas de cosas naturales* (Valladolid, en casa de Francisco fernandez de Cordoua, 1546). 4.to. British Library. Rhodes, p. 118. Could the makers of the inventory have mistaken "trezientas" for "treynta"?

1 Titelman sup[er] epistolas Pauli[1285] pp 68		068
1 Tercia quinquageno del Antonio[1286] 34		034
1 Tractado de misericordia[1287] in fol. 85		085
1 Thomas de anima[1288] in fol. 204		204
2 Tragedie Senece qqto.[1289] in fol. 153		306
1 Tomas de generatione[1290] in fol. 153		153
1 Tartaretus in sumulas Petri Hispani[1291] in 4to 136		136

(f. 57)

1 Tarifa de peso y medida[1292] en Italiano 34		034
1 Tractado del sacramento in 8° 8		008
1 Titus Livius[1293] in fol. pre 340		340

[1285] Tittelmans, Franciscus, 1502-1537. *Elvcidatio in omnes Epistolas apostolicas, per F. Franciscum Titelmannum, Minoritam* (Lvgdvni, apud Gulielmum Rouillium, 1554). 16.mo. Library Company of Philadelphia. Baudrier, IX, p. 213. The Bibliothèque Nationale, Paris, lists a 1553 edition.

[1286] Nebrija, Elio Antonio de. *In quinquaginta Sacrae Scripturae locos non vulgariter enarratos, tertia quinguagena* (Garnata, 1535. 4.to. Univ. of Illinois.

[1287] Alexander, *Anglicus*. Tractado muy utile de las obras de misericordia fidelissamamente traduzido de latin en romance de las obras del famoso doctor Alexãdro Anglico (Toledo, en casa de micer Lazaro Saluago ginoues por Iuan de villaquiran τ Iuan de Ayala. A costa del venerable Pero gonçalez de la torre Cura de Valdemora, 1530). Folio. British Library. Pérez Pastor, *Toledo*, p. 68, no. 156. Rhodes, p. 5.

[1288] Thomas Aquinas, Saint. *De anima Aristotelis expositio* (Uenetijs in officina heredum Luce Antonij Iunte, 1549). Folio. Camerini, I, p. 376.

[1289] Seneca, Lucius Annaeus. *L. Annei Senecae Tragoediae septem pristinae integritati restitutae... post Avantium et Philologum: D. Erasmum Roterodamum* ([Paris] Industria Ascensiana, 1514). Folio. British Library. Bibliothèque Nationale, Paris. This edition by Jod. Badius contains the commentary of G. B. Marmita and others. The Bibliothèque Nationale, Paris, has a 1522 folio edition published in Venice (Venetiis, per Bernardinum de Vianis de Lexona, 1522).

[1290] Thomas Aquinas, Saint. *Aristotelis de generatione et corruptione ... commentaria* (Venetiis, apud Iuntas, 1551). Folio. Camerini, I, p. 388. An earlier folio edition was published in Paris (Parisiis, apud J. Kerver, 1537). Bibliothèque Nationale, Paris.

[1291] Tartaretus, Petrus, 15th cent. *Expositio ... in summulas Petri Hispani* (Venice, Melchor Sessa, 1520). 4.to. Another possibility is the earlier quarto edition published by Lazarus de Soardis in Venice in 1515 or the undated Paris edition of F. Regnault. British Library. Bibliothèque Nationale, Paris.

[1292] Paxi, Bartholomeo de. *Tariffa de i pesi, e misvre corrispondenti dal Leuante al Ponente: e da una terra, e luogo allaltro, qua si p[er] tutte le parti dil Mondo* (Vinegia. Nelle case di Pietro di Nicolini da Sabbio, [1540]). 8.vo. British Library. For other editions, see *Rara Arithmetica*, pp. 77-80.

[1293] Five-part folio editions of Livy were produced in Basel in 1531, 1534-1535, 1539, 1543 and 1549. The editor was Desiderius Erasmus. British Library.

INVENTARIO DE LOS LIBROS

1 T[h]emistius in Aristo[telis]¹²⁹⁴ in fol. ligat. 136	136
1 Tesoro de misericordia¹²⁹⁵ in 4ᵗᵒ 85	085
1 Tesoro de pobres¹²⁹⁶ in fol. 17	017
1 Terentius qqto.¹²⁹⁷ in 4ᵗᵒ 85	085
1 Thomas de Garbo¹²⁹⁸ in 4ᵗᵒ 85	085
2 Termini Mayoris in 4ᵗᵒ 34	068
1 Textus misue¹²⁹⁹ in 8° 68	068
	926
/ ij,cmlvi /	1,530
	L. 2,456
1 Vocabularium ecclesiasticum¹³⁰⁰ in 4ᵗᵒ 119	119
23 Virgilius¹³⁰¹ in 8° 95	2,185
1 Virgilius in¹³⁰² 8° viejo 68	068
1 Vocabularium utriusq[ue] Juris¹³⁰³ in 8° 51	051

---

¹²⁹⁴ Themistius, Euphrada. *Commentaria in posteriora Aristotelis* (Venetijs, Luceantonij de Giunta, 1520). Folio, 2 parts. Camerini, I, p. 190. This may also be his *Themistii paraphrasis in Aristotelis posteriora* (Venetiis, Apud H. Scotum, 1542, 1549) or the 1528 edition, *Themistii... in libros quindecim Aristotelis commentaria* (Parisiis, apud S. Colinaeum, 1528). Folio. Bibliothèque Nationale, Paris. British Library.

¹²⁹⁵ See footnote 1015.

¹²⁹⁶ Joannes XXI, pope. *Libro de medicina llamado Tesoro delos pobres* (Seville, Cromberger, 1535, 1543, 1547). Folios. Griffin, Appendix One, nos. 391, 478, 510.

¹²⁹⁷ Terentius Publius, afer. Quarto editions of the *Comoediae sex*, with commentary by Aelius Donatus, Desiderius Erasmus and Giovanni Calfurnio, were published in Paris (Parisiis, ex officina Roberti Stephani, 1541) and Lyons (Lugduni, [Vincent de Portonariis], 1532).

¹²⁹⁸ Garbo, Tommaso del, d. 1370. *Thome de Garbo, filii Dyni... Commentaria non parum utilia in libros Galeni de febrium differentiis cum ipsius galeni textus, seu commentariorum annotatione secundum duplicem (antiquam scilicet et Nicolai Leoniceni traductionem) nondum alibi in lucem traducta: & summo cum labore impressioni data* (Lugduni, [S. Vincent] 1514). 4.to. National Library of Medicine. Bibliothèque Nationale, Paris. Durling, no. 4376.

¹²⁹⁹ Yuhanna ibn Mesawayh or Mesuë. *Textus Mesue. Doctorum celeberrimorum artis peonie cognomina... Mesue vita. Canones universales...* (Lugduni, Impressa per Benedictum Bonnyn, 1540). 8.vo. National Library of Medicine. Durling, 3138.

¹³⁰⁰ See footnote 659.

¹³⁰¹ Virgilius Maro, Publius. An octavo edition of the *Opera* was published in Lyons (Lugduni, Apud S. Gryphium, 1543). British Library.

¹³⁰² The "old" octavo copy might be the 1521 edition, *Vergiliana poemata* (Lugduñ., G. Huyon) or *Virgilius* (Parisiis, Apud S. Colinaeum, 1526). Both British Library.

¹³⁰³ See footnote 668.

1 Vita Christi[1304] falto		~~204~~
1 Vergel de n[uest]ra Señora[1305]	25	025
1 Vergel de virginidad[1306] in 4ᵗᵒ	51	051
1 Vida de S. J[uan] bap[tis]ta[1307]	34	034
1 Vida de S. Francisco y Sancta Clara	17	017
1 Virtutum Vitior[um]q[ue] exempla[1308] pp	68	068
1 Valerius Maximus[1309] in 8° en papel	51	051
1 Versor in Sumulas Petri Hispani[1310]	51	051
1 Viaje de la tierra sancta[1311] in fol.	102	102
2 Vocabulario del Antonio[1312] in fol.	500	1,000
2 Vocabularium grecum in 4ᵗᵒ en papel	238	476
1 Vocabularium grecum in fol. en papel	408	408

[1304] Ludolph of Saxony. *Vita Christi cartujano*. Jácome Cromberger printed editions of this four-volume folio work in Seville in 1530-31, 1536-37, 1543-44, 1551. Griffin, Appendix One. It was also published in Lyons in a quarto edition by Jacobus Giunta in 1536. Baudrier, VI, p. 174. See Lucien Febvre, *Erasmo, la contrarreforma y el espíritu moderno* (Barcelona, Ediciones Martínez Roca, 1971) pp. 56-57, on this influential work on the life of Christ which was published in several translations and in the Latin text in the sixteenth century.

[1305] Pérez, Miguel. *Vergel de nuestra señora* (Seuilla, por Domenico de Robertis, 1542). 4.to. British Library. Rhodes, p. 151. Palau, 219437. This work was condemned. De Bujanda, V, p. 548. See footnote 1046.

[1306] See footnote 1039.

[1307] Carvajal, Pedro de. *Libro d'la vida sanctidad y excellēcias de san Juā baptista* (Salamanca, Rodrigo de Castañeda, 1533). 4.to. Hispanic Society of America. Penney, p. 96. Ruíz Fidalgo, no. 38.

[1308] Nikolas de Hanneppas, Patriarch of Jerusalem. See footnote 673.

[1309] Valerius Maximus. There are several possible octavo editions from Lyons and Paris.

[1310] Joannes XXI, pope, d. 1277. *Petri Hispani Svmmvlae Logicales cvm Versoris Parisiensis ... Expositione* (Venetijs, apud haeredes Lucaeantonij Iuntę, 1550). Folio. University of Pennsylvania, Philadelphia. Camerini, I, p. 379. The Bibliothèque Nationale, Paris, also has a 1518 folio edition by Lucantonio Giunta. The commentary is by Versor, Johannes, d. ca. 1485.

[1311] The *Opus transmarinae peregrinationis ad sepulchram dominicum in Hierusalem*, by Bernhard von Breydenbach (c. 1440-1497) was translated into Spanish by Martín Martínez Dampies and published under the title *Viaje de la tierra sancta* (Çaragoça de Aragõ, Pablo Hurus, 1498). Folio. Biblioteca Nacional, Madrid. Palau, 35731. De Bujanda identifies this with *Passagium terrae sanctae* which the Spanish *Index* of 1559 condemned. De Bujanda, V, p. 426.

[1312] Nebrija, Elio Antonio de. *Dictionarium* (Compluti, in officina Arnaldi Guillelmi de brocario, 1520). Folio. British Library. Norton, 75. Rhodes, p. 12. This is another edition of the *Vocabulario de romāce en latin* published by Varela in Seville.

1 Viaje del Principe[1313] in 8°	34	034
3 Vita Christi in metro in 8°	25	075
1 Valerio de las historias[1314] in fol.	85	085
1 Vocab[ularium] Nebriss[ensis] gallico latinum[1315] in 4to	68	068
1 Vitae patrum[1316] in fol.	170	170
1 Vocabularium arabicum[1317] in 4to ligat.	204	204
1 Vocabularium Nebrissensis in 4to	340	340
1 Vita de Plutarcho[1318] in 4to en Italiano	204	204
1 Virgilius qqto.[1319] in fol. viejo	272	272
1 Vida de n[uest]ra Señora[1320] in papel in 8°	25	025
1 Viola Sanctor[um][1321] in fol.	51	051
1 Vita honesta Platine[1322] in fol.	34	034
1 Vives Introductio ad sapientiam[1323]	34	034
		6,302

[1313] Calvete de Estrella, Juan Cristóbal. *El felicissiimo viaje del muy alto y muy poderoso principe Don Phelippe, hijo del Emperador Carlos Qunto Maximo, desde España a sus tierras de la baxa Alemaña: con la descripcion de todos los estados de Brabante y Flandes.* (Anvers, en casa de Martin Nucio, 1552). Folio. British Library. Bibliothèque Nationale, Paris. Library of Congress. Hispanic Society of America. Palau, 40491. I cannot explain the difference in format.

[1314] See footnote 1047.

[1315] Nebrija, Elio Antonio de. *Vocabularius Nebrissensis ... ex hispaniēse in gallicū traductū* (Parisii, R. Chaudiere, 1516; Parisii, J. Petit, 1523; [and] Lugduni, 1524). 4.to. British Library. Bibliothèque Nationale, Paris.

[1316] Jerome, Saint. *Vitae patrum.* Folio editions were published in the 16th century in Lyons in 1509, 1520 and 1536. The Spanish translation of this work is on the *Index* of 1559. De Bujanda, V, pp. 550-51.

[1317] Alcalá, Pedro de. *Arte para ligeramēte sauer la lēgua arauiga* (Granada, 1505). 4.to. This work contains a grammar, vocabulary and a catechism for new converts. Biblioteca Nacional, Madrid. Guerrero, no. 1.

[1318] The British Library has a quarto edition, in Italian, of Plutarch's Lives, *La prima parte delle uite* (Vinegia, G. Giolito & fratelli, 1555). 4.to.

[1319] Virgilius Maro, Publius. *Uergilius cum cōmētarij* (Venetis, per Gregorium de Gregoris. Impensis vero D. Lucae Antonii de giunta, 1522). Folio. Camerini, I, p. 202. An earlier edition was produced by the Venetian firm in 1519. The works, with the commentary of Servius Honoratus, were also published in folio editions in Lyons in 1528 and 1529, and in Paris by Estienne in 1529-1532.

[1320] See footnote 1046.

[1321] *Viola Sanctorum.* Folio editions of this title were produced in Lyons in 1480 by Philippi and Reinhard, in Basel (B. Richel, 1475?) and in Augsburg (J. Keller, 1482). British Library.

[1322] Platina, Bartolomeo, 1421-1481. *Platine de honestate* (Venetiis, per Ioannem de Cereto de Tridino, 1503). Hispanic Society of America.

[1323] See footnote 368.

(f. 58)

1 Valois in Augusti[ni] de Civitate dei in fol.	51	051
		6,302
vj,cccliij		L. 6,353

2 Libros en blanco marca mayor ligat. p[ergamin]o a	8	736
1 Libro en blanco de marquilla a 8 manos		340
1 Libro en blanco de marquilla a 6 manos		272
1 Apotelesmata in fol. astrologie ligat.		051
		1,399
36 arrobas y media de pergamino escritto que no a de vender		----
16 Pieles de pergamino blanco para enquad.	30	480
41 Medias pieles de pergamino de Flandres	17	697
11 Pieles enteras de perg[amino] de Flandres	51	561
17 pares de tablas de marca mayor	13	231
14 pares de tablas de marquilla	10	140
91 pares de tablas de fol.	9	819
257 pares de tablas de a quarto	6	1,542
3 Palos de box	68	204
57 Manos 18 pliegos de crucifixos negros	25	1,343
10 Manos de crucifixos colorados	45	450
12 Aras encajadas grandez	51	612
8 Aras encajadas pequeñas	34	272
49 Aras por encajar grandez	15	735
		8,086

Lectura vieja con su caja y dos tablas de haya peso @ vij lib x@ 7 lib. 10
La letra del romance nuevo con una arca y dos cajas y tres tablas de ymponer pesa @ 21 lib. @ 21 lib.
La letra del rromance viejo con una caja y una arquita en que estavan los cornetes pesa a ix lib. viij@ 9 lib. 08
La letra dela cartilla nueva con una caja y una arca en que estavan los cornettes pesa @ x lib. ix @ 10 lib. 09
La letra de la lectura nueva con una arquita y una caja y tres tablas de ymponer xii @ xiij lib. @ 12 lib. 13
La letra del canon con dos galeones pesa a v lb. 24 @ 5 lib. 24
La letra de la nomina con su caja y una tabla en que esta la forma de los evang. @ iiij lb. x @ 4 lib. 10
Item otras tres arrobas del romance nuevo @ 3 lib.
Letra vieja para metal con una arquita y una tabla de ymponer @ ix lib. xiiij 9 lib. 14

(f. 59)

La letra dela glosa dela cartilla con una tabla larga de pino pesa @ i lb. xvij @ 1 lib. 17
La lectura cursiva con su caja y una arquita pesa @ v lb. xxiiij @ 5 lib. 24
La letra lectura antigua con su caja y una tabla de ymponer pesa @ vij lib. iij @ 7 lib. 03
La letra de la cartilla vieja con las formas de la cartilla pesan y su caja y dos tablas de ymponer y dos de haya pesa xij @ xx @ 12 lib. 20
La letra del breviario antigua con su caja y una arquita pesa @ vj lb xiiij @ 6 lib. 14
La letra del breviario nuevo con su arca y una arca en que estavan los cornettes pesa @ xj lb xix @ 11 lib. 19
La letra del romance pequeño que esta en un cofre en cornettes pesa @ ix lb xx @ 9 lib. 20
La letra del missal con su caja y una arca y quatro tablas de aya y una galera grande pesa @ xvij lb ix@ 17 lib. 09
La letra del breviario viejo en una forma compuesta con su rama y guarniciones y tabla de ymponer y con su caja pesa @ vj lb x @ 6 lib. 10
La letra antigua del tamaño del romance con una caja y unas galeras largas peso a v lb x @ 5 lib. 10
La letra de los conteros con una arca pequeña en que estavan los cornettes y su forma peso @ iij lb x@ 3 lib. 10
Item [h]ay otras xx libras de la lectura @   lib. 20

Dos ollas la una de campanil la otra de cobre/ una tinaja grande de cobre/ un moledor con su muletta/ un lavador/ una pila de piedra/ un junco de hierro/ un masso de hierro/ dos prensas/ Cinco ramas/ ocho flasquettas nuevas y viejas/ dos tejos/ dos matrices en las prensas/ dos tablas para poner el papel/ dos tinteros/ dos mulettas/ quatro pares de balas viejas/ una prensa de mojar papel/ nueve tablas de ymponer/ una vacina de cobre para mojar los panos/ un ? para poner las cajas/ un cajon con xviij zenas para poner historias/ otro cajon con quatro zenas/ dos bancos en que estan puestos quatro cajas/ dos bancos largos para se assentar los companeros/ dos bancos pequeños/ un tintero para colorado con su aparejo/ onze tablas para ymponer, buenas y malas/ dos piedras grandes/ otras dos piedras grandes para moler/ ocho tablas que estan puestas en la pared para cosas necessarias/ una arca grande adonde estan ciertas historias/ seys galeras viejas/ quatro cajuelas para

(f. 60)

poner los quadrados/ quatro llaves para ramas/ ocho componedores pequeños y grandez/ una tabla grande del Calendario/ un quadrante para astrologos. Un principio grande cortado en madera/ una piedra grande para moler vermellon/ lxiiij panos panos para mojar papel/ dos pares de tijeras unas grandes y otras pequeñas/ unas tenazes/ una olla de cobre con su cobertor/ en que se haze el verniz/ dos martillos chicos/ un bareño/ dos limas/ dos formoncillos/ un rodette un componedor de hierro/ un arca vieja/ lxvj historias viejas que estan en la carpenteria/ todas las reglettas y guarniciones con su cajon pesaron arrobas seys/ dos cajones de guarniciones de madera/ xij hierros tambien para guarniciones/ una mesa larga adonde comen los companeros/ un banco adonde se assientar/ una piedra grande para chiflar cuero/ clxxxvi historias de las hora viejas/ xlij babuines/ clvij viñettas para principios/ xxiiij letras grandez/ cinquenta letras grandez/ xlvij letras mas pequeñas/ un principio de 4to cerrado/ lxv historias para coplas de ambos cabos/ dos principios de 4to cerrados/ otro principio de 4to cerrado con el sacramento/ dos principios de octavo/ dos principios de octavo de Cartillas/ un principio del missal/ dos armas reales/ una donzella theodor[1324] / tres crucifixos en 4to/ otro mas pequeño/ un aba.. ? don fil/ las armas de Juan de Junta/ un principio de Caton/ xij signos pequeños/ cclxx letras de todas suertes/ un abecedario de cobre de quatro renglones/ un abecedario de madera de quatro renglones/ xxxvj letras de diversas maneras/ cv historias viejas de todas suertes/ unas paginas del romance que sierven en las horas para la letra dominical, pesaron xxxv libras/ unas viñettas de romance de estaño y plomo, pesaron xv libras/ xij apostolos/ una cazuela de cobre grande para tinta/ un calderon para calentar lejia/ un cucharon de hierro para deretir metal/ una rama sin cruzera/ un sacco de hacer humo/ xx savanas/ tres masseras/ quatro tablas de manteles delgadas/ quatro tablas de manteles gruessas/ seys tablas de manteles viejas/ siete panos de manos/ seys tovajas/ tres arcas de pino/ una cama de madera/ dos colchones/ una mudra de terliz/ una manta blanca/ una almohada de terliz/ una cifrador/ una mesa de nogal con sus dos pies/ dos tablas de nogal con sus pies/ un cofre de flandres viejo/ una mesilla de pino con su pie/ un cofre de Flandres pequeño viejo/ quatro syllas syn espaldar de cuero/ cinco candeleros/ un armario grande viejo/ un arca de aya para harina/ cinco picas/ dos sartones/ una paleta de freyr/ cinco assadores/ una cuchar de hierro/ tres trevedes/ una caldera grande/ una caldera pequeña/ un almirez con su mano/ dos calderones de traer agua/ dos tinajas para agua/ una carpetta/ un cajon de nogal/ un copero con quatro vidrios/ una arca de pino/ dos coracas/ dos rodelas/ quatro escopetas encajadas/ una escopeta por encajar/ un pavez/ un montante/ quatro ballestas/ una calderilla de ?

[1324] *Historia de la doncella Teodor* was published in Toledo (en casa de Fernando de Sancta Cathalina, 1543) and in Seville (Cromberger [1526-1532?]). Pérez Pastor, *Toledo*, p. 81, no. 198. Griffin, Appendix One, no. 338. This may be a woodcut illustration for that work, but I do not know of a Junta edition.

(f. 61)

una arca adonde duermen los companeros/ un armario de pino/ dos camas de madera/ un almofi de canamaça/ una coçedra de stopa con su pluma/ un colchon de lienço con su lana/ un cabeçal de pluma de stopa/ tres mantas de color/ un pagero/ un colchon de terliz con su lana/ un cosmeo de terliz con su pluma/ un cabeçal de stopa/ dos mantas blancas/ un repostero de Castilla/ dos arteças/ tres escriños/ quatro cedaços/ una mesa redonda con su juego de ajedrez/ una escriñola/ una media hanega/ un cedaço/ una coçina largilla/ una circa/ un embudo/ un argadillo/ un costal de lana/ un banco de nogal/ un banco para assentar/ un arca grande adonde estan los missales de pergamino/ una arquilla de haya syn cobertura/ una banca larga/ otra media hanega/ una arca larga de pino syn cobertera/ una mesa de hierro/ un morillo grande/ otro pequeño/ una arca grande que esta en la tienda con mucha herramienta para enquadernar de la qual no se hizo inventario por ser cosas muchas y menudas y queda en fidelidad del dicho Juan de Valdivielso/ una camara llamada la Carpenteria con mucha herramienta de entallador/ una camara llamada la funderia con ciertas baratijas y otras muchas cosas de por casa que no se inventariaron por ser diversas y quedan en fidelidad del dicho Juan de Valdivielso.

De manera que los libros tablas y otras cosas apreciadas montan un quiniento y onze myl mrs. en la qual suma no entran las prensas ny aparejos d'ellas ny pergamino escritto ni ajuar de casa por que no se ha de vender y por esto no estan apreciados.

Juan Gomez de Valdivielso
Matthias Gast.

Todos los quales dichos libros, casa, enprenta, tienda y libreria y los demas bienes susoinserados y yncorporados, yo el dicho Matias Gast en nonbre del dicho Juan de Junta mi señor y suegro y usando del dicho poder susoyncorporado, los doy a vos el dicho Juan Gomez de Valdivielso en el dicho cargo de factor y manifiçiador con los capitulos condiciones penas y posturas del thenor siguente:

(f. 62)

Los capitulos siguientes son las condiciones con que Juan Gomez de Valdivielso librero rrezibe la casa y tienda y emprenta de Juan de Junta por mano de Matias Gast

Primeramente conosco yo Juan Gomez de Valdivielso aver recibido de vos el dicho Matias Gast todos aquellos libros y cosas contenidos en dos ynventarios, el uno conforme al otro con sus precios a precios apreciados. Los quales estan firmados de n[uest]ros nonbres y signados de Pedro d' Espinosa escrivano publico del numero d'esta ciudad ante quien esta escriptura se otorga y que se obligado y me obligo a vender de los dichos libros todos los mas que pudiere a los precios contenidos, en los dichos ynventarios con que si en mas los vendiere, que sea para mi el dicho fulano y ansi mesmo me obligo que si los vendiere en menos de lo pagar de mi casa, hacienda hasta en complimento y valor de como estan apreciados en los dichos ynventarios sin que vos el dicho Matias Gast ni Juan de Junta v[uest]ro mayor ni otra alguna persona seays obligado a pagarme cosa alguna por mi trabajo ni comision aun que al tiempo que se me tomare la cuenta me descarguen y descuenten todos los libros que no se hubieren vendido a los mesmos precios como estan puestos enlos dichos ynventarios y aunque si vos el dicho Matias Gast o el dicho Juan de Junta v[uest]ro mayor me enviaredes algunos libros para asurtimiento de la tienda tambien me sean descargado al tiempo de la dicha cuenta a los mesmos precios que me los ubieren cargados con mas el porte que pareciere valer los libros que no avre vendido de los que me avra enviados y no de los otros

ii

Otrosi yo el dicho Matias Gast en nonbre de Juan de Junta mi señor y suegro y por virtud del poder que d'el tengo nonbro a vos el dicho Juan Gutierrez de Valdivielso por manificiador dela dicha casa, enprente y tienda y libreria para que lo tengays a v[uest]ro cargo en lugar del dicho Juan de Junta como yo lo tengo por tiempo de un año conplido primero seguiente que comienca a correr y corre desde el dia de la fecha y no mas si no fuera con expreso consentimiento

(f. 63)

y voluntad del dicho Juan de Junta y de vos el dicho Juan Gomez. Y yo el dicho Juan Gomez ansi acepto la dicho manificiacion y la afirmo y la apruebo

iij

Otrosi digo yo el dicho Matias Gast en nonbre del dicho Juan de Junta mi mayor que por quanto no doy ninguna ganancia a vos el dicho fulano por vender los libros que estan en los dichos dos ynventarios quiero y es mi voluntad que [h]ayays para vos todo el provecho que pudieredes aver o ganar en las enquadernaciones que hizieredes, aora sea de los libros de la tienda, ora sea delos que de fuera pudiere traer para los enquadernar con que vos el dicho fulano pongays toda la costa y trabajo y guardeys, mejoreys, y rrenoveys la herramienta que es del dicho Juan de Junta de tal manera que claramente conste no ser ella deminuyda mas antes mejorada so pena de pagar al tiempo de hacer las cuentas todo aquello que pareciere valer menos con mas la pena en el ultimo cap[itul]o contenida y no lo quieriendo pagar luego por ello pueda ser executado

iiij

Otrosi por quanto no es voluntad del señor Juan de Junta ni de vos el dicho Matias Gast que yo el dicho Juan de Valdivielso compre libros ningunos por no me endeudar digo y prometo so la pena en el ultimo cap[itul]o con[tenid]a de no comprar in fiado ni de contado ni libros ni otra cosa alg[un]a syn espresa licencia del dicho Juan de Junta o de vos el dicho Matias Gast su mandado excepto papel y mantenimientos para la arte ympresoria y esto a mi cargo y rrisgo y que vos el dicho Matias (o por que me [h]aceis o otra persona alguna sea obligado a pagar cosa alguna y en caso que yo quisiere obligar al dicho Juan de Junta vro. mayor o alguna otra persona o bienes, que la tal oblig[aci]on no valga

v

Otrosi que yo al dicho Juan de Valdivielso sea obligado y me obligo de dar a vos el dicho Matias Gast (o a cualquier mandado de Juan de Junta todos y cualesquier libros de la manera que me seran pedidos delos que yo el dicho Juan de Valdivielso

(f. 64)

[H]abre ymprimido de negro solamente y papel comun a rrazon de un ducado de a treci[ento]s y setenta e cinco mrs. cada rrezma ympresa y delo negro y colorado junto de papel comun a rrazon de qui[niento]s e veynte y cinco mrs. cada rrezma syn otra cosa alg[un]a y los p[ro]meto de enviar adonde me mandaren los dichos pagando el porte dende Burgos en adelante hasta llegar adonde quisieren quedando en casa cinquenta por suerte poco mas o menos para asurtimento de la tienda

vi

Otrosi yo el dicho Juan de Valdivielso sea obligado y me obligo a acer toda la costa a mi cargo y mision que fuere menester para sustentam[ient]o dela dicha casa, tienda y prensas como el comprar papel mantenimentos y pagar salarios asi a los companeros de la prensa como a los de la tienda y d'ellos y d'ellas para el servicio comun de la dicha casa por q[uan]to todo ello entra en el concierto de los trezi[ento]s y setenta e cinco mrs. por la rezma ympresa de negro solam[ent]e y en los qui[nient]os y veynte y cinco mrs. por la rezma ympresa de negro y colorado papel comun syn que vos el dicho Matias Gast ni vuestro mayor ni otra persona alg[un]a sean obligados a pagar cosa alguna syno que lo pague yo el dicho Juan Gomez a mi costa y mision como dicho es y que vos el dicho Matias Gast y Juan de Junta v[uest]ro mayor y otras quales quier persons seays libres y quitos de todo

vii

Otrosi que yo el dicho Juan Gomez no pueda vender ni trocar y enviar ning[un]os libros por grueso ni menudo en la dicha casa ymprensos a mercader ninguno para que pasen de Torquemada adelante para Vall[adol]id ni Medina del Campo, Salamanca o Segovia sy no que los libros que vendiere ansy por grueso como por menudo sean de Torquemada para ca y de aca para Montana y Navarra hasta la mar y al rreyno de Francia y al rreyno de Toledo y por el mismo caso yo el dicho Matias Gast ni Juan de Junta mi mayor

(f. 65)

ni otra persona alguna por el no podamos enviar ni vender ni trocar libros de Torquemada hazia Burgos y de ay adelante [h]acia la mar ni Navarra entiendese de los que fueren ymprimidos en la dicha casa de Juan de junta

viij.

Otrosi que si fuere menester que yo el dicho Juan Gomez comprase papel de marquilla o bastardo que vos el dicho Matias Gast o Juan de Junta v[uest]ro mayor sea obligado a me pagar mas por cada rrezma todo aquello que el papel en blanco pareciere aver costado mas de siete o siete reales y medio y no otra cosa pues la ympresion no cuesta mas que el papel, sea grande o pequeño y que si el papel comun valiere mas de a los dichos syete reales, o siete r[eale]s y m[edi]o, que yo el dicho Juan Gomez no ymprimire, y si ymprimere no por esto pueda pedir ni pedire mas de a ducado por la rrezma de lo negro y qui[nien]tos y veynte y cinco por la de negro y colorado papel comun

ix

Otrosi que yo el dicho Juan Gomez no pueda ymprimir por mi en particular ni por alguna otra persona, libros ni otras cosas ansy libros de obispados como de otros comunes (o menudencias y asi de pergamino como de qualquiera suerte de papel que sea salvo por el dicho Juan de Junta o su mandado ecepto sy no fuese con espresa licencia del dicho Juan de Junta y firmada de su nonbre y por qual dicho Juan de Junta señor y dueño de la dicha casa y azienda, me obligo de no ymprimir libro grande ni pequeño sin poner en principio o fin un titulo en que diga ser ympreso en casa del dicho Juan de Junta en tal año y tal mes y sy necesario fuere tal dia y esto se entiende en todos aunque se ympriman para personas particulares

x

Otrosi que yo el dicho Juan Gomez prometo y me obligo mi persona y b[ien]es de pagar en cada un año nueve mill mrs.

(f. 66)

e nueve pares de gallinas al mayordomo de la yglesia mayor d'esta cibdad y si costas de pleitos o execuciones me hiziere por no pagar a tiempo o pagar mal me hiziere que sea a costa de mi el dicho Juan Gomez y no de vos el dicho Matias ni de Juan de Junta v[uest]ro mayor y sera la primera paga por San Juan C[hrisosto]mo ? que vendra d'este presente año de mill y quin[ient]os y cinquenta y siete años e la otra para navidad del dicho año con sus gallinas y ansi en adelante y yo el dicho Matias Gast doy y concedo licencia a vos el dicho Juan Gomez para que vos por vos mismo podays cobrar y aver y que cobreys y [h]ayais todos los dineros que rentaren tres casillas que estan debajo de la dicha casa y del quarto delantero con que vos el dicho Juan Gomez seays obligado a repartir las cosas que fueren necesarias. Se entiende menudas fuera de viga y pared hasta dos ducados

xi

Otrosi que si caso fuere que yo el dicho Juan Gomez hubiese de ynprimir por alg[un]a persona en particular como muchas vezes se ofrece delos quales libros no podria dar ninguna parte a vos el dicho Matias o a Juan de Junta v[uest]ro mayor que en tal caso que me ayan de descontar otro ? ymprimido de negro solamente y seys R[eale]s de negro y colorado por mi caudal de la ympresion de cada rezma y lo que mas me pagaren se parta por yguales partes, la una para el dicho Juan de Junta y la otra para mi el dicho Juan Gomez y si pusiere papel de mi casa sea cumplido el cap[itul]o quinto

xij

Otrosi que yo el dicho Juan Gomez me pueda servir de las prensas de ymprimir letras, historias, artificios asi anejos al arte ympresoria como ala enquadernacion con todo lo que mas en la dicha casa [h]ay syn que por ello sea obligado a pagar cosa alg[un]a salvo entretener los dichos artificios y cosas bien reparadas a costa de mi el dicho Juan Gomez syn que vos el dicho

Matias Gast o Juan de Junta v[uest]ro mayor o otra persona sean obligados a pagar cosa alg[un]a so pena de pagar el menos cabo con la pena en el ultimo capitulo con[teni]da y yo el dicho Matias Gast asi lo concedo y quiero esto se entienda

(f. 67)

que os sirvays de todo lo suso dicho dentro de casa y que no podays serviros fuera de la dicha casa de cosa alguna ni podays, ni es voluntad del dicho Juan de Junta mi señor ni mia, que inpresteis ni saqueis dela dicha casa cosa alguna so la pena en el ultimo capitulo contenida y yo el dicho Juan Gomez ansy lo acepto y quiero

xiij

Otrosi que si n[uest]ro querer ? fuere servido que este contrato page de quatro años adelante que yo el dicho Juan Gomez sea obligado y me obligo de tornar a fundir las letras que menester lo ovieren dentro de Salamanca en casa del dicho Juan de Junta a mi costa con que el dicho Juan de Junta de y enpreste al fundidor las matrizes y que sea obligado a pagar el menos cabo de las letras que no sera menester tornar a fundir esto se entienda de las letras con que abre trabajado y no de otras

xiiij

Otrosi que durante todo el tiempo que estuviere la dicha casa y enprenta de Juan de Junta a cargo de mi el dicho Juan Gomez, que yo el dicho Juan Gomez no pueda acer y que no [h]are contrato de compania de libros ni prensas ni tablas ni otra manera de compania con persona alguna ni comprare letras ni matrizes ni aparejos para ymprimir so la pena de los veynte y cinco mill mrs. contenidos en el ultimo capitulo demas, y allende que todo lo que ymprimere o ganare sea para el dicho Juan de Junta como sy lo oviera ymprimido con sus aparejos del dicho Juan de Junta syn aver yo el dicho Juan Gomez probecho alguno y para ello, renuncio mi propiedad en el dicho Juan de Junta o quien su poder oviere asi al dicho Juan de Junta o su mandado le estuviere bien

xv

Otrosi por q[uan]to yo el dicho Juan de Valdivielso no tengo comision de fiar cosa alguna digo que todo lo que fiare sea obligado a dar cobrado a mi costa dentro de seys meses proximos siguientes contando dende el dia que me fuere quitada la manificiacion de la dicha casa y azienda y si las deudas fuesen tales que se perdiesen o no se cobrasen que se pierdan por mi el dicho Juan de Valdivielso, y no por el dicho Juan de Junta ni otra alg[un]a persona y que yo el dicho Juan de Valdivielso me obligo a mi p[erson]a y b[ien]es de mas y aliende de la fianca que tengo de dar

(f. 68)

de los pagar al dicho Juan de Junta o su mandado dentro delos dichos seys meses siguentes como dicho es esto se entiende de las deudas que yo el dicho Juan de Valdivielso hubiere hecho y no de las que de antes estavan o se devian en la dicha casa

xvi

Otrosi que yo el dicho Juan Gomez de Valdivielso sea obligado y me obligo de tener quenta con dia, mes, año de todo lo que ymprimere y el nombre del libro y quantos pliegos tiene y la cantidad que se hiziere y asi mismo de lo que vendiere y si algo fiare asentar el nombre propio y el plazo de la paga y en cada dos meses sacar una copia d'ello y enviarla al dicho Juan de Junta firmada de mi el dicho Juan Gomez y asimismo sea obligado de asentar de mi mano todas las cosas que comprare so p[en]a que si no fuere asy ? que al tiempo de la quenta sean vistas ser de la dicha casa del dicho Juan de Junta aun que no esten en los dichos ynventarios por q[uan]to quedan muchas cosas menudas por ynventariar las quales quedan a la fideledad de vos el dicho Juan Gomez de Valdivielso

xvij

Otrosi que todo lo que yo el dicho Juan Gomez de Valdivielso vendiere de los libros por mi ympresos en la dicha casa [h]aya y deva rrepartir y me obligo a rrepartir con vos el dicho Matias o Juan de Junta v[uest]ro mayor la mitad de la ganacia de los que abre vendido y es descontando prometo onze rreales de lo negro solamente y qu[inient]os y veynte y cinco mrs. de lo negro y colorado que tengo de aver por mi caudal como esta dicho de cada rrezma y lo que mas se vendiere sea una mitad para el dicho Juan de Junta y la otra para mi el dicho Juan Gomez y esto se entiende de lo en casa ymprimido y vendido por mi el dicho Juan Gomez y no de lo que abre enviado al dicho Juan de Junta ni su mandado y de la menudencia la mitad. Entiendese que el ducado a de ser del dicho Juan Gomez y si vendiere la rrezma a catorze reales que los tres reales de onze a catorze se parta entre mi y el dicho Juan de Junta y si en mas vendiere de a catorze que los reales la demasya sea para mi el dicho Juan Gomez y esto se entienda en la menudencia y no en los libros de prensa

xviij

Otrosi yo el dicho Matias Gast en nonbre del dicho Juan de Junta mi mayor doy licencia a vos el dicho Juan Gomez que podays enquadernar hasta veynte e cinco

(f. 69)

libros por suerte de los buenos y vendibles como son missales del obispado, oras de content. mundi, epistolas y evangelios y otras tales y obligo al dicho Juan de Junta y si neces[ari]o es, a mi el dicho Matias Gast y mis b[ien]es particularmente este capitulo y no en otra cosa alguna de tomar en desquenta o pagar el valor de las dichas encuadernaciones conforme fueren tasados de dos honbres de como entre libreros valieren las dichas encuadernaciones que rrestaren al t[iem]po de la cuenta

xx

Otrosi por q[uan]to vos el dicho Juan Gomez no podeys comprar libros de ninguno digo yo Matias Gast que el dicho Juan de Junta os provejera de los libros necesarios lo qual buenamente pudiere aver segun los dineros que vos el dicho Juan Gomez de Valdivielso le enviaredes y esto quede en libre voluntad del dicho Juan de Junta mi mayor

xxi

Otrosi yo el dicho Matias Gast en nombre del dicho Juan de Junta mi mayor sea obligado a tomar en descargo y descuenta todas las rrezmas ympresas que quedare al fenecimiento de las cuentas a trezientos y setenta y cinco mrs. la rrezma de lo negro, y a quinientos y veynte y cinco mrs. la rrezma de lo negro y colorado, papel comun, y no lo tomando en descargo que vos el dicho Juan Gomez las podays llevar como v[uest]ras al dicho precio de los mismos onze reales por cada rrezma

E nos los dichos Matias Gast en el dicho n[omb]re y yo el dicho Juan Gomez de Valdivielso por mi cada uno por lo quales personas nos oblig[am]os con n[uest]ras personas y b[ien]es y del dicho Juan de Junta a guardar y cumplir los dichos cap[itul]os y cada uno d'ellos so pena de veynte cinco mill mrs. por cada cap[itul]o que quebraremos o no cumplieremos, la una mitad para la camara y fisco de su mag[esta]d e la otra para la p[ar]te de nos obediente. Con los quales dichos capitulos que suso van yncorporados y con cada uno d'ellos yo el dicho Matias Gast en el dicho nonbre nonbro a vos el dicho Juan Gomez de Valdivielso por manificiador dela dicha casa, ymprentas, tienda y libreria por tiempo del dicho un año primero siguiente que comienca a correr y corre desde [h]oy dia dela fecha d'esta carta en adelante y os doy en el presente entero poder cumplido y como de der[ech]o es necesario para que seays tal manificiador de la dicha hazienda en la forma y manera que en los dichos cap[itul]os se declara. E obligo al dicho Juan de Junta mi s[eñ]or y suegro y a sus b[ien]es avidos y por aver a mi por el dicho poder obligados a que lo que dicho es lo avra por firme, estable y valedero para agora y siempre jamas donde no que vos dara y pagara las costas y

(f. 70)

daños ynteresses y menoscabos que a la causa se vos siguieren y rrecrezieren y la pena pagada o no que lo que dicho es valga y sea firme so la clausula radomanente pato (?) y qualesquier juezes y justicias de su Mag[esta]d de qualesquier partes que sean acuya juraron que le someto a ello le apremen como sy por suya difinitiva de juez conp[eten]^{te} lo oviesemos llevado e por el y yo en su nonbre fuese consentida y pagada en cosa juzgada sobrelo qual renuncio todas y quales quier leyes, fueros y der[ech]os que sean en su favor especial la ley del d[e]r[ech]o. en que dize que general Rondeleys fecha que non vala y yo el dicho Juan Gomez de Valdivielso que estoy presente confesando como confieso ser mayor de veynte y cinco años acepto esta escriptura en mi favor y por lo que a mi toca me obligo de guardar y cumplir y mantener y aver por firme y valedero todo lo con[teni]do en los dichos cap[itul]os y en cada uno d'ellos so las penas en ellos contenidos y para que el dicho Juan de Junta y vos el dicho Mathias Gast esteys cierto y seguro de lo cumplire lo que dicho es, doy por mi fiador a Pero Gomez de Valdivielso mi hermano vez[in]o del dicho lugar Dehoz de Valdivielso que esta pres[ent]e, al qual ruego salga por mi fiador que yo me obligo con mi per[son]a y b[ien]es avidos y por aver de le sacar a paz y a salvo y inpdenedo ? d'esta fianca syn daño ni costa alg[un]a, y yo el dicho Pero Gomez de Valdivielso acepto ser tal fiador y ansy yo el dicho Juan Gomez de Valdivielso como principal y yo el dicho Pero Gomez de Valdivielso su her[ma]no como su fiador, y principal pagador aziendo como para ello hago de deuda agena

(f. 71)

mia propia nos ambos a dos juntam[ent]e de mano comun a voz de uno y cada uno de nos por sy e por el todo ynsolidun renunci[an]do como renunc[iam]os las autenticas presentes de fide in socibus hoc hita de duobus rreys con el beneficio de la division y excusion de bienes e la epistola de dibondriano en todo y por todo com en ellas ue co[mparec]e otorg[am]os e conoscemos por esta presente carta que nos oblig[am]os con n[uest]ras personas y b[ien]es muebles, y rraizes der[ech]os y aciones avidos y por aver de que yo el dicho Juan Gomez de Valdivielso [h]are y cumplire de mi parte todo lo con[teni]do en los dichos cap[itul]os suso yncorporados, y cada una cosa, y parte d'ellos so las penas en ellos y en cada uno d'ellos puestas y declaradas y pagaremos todo y qualquier alcanze que fuere hecho a mi el dicho Juan Gomez de Valdivielso en fin del dicho año en que espira este contrato, y mas todas las costas y daños que de no lo acer asi ala causa se vos siguieren y rrecrezieren llanamente que in pleito alguno y sin que contra persona alguna sea fecha ni se haga diligen in excusion de bienes alguna y para lo asi cumplir pagar y mantener y aver por firme y no lo contravenir obligamos las dichas n[uest]ras personas y bienes muebles raizes d[e]r[ech]os y aciones avidos y por aver e damos poder cump[li]do a quales quier juezes y justicias de su Mag[esta]d de qualesquier partes que sean d'estos sus reynos e señorios acuya jur[ar]on nos sometemos y renuncianmos n[uest]ro propio fuero juraron domizilio y la ley si conveneriõn de juridicione comun judiciarum y todo bene

(f. 72)

de restitucion yn yntegrum para que por todo rremedio y rrigor del d[e]r[ech]o y via mas brebe y executiva nos conpelan y apremen a lo asi cunplir y pagar haz[ien]do sobre ello todas las execuciones, prisiones, venciones, tranzes, y rremates de bienes que para ello convengan bien asy como sy lo [h]oviesemos llevado por sentencia definitiva de juez conp[eten]te y aquella fuese pasada en cosa juzgada, y por nos consentida sobre lo qual r[enunciam]os todas y quales quier leyes, fueros y d[e]r[ech]os, ferias y mercados trancas que sean en n[uest]ro favor especial la ley del d[e]r[ech]o en que dize que general Rondeleyo fecha que no vala y por questo sea cierto y firme y no venga en dubio nos ambas las dichas partes otorgamos esta carta que a el escribano pu[bli]co y t[estig]o yuso escripto que fue ella, y otorgada en la dicha ciudad de Burgos a veynte y quatro dias del mes de febrero de mill y quin[ient]os y cinq[uen]ta siete años + Que fueron presentes a lo que dicho es Juan de Leyva tintorero y Pablo de San Millan v[ezin]o y est[udiant]e en Burgos y Lope de Cuvelcu criado de mi el dicho Alonso y los dichos tres otorg[ad]os lo firmaron de sus n[omb]res en el reg[istr]o d'esta carta a los quales dichos Matias Gast y Juan Gomez de Valdivielso yo el escribano doy fe los conozco

P[edr]o Dellanos librero v[ezin]o de Burgos y Diego Rruiz de Castresana estudiante, hijo de Di[eg]o Rruiz de Castresana v[ezin]o de la villa o ni ? juraron en forma de d[erech]o conocer al dicho P[edr]o Gomez de Valdivielso otorgue y que es el mismo como de suso se nonbra y lo firmaron de sus n[omb]res

Piedro Dellano
Diego de Castresana

INDEX OF WORKS IN INVENTORY

Abū Ma'shar 150
Acta concilii Tridentini 40
Actiona Christiana 38
Ad libros tres predictionum Hippocr. (Cuellar) 50
Adagiorvm ... epitome (Erasmus) 38, 60
Adrian VI, pope
    Quaestiones duodecim quodlibeticae 89
    Quaestiones in Quartum sententiarum 89
Aesop
    Fabulae 61
    Favole d'Isopo 158
Aggregator (Dondi) 153
Agricola, Rudolf
    De inuentione dialectica 52
Agricultura 150
Alabança de la Pulga 135
Alarcón, Luis de
    Camino del cielo 110
Alardus Amstelredamus
    Similitudines sive collationes ex Biblijs sacris 93
Alberti, Leon Baptista
    El Momo 121
Albertini, Francisco degli
    Mirabilia Rome 163
Alberto Pio, prince of Carpi
    In locos lucubrationum Erasmi 51
Albertus, Magnus, Bp. of Ratisbon
    Secreta mulierum τ virorum 94
Alcalá, Pedro de
    Arte para ligeramēte sauer la lēgua arauiga 175
Alciati, Andrea
    Emblemas 121
    Emblemata 40, 57
Alcocer, Fernando, trans.
    Ariosto, Ludovico. Orlando Furioso 134
Alexander, Anglicus
    Tractado de las obras de misericordia 172
Ali ibn al-Abbas, al-Majusi al-Arrajani
    Liber totius medicine 160
Alliaco, Petrus de
    Posteriora roberti cenalis 90, 169
    Questiones super libros sententiarū [of Petrus Lombardus] 87
Almain, Jacques
    Libellus de auctoritate ecclesie 149
    Almanach perpetuum 40
    Almanach perpetuum (Zacuto) 40

Alonso de Madrid
> Espejo de illustres personas 120
> Alphabetum hebraicum 150
> Alphonsina (Enríquez) 38
> Altercatio Synagogae et Ecclesiae 39

Álvarez de Ayllón, Pedro
> Comedia de Preteo y Tibalda 113

Álvarez, Vicente
> Relacion del camino y buē viaje que hizo el Principe de Espa 100
> Amadís de Gaula, Book 5 142

Ambrosius, Saint, bp. of Milan
> Commentarij in omnes divi Pauli epistolas 40
> Ameto (Boccaccio) 150
> Amicvs medicorvm (Ganivet) 40

Andreae, Joannes
> Declaratio arboris consanguinitatis 53, 149
> Andria (Terentius) 105

Aneau, Barthélemy
> Picta poesis 84
> Angela, of Foligno 106, 149, 170
> Angelus Aretinus de maleficiis (Gambilionibus) 38

Angelus Carletus, de Clavasio
> Summa Angelica de casibus conscientiae 91, 171

Anghiera, Pietro Martyre d',
> De orbe novo decades 61, 84
> Annotationes in Dioscoridem Anazarbeum (Laguna) 55
> Annotationes in interpretes Pauli Aeginetae (Orozco) 38
> Anothomia Mundini 38

Anselm, Saint, Abp. of Canterbury
> Divi Anselmi in Matthaeum evangelistam 39
> Meditaciones de San Anselmo 131
> Anthidotarius animae (Salicetus) 39

Antoninus, Saint, Abp. of Florence
> Chronica Antonini. 48
> Summa Confessionalis 46
> Summa de confession llamada Defecerunt 114, 155

Antonio da Padova, Saint
> Sermones 91, 95
> Aparejo para bien morir (Erasmus) 104
> Aphorismi Hippocratis 70

Apianus, Petrus
> Libro de Cosmographia 50
> Apocalypsis en rromance 149
> Apologia adversus rhapsodias calumniosarum (Erasmus) 60
> Apologiae Erasmi Roterodami omnes 39
> Apophthegmata (Erasmus) 38, 104

Appianus, of Alexandria
> Historia de todas las guerras civiles 106

Apuleius, Lucius

De asino aureo 37
Lucio Apvleyo del Asno de oro 149
Aranda, Antonio de
Informacion de la Tierra Santa 126
Loores de la Virgen nuestra Señora 128
Loores del dignissimo lugar del Calvario 128, 162
Aranzel. Quaderno delas ordenancas 105
Arboreus, Joannes
Primus (Tertius ...) tomus theosophiae 100
Arderique 152
Argellata, Petrus de
Petri de Largelata chirurgie libri sex 168
Argomanas, Juan de
Tratado delas indulgencias, y perdones 145
Ariosto, Ludovico
Orlando Furioso nueuamente traduzido 133, 134
Orlando Furioso traduzido en Romance Castellano 165
Aristides, Aelius
Λόγοι 82
Aristoteles
Aristotelis et Theophrasti historias 39
De generatione et corruptione 157
Libri artis Porphyrij et Aristotelis 150
Libri Meteororum 39
Organon 44
Pedro, de Castrovol. Incipit tractatus super libros phisicorum 48
Peri zoön ... Περί ζώων ιστ 40
Perihermenias 98
Posteriorum analyticorum 98
Rhetorica 169
Textus abbreuiatus Aristotelis super octo libris phisicorum 96
Aristotelis de generatione et corruptione (Thomas Aquinas, St.) 172
Aristotelis [Dialectica] cū explanatiōe Iohānis de lap 150
Arithmetica brevis 40
Armandus de Bellovisu
De declaratione difficilium terminorum 162
Arnaldus de Villanova
Commentum novum in parabolis divi Arnaldi 54
Opera 37
Arredondo y Alvarado, Gonzalo de
Castillo inexpugnable 110
Ars chirurgica (Guidi) 46
Ars chirurgica (Guy de Chauliac) 49
Ars medicinalis (Galenus) 66
Ars notariatus 40, 41
Arte breue de cuenta Castellana y Arismetica (Gutiérrez) 106
Arte de Amistad (Cicero) 105
Arte de Antonio (Nebrija) 149
Arte de bien morir (Fernández de Santaella) 105

Arte de canto llano   105
Arte de canto llano (Alcalá de Henares)   104
Arte del Computo (Valencia)   107
Arte para bien confessar (Ciruelo)   111
Arte para ligeramēte sauer la lēgua arauiga (Alcalá)   175
Arte para servir a Dios (Madrid)   105
Articella   39, 161
Artis veterinariae, sive mulomedicinae (Vegetius Renatus)   102
Asno de oro, corregido y añadido (Apuleius)   149
Astesanus, de Ast
    Summa Astensis   93
Astudillo, Diego de
    Quaestiones super octo libros Phisicorum   41
Auctores cum suis commentis   37
Auctoritates philosophorum   37
Augustinians
    Regvla beati Avgvstini   90
Augustinus, Aurelius, Saint   162
    Confessiones   112
    Epitome Omnivm Opervm   157
    Las meditaciones   131
    Libro de las meditaciones y soliloquios   130
    Meditationes, Soliloquio   73
    Regla siue declamatio d. Augustini   169
    Sermones   94
Aurea Rosa super euangelia   81
Aureum ac perutile opus practice medicine (Balescon de Tarente)   86
Ausonius, Decimus Magnus
    Avsonii Galli poetæ disertissimi Omnia opera   41
Aventuras del Caballero determinado (La Marche)   107
Avicenna   155
    De viribus cordis cum cōmentarijs   40
    Flores Avicenne   62
Ávila y Zúñiga, Luis de
    De la Guerra de Alemaña   123
Aviso de caçadores, y de caça (Núñez de Avendaño   104
Aviso de curas ... Agora nuevamēte añadido (Díaz de Lu   104
Aviso de curas (Díaz de Lugo)   104
Aviso de penitentes   105
Avsonii Galli omnia opera   41

Baculo de nuestra peregrinacion   106
Baculus clericalis (Cucala)   43
Badius, Jodocus
    see Sallustius   96
Balbi, Giovanni
    Catholicon   45
    Tractatus de praescriptionibus   99
Baldo degli Ubaldi

        Super feudis 43
Balescon de Tarente
        Aureum ac perutile opus practice medicine 86
Banquete de caualleros 147
Baptismale mantuani opuscula 150
Baptista Mantuanus
        Parthenice prima 167
        Parthenice septem 167
Barbo, Paolo
        Quaestionum in quatuor libros Sententiarum 93
Bartholomaeus Anglicus
        De proprietatibus rerum 43
Bassolis, Joannes de
        In quatuor libros sententiarum 53, 151
Batalla de dos 106
Batalla de perros 106
Belial de consolatione peccatorum (Palladinus) 43
Belloni, Niccolò
        Consiliorum liber primus 44
Bembo, Pietro
        Los Asolanos 106
        Petri Bembi Epistolarum 59
Benoît, Guillaume
        Repetitio Capituli, Raynuntius de testamentis 90
Bermudo, Juan
        Declaraciõ de instrumẽtos musicales 117
Bernabé de Palma
        Fuente de vida 123
Bernard, Saint, Abbot of Clairvaux
        Opera quae colligi potuere omnia 42
        Sermones 144
        Sermones de tempore et de sanctis 169
        Stimulus amoris 121
Beroaldo, Filippo, comm.
        Cicero. Tusculanae quaestiones 43
        Cicero, Marcus Tullius. In omnes M. Tullii Ciceronis orationes 81
Bertachini, Giovanni
        Tractatus de episcopo 100
Bertrucius, Nicolaus
        Collectorium totius fere medicine 80
Biblia (Alemaña) 43
Biblia (Antwerp) 42
Biblia (Cologne) 42
Biblia (Louvain) 42
Biblia graeca et latina 43
Biblia sacrosancta 43
Biel, Gabriel
        Gabriel Biel super canone misse 64, 160
        Gabriel Biel super primũ librum Sententiarum 63, 64

Biondo, Flavio
    De Roma triumphante 43
Boccaccio, Giovanni
    Ameto 150
    Cayda de principes 110
    La Fiameta 63, 158
    Las cientnouellas 133
Boethius, Anicius Manlius Severinus
    Consolacion de la philosophia 106, 151
    Opera omnia 151
Bonaventura, Saint
    Cruz de Christo 108, 166
    Dieta salutis 156
    Doctrina cordis 117
    Meditationes vitae Christi 107
    Obras 164
    Sermones 170
    Tratado de la pureza de la conciencia 107
Bonaventura, St.
    Estimulo de amor 121
Boscán Almogáver, Juan
    Las obras 150
Botteo, Enrico
    Tractatus de Synodo episcopi 99
Bouelles, Charles de
    Theologicarum conclusionum 51
Brant, Sebastian
    Expositio titulorum 58
    Navis stultifera 79
Brasavola, Antonio Musa
    Examen omnium syruporum 77
Breue summa llamada Sossiego y descanso del anima (Fuensalida) 143
Breviarium Carmelitarum 42
Breviarium Cisterciense 41
Breviarium de las plagas 42
Breviarium de mercede 151
Breviarium del Calice 42
Breviarium medinense 41
Breviarium ord. Carthusiensis 41
Breviarium Praedicatorum 41, 42
Breviarium romanum 41, 42, 151
Breviarium Romanum de las armas 42
Breviarium Salmanticensis 43
Breviarium Santi Petri 42
Breviarium secundum consuetudinem ecclesie Valentine 42
Breviarium secundum ordinationem ecclesie Segobiensis 151
Breviarium secundum Ordinem Inmaculatae Concepcionis 41
Bruni, Giovanni
    Le cose uolgari 72
Bucolica (Virgilius Maro) 42

Budé, Guillaume
   Commentarii linguae graecae 49
   Epistolae 60
Buen plazer trobado (Hurtado de Mendoza) 106
Buen Talante
   Sermon de amores 170
Burchard, Johann
   Ordinarivm Missae 79
Buridan, Jean
   Sophismata 170
Busto, Bernabé de
   Introductiones grammaticas 67

C. Ivlii Caesaris rerum ab se gestarum commentarii 49
Caesar, Caius Julius
   Caesaris rerum ab se gestarum commentarii 49
   Comentarios de Cesar 112, 153
   Commentaria 51
   Commentarii [De bello gallico] 153
Cagnazzo, Giovanni
   Summa summarum 93
Calendarium franciscanorum 153
Calendarium Romanum (Stoffler) 46
Calepino, Ambrogio 45
   Ambrosii Calepini Bergomatis Lexicon 45
   Dictionarum linguarum septem 103
Calisto y Melibea (Rojas) 109
Camino del cielo (Alarcón) 110
Campen, Jean de
   Enchiridion Psalmorvm 59
Canamor
   La historia del rey Canamor 169
Cancionero espiritual 112
Cano, Melchor
   Relectio de Poenitentia 49
   Relectio de sacramentis 49
   Tractado de la victoria de si mismo 147
Canones Consiliorum 52
Cantiuncula, Claudius
   Topica legalia 99
Canzoniere et triomphi (Petrarca) 51
Caoursin, Gulielmus
   La conquista y cruenta batalla de Rhodas 112
Capella, Martianus Mineus Felix
   De nuptiis Philologiae et Mercurii 76
Capitulos de Corregidores 113
Capitulos de Toledo 113
Capreolus, Johannes
   Quaestiones in IV libros Sententiarum 154
Caraccioli, Roberto 169

Carcel de amor (San Pedro) 108
Cardano, Girolamo
    Liber de immortalitate animorum 48
Carerio, Luigi
    Practica nova causarum criminalium 84
Carion, Johann
    Chronica 112
    Suma y compendio de todas chrónicas del mundo 112
Carmen de floribus (Mancinelli) 44
Carranza de Miranda, Bartolomé
    Controversia de necessaria residentia personali Episcoporum 53
    Summa Conciliorum et Pontificum 93
Carranza de Miranda, Sancho
    Progymnasmata logicalia 167
Cartagena, Antonius de
    Liber de peste, de signis febrium 38
Cartas de Rhua 112
Carvajal, Pedro de
    La vida sanctidad y excellēcias de san Juā baptista 174
Cassador, Guilielmus
    Decisiones ac intelligentiae ad regvlas cancellarie 55
    Decisiones seu cōclvsiones avreae 55
Cassianus, Joannes
    Opus ... de Institutis cenobiorum 153
Cassiodorus Senator, Flavius Magnus
    Historia tripertita 69
Castiglione, Baldassare
    Libro llamado el cortesano 110
Castilla, Francisco de
    De los tratados de philosophia moral 137
    Theorica de virtudes en coplas 146
Castillejo, Christóbal de
    Sermon de amores del maestro buentalante 170
Castillo de Villasante, Diego del
    Doctrinal de confessores 115
    Las leyes de Toro glosadas 51
    Tratado de cuentas 145
Castillo inexpugnable defensorio d'la fe (Arredondo y Alvarado) 110
Castrillo, Alonso de
    Tractado de republica cō otras hystorias 146
Castro, Alphonso de
    De iusta hæreticorum punitione 44
    In psalmū miserere mei deus 46
    super psalmū Beati quor. remisse sunt iniquitates 44
Catalogus Sanctorum (Natalibus) 44
Catecismo Christiano (Ponce de la Fuente) 111
Caterina da Siena, Saint
    Las epistolas y oraciones 122
Cathacumenus Romanus 50
Cathechismo 111

Cathena aurea super Psalmos 46
Catholic Church. Cancellaria Apostolica
    Regulae cancellariae 90, 91
Catholicon (Balbi) 45
Cato, Dionysius, pseud.
    Disticha de moribus 51
Catolico 45
Catullus Tibullus Propertius 45
Catullus, Gaius Valerius
Catullus Tibullus Propertius 45
Cavallero de la 4 109
Cavallero de la Cruz (Salazar?) 109
Cayda de principes (Boccaccio) 110
Cazalla, Juan de
    Lumbre del alma 127
Cei, Francesco
    Sonecti, capituli, canzone, sextine, stanze et strambocti 95
Celaya, Juan de
    Magna exponibilia 157
Celestial Jerarquia y inffernal labirintho 118, 125
Celestina segunda (Silva) 109
Celestina tercera 113
Celsus, Aulus Cornelius
    De re medica libri octo 50
Centiloquio de problemas 111
Centum modi argumentandi (Everardi) 49
Cervantes de Salazar, Francisco
    Obras 134
Cessolis, Jacobus de
    Dechado de la vida humana 115, 155
Champier, Symphorien
    Floriani Campegii opuscula Symphoriani 63
    Speculum Galeni 91
Chanca, Diego Álvarez
    Commentum novum in Parabolis divi Arnaldi de Villa Nova 54
Châteillon, Sébastien
    Dialogorum sacrorvm ad linguam 53
Cherubino de Florencia
    Confessionario 114
Chirino de Cuenca, Alonso
    Tractado llamado menor daño de medicina 132
Chirurgie libri sex (Argellata) 168
Christiani matrimonii institutio (Erasmus) 157
Christopathia (Quirós) 110
Christophorus, de Sancto Antonio
    Triumphus Christi contra infideles 96
Chronica Antonini 48
Chronica del Peru (Cieza de León) 107
Chronica del rey don Alonso 107
Chronica del rey don Guiliermo de Inglaterra 112
Chronica Ioannis Carionis 112

Chronica del rey don Guiliermo de Inglaterra 112
Chronica Ioannis Carionis 112
Chronici rervm Memorabilivm Hispaniae (Vasaeus) 44
Chrysostomus, Joannes, Saint
    in Acta apostolorum 47
    in D. Pauli Epistolas 47
    in Euang. Matthaei 47
    Lucubrationes 72
    Sermon de Chrisosthomo 144
Chyrurgia (Guy de Chauliac) 50
Cicero, Marcus Tullius
    Arte de Amistad 105
    De natura deorum 51
    De oratore 50
    De oratore ad Q. Fratrem 46
    Epistolae ad Atticum 154
    Epistolae familiares 59
    Familiares epistolae ... Pauli Manutij scholia 91
    In omnes M. Tulii Ciceronis orationes 81
    Officios 146
    Opera 48
    Orationes 165
    Philippicae 84, 167
    Tusculanae quaestiones 43, 48
    [De Inventione Rhetorica] 154
Cieza de León, Pedro
    Chronica del Peru 107, 153
Cifuentes, Miguel de
    Glosa de Cifuentes 68
Cipolla, Bartolomeo
    Commentaria ... De ædilitio edicto 48
Circe, La (Gelli) 128
Ciruelo, Pedro
    Arte para bien confessar 111
    Confesionario 111
    Contemplaciones sobre los mysterios de la Passion 112
    Expositio libri missalis 73
    Hexameron theologal 110
    Musica 75
    Reprouaciõ de las supersticiones 142, 170
Cisneros, Garsías de
    Exercicios de la vida spiritual 121
Clarian de Landanis
    El segundo libro del muy valiẽte don Clarian 116
Clemente, Dionís
    Cronica del cavallero Valerian de Ungria 147
Clemente, Juan
    Liber super praedicamenta Arist. 70
Clementinae (Covarrubias y Leyva) 154
Cleynaerts, Nicolaus

    Institutiones absolutissimae in graecam linguam 70
    Institvtiones grammaticae Latinae 64
    Meditationes Graecanicae in artem grammaticam 162
Clichtove, Josse van
    Elucidatorium ecclesiasticum 60
    Introductiones 99
    Propugnaculum ecclesie 87
Clypeus thomistarum (Petrus Nigri) 49
Colloquia (Schottenius) 49
Colloquia (Vives) 52
Colloquio espiritual 152
Colloquios o Dialogos (Mejía) 109
Columella, Lucius Junius Moderatus
    De re rustica libri xii 49
Comedia de Nicolao Graffo 152
Comedia de Preteo y Tibalda (Álvarez de Ayllón) 113
Comedia llamada Florinea (Rodríguez Florián) 114
Comedia llamada Seluagia (Villegas Selvago) 107
Comentario de Marco Polo veneciano 110
Comentarius pverorvm de latine linguae elegantia (Cordier) 159
Commentaria (Caesar) 51
Commentaria in regulas Cancellariae Iudicales (Gómez) 65
Commentaria Schodrensis in Plinium 50
Commentarii in Ecclesiasten Salomonis (Tittlemans) 99
Commentarii in VII libros Aphorismorum Hippocratis (Dryvêre) 69
Commentarii initiatorii in Evangelia (Le Fèvre d'Étaples) 62
Commentarii linguae graecae (Budé) 49
Commentarij ... in Euangelium secundum Marcum & Lucam 47
Commentarij in omnes divi Pauli epistolas (Erasmus) 40
Commentarij in omnes Psalmos (Euthymius Zigabenus) 58
Commentariorum in centum Ptolemaei sententias (Pontanus) 84
Commentariorum in Evang. Matthaei (Chrysostomus) 47
Commentarios de la Guerra de Alemaña (Ávila y Zúñig 123
Commentarium in Acta apostolorum (Chrysostomus) 47
Commentarius in Psalmum CXXX (Huelga) 45
Commentum novum in parabolis divi Arnaldi 54
Commentum super prologum naturalis historie Plinii (Figueretus) 62
Comœdiæ omnes (Plautus) 87
Comoedia de Samaritano Evangelico (Papeus) 44
Comoediæ sex (Terentius) 171
Comoediæ: cum cõmmentarijs famatissimorum oratorum (Teren 96
Comoediae, Multo maiore uigilantia repurgatae (Terentius) 96
Compendium dialecticae Aristotelis (Tittlemans) 97
Compendium ethices 48
Compendium in chyrurgia (Santo) 163
Compendium musices 45
Compendium naturalis philosophiae (Tittlemans) 97
Compendium previlegiorum fratrum minorum 45
Compendium super francorum gestis (Gaguin) 154

Conciones de sanctis sive de imitatione sanctorum (Pepin) 88
Concordantiae maiores Sacrae Bibliae 44
Concordantie biblie 152
Concordia evangelica Janseni 48
Confesionario 111
Confessio theologica 44
Confessional del Tostado 108, 152
Confessionale Jacobi Phillipi 46
Confessionale pro instructione confessorum (Savonarola) 45
Confessionario (Florencia) 114
Confessionario (Segura) 107
Confessionario del Hieronymo 113
Confvtatio cavillationvm (Gardiner) 101
Conjugationes 45
Conqueste du Charlemagne des Espaignes 110
Consentius, grammarian 103
Consentius, Publius
 De re grammatica breuissimo institutio 64
Consilia Guid. pape (La Pape) 45
Consilia Montagnane (Montagnana) 152
Consiliorum criminalium 68
Consiliorum liber primus (Belloni) 44
Consilium cardinalium 44
Consilium contra pestilentiam (Gentilis Fulginas) 65
Consolaciō de la philosophia (Boethius) 106
Consonantie Christi et Prophetarum 51
Constituciones de la Congregacion de san Benito de Ualladolid 111
Constitutiones dominice 51
Consuelo de la vejez 109
Consuetudines premonstratenses 50
Contemplacion de la vida de Iesu Christo (Bonaventura, St.) 107
Contemplaciones sobre el psalmo miserere 110
Contemplaciones sobre los mysterios de la Passion (Ciruelo) 112
Contemptus Mundi 108, 114, 153
Contemptus mundi, nueuamente romançado 108
Contextus vniversae grammatices Despavterianae 98
Contra la condicia delas riquezas (Plutarch) 136
Contra la pestilencia 110
Copilacion de todas las obras del poeta Juan de mena 135
Coplas de Mingo Revulgo 163
Coplas sobre el psalmo miserere 114
Coras, Jean de
 In universam sacerdotiorum materiam 48
Cordial de las 4 cosas postrimeras (Denis le Chartreux) 111
Cordial del Anima (Denis le Chartreux) 111
Cordier, Mathurin
 Comentarius pverorvm de latine linguae elegantia 159
 De corrupti sermonis emendatione 55
 Regulae speciales de syllabarum quantitate 155
Córdoba, Antonio de

>Libellus de detractione 37
>Opus de indulgentijs 37

Cordus, Valerius
>Pharmacorum conficiendorum ratio 56

Cornazano, Antonio
>De re militari 51

Cornucopiae: opus commentariorum (Martialis) 163
Corona beate Marie 153
Corona florida (Gazio) 47
Coronel, Antonio
>In posteriora Aristotelis commentaria 88
>Physice perscrutationes 85
>Prima [-secunda] pars Rosarii 165
>Quaestiones Logicae 73

Coronel, Petrus
>Petrus Coronel in predicamenta (Aristotelis) 85

Coronica del cauallero Florambel 122
Coronica delas Indias 108, 109
Coronica general de España (Ocampo) 111
Corporales de Daroca (Cueva) 152
Corpus juris civilis. Digestum novum (Justinian I) 155
Corral, Pedro del
>La Cronica del Rey dō Rodrigo 108

Cortes de Valladolid (1523) 113
Cortes de Valladolid [1537] 139
Costerus, Joannes, of Louvain. ed.
>De veritate corporis et sanguinis 72

Cousturier, Pierre
>De tralatione Bibliae 95
>[Vita carthusianorum] 95

Covarrubias y Leyva, Diego de
Clementinae 154
>In librum Quartum Decretalium Epitome 44, 152

Cravetta, Aimone
>Tractatus de antiquitate temporis 48

Crinitus, Petrus
>Commentarii de honesta disciplina 86
>De poetis Latinis 86

Cristalian de España 115
Cronica de Don Florisel de Niquea y el fuerte Anaxartes (Silva) 117
Cronica de los frayles ... sant Hieronymo (Vega) 109
Cronica de los frayles de S. Hieronymo 153
Cronica del cavallero Valerian de Ungria (Clemente) 147
Crónica del valeroso caballero Lucidante de 128, 129
Cronica granatensis 46
Cronica Saxonie 154
Cruz de Christo (Bonaventura, St.) 108
Cucala, Bartolomé
>Baculus Clericalis 43

Cuellar, Enrique
    Aphorismos [Hippocrates] 154
    Opus ad libros tres predictionum Hippocr. 50
Cueva, Gaspar Miguel de la
    Historia del misterio del altar 152
Cursus Canonicus 52
Cursus librorum philosophie naturali (Orbelli) 168
Curtius Rufus, Quintus
    De rebus gestis Alexandri magni 89
    Opera 168
Cyrillus, Episcopus
    Speculum sapientiae 171
Cyrillus, Saint, Patriarch of Alexandria
    Opervm Divi Cyrilli 46

Dante Alighieri 56
Dati, Agostino
    Elegantiarum linguæ Latinæ 59
De acquirend. possess. (Ferretti) 58
De ædilitio edicto (Cipolla) 48
De anima Aristotelis expositio (Thomas Aquinas, St.) 172
De antiquitatibus Ivdaeorvm (Josephus) 71
De architectura (Vitruvius Pollio) 101
De Arte grammatica (Diomedes) 66
De asino aureo 37
De bello punico secundo (Silius Italicus) 169
De Civilitate morum (Maldonado) 74, 162
De contemptu mundi (Innocent III, Pope) 45
De copia verborum et rerum in iure civili (Oldendorp) 51
De corrupti sermonis emendatione (Cordier) 55
De crisibus (Galenus) 66
De curandi ratione libri XIII (Fuchs) 63
De curis egritudinum particularium (Gatinaria) 167
De declaratione difficilium terminorum (Armandus de Bellovisu) 162
De detractione et famae restitutione (Córdoba) 37
De dictis factisque memorabilibus collectanea (Fregoso) 63
De differentiis febrium (Galenus) 66
De disciplinis (Vives) 103
De dissectione partium corporis humani (Estienne) 150
De divina providentia (Seyssel) 95
De divinis traditionibus 54
De divino nomine Iesus (Martinus Silicaeus) 94
De docendi studendique modo (Roscius) 102
De donationibus (López de Palacios Rubios) 88
De duabus hodie medicorum sectis (Dryvêre) 70
De duplici copia verborum ac rerum (Erasmus) 51
De elegantia linguae Latinae (Valla) 56
De elementis (Galenus) 66
De felicitate Christiana (Maldonado) 163

INDEX

De haereticis aurevs tractatus (Nicolaus Arelatanus) 40
De herbarum virtutibus (Macer Floridus) 74
De homine (Martius) 67
De honesta volvptate (Platina) 162
De honestate (Platina) 175
De immensa misericordia Dei (Erasmus) 120
De indulgentijs (Córdoba) 37
De institutio grammatica (Nebrija) 149
De institutione oratoria (Quintilianus) 89
De Institutis cenobiorum (Cassianus) 153
De intensione τ remissione formarum (Pomponazzi) 81
De interdictum esu carnium (Erasmus) 60
De inuentione dialectica (Agricola) 52
De iusta hæreticorum punitione (Castro) 44
De iusticia ... retentionis regnis Nauarre (López) 83
De la Guerra de Alemaña 123
De lingua latina (Varro) 102
De litteris, syllabis, pedibus et metris (Terentius Maurus) 96
De locorvm affectorvm (Galenus) 66
De los mysterios de la missa (Tittelmans) 144
De los tratados de philosophia moral (Castilla) 137
De lumbricis alvvm occvpantibus (Gabuccini) 72
De maleficiis (Gambilionibus) 38
De medica materia libri sex (Dioscorides) 53
De medicamentorum quomodocunque purgantium (Dupuis) 85
De methodo ac ratione studendi (Gribaldi) 65
De misericordia dei (Erasmus) 60
De modo generalis concilij celebrandi (Durantis) 55
De morbo gallico (Vittori) 63
De morborum et symptomatum (Galenus) 66
De natura deorum (Cicero) 51
De necessaria residentia Episcoporum (Carranza de Miranda) 53
De nobilitate civili et Christiana (Osorio) 82
De nuptiis Philologiae et Mercurii (Capella) 76
De Octo Partibvs Orationis (Donatus) 56
De octo partium orationis constructione (Erasmus) 55
De Oratore (Cicero) 50
De oratore ad Q. Fratrem (Cicero) 46
De orbe novo (Anglerius) 61
De orbe novo decades octo (Anghiera) 84
De ordinaria conversione Peccatoris (Pico) 54
De ornatu animae (Ortiz) 82
De partitione oratoria M. T. Ciceronis (Strebée) 92
De peste, de signis febrium (Cartagena) 38
De plantis ecclesie 54
De poetis Latinis (Crinitus) 86
De principiis (López de Villalobos) 103
De proprietatibus rerum (Bartholomaeus Anglicus) 43
De prudentia (Pontanus) 84

De pueris statim ac liberaliter instituendis (Erasmus) 57
De quantitate syllabarum 74, 163
De quantitate syllabarum (Gomiel) 65
De quatuor nouissimis (Denis le Chartreux) 116
De ratione minuendi sanguinem (Gómez) 65
De ratione studii (Erasmus) 52
De re grammatica (Consentius) 64
De re medica (Celsus) 50
De re medica (Luiz) 38
De re medica (Mesue) 75
De re militari (Cornazano) 51
De re militari (Macchiavelli) 77
De re militari (Puteo) 106
De re rustica (Columella) 49
De rebus gestis Alexandri magni (Curtius Rufus) 89
De rebus Hispaniae (Marineo) 75
De recta Latini Graeciqve sermonis pronuntiatione (Erasmus) 61
De Regulis juris (Decio) 54
De regulis juris (Novella?) 79
De Roma triumphante (Biondo) 43
De salubri victus ratione (Polybus) 85
De scriptoribus ecclesiasticis (Trithemius) 96
De senectute Christiana (Maldonado) 74
De septem Verbis (Jodar) 103
De simplicitate vitæ Christianę (Savonarola) 94
De situ orbis (Mela) 87
De situ orbis (Strabo) 93
De statu ecclesie (Seyssel) 95
De tralatione Bibliae (Cousturier) 95
De urbibus, arcibus, castellisque (Dürer) 39
De usu partium corporis humani (Galenus) 159
De utroqve retractu, municipali, et conventionali (Tiraqueau) 98
De verborum obligationibus (Duaren) 52
De verborum proprietate (Nonius Marcellus) 75
De veritate corporis et sanguinis Domini Nostri (Costerus) 72
De viribus cordis (Avicenna) 40
Decachordum Christianum (Vigerius) 54
Dechado de la vida humana (Cessolis) 155
Dechado de la vida humana (Xerxes, pseud.) 115
Decio, Felipe
De Regulis juris 54
Decisiones ac intelligentiae (Cassador) 55
Decisiones capelle tholose 56
Decisiones seu conclusiones aureae (Cassador) 55
Declamatio sive regule Augustini 54
Declaracio officij misse 156
Declaracion de instrumentos musicales (Bermudo) 117
Declaracion del decalogo 116
Declaracion del pater noster (Erasmus) 116, 155

INDEX

Declaracion sobre los 7 peccados mortales 116
Declaratio arboris consanguinitatis (Andreae) 53
Declaratio articulorvm adversus Haereses (Tapper) 90
Decreta Augustana 54, 155
Decreta et acta sacrosancti oecumenici et Generalis Concilii Tr 38
Dedekind, Friedrich
    Grobianus et Grobiana 67
Del Anima (Denis le Chartreux) 111
Del divino nombre de Iesus (Guijeño) 119
Del divino nombre de Iesus (Martínez Siliceo) 119
Deliberacion en causa delos pobres del Benedictino 118
Deliberacion en la causa de los pobres (Soto) 118
Demandas y respuestas 115
Denis le Chartreux
    Cordial de las 4 cosas postrimeras 111
    Cordial del Anima 111
    Libro de quatuor nouissimis 116
    Svmmae fidei orthodoxae 54
Desafio de los reyes de Francia y Inglaterra 115
Descousu, Celse Hugues
    Reportorio universal de todas las leyes 124
Description del reyno de Galicia 118
Despautère, Jean
    Contextus vniversae grammatices 98
    Grammaticae prima pars 65
Despertador del anima (Raymundus de Sabunde) 117
Despertamiento del anima en dios (Vives) 116
Deza, Diego de
    Exposicion del Pater Noster 120
Dialogo entre un penitente y un confessor 117
Dialogorum sacrorvm (Châteillon) 53
Dialogus Ciceronianus (Erasmus) 45
Diatriba de hominis justificatione (Smith) 53
Diatriba de Justificatione 53
Díaz de Lugo, Bernardo
    Regulae iuris 90
Díaz de Lugo, Juan Bernardo
    Aviso de curas 104, 149
    Aviso de curas ... Agora nuevamēte añadido 104
Díaz de Montalvo, Alonso
    Ordenanças reales de Castilla 165
    Repertorium notabilium questionum 90
Díaz del Castillo, Bernal
    Soliloquios 142
Díaz Tanco de Frexenal, Vasco
    Jardin del Alma christiana 125
    Los veinte triumphos 147
Díaz, Hernando
    La vida y excelentes dichos 115

Dictionarium juris 55
Dictionarium Latinohispanicum (Nebrija) 101
Dictionarium poeticum apud Gryphium 56
Dictionarum linguarum septem (Calepino) 103
Dictorum Factorumque (Valerius Maximus) 102
Dieç, Manuel
    Libro de Albeytería 106
Dieta salutis (Bonaventura, St.) 156
Differētie excerpte ex Laurētio valla (Nebrija) 54
Dilucidariū propositionm exponibilium (Naveros) 79
Dinus in chirurgia (Garbo) 156
Diomedes, the Grammarian
De Arte grāmatica 66
Dionysius, Areopagita
D. Dionysii Areopagitæ scripta 55
Dionysius, Nestor
    Vocabula suis locis & secundum alphabeti ordinem collocata 79
Dioscorides, Pedanius, of Anazarbos
De medica materia libri sex 53
Directorio delas obras canonicas 118
Directorium humanae vite 157
Discursos de la vida humana (La Marche) 107
Dispensarium ad aromatarios (Prévost) 78
Dispensarium medicine 56
Disputationes viginti adversus Lutherana dogmata (Ruíz de Vi 102
Disputatorum in quatuor libros Sententiarum (Rubio) 67
Disticha de moribus, nomine Catonis inscripta 51
Distinctiones Vincentii 55
Diuisiones decem nationum totius christianitatis 56
Diurnal de Astorga 54, 155
Diurnale burgense 155
Diurnale Cisterciense 54
Diurnale de San Pedro 52
Diurnale Hieronymi 54
Diurnale predicatorum 54
Diurnum Ordinis fratrum predicatorum 54
Diurnum Romanum 52
Diurnum Romanum (Alcalá) 52
Divi Anselmi in Matthaeum commentarius 39
Divina commentaria solennesque repetitiones decem (Segura) 89
Divisiones decem nationum 56
Doctrina cordis d'l serafico dotor Sant Bonaventura 117
Doctrina mense (Sulpitius) 52
Doctrinal de confessores (Castillo de Villasante) 115
Doctrinale contra Witclevistas & Hussitas (Netter) 101
Dominicae Precationis Explanatio 85
Don Cirongilio de Tracia (Vargas) 116
Don Clarian de landanis 116
Don Felisbian 116

INDEX

Don Florisel de Niquea (Silva) 117
Don Roselao de Grecia 116
Donation of Constantine 56
Donatus, Aelius
    Commentarii grammatici tres 67
De Octo Partibvs Orationis 56
Dondi, Jacopo
    Aggregator 153
Dorbellus, Petrus
    Sermones hortuli conscientie 170
Dorland, Pierre
    Viola animae 148
Dotrina de religiosos (Humbert de Romans) 118
Dryvêre, Jérémie de
    Commentarii in VII libros Aphorismorum Hippocratis 69
De duabus hodie medicorum sectis 70
    In omnes Galeni De temperamentis libros 68
    Novi commentarii in omnes Galeni libros 68
Duaren, François
De verborum obligationibus 52
    Opera omnia 52
Dueñas, Juan de
    Espejo de consolacion 119, 120, 158
    Tercera parte del Espejo de consolacion 120
Dullaert, Joannes
    Super octo libros Aristotelis de Phisico 55
Duns, Joannes, Scotus
    Questiones quodlibetales ex quattuor Sententiarum 92
    Universalia Scoti 102
Duodecim Caesares (Suetonius) 94
Dupuis, Guillaume
De medicamentorum purgantium 85
Durán, Domingo Marcos
    Tractado dela musica llamado Lux bella 127
Durantis, Gulielmus
De modo generalis concilij celebrandi 55
    Rationale divinorum officiorvm 89
Dürer, Albrecht
De urbibus, arcibus, castellisque 39
Dynus super quarta primi (Garbo) 155

Ecclesiasticae historiae (Eusebius) 59
Eck, Johann
Enchiridion locorvm commvnivm aduersus Lutherum 59
Edificio spiritual de la caridad (Maluenda) 147
Egloga real 122, 157
El arcipreste de Talavera 105
El cavallero determinado (La Marche) 153

El cortesano (Castiglione) 110
El Desseoso 115
El Momo (Alberti) 121
El triumpho de la cruz (Savonarola) 146
El vellocino dorado (Gómez de Ciudad Real) 148
Elegancias romançadas (Nebrija) 121
Elegantiarum linguæ Latinæ (Dati) 59
Elogia veris clarorum virorum (Giovio) 58
Elucidatio in librum D. Iob (Tittelmans) 99
Elucidatio in omnes Epistolas apostolicas (Tittelmans) 172
Elucidatorium ecclesiasticum (Clichtove) 60
Emblemas (Alciati) 121
Emblemata (Alciati) 40, 57
Enarratio rei medice 60
Enarrationes (Chrysostomus) 47
Enchiridion de los tiempos (Venero) 120
Enchiridion militis Christiani (Erasmus) 57, 59, 60
Enchiridion Psalmorum 157
Enchiridion Psalmorum (Campen) 59
Enchiridion, (Dispensarium vulgo vocant) (Lespleigney) 56
Enchiridion, o manual de Doctrina christiana (Jiménez) 130
Enchyridio psalmorum 157
Enchyridion confessorum 57
Enquiridio o manual del cavallero christiano (Erasmus) 120
Enríquez de Valderrávano, Enrique
    Libro de musica de vihuela 124
Enríquez, Alfonso
    Alphonsina 38
Enzinas, Ferdinandus de
    Tractatvs sillogismorvm 98
Epata 158
Epistolae (Budé) 60
Epistolae ad Atticum (Cicero) 154
Epistolae diui Pauli apostoli (Le Fèvre) 62
Epistolae familiares (Piccolomini) 58
Epistolae familiares (Symmachus) 157
Epistolae heroides (Ovidius Naso) 157
Epistolae Hieronymi 156
Epistolae Pauli 56, 156
Epistolae Pauli et aliorum Apostolorum (Vio) 47
Epistolarum libri decem (Plinius Caecilius Secundus) 57, 87
Epistolarum medicinalium (Manardi) 61
Epistolarvm opvs complectens (Erasmus) 57
Epistolas familiares (Guevara) 119, 121
Epistolas familiares (Ortiz) 119, 156
Epistolas y evangelios por todo el año (Montesino) 119
Epistolas y oraciones (Caterina da Siena) 122
Epistole ex registro beatissimi Gregorij 57
Epistole selecte 60

INDEX

Epitheta (Tixier) 157
Epitome grammaticæ græcæ (Hummelberger) 68
Epitome Juris 58
Epitome Omnivm Opervm Divi Avrelii Avgvstini 157
Erasmi Juris 57
Erasmus, Desiderius
    Adagiorum epitome 38, 60
    Ambrosius, Saint. Commentarij in divi Pauli epistolas 40
    Apologia adversus rhapsodias calumniosarum Alberti Pii 60
    Apologiae Erasmi Roterodami omnes 39
    Apophthegmata 103, 104
    Apophthegmatum 38
    Christiani matrimonii institutio 60, 157
    Chrysostomus. Commentarium in Acta apostolorum 47
    De duplici copia verborum 51
    De interdictum esu carnium 60
    De matrimonio 157
    De misericordia dei 60, 120
    De octo partivm orationis constrvctione 55
    De pveris statim ac liberaliter instituendis 57, 156
    De ratione studii 52
    De recta Latini Graeciqve sermonis pronuntiatione 61
    Declaracion del Pater noster 122, 155
    Dialogvs qui titul. Ciceronianvs 45
    Enchiridion militis Christiani 57, 59, 60
    Enquiridio o manual del cavallero christiano 120
    Epistolarvm opvs complectens 57
    Erasmi Juris 57
    Erasmus contra Carpium 60
    Exposicion sobre el psalmo, Miserere mei, Deus 110
    Hyperaspistes diatribae adversus Seruum Arbitrium 57
    La lengua de Erasmo nueuamente Romançada por muy elegante esti 127
    La oracion del Señor que llamamos Pater noster 122
    Moria 163
    Novum Testamentum 78
    Opus de conscribendis epistolis 155
    Paraphrases in Novum Testamentum 83
    Preparacion y aparejo para bien morir 104, 105
    Sermon ... dela grādeza delas misericordias de Dios 120
    Silenos de Alcibiades 143
    Tractado de las querellas de la Paz 140
    Tratado de la oracion 144
Escala espiritual (John Climacus, St.) 121
Escobar, Luis de
    Las qvatrocientas respvestas 137
Espejo de bien vivir 121
Espejo de Caballerías 116
Espejo de cauallerias (López de Santa Catalina) 122

Espejo de consolacion (Dueñas) 119
Espejo de consolacion: parte primera (Dueñas) 120
Espejo de illustres personas (Alonso de Madrid) 120
Espejo de la vida 122
Espejo de perfecion (Herp) 97, 119
Espejo de religiosos 115
Espejo del anima (Evia) 121
Espejo del principe christiano (Monzón) 122
Espina, Alfonso de
    Fortalitium fidei contra Judeos 61
Estienne, Charles
    De dissectione partium corporis humani 150
Estilo de escrivir cartas mēsageras (Yciar) 120
Estimulo de amor (Bonaventura, St.) 121
Estymulo de humildad 121
Ethica, seu moralia opuscula (Plutarch) 81
Eusebius Pamphili, bp. of Caesarea
    Chronicon 153
Ecclesiasticae historiae 59
    Opera 58
Euthymius Zigabenus
    Commentarij in omnes Psalmos 58
Evangelia cum commentariis (Vio) 47
Evangelios epistolas leciones y prophecias 118
Everardi, Nikolaus
    Centum modi argumentandi 49
Evia, Francisco de
    Preparatio mortis 88
    Thesoro de los Angeles 121, 146
Examen omnium syruporum (Brasavola) 77
Exemplario contra los engaños y peligros del mundo 157
Exercitario de vida spiritual (Cisneros) 121
Exercitio de la Vida Spiritual 121
Exercitio del verdadero christiano 122
Exposicion de la passion 119
Exposicion del Pater Noster (Deza) 120
Exposicion del Pater noster (Savonarola) 121
Exposicion del primer Psalmo de David (Ponce de la Fuente) 113
Expositio in summulas Petri Hispani (Tartaretus) 172
Expositio libri missalis peregregia (Ciruelo) 73
Expositio super libros posteriorū Aristotelis (Coronel) 88
Expositio super toto psalterio (Torquemada) 98
Expositio super totum corpus evangeliorum (Simone Fidati) 92
Expositio titulorum (Brant) 58
Externae historiae (Justinus) 70

Fantis, Antonio de, comm.
    Formalitates Scoti 62

INDEX

Fasciculus mirrhe 123
Favole d'Isopo 158
Felix, Magno
    Los quatro libros 122
Fernández de Enciso, Martín
    Suma de geografía 143
Fernández de Oviedo y Valdés, Gonzalo
    Coronica delas Indias 108, 109
Fernández de Santaella, Rodrigo
    Arte de bien morir 105
    Vocabvlarivm Ecclesiasticvm 100
Fernández de Villegas, Pedro
Flosculus sacramentorum 61, 159
Fernández, Sebastián
    Tragedia llamada Claudina 108
Ferrari, Giovanni Pietro
Practica noua iuris 166
Ferretti, Emilio
    De acquirend. possess. 58
Figueretus, Martinus
    Commentum super prologum naturalis historie Plinii 62
Figure biblie (Rampegolo) 61
Firmamenta trium ordinum ... Francisci 63
Flor de virtudes 158
Flores Avicenne 62
Flores de Consolacion 123
Flores legum 63
Flores poetarum 62
Flores ultimarum voluntatum (Rolandinus de Passageriis) 62
Flos sanctorum 122, 159
Flosculi lingue latine 158
Flosculus sacramentorum (Fernández de Villegas) 61, 159
Fontanus, Jacobus
    La muy lamentable conquista y cruenta batalla de Rhodas 112
Forma libellandi (Infante) 123
Formalitates Scoti 62
Formulare Advocatorum et Procuratorum Romane Curie 63, 159
Formulare instrumentorum 63
Formularium diuersorum contractuum 64
Formularium instrumentorum 63
Formularium procuratorum 63
Fortalitium fidei contra Judeos (Espina) 61
Francini, Antonio 69
Francisco de Borja, Saint
    Segunda parte de las obras 134
Franciscus, de Mayronis
    In sententias 76
Fregoso, Battista
    De dictis factisque memorabilibus collectanea 63

Frías, Martinus de
    Tractatus perutilis 98
Fuchs, Leonhart
    De curandi ratione libri XIII 63
    De sanandis totivs humani corporis malis 63
Fuensalida, Francisco de
    Sossiego del anima 143
Fuente de vida (Bernabé de Palma) 123
Fuentes, Alonso de
    Summa de philosophia natural 143
Fuero real de España glosado por Alonso díaz de Montalvo 123
Fugicrettus in Plinium 62
Fusch, Remaclus
    Plantarum omnium quarum apud pharmacopolas usus est 53

Gabriel Biel super primū librum Sententiarum 64
Gabriel of Barletta
    Sermones 92
Gabuccini, Girolamo
    De lumbricis alvvm occvpantibus 72
Gaguin, Robert
    Compendium super francorum gestis 154
Galenus
    Aliquot opuscula 66
    Ars medicinalis 66
    De crisibvs 66
    De differentiis febrium 66
    De elementis libri dvo 66
    De locorvm affectorvm 66
    De morborvm et symptomatvm 66
    De usu partium corporis humani 159
Gambilionibus, Angelus de
    De maleficiis 38
Ganivet, Jean
    Amicus medicorum 40
Garbo, Dino del
    Dinus in chirurgia 156
    Dyni Florentini in quarta Fen primi Avicen. 155
Garbo, Tommaso del
    Commentaria in libros Galeni de febrium 173
García de Villalpando, Antonio
    Instruccion de la vida christiana 125
Garcilaso de la Vega 150
Gardiner, Stephen (pseud. Winton), bp. of Winchester
    Confutatio cavillationum 101
Gatinaria, Marcus
    De curis egritudinum 167
Gaza, Theodorus

INDEX

    Introductionis grammaticae libri quatuor 68
    Theodori Grammatices Libri IIII 159
Gazio, Antonio
    Corona florida 47
Gelli, Giovanni Battista
    La Circe 128
Gellius, Aulus
    Noctes Atticae 39
Gentilis Fulginas
    Consilium contra pestilentiam. 65
    Questiones & tractatus extravagantes 67
Gesta Romanorum 64
Ghaligai, Francesco
    Practica d'Arithmetica 40
Giganti, Girolamo
    Tractatus de pensionibus ecclesiasticis 96
Giovio, Paolo
    Elogia veris clarorum virorum 58
Glosa de Cifuentes 68
Glosemata: legum Tauri (López de Palacios Rubios) 167
Glossa literalis in naturalis historiae (López de Villalobos 102
Godschalk, Jean
    Latini sermonis observationes 94
Gómez de Ciudad Real, Álvaro
    El vellocino dorado 148
    Musa Paulina 77
Gómez de Toledo, Gaspar
    Tercera parte de la tragicomedia de Celestina 113
Gómez, Jorge
    De ratione minuendi sanguinem in morbo laterali 65
Gómez, Luís
    Commentaria ... in regulas Cancellariae 65
Gomiel, Pedro de
    De quantitate syllabarum 65
Gracian, Diego, trans.
    Las obras de Xenophon 134
Gracioso convite delas gracias del sancto sacramento (Osuna) 107
Graecae institutiones (Lascaris) 65
Gramatica del ciego 64
Gramatica Donati 67
Gramatica Eduardi Lusitani 65
Grammatica brevis (Marineo) 67
Grammatica hebraica 159
Grammaticae prima pars (Despautère) 65
Grammaticarum institutionum (Valerius) 65
Grammatices compendium (Sulpitius) 160
Greek Anthology 57
Gregorius I, the Great, Saint
    Epistole ex registro beatissimi Gregorij 57

Homeliae diui Gregorii super Ezechielem 64
In summulas Petri Hispani 64
Los Morales de Sant Gregorio papa 131
Moralia diui Gregorij 76
Treynta y seys amonestaciones del Pastoral 136
Gregory, of Nazianzus, Saint
    Mystica Mosicae uitae enarratio 79
Gribaldi, Matteo
    De methodo ac ratione studendi 65
Grobianus et Grobiana (Dedekind) 67
Guerra de Alemaña (Ávila y Zúñiga) 123
Guerra de Milan 123
Guerricus, Abbot of Igny
    Sermones 95
    Sermones antiqui 95
Guevara, Antonio de
    Libro aureo de Marco Aurelio 131, 132
    Libro llamado Monte Calvario 131
    Libro primero de las Epistolas familiares 119, 121
    Oratorio de religiosos y exercicio de virtuosos 134
    Segunda parte de las epistolas 119
    Vida de los césares 108
Guia del cielo (Léon) 123
Guidi, Guido
    Ars chirurgica 46
Guido de Caulhiaco: cirurgiano y maestro en mediciina 123
Guilelmus Parisiensis
    Rhetorica divina 90
Guilliaud, Claude
    In canonicas apostolorum septem epistolas 65
Gutiérrez de Gualda, Juan
    Arte breue ... de cuēta Castellana 106
Guy de Chauliac
    Ars chirurgica Guidonis Cauliaci 49
    Chyrurgia 50
Guido de Caulhiaco: cirurgiano y maestro en medicina 123

Hanapus, Nikolaus
    Virtvtvm vitiorvmqve exempla 174
Harmenopoulos, Konstantinos
    Promptvarivm ivris civilis 85
Hebraicas institutiones (Pagnino) 67
Henricus Gandavensis
    Quodlibeta Henrici Goethals a Gandavo 89
Henricus, de Herph
    Espejo de perfeciō 119
Herborn, Nikolaus
    Paradoxa seu theologice assertiones 83

INDEX

Sermones quadragesimales 95
Hernández de Velasco, Gregorio, trans.
    [Virgilius] Los doze libros de la Eneida. 119
Hernando de Talavera
    Misterios de la misa 132
Herodianus
    Historiae 68
Heroides Epistolae (Ovidius Naso) 59
Herp, Hendrik
    Espejo de Perfecion 97
Herrera, Gabriel Alonso de
    Libro de agricultura 150
Hesychius of Alexandria
    Lexikon (Gr.) 56
Hevia, Francisco de
    see Evia, Francisco de 88
Hexameron theologal (Ciruelo) 110
Hippocrates
    Aphorismi Hippocratis Graece et Latine 70
    Aphorismos 154
    Libri epidemiorvm 59
    Opera omnia 69
Hispaniola (Maldonado) 74
Historia de la doncella Teodor 178
Historia de la tomada de oran 124
Historia de todas las guerras civiles (Appianus) 106
Historia del inuencible cauallero don Polindo 115
Historia del misterio divino (Cueva) 152
Historia dela bendita Magdalena 128
Historia rerum Venetarum (Sabellico) 47
Historia tripertita (Cassiodorus) 69
Holkot, Robertus
    Super librū Sapientie 160
Homeliae diui Gregorii super ezechielem 64
Homer
    Ilias 161
    Odyssea 165
    Opera 69
    Ulixea 160
Horae beatae Mariae virginis 68
Horae conceptionis (Segovia) 68
Horae hierosolimitane 69
Horae predicatorum 69, 160
Horae romanae 69
Horae Romanae (Lisbon) 69
Horae Romanae (Lyons) 70
Horae romanae (Zaragoza) 68
Horae romanae romance portugues 160
Horas dela passion 124

Horas Romanas   124, 160
Horatius Flaccus, Quintus
    Opera   68
Hore Marie Virginis in metro   69
Horologiographia (Münster)   69
Horozco, Alonso de
    Regimiento del alma   142
Hortulus animæ   68
Huelga, Cipriano de la
    Commentarius in Psalmum CXXX   45
Huerta, Roque de
    Recopilacion de notas de escripturas publicas   133
Hugo de Balma
    Sol de contemplatiuos   144
Hugo de Sancto Charo
    In Dauiticum psalterium   69
    Speculum sacerdotum ecclesie   94
Humbert de Romans
    Doctrina de religiosos   118
Hummelberger, Michael
    Epitome grammaticæ græcæ   68
Hurtado de Mendoza, Juan
    Buen plazer   106
Hymni et orationes   69, 160
Hymni heroici (Pico della Mirandola)   69
Hyperaspistes diatribae adversus Arbitrium Lutheri (Erasmus)   57
Hystoria de como fue hallada la ymagen del sancto Crucifixo   132
Hystoria del Emperador carlo magno   110

Iardin delas nobles donzellas (Martín de Córdoba)   125
ibn Serapion
    Practica   83
Imitatio Christi   65, 108, 114, 153
In Apocalypsim Ioannis Evangelistae (Primasius)   87
In Burbonias consuetudinis commentaria (Papon)   84
In canonicas apostolorum septem epistolas (Guilliaud)
In canonicas apostolorvm septem epistolas   65
In cavsa pavpervm deliberatio (Soto)   52, 171
In Dauiticum psalterium (Hugo de Sancto Charo)   69
In Hippocratis Prognostica commentarii (Vittori)   61
In libros tres Augustini nimphi (Rocha)   98
In librum Quartum Decretalium Epitome (Covarrubias y Leyva)   44
In locos lucubrationum D. Erasmi Rhoterodami (Alberto Pio)   51
In omnes D. Pauli Apost. Epistolas (Petrus Lombardus)   72
In omnes D. Pauli Epistolas cōmentarij (Primasius)   87
In omnes Diui Pauli epistolas enarrationes (Theophylactus)   97
In omnes Divi Pauli Apostoli Epistolas (Theophylactus)   98
In omnes Epistolas Pauli (Sedulius Scotus)   94

INDEX

In omnes Galeni De temperamentis libros (Dryvêre) 68
In omnia L. Annei Senecæ scripta castigationes (Nuñez de 88
In Petri hyspani summulas commentaria (Major) 78
In primam secundae partis Summae theologicae (Vio) 47
In psalmum miserere mei deus (Castro) 46
In psalterio expositio (Ludolphus de Saxonia) 71
In quinquaginta Sacrae Scripturae locos (Nebrija) 172
In Somnium Scipionis (Macrobius) 73
In tertium (-quartum) sentētiarum (Bassolis) 53
In tractatū formalitatum Scoti sententia (Trombeta) 62
In universam sacerdotiorum materiam (Coras) 48
Index operum Aristoteles 70
Index operum Tostati 70
Infante, Juan
    Forma libellandi 123
Informacion de la Tierra Santa (Aranda) 126
Innocent III, Pope
    De contemptu mundi sive miseria conditionis humane 45
Instituciones y doctrina del Theologo Taulero 125
Institutiones absolutissimae in graecam lingvam 70
Institutiones grammaticae Latinae (Cleynaerts) 64
Institutiones grammatice (Priscianus) 65
Institutiones in linguam sanctam (Martínez) 67
Institutiones oratoriae (Quintilianus) 161
Institutionum grammaticarum (Manutius) 66
Institvtionvm libri septem (Lactantius) 162
Instruccion de la vida christiana (García de Villalpando) 125
Instrucion de Mercaderes (Saravia de la Calle) 145
Instruction de guerra 125
Instruction de la vida Christiana 125
Instruction del anima 125
Instruction y refugio del anima (López de Stuniga) 126
Interpretatio in Somnium Scipionis 77
Interpretationes nominum hebraicorum 71
Intonario 125
Introductio ad sapientiam (Vives) 70
Introduction ala sabiduria (Vives) 125
Introductiones (Nebrija) 64
Introductiones artis grammatice hebraice (Zamora) 64
Introductiones grammaticas Busto) 67
Introductiones. In terminos ... (Clichtove) 99
Introductionis grammaticae (Gaza) 68
Irenaeus, Saint, Bp. of Lyons
Opus eruditissimum 70
Isagoge ad sacras Literas (Pagninus) 161
Isagoge Ioannicii (Articella) 161
Isla, Alonso de la
    Thesoro de virtudes 146

Isocrates
    Orationes 82
Itinerario del varon miser Luis (Varthema) 126
Itinerarium prouinciarum omnium (Antoninus) 71
Iuego de damas 126
Iustini ex Trogi Pompeii historijs externis (Justinus) 161

Jacobus de Voragine
    Legenda sanctorum 72
Jarava, Hernando de
    Las liciones de Job con los nueve psalmos 127
    Los siete psalmos penitenciales 143
Jarava, Juan de
    Problemas, o Preguntas problematicas 135
Jarava, Juan de, trans.
    Libro de vidas y dichos graciosos (Erasmus) 104
Jardin del Alma Christiana (Díaz Tanco de Frexenal) 125
Jerome, Saint
    Liber aepistolarvm 59
    Opus epistolarum divi Hieronymi cum scholiis Erasmi 58
    Scala celi 171
    Vitae patrum 175
Jiménez, Diego
    Enchiridion, o manual de Doctrina christia 118, 130
Joannes Climacus, Saint
    Scala paradisi 70
Joannes XXI, pope
    Dialectica Petri Hispani 156
    Interpretatio Georgij Bruxcellēsis in summulas Petri Hyspani 151
    Libro de medicina llamado Tesoro delos pobres 173
    Petri Hispani Svmmvlae Logicales 174
Joannes, de Imola
    Super Clementinis cōmentaria 154
Jodar, Juan de
    De septem Verbis 103
Johannes de Verdena
    Sermones dormi secure 91
John Climacus, Saint
    Escala espiritual 121
Jordan von Quendlinburg
    Opvs sermonvm 92
Josephus, Flavius
    De antiquitatibus Ivdaeorvm libri X 71
Juan, de Aviñón
    Seuillana medicina 132
Justinian I, Emperor of the East
    Corpus juris civilis. Digestum novum 155
    Las instituciones imperiales 126

INDEX

Justinus, Marcus Justinus
    Externae historiae 70, 161
Justino abreviador de la historia del Trogo Pompeyo 125
Juvenalis Familiares commentum (Juvenalis) 161
Juvenalis, Decimus Junius
Iuuenalis familiare commentum 70, 161

La chronica del conde fernan gonçalez 152
La Circe 128
La comedia llamada Thebayda 145
La conquista y cruenta batalla de Rhodas 112
La coronacion (Mena) 110
La Cronica del Rey don Rodrigo (Corral) 108
La gran conquista de vltramar 114
La historia de la reyna Sebilla 169
La historia del rey Canamor 169
La historia que escrivio el poeta Lucano 127
La hystoria breue del conde fernā gōçales 152
La hystoria de Cristalian de España 115
La lengua de Erasmo nueuamente Romançada (Erasmus) 127
La Marche, Olivier de
    Caballero determinado 107, 153
    Discursos de la vida humana 107
La natura angelica (Ximénes) 133
La Pape, Guy de
    Consilia Guid. pape 45
La passion de nuestro redemptor (San Pedro) 166
La prima parte delle uite (Plutarch) 175
La vida de Santana 148
La vida y excelencias y milagros de la virgen Maria (Pérez) 148
La vida y excelentes dichos delos Filosofos (Díaz) 115
La vida y excellēcias de san Juan baptista (Carvajal) 174
La Visitacion de Nra. Señora a Santa Ysabel (Morejón) 148
Laborintho de amor 128
Lactantius, Lucius Caecilius Firmianus
    Institutionum libri septem 162
Laguna, Andrés de
    Annotationes in Dioscoridem 55
Lando, Ortensio
    Paradoxas o sentencias 136
Lapide, Johannes de, comm.
Libri artis Porphyrij et Aristotelis 150
Laredo, Bernardino de
    Metaphora medicine τ chirurgie 163
Las Catorze Questiones del Tostado 139
Las cientnouellas de micer Iuan Bocacio 133
Las cortes de Madrid 113
Las cortes de Madrid (1534) 114

Las cortes de Segouia (1532)   114
Las Cortes de Valladolid (1548)   113
Las diferencias de libros en el uniuerso (Vanegas de Busto)   117
Las fiestas que se hizierō en Roma   129
Las instituciones imperiales (Justinian)   126
Las leyes de Toro glosadas (Castillo de Villasante)   51
Las liciones de Job con los nueve psalmos (Jarava)   127
Las meditaciones, Soliloquios y Manual (Augusine, St.)   131
Las obras spiritvales de Don Seraphino d' Fermo   117
Las ocho questiones del tēplo   139
Las pragmaticas del reyno   136
Las Pregmaticas y Capitulos ... Cortes de Valladolid [1537]   139
Las preguntas que el emperador Adriano hizo al infante Epitus   158
Las prematicas ... de ...Caça y Pesca   135
Las quatrocientas respuestas a otras tantas preguntas (Escobar)   137
Las sergas de Esplandian   142
Lascaris, Constantino
    Graecae institutiones   65
Lasso de Oropesa, Martín, trans.
    La historia ... Lucano   127
Latini sermonis observationes (Godschalk)   94
Latomus, Jacobus
    Opera   72
Le cose uolgari (Bruni)   72
Le Fèvre, Jacques, d'Étaples
    Commentarii initiatorii in Evangelia   62
    Epistolae diui Pauli apostoli   62
    Super institutionibus Iustiniani   62
Legenda divi Francisci   72
Legenda sanctorum (Jacobus de Voragine)   72
Lemnius, Levinus
L. L. libelli tres   71
León, Pablo de
Libro llamado Guia del cielo   123
Lespleigney, Thibault
    Enchiridion, (Dispensarium vulgo vocant)   56
Lexicon grecum   73
Ley de amor (Osuna)   104
Leyes de hermandad   129
Leyes de los abogados y procuradores   129
Leyes de Toro   129
Leyes del estylo   127
Leyes, ordenanças prematicas del obraje delos paños   138
Li, Andrés de
    Repertorio de los tiempos   141
    Tesoro de la Passion sacratissima de Nuestro Redenptor   146
Libellus de auctoritate ecclesie (Almain)   149
Liber de immortalite animorum (Cardano)   48
Liber de peste, de signis febrium (Cartagena)   38

INDEX

Liber hysagoge Joannicii 161
Liber totius medicine necessaria continens (Ali ibn al-Abbas) 160
Libri Meteororum (Aristoteles) 39
Libro aureo de Marco Aurelio (Guevara) 131, 132
Libro d' cozina (Nola) 129
Libro de agricultura (Herrera) 150
Libro de Albeyteria (Dieç) 106
Libro de coplas en loor de nuestra Señora 162
Libro de Cosmographia (Apianus) 50
Libro de Instrucion Christiana (Segura) 125
Libro de la Imitaciõ de Christo: llamado Cõtemptus Mundi 108
Libro de la verdad de la fe (Soares) 126, 128
Libro de las meditaciones y soliloquios (Augustine, St.) 130
Libro de los sacratísimos misterios (Hernando de Talavera) 132
Libro de lucio apuleyo del asno de oro 149
Libro de medicina llamado Tesoro delos pobres (Joannes XXI) 173
Libro de musica de vihuela (Enríquez de Valderrávano) 124
Libro de musica de vihuela de mano (Milán) 127
Libro de pestilencia 128
Libro de pestilencia curativo (Lobera de Ávila) 128
Libro de vidas y dichos graciosos (Erasmus) 104
Libro del esforçado cavallero cõde Partinuples 152
Libro del invencible cauallero Lepolemo (Salazar?) 109
Libro del juego de las suertes (Spirito) 128
Libro del regimiento de la salud (Lobera de Ávila) 141
Libro delas quatro enfermedades cortesanos (Lobera de Ávila) 130
Libro intitulado los problemas (López de Villalobos) 135
Libro llamado batalla de dos (Puteo) 106
Libro llamado el cortesano (Castiglione) 110
Libro llamado Fiameta (Boccaccio) 158
Libro llamado Guia del cielo (Léon) 123
Libro llamado lumbre del alma (Cazalla) 127
Libro llamado Monte Calvario (Guevara) 131
Libro llamado Thesoro de virtudes (Isla) 146
Libro primero de Morgante, Roldan y Reynaldos (Pulci) 132
Libro primero del cauallero Don Clariã de landanis (Veláz 116
Libro segundo de espejo de cauallerias (López de Santa Catal 122
Licier de primagenitura 71
Linacre, Thomas
    Rudimenta grammatices 66
Livius, Titus
    Ab vrbe condita decadis prime 98
    Decades 100
Lobera de Ávila, Luis
    Libro de pestilencia curativo 128
    Libro delas quatro enfermedades cortesanos 130
    Regimiento de la salud 141
    Vergel de sanidad 147
Locorvm commvnivm aduersus Lutherum (Eck) 59

Longolius, Christophorus
    Orationes 81
Loores de la Virgen nuestra Señora (Aranda) 128
Loores del dignissimo lugar del Calvario (Aranda) 128
López de Corella, Alonso
    Trezientas preguntas de cosas naturales 171
López de Mendoza, Iñigo
    Prouerbios 137
López de Palacios Rubios, Juan
    De donationibus inter virum et uxorem 88
    De iusticia et iure obtētionis 83
    Glosemata: legum Tauri 167
    Repetitio rubricae de donationibus 90
López de Santa Catalina, Pedro?
    Libro segundo de espejo de cavallerias 122
López de Stuniga, Diego de
    Instruction y refugio del anima 126
López de Villalobos, Francisco
    Glossa literalis in primum [Plinii] naturalis historiae 102
Los problemas 135, 168
Los Asolanos (Bembo. Gli Asolani) 106
Los discursos (Macchiavelli) 117
Los doze triumphos de los doze apostolos (Ludolphus de Saxonia) 146
Los Morales de Sant Gregorio 131
Los problemas de Villalobos 168
Los quatro libros del cauallero Felix mag 122
Los quatro libros del don Cirongilio de Tracia (Vargas) 116
Los sacratísimos misterios de la misa (Hernando de Talavera) 132
Los seys libros de musica de cifras para tañer Vihuela (Narv 130
Los trivmphos de Francisco de Petrarcha 129
Los veinte triumphos (Díaz Tanco de Fregenal) 147
Lucanus, Marcus Annaeus
    Ciuilis belli libri X 73
    La historia que escriuio Lucano 127
    Pharsalia 72, 73
Lucena, Juan de
    Tratado de Vita beata 148
Lucerna fratrum minorum 72
Lucian
Luciani Opera 73
Luciani Samosatensis opera 72
    Opuscula quaedam 73
Lucubrationes (Valla) 72
Lucubrationes aliquot (Chrysostomus) 72
Ludolphus de Saxonia
    In psalterio expositio 71
    Los doze triumphos de los doze apostolos 146
        Vita Christi cartujano 174

INDEX

Luiz, Antonio
    De re medica opera 38
Lumbre del alma (Cazalla) 127
Lux bella (Durán) 127
Luz de religiosos 126
Luz del alma Christiana (Meneses) 130
Luzero de la vida christiana (Ximénez de Prexano) 126

Macchiavelli, Niccolò
    De re militari 77
    Los discursos 117
Macer Floridus
    Aemilius Macer De herbarum virtutibus 74
Macrobius, Ambrosius Aurelius Theodosius
    In Somnium Scipionis libri duo 73, 77
    Interpretatio in Somnium Scipionis 77
    Somnium Scipionis Saturnaliorum libri 75
Madrid, Alonso de
    Arte para servir a Dios 105
Magistris, Joannes de
    Quaestiones super tota philosophia naturali 166
    Summularum Petri Hispani glossulae 170
    Textus magistri sentētiarum 77
Magna exponibilia (Celaya) 157
Major, Joannes, Scotus
    Quartus sentētiarū 76
Major, John
    In Petri hyspani summulas commentaria 78
Maldonado, Juan
    De Civilitate morum 74
    De felicitate Christiana 163
    De senectvte Christiana 74
    Hispaniola 74
    Opvscvla quaedam 74
    Paraenesis ad politiores literas 74
    Pastor bonus 74
    Vitæ sanctorvm 74
Maluenda, Luis de
    Tratado llamado excelencias de la fe 119
    Tratado llamado leche de la fe 126
    Vergel de virginidad 147
Mammotrectus super Bibliam (Marchesinus) 164
Manardi, Giovanni
    Epistolarum medicinalium 61
Mancinelli, Antonio
    Carmen de floribus 44
Manipulus Medicinarum (Sepulveda) 75
Manual Christiano 132

Manuale chori apuntado 162
Manuale predicatorum 76
Manuale romanum 75
Mar de istorias (Pérez de Guzmán) 131
Marchesinus, Joannes
    Mammotrectus super Bibliam 164
Margarita decreti (Martinus Polonus) 78
Margarita doctorum 76, 162
Margarita philosophica (Reisch) 76
Marineo, Lucio, Siculus
    De rebus Hispaniae memorabilibus 75
    Grāmatica breuis ac perutilis 67
Marsiliis, Hippolytus de
    Consiliorum criminalium 68
Martialis, Marcus Valerius
    Cornucopiae: opus cōmētariorum 163
    Epigrammaton libri XIIII 75, 77
Martín, de Córdoba
    Iardin delas nobles donzellas 125
Martínez de Bizcargui, Gonçalo
    Arte de canto llano 105
Martínez de Burgos, Andrés 142
Martínez de Toledo, Alfonso
    Vicios de las malas mujeres 105
Martínez Guijeño (or Guijarro), Juan
    Del divino nombre de Jesus 119
Martínez, Martinus
    Institutiones in linguam sanctam 67
Martinus Polonus
Margarita decreti 78
Martinus Silicaeus, Joannes Blasius
    De diuino nomine Iesus 94, 170
    [Syliceo sobre el pater noster?] 144
Martius, Galeottus
    De homine libri duo 67
Mazzolini da Prierio, Sylvestro
    Sylvestrinae Svmmae 93
Medicina spiritual preservativa 130
Medidas d'l Romano Vitruvio (Sagredo) 132
Meditaciones de San Anselmo 131
Meditationes Graecanicae (Cleynaerts) 162
Meditationes, Soliloquio (Augustinus) 73
Meditationum, confessionum, ac deuotarum orationum (Salicetus) 49
Medulla dyalectices (Pardo) 161
Mejía, Pedro
    Colloquios o Dialogos nuevamente cōpuestos 109
    Coloquios o dialogos 115
Muestra de la pena y gloria perpetua 131
    Silua de varia lecion 143

INDEX

Mela, Pomponius
    De situ orbis [and other works] 87
Memorial de amor sancto 130, 163
Memorial de la Passion 132
Memorial de la vida de Christo 130
Memorial de la vida de nuestro Redemptor Iesu Christo (Herp) 119
Mena, Juan de
    Copilacion d' todas las obras 135
    La coronacion 110
    Todas las obras 134
Meneses, Felipe de
    Luz del alma Christiana 130
Menor daño de medicina (Chirino de Cuenca) 132
Mesuë
    De re medica libri tres 75
    Opera cum commentariis Variorum 74
    Textus Mesue 173
Metamorphoseos libri quindecim (Ovidius Naso) 165
Metaphora medicine τ chirurgie (Laredo) 163
Milagros de la pena de Francia 131, 163
Milagros de Nuestra Señora de Monserate 132
Milagros de S. Isidoro 132, 164
Milán, Luis de
    Libro de musica de vihuela 127
Mingo Revulgo, pseud.
    Coplas de Mingo Revulgo 163
Mirabilia Rome (Albertini) 163
Mirandula, Octavianus
    Viridarium illustrium poetarum flores 101
Missale Burgensis 77
Missale Carmelitanum 75, 76
Missale carthusianum 162
Missale de Astorga 75
Missale del Calice 75
Missale ecclesiae Toletanae 73
Missale ecclesie Salmanticensis 76
Missale hieronymi 78
Missale predicatorum 77
Missale romanum 74, 76
Missale romanum ordinis Sancti Hieronymi 78
Missale secundum ordinem Carthusiensium 77
Missale secundum ordinem fratrum Carmelitarum 75
Modus legendi abbreuiaturas 78
Mondino dei Luzzi
    Anothomia Mundini 38
Montagnana, Bartholomaeus
    Consilia Montagnane 152
Monte Calvario (Guevara) 131

Montesino, Ambrosio de
    Epistolas y evangelios   119
    Evangelios epistolas; leciones y prophecias   118
Monzón, Francisco de
    Libro primero d'l espejo del prīcipe christiano   122
Moraes, Francisco de
    Palmerin de inglaterra   137
Morejón, Diego de
    La Visitacion de Nra. Señora a Santa Ysabel   148
Morgante maggiore   132
Moria de Erasmo   163
Mudarra, Alonso
    Tres libros de Musica ... para vihuela   129
Mueller, Johannes Regiomontanus
    Scripta clarissimi mathematici   95
Muestra de la pena y gloria perpetua (Mejía)   131
Münster, Sebastian
    Horologiographia   69
Muñoz, Petrus sup[er] threnos
    Petrus Muñoz super threnos   85
Musa Paulina (Gómez de Ciudad Real)   77
Musaeus   164
Musica de vihuela de mano (Milán)   127
Mystica Mosaicæ uitæ enarratio (Nazianzus)   79

Nani Mirabelli, Domenico
    Polyanthea   84
Narváez, Luís de
    Los seys libros del delphin de musica   130
Natalibus, Petrus de
    Catalogus Sanctorum   44
Natura angelica   164
Naveros, Jacobus
    Dilucidariū propositionm exponibilium   79
    Preparatio Dialectica   53, 54
Navis stultifera (Brant)   79
Nebrija, Elio Antonio de
    Aelii Antonii Nebrissensis introductiones   64
    De institutio grammatica   149
    Dictionarium   174
    Dictionarium Latinohispanicum   101
    Differētie excerpte ex Laurētio valla   54
    Elegancias romançadas   121
    In quinquaginta Sacrae Scripturae locos   172
    Libri minores   161
    Pvblii Vergilii Maronis Partheniae Mantuani opera   101
    Rerum a Fernando et Elisabe hispaniarum ...   44
    Vocabulario de romāce en latin   174

INDEX

    Vocabularius Nebrissensis 175
    Vocabularius utriusque iuris 101
Negri, Francesco
    Epistole 58
Nellus, a Sancto Geminiano
    Tractatus insignis de Bannitis 99
Netter, Thomas
    Doctrinale fidei Ecclesie Catholicae 101
Niccolò de' Tudeschi
    In Clementinas 88
Nicolas de Hannapes
    Virtvtvm vitiorvmqve exempla 102
Nicolaus Arelatanus, Joannes
    De haereticis aureus tractatus 40
Nicolaus de Plove
    Tractatus sacerdotalis 97
Nicolaus, de Lyra
    Postilla super psalterium 86
    Tabula super bibliam 97
Noctes Atticae (Gellius) 39
Nola, Roberto de
    Libro d' cozina 129
Nonius Marcellus
    De verborum proprietate 75
Nonnus Panopolitanus
    Νοννου ποιητου με 79
Norte de Confessores 133
Norte delos estados (Osuna) 133
Novelas (Boccaccio) 63
Novi commentarii in omnes Galeni libros (Dryvêre) 68
Novi Testamenti Ientaculis Tractatus (Vio) 161
Novum Testamentum 78
Novum Testamentum (Erasmus) 78, 164
Novum Testamentum cum annota. Isidori 78
Novus orbis regionum 79
Núñez de Avendaño, Pedro
    Auiso de caçadores 104
Nuñez de Guzmán, Fernando
    Castigationes in Pomponium Melam 88
    In omnia L. Annei Senecæ scripta castigationes 88
    Pomponii Melae. Castigationes 88

Observationes lingue latine 82
Ocampo, Florián de
    Coronica general de España 111
Officinae Ioannis Ravisii Textor epitome (Tixier) 80
Officio de la Cemana sancta 165
Officium angeli custodis 133

Officium de nomine Jesu 79
Officium Hebdomadae sancte 80
Officium quinque plagarum 79
Oldendorp, Johann
    De copia verborum et rervm in iure civili 51
Olivier de Castile
    La historia d'los dos nobles Oliveros de Castilla ... 164
Opera in arte chyrurgia (Vigo) 166
Opera quae colligi potuere omnia (Bernard, St.) 42
Opus de conscribendis epistolis (Erasmus) 155
Opus regale (Vivaldus) 82
Opus sermonum (Jordan von Quendlinburg) 92
Opuscula quaedam (Maldonado) 74
Oratio apologetica 165
Orationes (Longolius) 81
Oratorio de religiosos (Guevara) 134
Oratorio del Toledano 134
Orbelli, Nicolaus de
    Cursus librorum philosophie naturali 168
    Sumule philosophie rationalis 168
Ordenanças de los tres adelantamientos 134
Ordenanças que hablan cerca del Calçado y Corambre 135
Ordenanças reales de Castilla 165
Ordenanças sobre el obraje delos paños 138
Ordenances reales en frances 164
Ordinarium fratrum predicatorum 80
Ordinarium Missae (Burchard) 79
Ordo divini officii de mercede 80
Ordo divini officij 81
Oriano, Lanfrancus de
    Practica 86
    Praxis ivdicaria 86
Orlando Furioso (Ariosto) 133
Orlando Furioso nueuamente traduzido 134
Orlando Fvrioso traduzido en Romance (Ariosto) 165
Orozco, Alonso de
    Recopilacion de todas las obras 134
    Vergel de oracion 147
Orozco, Cristóbal
    Annotationes in interpretes Pauli Aeginetae 38
Ortiz, Francisco
    De ornatu animae 82
    Epistolas familiares 119, 156
    Homiliarum 82
Osorio, Jeronymo
    De nobilitate civili et Christiana 82
Osuna, Francisco de
    Evangeliorum Dominicalium totius anni. 54
    Evangeliorum Quadragesimalium 82, 168

INDEX

    Gracioso convite   107
    Ley de amor y quarta parte del abecedario spiritual   104, 150
    Norte delos estados   133
    Pars occidentalis   82
    Primera parte del libro llamado Abecedario spitritual   104
    Quinta parte del abecedario spiritual   104
    Segunda parte del abecedario spiritual   103
    Sexta parte del abecedario spitritual   105
    Tercera parte del Abecedario spiritual   103
    Trilogium evangelicum Primum Christi Passionem   82
Ovidius Naso, Publius
    Amatoria   80
    Ars amatoria   80
    De arte amandi   80
    De fastis   164
    Epistolae heroides   157
    Epistolas Ouidij   59
    Epistole cum commento   59
    Epistole Ovidij   156
    Fasti   81
    Fastorum lib. VI   82
    Libri de Ponto cum commentariis Merulae   81
    Metamorphoseon libri XV   80
    Metamorphoseos   165
    Opera   164

Pagnino, Santi
    Hebraicas institutiones   67
Pagninus, Santes
    Isagoge ad sacras Literas   161
Palladinus, Jacobus
    Belial de consolatione peccatorum   43
Palma, Bernabé de
    Via espiritus: o dela perfecion del anima   147
Palmerin de inglaterra (Moraes)   137
Pandectae medicinae   167
Pandectae medicinae (Silvaticus)   85
Panis quotidianus   168
Papelones d'España   139
Papelones de Flandres   139
Papeus, Petrus
    Samarites Comœdia de Samaritano Euangelico   44
Papon, Jean
    In Burbonias consuetudinis commentaria   84
Paradoxa seu theologice assertiones (Herborn)   83
Paradoxas o sentencias (Lando)   136
Paradoxas o sentencias fuera del comun parecer   136
Paraenesis ad politiores literas (Maldonado)   74

Paraphrases in Novum Testamentum (Erasmus) 83
Paraphrasis in elegantias Valle 167
Pardo, Gerónimo
    Medulla dyalectices 161
Pars Meridionalis Euangeliorum Dominicalium (Osuna) 54
Parthenice prima (Baptista Mantuanus) 167
Parthenice septem (Baptista Mantuanus) 167
Partinuples 152
Paschale cum Aelii Antonii Nebriss. interpretatione (Sedulius) 91
Passagium terrae sanctae 174
Pastor bonus (Maldonado) 74, 164
Patavinus ·
    see Antonio da Padova, Saint 91
Paulus Venetus
    Quadratura magistri Pauli Veneti 89
    Super libris posteriorum 162
Paxi, Bartholomeo de
    Tariffa de i pesi, e misvre 172
Pedro, de Castrovol
    Economica 153
    Formalitates 63
    Tractatus super libros phisicorum 48
    Tractatus sup[er] psalmum: "Quicumque vult" 48
Pelegromius, Simon
    Synonimorum sylva 96
Pepin, Guillaume
    Conciones de sanctis 88
    Opusculum ... super confiteor 84
    Sermones quadragesimales super evangelia 86
    Sermonum dominicalium 86
Pérez de Guzmán, Fernando
    Mar de istorias 131
    Valerio d'las hystorias escolasticas 148
Pérez, Diego
    Pragmaticas y leyes hechas por mandado de los Principes 136
Pérez, Juan
    see Petreius, Joannes 166
Pérez, Miguel
    La vida y excelencias y milagros de la virgen Maria 148
    Vergel de nuestra señora 174
Perihermenias (Aristoteles) 98
Perla preciosa 135, 136
Perla preciosisima 166
Perla y cruz de Christo 166
Perottus, Nicolaus
    Martialis, Marcus Valerius. Cornucopiae 163
Persius Flaccus, Aulus
    Satyrae sex 86
    Satyrae sex cvm qvinqve commentatorib 166

INDEX

Satyrae sex, Ioanne Murmelio scholiaste 166
Petrarca, Francesco
    Canzoniere et triomphi 51
    Los trivmphos 129, 145
Petreius, Joannes
    Progymnasmata artis rhetoricae 166
Petri Bembi Epistolarum 59
Petri Hispani Svmmvlae Logicales 174
Petrus de Palude, patriarch of Jerusalem
    Sermones thesauri novi 95
Petrus Hispanus
    see Joannes XXI, pope 156
Petrus Jacobus a Montepessulano
    Practica Petri Jacobi 86
Petrus Lombardus
    In omnes D. Pauli epistolas 72
Petrus Nigri
    Clypeus thomistarum 49
Petrus, Comestor
    Scolastica historia 69
Pharmacorum conficiendorum ratio (Cordus) 56
Pharsalia 72
Philippicae (Cicero) 84, 167
Physice perscrutationes (Coronel) 85
Piccolomini, Enea Silvio 58
    Epistolae familiares 58
Pico della Mirandola, Giovanni
    Hymni heroici 69
Pico, Domingo del
    De ordinaria conversione Peccatoris 54
Picta poesis (Aneau) 84
Pierre le Vénérable
    Epistolarum libri VI 58
Pindar 166
Pius II, Pope
    Epistolae familiares 58
Pizarro, Diego
    Tractado sobre los Censos 145
Plantarum omnium (Fusch) 53
Platina, Bartolomeo
    De honesta voluptate 162
Platine de honestate 175
Plautus, Titus Maccius
    Comœdiæ omnes 87
Plinius Caecilius Secundus, Caius
    Epistolarum libri decem 57, 87
    Historia mundi 87
Plutarch
    Contra la condicia delas riquezas 136

    Ethica, seu moralia opuscula 81
    La prima parte delle uite 175
    Las vidas de dos illustres varones 147
    Opuscula 165
Polindo
    Historia del cavallero don Polindo 115
Poliziano, Angelo
    Angeli Politiani opervm 165
Polo, Marco
    Comentario de Marco Polo veneciano 110
Polyanthea (Nani Mirabelli) 84
Polybus
    De salubri victus ratione privatorum 85
Polyhistor (Solinus) 92
Pomponazzi, Pietro
    Tractatus ... mere peripatetici 81
Ponce de la Fuente, Constantino
    Catecismo Christiano 111
    Exposicion del primer Psalmo de David 111, 113
Pontanus, Joannes Jovianus
    Commentariorum in centum Claudij Ptolemaei sententias 84
    De prudentia 84
Porphyry
    Isagoge ... Aristotelous 44
Porras, Antonio de
    Tratado de la oraciō 146
Porta, Sancho
    Sermones festiuitatum ... virginis Marie 171
    Sermones festiuitatum beatissime virginis Mariae 95
Posteriora magistri roberti cenalis (Alliaco) 90
Posteriorum analyticorum (Aristoteles) 98
Postilla super psalterium (Nicolaus de Lyra) 86
Practica (Petrus Jacobus a Montepessulano) 86
Practica d'Arithmetica (Ghaligai) 40
Practica noua iuris 166
Practica nova causarum criminalium (Carerio) 84
Pragmatica ... por donde los herradores nueuamente 138
Pragmatica de Valladolid de vestido [1547] 139
Pragmatica de Valladolid [1537] 139
Pragmaticas de Valladolid (1548) 138
Praxis ivdicaria (Oriano) 86
Precationes biblicæ sanctorum virorū & mulierū 87
Precationes Psalorum 87
Prefacios 139
Prefacios toledanos 139
Pregmatica d'los paños 138
Pregmatica del pan 138
Prematica de la pena de los ladrones 138
Prematicas de como se han de comprar las lanas 138

INDEX

Prematicas y Ordenanças en la Caça y Pesca 135
Prematicas y Ordenanças sobre trages, Brocados, Oro y Sedas 135
Preparacion y aparejo para bien morir (Erasmus) 104
Preparatio Dialectica (Naveros) 53
Preparatio mortis (Evia) 88
Previlegium fratrum predicatorum 166
Prévost, Nicole
    Dispensarium ad aromatarios 78
Prima pars. s. tho. cū cōmē. car. Caietani 168
Primasius, bp. of Hadrumetum
    in Apocalypsim Ioannis Evangelistae 87
    In omnes D. Pauli Epistolas commentarii 87
Primera parte del libro llamado Abecedario spiritual (Osuna) 104
Priscianus 66, 159
    Institutiones grammatice 65
Priscianus, Theodorus
    Ad Timotheum fratrem, Phaenomenon euporiston 99
Problemas de la oration 135
Problemas, o Preguntas problematicas (Jarava) 135
Probus, Marcus Valerius 101
Processionale Romanuʒ 86
Processionarium benedictinum 168
Processionarium Romanum 166
Processionarium toletanum 166
Processionarius secūdum ordinē Cisterciensem 84
Processionarius secundum consuetudinem ordinis sancti ... Hiero 86
Processo Iudiciario 135
Prognosticon de euersione Europae (Torquatus) 85
Progymnasmata artis rhetoricae (Petreius) 166
Progymnasmata logicalia (Carranza de Miranda) 167
Promptuarium iuris civilis (Harmenopoulos) 85
Propalladia 136
Propalladio de Bartholome de Torres Naharro 136
Propertius, Sextus 45
Propugnaculum ecclesie. Aduersus Lutheranos (Clichtove) 87
Prosopopeia animalium aliquot (Ursinus) 88
Prosper, Tiro, Aquitanus, St.
    Opera 87
Prouerbios de dō Iñigo lopez de mendoça 137
Proverbia Salomonis 85
Proverbios de Seneca 136
Prudentius Clemens, Aurelius
    Opera 84, 165
Psalmi cum hymnis 136
Psalmi Davidici ad hebraicam veritatem castigati (Vio) 50
Psalmi penitentiales 85
Psalmos in Prosa 136
Psalterio de Dauid 136
Psalterium burgense 83

Psalterium carmelitanum 86
Psalterium Jeronimi 166
Psalterium romanum 83, 166
Psalterium romanum cum hymnis 86
Pulci, Luigi
    Libro primero de Morgante, Roldan y Reynaldos 132
    Morgante maggiore 132
Pulgar, Hernando de
    Mingo Revulgo, pseud. Coplas de Mingo Revulgo 163
Pureza de la conciencia (Bonaventura, St.) 107
Puteo, Paris de
    Libro llamado batalla de dos 106

Quaderno ... cortes (Madrid) 140
Quaderno de alcavalas 140
Quaderno de las cortes: Valladolid (1523) 113
Quaderno de las leyes ... de Toro 140
Quaderno de las leyes de Madrid (1528) 113
Quadernos de las cortes de Segouia (1532) 114
Quadratura magistri Pauli Veneti 89
Quaestiones duodecim Quodlibeticae (Adrian VI, pope) 89
Quaestiones in IV libros Sententiarum (Capreolus) 154
Quaestiones in Quartum Sententiarum (Adrian VI, pope) 89
Quaestiones Logicae (Coronel) 73
Quaestiones super octo libros Phisicorum (Astudillo) 41
Quaestiones super tota philosophia naturali (Magistris) 166
Quaestiones tusculanarum (Cicero) 48
Quaestionum in quatuor libros Sententiarum (Barbo) 93
Quarta parte del abecedario spiritual (Osuna) 104
Quarta parte del espejo de consolacion (Dueñas) 119
Querellas de la Paz (Erasmus) 140
Questión de amor 140
Questiones & tractatus extravagantes (Gentilis Fulginas) 67
Questiones quodlibetales ex quattuor Sententiarum (Duns Scotus) 92
Questiones super libros sententiarum (Alliaco) 87
Quinque libri minores 89
Quinta parte del abecedario spiritual (Osuna) 104
Quinti Calabri derelictorum ab Homero (Quintus Smyrnaeus) 168
Quintilianus, Marcus Fabius
    De institutione oratoria 89, 168
    Institutiones oratoriae 161
Quintin, Jean
    Sermones 92
Quintus, Smyrnaeus
    Quinti Calabri derelictorum ab Homero libri quatuordecim 168
Quiros sobre la passion 168
Quirós, Juan de
    Christopathia 110

INDEX

Quodlibeta (Thomas Aquinas) 169
Quodlibeta Henrici Goethals a Gandavo 89

Rabirius, Junius, comm. 55
Rampegolo, Antonio
    Figure biblie 61
Ratio accentuum omnium (Robles) 50
Rationale divinorum officiorvm (Durantis) 89
Raulin, Jean
    Opus sermonū quadragesimaliū 90
Raymundus de Sabunde
    Despertador del anima 117
    Violeta del anima 148
Recopilacion de notas de escripturas publicas (Huerta) 133
Recopilacion de todas las obras (Orozco) 134
Refranes glosados 141
Regimiento de la salud (Lobera de Ávila) 141
Regimiento del alma (Horozco) 142
Regla de la confradia de nombre de Dios 141
Reglas de S. Augustin 141
Regulae cancellariae apostolicae 90, 91
Regulae iuris, cum suis ampliationibus (Díaz de Lugo) 90
Regulae speciales de syllabarum quantitate (Cordier) 155
Regule cum suis ampliationibus (Soccini) 158
Regule divi Hieronymi 90
Regule sacre scripture 90
Regvla beati Avgvstini et constitntiones ordinis Praedicatorum 90
Reisch, Gregor
    Margarita philosophica 76
Relacion de las yndias 141
Relacion del viaje que hizo el Principe de España (Álvare 100
Relectio de Poenitentia (Cano) 49
Relectio de sacramentis in genere (Cano) 49
Repertorio d'los tiempos (Li) 141
Repertorio de todas las prematicas y capitulos de cortes 142
Repertorio de todos los caminos de España (Villuga) 141
Repertorium notabilium questionum (Díaz de Montalvo) 90
Repetitio Capituli, Raynuntius de testamentis (Benoît) 90
Repetitio rubricae de donationibus (López de Palacios Rubios 90
Repetitio valde subtilis (Urzurrum) 91
Reportata super libros ethicorum Aristotelis (Tartaretus) 90
Reportorio Universal de todas las leyes (Descousu) 124
Reprobacion de la astrologia judiciaria (Savonarola) 141
Reprouacion delas supersticiones y hechizerias (Ciruelo) 142, 170
Rerum a Fernando et Elisabe hispaniarum (Nebrija) 44
Rhetorica (Aristoteles) 169
Rhetorica divina (Guilelmus Parisiensis) 90

Rhua, Pedro de
    Cartas de Rhua 112
Robles, Franciscus
    Ratio accentuum omnium 50
Rocha, Thomas
    In libros tres Augustini nimphi 98
Rodríguez Florián, Juan
    Comedia llamada Florinea 114
Rojas, Fernando de
    Tragicomedia de Calisto y Melibea 109
Rolandinus de Passageriis
    Flores ultimarum voluntatum 62, 63
    Summa artis notariae 93
Rosarii magistri Anthonij Coronel 165
Roscius, Lucius Vitruvius
    De docendi studendique modo, ac de claris puerorum moribus 102
Rosiglia, Marco
    Opera 80
Rromances 141
Rromances de Sevilla 141
Rubio, Guillermo de
    Disputatorum in quatuor libros Magistri Sententiarum 67
Rudimenta grammatices (Linacre) 66
Ruescas, Agustín de
    Dialogo intitulado Centiloquio 111, 113
Ruíz de Virués, Alonso
    Disputationes viginti 102
    Tractatus de matrimonio Reg. Angliæ 100

Sabellico, Marco Antonio
    Historia rerum Venetarum 47
Sacrarum orationes 93
Sacro Bosco, Johannes de
    Spherae tractatus 170
    Tractado de la Sphera 142
Sagredo, Diego de
    Medidas d'l Romano 132
Salazar, Alonso de (possible author)
    Libro del invencible cavallero Lepolemo 109
Salazar, Diego de
    Tratado de re militari 146
Salicetus, Nicolaus
    Anthidotarius animae 39
    Meditationum, confessionum, ac deuotarum orationum 49
Sallustius Crispus, Caius
    De L. Sergij Catilinæ coniuratione 92
    Opera Sallustiana 96
Salustio Cathilinario τ Jugurgurta. Con glosa en romance 143

INDEX

Saludable y deuoto dialogo entre vn penitente y un cōfessor 117
San Benito de Ualladolid
    Constituciones 111
San Pedro, Diego de
    Carcel de amor 108, 140
    La passion de nuestro redemptor 166
Sancta Sophia, Marsilius de
    Signa, causas et curas febrium 75
Santo, Mariano
    Compendium in chyrurgia 163
Saravia de la Calle
    Instrucion de Mercaderes muy provechosa 145
Satyrae sex (Persius Flaccus) 86, 166
Satyrae sex cvm qvinqve commentatoribvs (Persius Flaccus) 166
Savonarola, Girolamo
    Confessionale pro instructione confessorum 45
    El triumpho de la cruz 146
    Exposicion del Pater noster 121
    Las obras que se hallan romançadas 133
    Opuscula, De simplicitate vitæ Christ 94
    Reprobacion de la astrologia 141
Scala celi 171
Scala paradisi (Joannes Climacus, Saint) 70
Schottenius, Hermann
    Colloquia sive confabulationes Tyronum Literatorum 49
Scolastica historia (Petrus, Comestor) 69
Scripta clarissimi mathematici M. Ioannis Regiomontani (Mueller 95
Scriptum Sancti Thome 92
Sebilla 169
Secreta mulierum τ virorum (Albertus Magnus) 94
Sedeño, Juan
    Summa de varones illustres 143
Sedulius Scotus, 9th cent.
    In omnes Epistolas Pauli Collectaneum 94
Sedulius, Coelius
    Sedulii Paschale 91, 170
Segunda comedia de Celestina (Silva) 109
Segunda parte del abecedario spiritual (Osuna) 103
Segura, Diego de
    Divina commentaria 89
Segura, Juan de
    Confessionario 107
    Libro de Instrucion Christiana 125
Segvnda parte del Espeio de consolacion (Dueñas) 120
Seneca (pseud.)
    Proverbios de Seneca. 136
Seneca, Lucius Annaeus 166
    Tragoediae decem 97
    Tragoediae septem 172

Sententie juris selecte 95
Sepulveda, Fernando de
    Manipulus Medicinarum 75
Serafino, da Fermo
    Las obras spiritvales 117, 170
Serapionis medici arabis celeberrimi practica 83
Sermon de amores (Buen Talante) 170
Sermon de la Madalena 144
Sermonario Quadragesimal Medicinal (Vaca) 140
Sermones (Antonio da Padova, St.) 91
Sermones (Augustine, St.) 94
Sermones (Bernard, St.) 144
Sermones (Gabriel of Barletta) 92
Sermones (Guerricus) 95
Sermones abbatis ab Aguilar 95
Sermones antiqui (Guerricus) 95
Sermones de la passion 142
Sermones de tempore (Bernard, St.) 169
Sermones Domini Petri de Palude 95
Sermones dormi secure (Johannes de Verdena) 91
Sermones estivales de tempore (Porta) 95
Sermones festiuitatum virginis marie (Porta) 171
Sermones hortuli conscientie (Dorbellus) 170
Sermones quadragesimales (Herborn) 95
Sermones quadragesimales (Pepin) 86
Sermones quattuor nouissimorum perutiles (Bonaventura, St.) 170
Sermonum dominicalium totius anni (Pepin) 86
Sermonum quadragesimalium (Raulin) 90
Servius (commentator) 175
Sevillana medicina (Juan de Aviñón) 132
Sexta parte del abecedario spitritual (Osuna) 105
Seyssel, Claude de
    De divina providentia 95
    De statu ecclesie 95
Siete psalmos penitenciales (Jarava) 143
Siette Psalmos con glosa 143
Signa, causas et curas febrium complectens (Sancta Sophia) 75
Silenos de Alcibiades (Erasmus) 143
Silius Italicus, Caius
    Opus de bello punico secundo 169
Silij italici Vita [and other works] 93
Silva de varia lecion (Mejía) 143
Silva, Feliciano de
    La Cronica de don Florisel de Niquea 117
Segunda comedia de Celestina 109
Sueno de Feliciano 143
Silvaticus, Mattheus
    Pandectae medicinae 85
Similitudines sive collationes ex Biblijs sacris (Alardus) 93

INDEX

Simone Fidati, da Cascia
    Expositio super evangeliorum 92
Singularia doctorum 92
Smith, Richard
    Diatriba de hominis justificatione 53
Soares, João
    Libro de la verdad de la fe 126, 128
Soccini, Bartolommeo
    Regule cum suis ampliationibus et fallentiis 158
Sol de contemplatiuos (Hugo de Balma) 144
Soliloquios (Díaz del Castillo) 142
Solinus, Caius Julius
    Polyhistor 92
Solis mundo 143
Sonecti et strambocti ... in laude de Clitia (Cei) 95
Sonetti: Capituli: Egloghe: Strabotti (Rosiglia) 80
Sophismata (Buridan) 170
Sophocles
    Sophoclis Tragoediæ septem 100
Sossiego y descanso del anima (Fuensalida) 143
Soto, Domingo de
    Deliberacion en la causa de los pobres 118
    In causa pauperum deliberatio 52, 171
    Super octo libros physicorum Aristotelis 84
Spain. Laws
    Pragmatica de arrendadores 138
    Pragmatica de telas de oro y plata 138
Speculum Galeni (Champier) 91
Speculum sacerdotum ecclesie (Hugo de Sancto Charo) 94
Speculum sapientiae 94
Speculum sapientiae (Cyrillus) 171
Spherae tractatus (Sacro Bosco) 170
Spirito, Lorenzo
    Libro del juego de las suertes 128
Stimulus amoris (Bernard, St.) 121
Stoffler, Joannes
    Calendarium Romanum 46
Strabo
    De situ orbis 93
Strebée, Jacques Louis
    De partitione oratoria Ciceronis 92
Sucesso de Inglaterra 144
Sueño de Feliciano (Silva) 143
Suetonius Tranquillus, Caius
    Duodecim Caesares 94
Sulpitius, Joannes, Verulanus
    Doctrina mense 52
    Grammatices compendium 160
    [opera diversa] 95

Suma de arithmetica (Texeda) 106
Suma de geografía (Fernández de Enciso) 143
Suma y compendio de todas chrónicas del mundo (Carion) 112
Summa Angelica (Angelus Carletus) 91
Summa angelica de casibus conscientiae (Angelus Carletus) 171
Summa artis notariae (Rolandinus de Passageriis) 93
Summa Astensis (Astesanus) 93
Summa Conciliorum et Pontificum (Carranza de Miranda) 93
Summa Confessionalis (Antoninus, St.) 46
Summa de confession llamada Defecerunt (Antoninus, St.) 114
Summa de philosophia natural (Fuentes) 143
Summa de varones illustres (Sedeño) 143
Summa de Virtudes 143, 171
Summa Mysteriorum Christianæ Fidei (Tittelmans) 99
Summa Petri Dolose 94
Summa Roselle De casibus conscientiae (Trovamala) 93
Summa summarum, qvæ tabienae dicitur (Cagnazzo) 93
Summae fidei orthodoxae (Denis le Chartreux) 54
Summularum Petri Hispani glossulae (Magistris) 170
Sumule philosophie rationalis (Orbelli) 168
Super canone misse (Biel) 64, 160
Super confiteor (Pepin) 84
Super feudis (Baldo degli Ubaldi) 43
Super institutionibus Iustiniani (Le Fèvre) 62
Super leges Tauri (Castillo de Villasante) 51
Super libris posteriorum (Paulus Venetus) 162
Super librū Sapientie (Holkot) 160
Super octo libros Aristotelis de Phisico (Dullaert) 55
Super octo libros physicorum Aristotelis (Soto) 84
Super praedicamenta Arist. (Clemente) 70
Super psalmum Beati quorum remisse sunt iniquitates (Castro) 44
Supplementum cronicorum 93
Sutor, Petrus
    see Cousturier, Pierre 95
Syliceo sobre el pater noster (Martinus Silicaeus) 144
Sylogismi Petri Doltz 171
Sylve morales 92
Sylvestrinae Svmmae (Mazzolini da Prierio) 93
Symmachus, Quintus Aurelius
    Epistolae familiares 157
Synonimorum sylva (Pelegromius) 96

Tapper, Ruard
    Declaratio articulorvm adversus haereses 90
Tariffa de i pesi, e misvre (Paxi) 172
Tartaretus, Petrus
    Expositio ... in summulas Petri Hispani 172
    Reportata super libros ethicorum Aristotelis 90

INDEX

Tauler, Johann
    Instituciones y doctrina   125
Tercera parte de la Celestina (Gómez de Toledo)   113
Tercera parte del Abecedario spiritual (Osuna)   103
Terentianus Maurus
    De litteris, syllabis, pedibus et metris   96
Terentius, Publius, afer
    Andria   105
    Comoediæ sex   171
    Comoediae sex   96
    Comoediae, Multo maiore, quam hactenus unquam, uigilantia repur   96
    Pvblii Terentij Aphri comicorū latinorū principis comœdi   96
Termini Mayoris   173
Tesaurus Spirituales   99
Tesoro de la Passion de Nuestro Redemptor (Li)   146
Tesoro delos pobres   173
Texeda, Gaspar de
    Suma de arithmetica   106
Textus abbreuiatus Aristotelis super octo libris phisicorum   96
Textus magistri sentētiarum   77
Textus Mesue (Yuhanna ibn Mesawayh)   173
Textus phisicorum Aristo[teles] abreviatus   96
Themistius, Euphrada
    Commentaria in posteriora Aristotelis   173
Theocritus   100
Theologicarum conclusionum (Bouelles)   51
Theophilus, antecessor   71
Theophrastus
    Aristotelis et Theophrasti historias   39
Theophylactus, Abp. of Okhrid
    In omnes Diui Pauli Apostoli enarrationes   97
    In omnes Divi Pauli Apostoli Epistolas   98
Theorica de virtudes (Castilla)   146
Theosophiae (Arboreus)   100
Thesoro de devocion   144
Thesoro de los Angeles (Evia)   146
Thesoro de misericordia (Toro)   144
Thesoro de virtudes (Isla)   146
Thomas Aquinas, Saint
    Aristotelis de generatione et corruptione   172
    De anima Aristotelis expositio   172
    Prima pars. s. tho. cū cōme. car. Caietani   168
    Quaestiones in IV libros Sententiarum   154
    Quodlibeta   169
[Aristoteles. Perihermenias]   98
[Aristoteles. Posteriorum analyticorum]   98
Tibullus, Albius   45

Tiraqueau, Andre
    De vtroqve retractv 98
Tittelmans, Franciscus
    Commentarii in Ecclesiasten Salomonis 99
    Compendium dialecticae 97
    Compendium naturalis philosophiae 97
    De los mysterios de la missa 144
    Elucidatio in librum D. Iob. 99
    Elvcidatio in omnes Epistolas apostolicas 172
    Mysteriorum missae 144
    Svmma Mysteriorvm Christianæ Fidei 99
Tixier, Jean
    Officinae Ioannis Ravisii Textor epitome 80
Tixier, Jean, seigneur de Ravisy
    Epitheta 157
Topica legalia (Cantiuncula) 99
Toro, Gabriel de
    Thesoro de misericordia diuina y humana 144
Torquatus, Antonius
    Prognosticon ... de euersione Europae 85
Torquemada, Juan de
    Expositio super toto psalterio 98
Torres Naharro, Bartholomé de
    Propalladia de Bartholome de Torres Naharro 136
Tostado sobre el eusebio 145
Tostado, Alonso
    Confessional 108, 152
    Las catorze questiones del Tostado 139
Tostado sobre el eusebio 145
Toulouse (Archdiocese)
    Decisiones capelle tholose 56
Tovar, Luis de
Triumphus Christi 96
Tractado de la Sphera (Sacro Bosco) 142
Tractado de la victoria de si mismo (Cano) 147
Tractado de la vida de Iesu Christo 145
Tractado de las obras de misericordia (Alexander, Anglicus) 172
Tractado de las querellas de la Paz (Erasmus) 140
Tractado de republica (Castrillo) 146
Tractado de vendemmia 144
Tractado de Vita Christi 145
Tractado del asino 145
Tractado del sacramento 172
Tractado dela musica llamado Lux bella (Durán) 127
Tractado intitulado Contemptus mundi 114
Tractado llamado menor daño de medicina (Chirino de Cuenca) 132
Tractado sobre los Censos (Pizarro) 145
Tractatus breuis de arte & modo audiendi confessiones (Frías 98
Tractatus de antiquitate temporis (Cravetta) 48

INDEX

Tractatus de conversione paganorum 98
Tractatus de episcopo (Bertachini) 100
Tractatus de matrimonio Reg. Angliæ (Ruíz de Virués) 100
Tractatus de pensionibus ecclesiasticis (Giganti) 96
Tractatus de praescriptionibus (Balbi) 99
Tractatus de Synodo episcopi (Botteo) 99
Tractatus de vera contritione 99
Tractatus formalitatum (Pedro, de Castrovol) 63
Tractatus insignis de Bannitis (Nellus) 99
Tractatus mysteriorum missae (Tittelmans) 144
Tractatus perutilis (Frías) 98
Tractatus sacerdotalis (Nicolaus de Plove) 97
Tractatus sillogismorum (Enzinas) 98
Tractatus super libros phisicorum (Castrovol) 48
Tractatus super psalmum: "Quicumque vult" nominatum (Castrovol) 48
Tragedia llamada la madre Claudina (Fernández) 108
Tragicomedia de Calisto y Melibea (Rojas) 109
Tragoediæ septem (Sophocles) 100
Tragoediae decem (Seneca) 97
Tragoediae septem (Seneca) 172
Tratado ... Doctrinal de confessores (Castillo de Villasante) 115
Tratado de cuentas (Castillo de Villasante) 145
Tratado de la oracion (Erasmus) 144
Tratado de la oracion (Porras) 146
Tratado de la pureza de la conciencia (Bonaventura) 107
Tratado de las ocho questiones del templo (Vergara) 139
Tratado de re militari (Salazar) 146
Tratado de Vita beata (Lucena) 148
Tratado del modo y estilo en la visitacion ordinaria (Frías) 98
Tratado del sacramento 146
Tratado delas indulgencias, y perdones (Argomanas) 145
Tratado delos rieptos τ desafios (Valera) 146
Tratado llamado el Desseoso 115
Tratado llamado excelencias de la fe (Maluenda) 119
Tratado llamado leche de la fe (Maluenda) 126
Trejo, Guterrius de
    Super epistolas Pauli 97
Trent, Council of
    Acta concilii Tridentini 40
Tres libros de Musica en cifras para vihuela (Mudarra) 129
Treynta y seys amonestaciones del Pastoral 136
Trezientas preguntas de cosas naturales (López de Corella) 171
Trilogium evangelicum Primum Christi Passionem (Osuna) 82
Trithemius, Johannes
    De scriptoribus ecclesiasticis 96
Triumphus Christi contra infideles (Christophorus) 96
Trombeta, Antonius, comm.
    In tractatū formalitatum Scoti sententia 62

Trovamala, Baptista
    Summa Roselle De casibus conscientiae 93

Universales Joannis Mesue 74
Universalia Scoti (Duns) 102
Ursin, Jean
    Prosopopeia animalivm aliqvot 88
Ursinus, Joannes
    Prosopopeia animalium aliquot 88
Urzurrum, Michael de
    Repetitio valde subtilis 91

Vaca, Gabriel
    Sermonario Quadragesimal Medicinal 140
Valencia, Hierónymo de
    Arte del Computo nueuamente compuesta 107
Valera, Diego de
    Tratado delos rieptos τ desafios 146
Valerio d'las hystorias escolasticas (Pérez de Guzmán) 148
Valerius Maximus 174
    Dictorum Factorumque 102
Valerius, Cornelius
    Grammaticarum institutionum libri IV 65
Valla, Lorenzo
    De elegantia linguae latinae 58
    Elegantiae linguae Latinae 56
    Lucubrationes aliquot ad Linguae Latinae restaurationem spectant 72
Vanegas de Busto, Alejo
    Las differencias de libros que ay en el universo 117
    Papeus, Petrus. Samarites Comœdia de Samaritano Euangelico 44
Vargas, Bernardo de
    Don Cirongilio de Tracia 116
Varro, Marcus Terentius
    De lingua latina 102
Varthema, Ludovico de
    Itinerario del miser Luis 126
Vasaeus, Joannes
    Chronici rervm Memorabilivm Hispaniae 44
Vega, Pedro de la
    Cronica de la orden sant Hieronymo 109
Vegetius Renatus, Flavius
    Artis veterinariae, sive mulomedicinae 102
Velázquez de Castillo, Gabriel
    Libro primero del ... don Clarian 116
Venero, Alonso de
    Aphorismos 105
    Enchiridion de los tiempos 120

INDEX

Verdad de la fe (Soares) 126
Verdadera informacion de la Tierra Santa (Aranda) 126
Vergara, Juan de
    Tratado de las ocho questiones del tēplo 139
Vergel de nuestra señora (Pérez) 174
Vergel de oracion y monte de contemplacion (Orozco) 147
Vergel de sanidad (Lobera de Ávila) 147
Vergel de virginidad (Maluenda) 147
Vergilius cum cōmētarij (Virgilius Maro) 175
Versor, Johannes, comm.
    Petri Hispani Svmmvlae Logicales cvm Versoris Expositione 174
Via espiritus (Palma) 147
Viaje de la tierra sancta 174
Viaje del Principe 175
Vicios de las malas mujeres (Martínez de Toledo) 105
Victoria de si mismo (Cano) 147
Victorius, Benedictus
    see Vittori, Benedetto 63
Vida de los césares (Guevara) 108
Vida de nuestra señora 148, 175
Vida de S. Francisco y Sancta Clara 174
Vida de Santa Maria Magdalena 128
Vigerius, Marcus
    Decachordū Christianū 54
Vigo, Giovanni de
    Opera ... in arte chyrurgia 166
    Opera īn chyrurgia 80
Villegas Selvago, Alonso de
    Comedia llamada Selvagia 107
Villuga, Pedro Juan
    Repertorio de todos los caminos de Españ 141
Vio, Tomaso de
    Epistolae Pauli et aliorum Apostolorum 47
    Evangelia cum commentariis 47
    In omnes authenticos veteris testamenti historiales libros comm 48
    Novi Testamenti Ientaculis Tractatus 161
    Prima pars summe thomae cum cōmē. card. Caietani 168
    Psalmi Davidici ad hebraicam veritatem castigati 50
    Thomas Aquinas, St. Prima secundae partis Summae theologicae 47
Viola animae 148
Viola Sanctorum 175
Violeta del anima (Raymundus de Sabunde) 148
Virgilius Maro, Publius 42, 102
Bucolica 101
Eclogae Vergilii 57
    Los doze libros de la Eneida de Vergilio 119
    Opera 102, 173
Vergilius cum cōmētarij 175
Viridarium illustrium poetarum flores 101

Virtvtvm vitiorvmqve exempla (Nicolas de Hannapes) 102
Vita Christi cartujano (Ludolph of Saxony) 174
Vita Christi in metro 175
Vita de Santa Maria Magdalena 148
Vitæ sanctorvm (Maldonado) 74
Vita y excellencias de S. Juan baptista 148
Vitae patrum (St. Jerome) 175
Vite et sentencie de philosophi 102
Vite patrum (Maldonado) 162
Vitoria de Christo 147
Vitruvius Pollio, Marcus
    De architectura 101
Vitruuius iterum 101
Vittori, Benedetto
    De morbo gallico 63
    In Hippocratis Prognostica commentarii 61
Vivaldus, Joannes Ludovicus
    Opus regale 82
Vives, Juan Luis
    Colloquia sive linguae latinae exercitatio 52
    Comentarios para despertamiento del anima en dios 116
    De disciplinis libri XX 103
    Introductio ad sapientiam 70
    Introduction ala sabiduria 125
Vocabula suis locis collocata (Dionysius) 79
Vocabularium arabicum 175
Vocabularium Ecclesiasticum (Fernández de Santaella) 100
Vocabularium grecum 174
Vocabularius utriusque iuris 173

Xenophon
    Las obras 134
    [Works] 103
Xerxes, pseud.
    Dechado de la vida humana 115
Ximenes, Francesch
    Natura angelica 133
Ximénez de Prexano, Pedro
    Luzero de la vida christiana 126
Xodar, Juan de
  see Jodar, Juan de. 103

Yciar, Juan de
    El estilo de escrivir cartas 120

INDEX

Zacuto, Abraham ben Samuel
    Almanach perpetuum 40
Zamora, Alonso de
    Introductiones artis grammatice hebraice 64

www.ingramcontent.com/pod-product-compliance
Lightning Source LLC
Chambersburg PA
CBHW080801020526
44114CB00035B/1